The UK financial system

third edition

MANCHESTER
UNIVERSITY PRESS

D0234204

The UK financial system

Theory and practice

third edition

Mike Buckle and John Thompson

Manchester University Press

Manchester and New York

distributed exclusively in the USA by St. Martin's Press

Published by Manchester University Press
Oxford Road, Manchester M13 9NR, UK
and Room 400, 175 Fifth Avenue, New York, NY 10010, USA

Distributed exclusively in the USA by
St. Martin's Press, Inc., 175 Fifth Avenue, New York,
NY 10010, USA

Distributed exclusively in Canada by
UBC Press, University of British Columbia, 6344 Memorial Road,
Vancouver, BC, Cananda V6T 1Z2

British Library Cataloguing-in-Publication Data
A catalogue record for this book is available from the British Library

Library of Congress Cataloging-in-Publication Data applied for

ISBN   0 7190 5412 5 *paperback*

First edition published 1992
Second edition published 1995
This edition first published 1998

05 04 03 02 01 00 99 98   10 9 8 7 6 5 4 3 2 1

Typeset by Ralph Footring, Derby
Printed by Bell and Bain Ltd, Glasgow

To Margaret and Fiona

Contents

Figures

Tables

Boxes

Preface

In this third edition we seek to build on our experiences and the helpful comments we have received from the users of the first and second editions. We are aware that the financial system is not static and a number of key changes have taken place since the second edition was published in 1995. The four most important of these changes have been:

(i)   the granting of operational independence to the Bank of England;
(ii) the transfer of the responsibility for prudential control of the banking system from the Bank of England to the new Financial Services Authority;
(iii) the new system of intervention in the money markets adopted by the Bank of England;
(iv) changes in the operation of the stock and gilt-edged markets.

In addition to these major changes, a number of less significant, but nevertheless important, changes have taken place (e.g. changes in building society regulation, European legislation). These have been incorporated into this edition and we have also taken the opportunity to incorporate additional material on the pricing of securities. Also, where appropriate, we have enlarged the evidence concerning the hypothesis of market efficiency.

Changes to the UK financial system are likely to occur in the future and we therefore recommend that the interested reader keeps abreast of such changes by perusal of the financial section of the quality press.

We are grateful to the following for their help in the preparation of the book: Peter Franklin, Nottingham Trent University; Bryn Gravenor, University of Wales, Swansea; Richard Harrington, University of

Manchester; Ken Holden, Liverpool John Moores University; and Kent Matthews, Cardiff Business School. Any errors and omissions are the responsibility of the authors.

Mike Buckle

John Thompson

August 1998

Chapter 1

Introduction to the financial system

1.1 Introduction

We begin our study of the UK financial system with an introduction to
the role of a financial system in an economy. We start this introduction
with a very simple model of an economy and then extend the analysis
throughout the rest of this and the next chapter. A second objective is to
establish some of the basic financial concepts which will be drawn upon
throughout this book. Finally, we hope to introduce readers to the many
sources of data available relating to the UK financial system. In particular we explain the relationships between the various sets of financial
statistics.

1.2 The role of the financial system

To help us to understand the role played by a financial system in a
mature economy such as that of the UK we start by constructing a
simplified model of an economy. In this model the economy is divided
into two distinct groups or sectors. The first is the household sector,
which is assumed to be the ultimate owner of all the resources of the
economy. In the early stages of development of an economy the household unit would have undertaken production of any goods consumed. As
economies developed, a form of specialisation has generally taken place
so that the proximate ownership and control of much of the productive
resources of the economy, such as land, buildings and machinery, have
been vested in units making up the second sector, which we call the
firms sector. We will examine the financial relationships between these
two sectors later. In our simple model it is the firms sector which
organises the production of goods and services in the economy. In
exchange for these goods and services, households hire out their

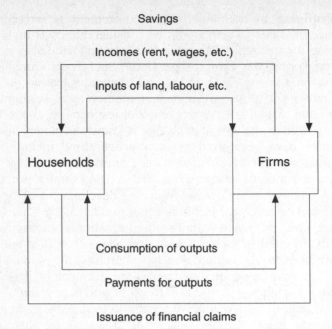

Figure 1.1   *The circular flow of income, expenditure and finance*

resources of land, labour, and so on. At this stage we ignore the role of
the government and we assume that the economy is closed, so that there
is no exchange of goods and services with other economies. The real
flows in this simple economy are set out in the inner loop of figure 1.1.

In this simple economy it would not be an easy task for households to
attempt to satisfy their wants. The greater the number of commodities
available in the economy, the greater would be the task. This can be seen
by considering the choices open to households. Households can con-
sume the commodities they own, they can exchange these commodities
for commodities owned by other households or they could use these
commodities as inputs to create new commodities. In the last situation
the household would have to hire out the commodities to an existing
firm in exchange for the firm's output or alternatively create a new firm.
In the case of exchanging commodities with other households there
would clearly be many difficulties. For a successful transaction to take
place between two parties in such a barter economy, it is necessary for
each of the two parties to want simultaneously that which the other

party is offering to exchange. This requirement is termed 'double coincidence of wants'. There would be considerable costs involved both in searching for a suitable party with which to trade and also in reaching an agreement over the terms of the trade. Such costs would limit the amount of trade taking place and would eventually lead to pressure for general agreement to use a single commodity as a standard unit of exchange into which all other commodities can be converted. The commodity used as the unit of exchange is known as money and various commodities have been used as money over time including cowrie shells, cattle, gold, silver and cigarettes. The main criterion for development of a commodity as money is that it is generally acceptable in exchange for other commodities. With the development of money, the act of sale can be separated from the act of purchase.

We can now introduce money into our simple economy so that households are paid in money for the resources they hire out to firms and in turn households use that money to purchase the outputs of firms. The middle circuit in figure 1.1 denotes these monetary flows and are the flows corresponding to the real flows of goods and services occurring in the opposite direction. We should note that by aggregating all firms into one sector we are considering flows taking place only between firms and households and are therefore ignoring the considerable flows which take place between firms. That is to say, we are considering only inter-sector flows and ignoring intra-sector flows.

In this simple economy any expenditure in excess of current income by a household or a firm could occur only if the household or firm had accumulated money balances by not spending all of its income received in past periods. This is clearly a constraint on economic development since firms need to invest, that is, replace, maintain or add to existing real assets such as buildings and machinery. As the economy becomes more sophisticated, investment requires larger amounts of accumulated funds. Various expedients were developed to enable firms to overcome such constraints. For example, partnerships were formed so that accumulated savings could be pooled. The next major stage in the development of financing arrangements came with borrowing. Those households which did not spend all of their current income on consumption, that is, saved some of their income, could lend these funds to firms, which in turn could use these funds to finance investment. In exchange for these funds, firms would issue claims, which are effectively sophisticated IOUs, which promise some benefits to the lender of funds at some date or dates in the future. The nature of financial claims and the various types of claims in existence are discussed in the next section.

The ability to finance investment through borrowing undoubtedly encourages economic development and the existence of financial claims would also stimulate household saving. The investment and saving flows in our simple economy are represented by the outer loop of figure 1.1. The non-spending of income (or saving) by households can be regarded as a leakage of funds from the circular flow of income and expenditure captured in the middle loop of figure 1.1. This household saving, though, finds its way into firms' investment and firms' investment involves the purchase of capital equipment from other firms, so the leaked funds are injected back into the circuit.

We can now see one of the main roles of a financial system, which is to provide the mechanisms by which funds can be transferred from those with surplus funds to those who wish to borrow. In other words, the financial system acts as an intermediary between surplus and deficit units. In terms of figure 1.1 this function is represented by the outer loop. It is clear therefore that the financial system plays an important role in the allocation of funds to their most efficient use amongst competing demands. In a market system such as the UK financial system this allocation is achieved through the price mechanism, with the various prices being set within the relevant financial markets, which are themselves part of the financial system. The existence of financial markets also enables wealth holders to alter the composition of their portfolios. A secondary role for a financial system is to provide the mechanisms for the inner money flows, that is, the payments mechanism. A further function of a financial system is the provision of special financial services such as insurance and pension services.

Before we consider in more detail the lending and borrowing flows (sections 1.7 and 1.8) represented by the outer loop of figure 1.1, we examine in the next section the nature of the financial claims which underlie these flows.

1.3   Financial claims

A financial claim can be defined as a claim to the payment of a sum of money at some future date or dates. A borrower of funds issues a financial claim in return for the funds. The lender of funds holds the borrower's financial claim and is said to hold a financial asset. The issuer of the claim is said to have a financial liability. By definition therefore the sum of financial assets in existence will exactly equal the sum of liabilities. To take an example, a bank deposit is a sum of money lent by an individual or company to a bank. The deposit is therefore a liability of the borrower of funds, which is the bank. The depositor holds a financial asset, that is, a financial claim on the bank. Another term commonly used to denote a financial claim is a financial instrument.

The existence of a wide variety of financial instruments in a mature financial system, such as the UK system, can be explained by reference to consumer theory. Traditional consumer theory explains the demand for a commodity in terms of utility and a budget constraint, with the implication that a particular good can be identified as separate from other goods. In contrast Lancaster (1966) argues that:

(i) all goods possess objective characteristics, properties or attributes;
(ii) these characteristics form the object of consumer choice.

In the same way, a financial instrument can be considered to be a 'bundle' of different characteristics. Because individual agents place different emphasis on the various characteristics, a wide range of financial instruments is supplied. It is now necessary to examine the different characteristics possessed by financial instruments. The most important of these are risk, liquidity, real value certainty, expected return, term to maturity, currency denomination and divisibility.

1.3.1 *Risk*

Risk is a fundamental concept in finance and it is one which we will return to many times throughout the book. What follows is a brief introduction to the nature of financial risk.

When we talk about risk in relation to a financial instrument we are referring to the fact that some future outcome affecting that instrument is not known with certainty. The uncertain outcome may, for example, be changes in the price of the security, or default with respect to repayment of capital or income stream. Although such outcomes are uncertain, an individual may have some view about the likelihood of particular outcomes occurring. Another way of stating this is that the individual will view some outcomes as more likely than others. Such views are likely to be formed on the basis of past experience of such outcomes occurring although other relevant information may also be used. The next step in assessing the particular risk of the financial instrument is to assign subjective probabilities to the different outcomes that may occur. The resulting probability distribution provides us with the individual's view as to the most likely outcome, that is, the expected value of the distribution. The spread of the distribution indicates the degree to which the outcome will be much greater or much less than expected. The greater the spread, the greater is the risk that an outcome far removed from that expected will occur. The most common measure of risk is in fact the standard deviation of the probability distribution, a measure which increases as the spread widens.

Figure 1.2   *Probabilities of the share price in one year's time*

To take an example, a person invests £1,000 in the ordinary shares of a company. The value of the shares in one year's time, that is, the price of those shares plus any income received from them in the form of dividends, is uncertain. The value may have risen or fallen; however, this person will believe some range of values are more likely than others. For example, he or she may believe that there is a 50 per cent chance that the value of the shares in one year's time will be in the range £1,000 to £1,200. Figure 1.2 illustrates one possible distribution of likely values.

The expected value of this distribution is £1,090 and the standard deviation, or measure of risk, is £161. A larger spread, that is, a larger standard deviation, would indicate the potential for a larger reward and, conversely, the potential for a larger loss around a particular expected value.

In these introductory remarks on the nature of risk, two types of risk were mentioned, namely price risk (or market risk, i.e. the risk that the price of the security will change) and the risk of not being repaid the sum lent or any interest promised in the claim, known as default risk. During the course of this book we will consider many other types of financial risk.

1.3.2 *Liquidity*

Liquidity refers to the ease and speed at which a financial instrument can be turned into cash without loss. This will depend upon on the asset being redeemable or marketable on an organised market. Thus for example a bank sight deposit can be withdrawn or redeemed on demand and is therefore very liquid. In contrast listed shares can be sold on a stock exchange but the precise amount of cash obtained will depend on the market valuation at the time of sale. Hence listed shares are less liquid than sight deposits. As a final example a bank loan is an agreement between two parties, the bank and the borrower, and so there is unlikely to be a third party willing to purchase the loan from the bank before it matures. That is to say, the bank loan is not marketable. (Note that since the 1980s there has been a growing trend towards packaging loan-type assets, such as mortgages, to make them marketable so they can be sold on; this process is part of a larger phenomenon termed securitisation – for further discussion see chapter 12.) The existence of an organised market for an instrument and the ability to deal at short notice therefore enhances the instrument's liquidity. It is possible to devise a spectrum of liquidity along which different financial instruments can be positioned. Such an analysis is crude and subject to a number of exceptions but is still illustrative. At the very liquid end we would find short-term deposits, moving through longer-term deposits, where funds are tied up for longer periods, through bonds and shares, where their marketability provides some degree of liquidity, to long-term loans, life policies and pension rights. Life policies and pension rights are considered to be very illiquid when they are held to maturity, although it has become increasingly easier to turn them into cash at short notice, albeit at considerable financial penalty, the further the date of encashment is from the maturity date.

1.3.3 *Real value certainty*

A third distinguishing characteristic of financial instruments is real value certainty, which refers to their susceptibility to loss due to a rise in the general level of prices. The maintenance of the real value of an asset is likely to be an important consideration for those who are lending funds over a long time period. An individual acquiring assets to draw upon in retirement will want to ensure that the purchasing power of those assets is at least as great in retirement as when the assets were acquired. Financial instruments whose values are fixed in money terms, for example a bank deposit, will find their real value eroded when the rate of inflation exceeds the rate of interest earned. Over most of the

1970s, inflation exceeded the interest rate earned on bank and building society deposits in the UK and as a consequence the real value of such deposits was eroded. Ordinary shares are an instrument which, if held over a few years, have tended to increase in value in line with or above the rise in the general price level. The asset which has tended to provide the best protection against erosion in value by inflation is not a financial asset but the physical asset of property. This is not to say that there are not times when the real value of property does decrease, and an example of this is the decline in the real value of residential property in the late 1980s and early 1990s. Rather, it is to say that if held over a number of years, the increase in value of property has tended to exceed inflation. This, as we shall see in chapter 6, explains why the long-term investment institutions are significant holders of property in their portfolios.

1.3.4 *Expected return*

Most financial instruments offer an explicit cash return to their holders. This return takes the form of a rate of interest or dividend and, for those instruments subject to changes in their market price, there is an additional element of return in the form of an appreciation in their value. Instruments subject to changes in price are termed capital uncertain and include bonds and equities. For such capital uncertain instruments it will be the expected return (see above section on risk) that is used to determine whether to purchase or hold on to the instrument. *Ceteris paribus*, the higher the expected return the greater will be the demand for the instrument. In practice, however, a high return on an asset may also indicate that there is a premium component to the return to compensate the holder for some disadvantage such as illiquidity or high risk.

1.3.5 *Term to maturity*

Financial instruments vary widely according to the characteristic of term to maturity. Sight deposits at banks have zero term to maturity, as they can be withdrawn on demand. At the other end of the spectrum 'consols' (a type of government bond) and equity have no redemption date and therefore possess an infinite term to maturity. Between these two extremes financial instruments are issued with a wide range of maturities. In general, returns on instruments identical except for their term to maturity will reflect both expectations of future interest rate changes and the loss of liquidity in holding long-term as opposed to short-term instruments. This is examined in more detail in chapter 9.

1.3.6 *Currency denomination*

With the general reduction in restrictions on the movement of capital across national boundaries, the currency denomination of a financial instrument has assumed greater importance. This adds a further component to the return on non-domestic instruments in the form of the appreciation or depreciation of the relevant exchange rate.

1.3.7 *Divisibility*

This characteristic reflects the degree to which the instrument can be subdivided into small units for transaction purposes. For example, a sight deposit is fully divisible whereas Treasury bills are sold in minimum denominations and hence are not divisible. The degree of divisibility is therefore an additional determinant of an instrument's liquidity.

The characteristics approach to analysing financial instruments can also provide some indication of why an economic agent, such as an individual or company, will desire to hold more than one type of financial asset. It is likely that economic agents will hold their wealth in different forms so as to meet a number of different financial objectives. For example, an individual may be uncertain about her or his level of income or consumption in the near future and so can meet this uncertainty by holding wealth in a form which can be drawn on at short notice. That is, some wealth will be held as liquid assets such as bank deposits. The individual may also have the objective of holding wealth over a long period of time, for the purpose of providing income in retirement, and will want these funds to keep their purchasing power. This may lead to the holding of some funds in the form of ordinary shares. From this analysis we can see that an economic agent is likely to hold a collection or portfolio of assets, where the mix of characteristics underlying the assets in the portfolio will satisfy the various objectives of the agent. We have referred to some specific types of financial instruments in this section, such as a bank deposit and an ordinary share. These are examples of the two general types of claim, namely debt and equity, which dominate the types of financial instruments in existence. We shall finish this section with a look at the characteristics of these two general types of claim.

1.3.8 *Debt*

Debt is a financial claim which is normally due to be repaid on a specified future date with interest being paid at regular intervals until repayment. Examples of debt instruments are deposits, loans, bills and bonds. A deposit is a claim which records the liability of a financial institution to repay a sum of money in the future to the depositor (the lender of funds to the institution). A variety of deposit types exist, differing mainly in the arrangements for repayment; so, for example, a sight deposit with a bank would be repayable on demand whilst a time deposit is repayable after a given period of notice. Deposits are generally considered to be at the liquid end of the spectrum of liquidity, although there are some exceptions to this where a deposit may have a repayment date of up to five years from the date of issue. Deposits are susceptible to default risk, though such risk is considered to be relatively low as financial institutions rarely default – exceptions do occur as in the case of BCCI.[1] Deposits can also be classified according to their size, so that retail deposits are small and wholesale deposits are large. Financial institutions have also issued certificates of deposits (CDs), which are instruments acknowledging the existence of a deposit for a fixed period but which can be sold in the money markets (i.e. possess the characteristic of marketability – see chapter 10 for further discussion).

The majority of loans are made by financial institutions and generally specify a fixed date for repayment. The term to maturity of the loan generally varies according to the purpose for which the finance is required, and may be up to 30 years hence in the case of a mortgage. Most bank loans though have a repayment date of less than ten years from the date they are issued. Loans are susceptible to default risk, though, as we shall see in the next chapter, financial institutions attempt to minimise such risks through a variety of methods. Loans which are secured, such as a mortgage on property, have a lower default risk than unsecured loans, as in the event of non-repayment the holder of the claim can sell the security to recover the debt. Loans are generally considered to be illiquid as they are agreements between two parties and therefore not marketable.

Bills of exchange can be considered to be promises to pay a certain sum of money at a fixed date and are analogous to postdated cheques. Commercial bills are used to finance trade and help to reconcile the competing interests of the buyer of the goods, who wishes to delay payment, and the seller, who desires prompt payments. The buyer issues a bill which promises to pay in the future, but the seller receives a financial instrument which can be resold in the money markets (i.e. it is

1   Note also deposits are insured against default to a limited extent – see chapter 18 for further details.

negotiable). The price received from the sale is less than the face value of the bill on maturity and so the bill is said to be discounted. For example, if a £1,000 bill due for redemption in three months' time is sold for £950, the rate of discount over three months is 5.3 per cent ((50/950)×100), or approximately 21 per cent per annum. Bills are also issued by central government (Treasury bills) and local authorities.

Deposits and loans are claims which generally pay variable rates of interest. In contrast, a bond is a claim which pays a fixed rate of interest, known as a 'coupon payment', at regular intervals. The bond may have a known repayment date, at which time the bond's par value, which is generally £100, is repaid. Some bonds though have no definite repayment date and are known as undated bonds, for example 2.5 per cent consolidated stock (consols) issued by the UK government in 1888. In the UK, central government, local government, public boards and companies issue bonds. Bonds issued by the UK government are commonly known as 'gilt edged', as the risk of default on such stocks is as close to zero as is possible on a financial instrument. Bonds issued by companies, known as debentures or loan stocks, do carry some risk of default, as do bonds issued by some foreign governments. Another type of bond traded in London are eurobonds. These are issued by international companies, governments and government agencies and are distinguished by not being subject to the tax and other regulations of the country in whose currency they are issued. This freedom from restrictions has led to many innovations in the characteristics of eurobonds and so there exists a wide variety of interest, currency denomination and repayment terms for these bonds (see chapter 12 for further detail on this). All bonds have the characteristic of marketability, which enhances their liquidity. The yield to maturity on a bond can be defined as the rate of discount, which equates the current market price of the bond with the future coupon payments and the repayment of the principal. Thus, for example, the yield to maturity on a five-year £100 bond with a coupon of 10 per cent paid once a year can be calculated by solving for i (the yield to maturity) in the following formula:

$$\text{Market price of bond} = \frac{10}{(1+i)} + \frac{10}{(1+i)^2} + \frac{10}{(1+i)^3} + \frac{10}{(1+i)^4} + \frac{10}{(1+i)^5} + \frac{100}{(1+i)^5}$$

The price at which bonds trade in a market will change as yields on other financial instruments change. It can be seen from the above formula that there is an inverse relationship between the price of a bond and its yield to maturity. This is more easily seen by examining the behaviour of the price of a non-redeemable bond such as a consol. This is equivalent to a perpetuity (a regular payment received without any time limit, i.e. forever). Thus the price of a consol paying a coupon value of £2.50 will be $2.5/i$, assuming that the coupon is paid once per year. Thus if the market rate of interest on similar securities (i) is 10 per cent per annum, the price of the consol will be £25. However, if the market rate falls to 5 per cent per annum, the price of the consol will rise to £50. If yields on competing financial instruments change then, given that the coupon is fixed, changes in the market price of a bond keep its yield in line with that of similar financial instruments. Consequently, if a bond is not held to maturity, there is a risk that the price at which the bond is sold will be less than the price at which the bond was bought; that is, bonds are subject to price risk.

A final point about the characteristics of debt instruments is that they are normally susceptible to a reduction in real value due to general price inflation (when the nominal rate of interest is less than the rate of general price inflation). There are some exceptions to this where debt instruments have been issued with yields that are linked to the retail price index. In the UK two examples of such instruments are index-linked government bonds and index-linked National Savings certificates.

1.3.9 *Equity*

Equities differ from the types of financial instruments so far described in that they represent a claim to a share in the ownership of a company, rather than evidence of debts. The principal type of equity instrument is the ordinary share issued by limited companies. The main characteristic of ordinary shares is that the income to be received from them is not fixed in any way. This income payment, known as dividends, constitutes a share in the profits earned by the company. The amount of the total profits earned by the company which is distributed to shareholders is determined by the company's management. The factors determining the dividend payment will include the financial performance of the company and the extent to which the company wishes to retain profits to finance investment. In addition to uncertainty about the income payments on ordinary shares, known as income risk, ordinary shares are also subject to price risk. Ordinary shares are marketable, though it is easier to trade listed shares in the larger, well known companies than it is in small companies. The liquidity of the particular ordinary share will therefore depend on its degree of marketability. In times of panic in share markets, for example October 1987, it may not be possible to sell a share without incurring a significant loss. One characteristic of ordinary shares which is highly valued is their real value certainty – when held over a sufficiently long period of time the value of shares has generally increased at a rate in excess of the rate of inflation.

1.4   Sectoral analysis of the financial system

In the simple circular flow model of the economy introduced in section 1.1 the economy was assumed to be made up of two separate groups of decision makers, or sectors, namely households and firms. To take our analysis of the financial system further we need to consider both a further disaggregation of these two sectors and an extension of the economy to introduce a government and trade with overseas economies. The further disaggregation involves splitting the firms sector into industrial firms and firms whose primary activity is financial. The other changes introduce a public sector and an overseas sector. We have now achieved a sectoral breakdown of the economy which roughly corresponds to that used by the Central Statistical Office (CSO) for the UK economy. The CSO in fact identifies five main sectors of the UK economy, with a further breakdown of two of these sectors:

(i)   personal,
(ii)   industrial and commercial companies (ICC),
(iii) financial institutions –
         banks,
         building societies,
         life assurance and pension funds,
         other financial institutions,
(iv)   public sector –
         central government,
         local government,
         public corporations,
(v)   overseas.

The personal sector consists mainly of households, along with some other groups such as unincorporated businesses, charities, universities and so on, which the statisticians find difficult to separate out. Ideally we would like data relating solely to households; however, it is not thought that these other groups distort the overall picture of household behaviour to any significant degree. As described above, the firms' sector is split into ICC and financial companies. The CSO then disaggregates further the latter group in the construction of sector financial accounts. The public sector represents government institutions and in most analysis by the CSO this is further split into central government, local government and public corporations.

1.5   National wealth

We begin our examination of the financial relationships within the UK economy with a look at the extent of national wealth. We will then move

Table 1.1   *UK national balance sheet for year end 1996*

	Value (£billion)
Tangible assets	2638.5
Intangible assets[a]	155.1
External assets	1665.8
External liabilities	1662.7
Net external wealth	3.1
Net national wealth	2796.7

[a] Non-marketable tenancy rights (includes housing and agricultural tenancy rights).
Source: CSO, *UK National Accounts*, 1997 edn, table 12.1.

on to examine a breakdown of this wealth by sector. The first assessment of wealth relating to the UK was the Domesday Book, which, just over 900 years ago and using a census approach, set out the value of the land, animals and mills of England. Over the last 30 years government statisticians and academics have adopted statistical techniques to provide an assessment of the nation's wealth today.

The tangible wealth of a nation consists of its national resources and its stocks of goods (which include buildings), durable equipment (which provides services to consumers and producers), stocks of finished goods, raw materials and work in progress. In addition, a nation also possesses intangible wealth, which includes the skill, knowledge and character of its people, otherwise described by economists as human capital. The final component of a nation's wealth is its claims on wealth in other countries net of other countries' claims on its own wealth. The statisticians have encountered many problems in estimating the value of these various components of national wealth and these are discussed in detail in an article in *Economic Trends* written by Bryant (1987). The main problems identified by Bryant are those of putting a value on natural resources such as oil, coal and gas and on valuing human capital. As a consequence these items are left out of the final national accounts published by the CSO. The complete UK national balance sheet for the end of 1996 is summarised in table 1.1.

From table 1.1 we can note that the net national wealth of the UK at the end of 1996 was approximately £2,800 billion. This is just over four times gross domestic product for the UK for that year. This figure for net national wealth is of course only an estimate because of the exclusion of certain items, mentioned above, and because many of the included items are measured with error.

Table 1.2   *Ownership of national wealth by sector, 1985*

Sector	% share of wealth
Personal	71.5
Industrial and commercial companies	11.3
Monetary sector	1.5
Other financial institutions	2.1
Total private sector	86.4
Total public sector	13.6

Source: Bryant (1987), table 6.

In a capitalist economy such as the UK most of the appropriable wealth is owned privately. The breakdown by sector of the ownership of national wealth for 1985 is given in table 1.2. Thus private sector ownership of net national wealth was estimated to be just over 86 per cent at the end of 1985. Persons are in fact the ultimate owners of most private sector wealth (i.e. more than the 71.5 per cent owned directly) through the equity claims they hold, either directly or indirectly, on the other parts of the private sector.

1.6   Sector balance sheets

The national balance sheet shown in table 1.1 hides most of the financial wealth held by the various groups which make up the UK economy. A person may be wealthy without possessing any of the wealth counted in national wealth. This is because, to take an example, wealth held in the form of a bank deposit by a person (i.e. an asset to that person) will have a corresponding liability held by the bank. So, assuming that the bank deposit is not held outside the UK, aggregation of the net wealth of the personal sector (which contains the person's bank deposit as an asset) with the net wealth of the monetary sector (which contains the bank deposit as a liability) to form national wealth causes the asset and liability to cancel each other out. The financial relationship between the person and the bank is said to be 'netted out'. It therefore follows that the only financial wealth appearing in the national balance sheet is those assets held by UK residents which are claims on the overseas sector (i.e. the corresponding liability is held overseas). These are included in the item 'External assets' in table 1.1. As we move down to the sectoral level of the economy, the more financial wealth is revealed. In this connection, balance sheets are now constructed for the domestic sectors

Table 1.3 *Personal sector balance sheet for year end 1996*

	Value (£billion)
Tangible assets	1293.8
Intangible non-financial assets	155.1
Financial assets	2126.1
Financial liabilities	583.3
Net financial wealth	1542.8
Total net wealth	2991.7

Source: CSO, *UK National Accounts*, 1997 edn, table 12.2.

of the UK economy identified in the earlier section and it is to these that we now turn our attention.

1.6.1 *Personal sector*

The personal sector balance sheet showing how its wealth was made up at the end of 1996 is shown in table 1.3. Tangible assets of the personal sector are principally houses. Intangible assets are as defined in table 1.1. The financial assets and liabilities of the personal sector are many and varied and will be examined more closely later in this chapter, when financial accounts are considered.

There are a number of important points to note about the personal sector's balance sheet. First, its financial assets greatly exceed its financial liabilities; therefore the sector has been a net lender of funds to other sectors of the economy. This is not to say that all members of the personal sector have been net savers but that in aggregate the personal sector has been a net saver. This highlights again the point about aggregation hiding information and that a disaggregation of the households of the personal sector by, for example, age would reveal more information about the ultimate lenders and ultimate borrowers in the economy. A second point not revealed by the figures in table 1.3 is that over the period 1975 to 1987, when personal sector net wealth rose by over £2,200 billion, over four-fifths of this increase was due to price changes of its tangible assets (mainly houses) and financial assets (mainly equities, held directly and indirectly). Therefore most of the increase in personal sector wealth was due to positive changes in the value of assets already held rather than increases in the quantity of assets held; this has not been so in more recent years.

The balance sheet described in table 1.3 can be rewritten in a more conventional format as in table 1.4, which shows us that net wealth,

Table 1.4   *Personal sector balance sheet for year end 1996: conventional format*

Liabilities	£billion	Assets	£billion
Net wealth	2991.7	Tangible assets	1293.8
Financial liabilities	583.3	Intangible non-financial assets	155.1
		Financial assets	2126.1
Total	3575.0		3575.0

Source: CSO, *UK National Accounts*, 1997 edn, table 12.2.

sometimes known as 'net worth', is the item which brings assets and liabilities of the sector into balance. This format of balance sheet is the one we adopt for the rest of this chapter.

1.6.2   *Industrial and commercial companies*

The balance sheet for the ICC sector for 1996 is shown in table 1.5. Tangible assets for the ICC sector are mainly the buildings, plant and machinery which provide the means of production along with any stocks of raw materials, finished goods and work in progress. Financial assets held by this sector are mainly funds held to meet short-term needs, loans to subsidiaries and trade credit provided. On the liabilities side the main item is issued share capital or equities, with the rest made up of loans from banks and trade credit received (this is approximately balanced by trade credit provided). The ICC sector, in contrast to the personal sector, has generally been a net borrower, as evidenced by the excess of financial liabilities over financial assets outstanding at the end of 1996. It should be noted that as equities are a liability of companies then the value of these liabilities can change as the prices of shares change. This

Table 1.5   *Industrial and commercial companies balance sheet for year end 1996*

Liabilities	£billion	Assets	£billion
Net wealth	-267.6	Tangible assets	829.8
Financial liabilities	1589.6	Financial assets	492.2
Total	1322.0		1322.0

Source: CSO, *UK National Accounts*, 1997 edn, table 12.3.

Table 1.6   *Financial institutions balance sheet for year end 1996*

Liabilities	£billion	Assets	£billion
Net wealth	7.8	Tangible assets	109.9
Financial liabilities	4119.6	Financial assets	4017.5
Total	4127.4		4127.4

Source: CSO, *UK National Accounts*, 1997 edn, table 12.4.

can lead to the rather curious result, seen over the 1980s, of an increase in equity prices, as the equity markets enjoyed a long period of boom, leading to an increase in the liabilities of companies greater than an increase in their assets, resulting in a reduction in the net wealth of the ICC sector. Indeed, the total net wealth of this sector was negative for 1996.

1.6.3   *Financial institutions*

For the purpose of this analysis of sectoral wealth we will take the four financial subsectors together as they are sufficiently similar in respect of their wealth structure. The balance sheet for this sector is summarised in table 1.6. The striking points about the balance sheet of this sector are the substantial financial assets and liabilities alongside a comparatively low net wealth. This follows from the nature of their activities as financial intermediaries. Their business is to lend and borrow funds, hence their substantial holdings of financial assets and liabilities. The near equality of the financial asset and liability positions again reflects the nature of their business as intermediaries. Unlike companies in the ICC sector they do not need substantial investment in plant, equipment and stocks to undertake this business, hence the relatively low level of tangible assets. These tangible assets are mainly buildings, for example the branch networks of the banks and building societies, and equipment such as computers.

1.6.4   *The public sector*

As with financial institutions, for this analysis we examine the combined public sector balance sheet, shown for 1996 in table 1.7. The public sector's tangible assets rose only slowly in value over the 1980s and hence its share of national wealth declined from 18 per cent in 1980 to under 14 per cent in 1985 (see table 1.2). This was due in the main to the policies of privatisation (sales of public corporation assets) and sales

Introduction to the financial system   19

Table 1.7   *Public sector balance sheet for year end 1996*

Liabilities	£billion	Assets	£billion
Net wealth	64.7	Tangible assets	405.0
Financial liabilities	517.0	Financial assets	176.7
Total	581.7		581.7

Source: CSO, *UK National Accounts*, 1997 edn, table 12.12.

of council houses (sales of local authority tangible assets) initiated by
the Conservative administration over this period. The policy of privatisation has continued over the 1990s, although at a slower pace as the
stock of saleable public sector assets is much smaller.

1.7   Sector financial transactions

The analysis of sectoral financial relationships has so far examined
balance sheets. These show the breakdown of wealth by sector and the
financial relationships between sectors at one point in time – the day the
balance sheet is constructed. In addition to information on stocks of
assets and liabilities it is also useful to have information on financial
transactions in these stocks, recorded over periods of time. By comparing the balance sheets of a sector at two different points in time and
noting the changes that have taken place, balance sheet data can be
converted from stock to flow form. However, the changes in stocks of
assets and liabilities observed from this process could have come about
either by transactions in those assets/liabilities or by revaluations of the
stocks (i.e. price changes). The sector financial transactions accounts
published by the CSO are not, at present, reconciled with the published
sector balance sheets. The financial transactions accounts that are published are part of the national accounting framework which relates
sector accounts for income, expenditure, capital and financial transactions. Thus, for a sector we have:

```
    Income               Income and
  + Inter-sector transfers   expenditure
  – Expenditure           account
    _____
  = Saving
    _____
  – Capital transactions   Capital account
    _____
  = Financial surplus/deficit
```

Table 1.8   *Example of household sector balance sheet as at 31 December 1996*

Liabilities	£million	Assets	£million
Net wealth	1,400	Tangible assets	800
Financial liabilities	200	Financial assets	800
Total	1,600		1,600

The income and expenditure accounts describe the economic identity of income, and income less expenditure gives the residual of saving. Capital transactions are mainly investments in physical goods. The financial surplus/deficit is then the link between the real transactions of the sector and its financial transactions. If a sector has a financial surplus then it has funds available to add to its financial assets or to reduce its financial liabilities. A financial deficit implies the sector needs to raise funds by selling financial assets or increasing its financial liabilities by borrowing.

To introduce the construction of sector financial transaction accounts we will consider a simple two-sector economy – households and firms – which has two financial instruments available for transactions – trade credit and equity. Trade credit is an asset of firms, that is, it represents funds lent from firms to households. Equity on the other hand is an asset of households. At 31 December 1996 our imaginary household sector is described by the balance sheet in table 1.8.

Over 1997 the household sector undertakes the following transactions:

income	£500 million
expenditure	£300 million
saving	£200 million
investment	£100 million
financial balance	£100 million

So for 1997 the household sector has a financial surplus of £100 million, which implies that it has funds available to enable it to acquire additional financial assets or reduce existing liabilities or both. For this example we take the situation where households acquire £200 million of company-issued equities as well as increasing their liabilities by £100 by borrowing from companies through the medium of trade credit. Any other collection of financial transactions is possible as long as the net transactions are consistent with the financial surplus. As a result of these

Table 1.9 *Example of household sector balance sheet as at 31 December 1997*

Liabilities	£million	Assets	£million
Net wealth	1,600	Tangible assets	900
Financial liabilities	300	Financial assets	1,000
Total	1,900		1,900

transactions the household sector balance sheet for the end of 1997 will be as shown in table 1.9.

The increase in tangible assets is the result of investment over the period. The value of financial assets and liabilities has increased by the value of the transactions over the period. The change in the value of net wealth comes about to bring the balance sheet of households back into balance. Another way to see the increase in net wealth is that it is equal to the value of saving over the period. Saving, which is the value of funds coming into the sector which are not consumed, is one way in which the size of the balance sheet of the sector can increase. The other way is for the value of assets already held to increase. In the case of households, the value of housing may increase as a result of an increase in house prices. So it is possible for the net wealth of a sector to increase without it saving any funds out of its income. However, changes in the value of assets are not captured within financial transaction accounts.

If we now consider the firms sector in our imaginary economy, its balance sheet for the end of 1997 is given in table 1.10.

The firms sector flows over 1997 are given below:

income	£200 million
consumption	–
saving	£200 million
investment	£300 million
financial balance	£-100 million

Table 1.10 *Example of firms sector balance sheet as at 31 December 1996*

Liabilities	£million	Assets	£million
Net wealth	300	Tangible assets	500
Financial liabilities	400	Financial assets	200
Total	700		700

Table 1.11   *Example of firms sector balance sheet as at 31 December 1997*

Liabilities	£million	Assets	£million
Net wealth	500	Tangible assets	800
Financial liabilities	600	Financial assets	300
Total	1,100		1,100

The firms sector has retained earnings of £200 million over 1997 but invests £300 million, leaving it with a financial deficit of £100 million. This implies that firms must sell existing assets or borrow new funds to finance the deficit. The financial decisions of the firms sector are implied by the household sector flows described earlier. This is because in a two-sector economy, as one sector increases its asset holdings the other sector must be increasing its liabilities by the same amount, for reasons explained in section 1.3. The financial decisions of firms are therefore to borrow funds through the issue of £200 million of equities and at the same time to increase holdings of financial assets by £100 million. The resulting balance sheet for the firms sector for the end of 1997 is given in table 1.11.

The financial transactions for the two sectors can be brought together in a financial account as shown in table 1.12.

The convention of financial accounts is:

(i)   a positive value implies an increase in financial assets or a decrease in financial liabilities,
(ii) a negative sign implies an increase in financial liabilities or a decrease in financial assets.

So in the financial account in table 1.12, a negative sign on trade credit transactions for the households sector implies that this sector is increasing

Table 1.12   *Financial account matrix for the two-sector economy (£million)*

	Households	Firms	Total
Saving	200	200	400
Investment	100	300	400
Financial balance	100	-100	–
Trade credit	-100	100	–
Equities	200	-200	–
Net financial transactions	100	-100	–

its liabilities, that is, it is borrowing more from companies through the medium of trade credit. It should be clear from this example that in order to interpret a particular figure in the financial transactions account we need to know not only the convention stated above, but whether the instrument transacted is an asset or liability of that sector.

From this simple financial account we can discern the accounting rules which underlie its construction and the construction of all financial accounts. First, the sum of the financial surpluses and deficits is zero, which reflects the fact that the financial assets of one sector are by definition the financial liabilities of another. Second, the net financial transactions of a sector will equal its financial balance. Third, the sum of transactions in a particular financial instrument will equal zero. This again follows from the fact that increased holdings of an asset of one sector will be balanced by increased liabilities of another. Finally, the sum of saving across sectors, that is, for the economy, will equal the sum of investment across sectors. In other words all saving will find its way into investment.

We now turn to examine the financial accounts for the complete UK economy.

1.8   Financial accounts for the UK economy

The CSO publishes financial accounts for the UK on a quarterly basis in *Financial Statistics* and annually in *National Accounts* (*The Blue Book*).

The financial accounts matrix for the third quarter of 1997 is presented in table 1.13. This matrix is fully disaggregated into the ten sectors described earlier. The total number of financial instruments is 45.[2] Whilst the matrix in table 1.13 is larger and more disaggregated than the matrix for our imaginary economy in table 1.12, its structure is essentially the same though the full matrix shows only the financial account (lines 1 to 5, showing the capital account, are not included).

There are problems with the data used to construct both national income and financial accounts. The figures making up these accounts are recorded with varying degrees of error. A sector's overall financial position, after calculating all income, expenditure and capital flows, is

---

2   The item 'accruals adjustment' refers to a gap between the actual payments and the incurring of a liability (or acquisition of an asset) to the government. For example, deduction of income tax by an employer creates a liability to make a payment to the Inland Revenue. The tax deduction is included in the government current account but an offsetting adjustment is made when the actual payment is delayed.

Table 1.13 Financial accounts: analysis by sector and type of asset, third quarter 1997 (£million)

	Line no.	Public sector			Financial companies and institutions				Industrial and commercial companies	Persons	Overseas
		Central government	Local authorities	Public corporations	Banks	Building societies	Life assurance and pension funds	Other financial institutions			
Notes and coins	6	-257		-13	52	-45		–	24	173	66
Sterling Treasury bills	7	-285	-5	47	3	-219	-5	-127	-35	1	597
British government securities	8	35	-9	307	832	-527	3,031	257	-123	-1,255	-2,548
National Savings	9	-392	–	-40	–	–	–		–	432	
Tax instruments	10	10			–	–		–	-14	4	
Net government indebtedness to Banking Department	11	27			-27						
Northern Ireland central government debt	12	4							–	-4	
Government liabilities under exchange cover scheme	13	-6	1	5					–		
Other public sector financing:	14										
non-marketable debt	14.1	-31		31					–		–
short-term assets	14.2	-446	175	-36		-112		397	24	-2	
Issue Department transactions in bills, etc.	15	-810						263	487	60	60
Government foreign currency debt	16	-269			907		-29	-75			-534
Other government overseas financing	17	1									-1
Official reserves	18	350									-350
Local authority debt:	19										
temporary	19.1	24	-63	10	10	–	48	10	-7	-32	–
foreign currency	19.2	12	12		–		-20	–			-12
sterling securities	19.3	–	12	–		-1		30		-21	–
other sterling debt	19.4	-130	166	5	-49		41	–	-1	-19	-13

20 Public corporation debt:										
20.1 foreign currency				64					-32	-64
20.2 sterling	-135	-4		8	132	17	6			–
21 Deposits with banks:										
21.1 sterling	1,048	88	403	-7,686	-512	2,139	6,447	1,334	-1,572	-1,689
21.2 foreign currency	-11	8	-13	-22,297	-29		1,402	784	146	20,010
21.3 sterling money-market instruments	-1			-1,475	1,085	1,792	-659	-26	53	-769
21.4 foreign currency money-market instruments				-6,534	-53	90	330	141	70	5,956
22 Deposits with building societies:										
22.1 sterling				-1	-4,682	42	-66	95	4,840	-228
22.2 sterling money-market instruments				-152	-220	46	192	-41	26	149
22.3 foreign currency money-market instruments				-174	473	23	-12	-8	-4	-298
24 Bank lending (excluding public sector)										
24.1 foreign currency				30,724			-10,132	-1,801	316	-19,107
24.2 sterling				6,029	361	-243	-3,110	-1,139	-610	-1,288
25 Credit extended by retailers								-30	30	
26 Identified trade credit:										
26.1 domestic	–	–	-562				112	613	-163	
26.2 import and export	–	–					947	–		-947
27 Loans secured on dwellings:										
27.1 building societies				3,189	3,303				-3,303	
27.2 other	-1								-3,396	
28 Other public sector lending	268	19				-10	239	-20	-144	-119
29 Other lending by financial institutions										
29.1 finance leasing	1		3	14		120	174	-180	-13	
29.2 other forms of lending					749	-329	-832	634	-671	
30 Unit trust units							-1,023		1,352	
31 UK company securities	-690	-17	1	-6,329	393	1,395	4,949	-5,453	-3,200	8,952

Table continued over

Table 1.13 *Continued*

	Line no.	Public sector			Financial companies and institutions				Industrial commercial companies	Persons	Overseas
		Central government	Local authorities	Public corporations	Banks	Building societies	Life assurance and pension funds	Other financial institutions			
Overseas securities	32	–			4,739	232	1,032	-7,834	4,313	43	-2,525
Life assurance and pension funds	33	631					-9,915			9,284	
Miscellaneous domestic instruments	34	-39	–	–	73	201	2,084	-3,622	1,006	-61	358
Direct and other investment abroad	35			-7	321		8	960	2,083	8	-3,373
investment in UK	36				-288		-26	-213	-596	-150	1,273
Miscellaneous overseas instruments	37	-632		26	44		427	5,338	-899		-4,304
Accruals adjustment	38	-3,709	-571	204	-311	-564	-553	-261	4,063	1,285	417
Total financial transactions	39	-5,444	-200	465	1,746	-167	1,205	-5,913	5,228	3,411	-331

Acquisition of assets or reduction in liabilities is shown positive: sale of assets or increase in liabilities negative.
Source: CSO, *Financial Statistics*, March 1998, table 8.1A.

Table 1.14   *Balancing items, 1990–96 (£billion)*

	Personal sector	ICCs	Overseas
1990	-866	8355	2203
1991	-9385	4101	509
1992	-5121	7925	5147
1993	-468	5275	-1532
1994	-3962	2904	5029
1995	-6491	6494	1992
1996	-7923	3956	2633

Source: CSO, *Financial Statistics*, November 1997, table 8.1L.

shown in its financial balance. If these flows were accurately recorded and if the sector's financial transactions were likewise identified in full, then the sum of financial transactions, shown in line 39 of table 1.13, should equal the financial balance. The effects of the errors and omissions in the flows recorded above and below line 5 lead to a difference between the financial balance and the sum of financial transactions. This difference is recorded in the summary accounts as the balancing item, details of which are shown in table 1.14. For the public sector and financial institutions, where most transactions have to be accurately recorded for policy or supervisory purposes, the balancing items have generally been small. For the other sectors, where there is less direct collection of statistics, the balancing items are often quite large and were particularly large in the latter part of the 1980s although they showed a tendency to fall in the 1990s as the CSO has devoted more resources to the compilation of these statistics. This can be seen in table 1.14, which shows the balancing items for the three sectors most prone to this problem.

There are other deficiencies with the published financial accounts although none as serious as that just described. One problem is that the data are published on a net basis, that is, a figure presented in the financial transactions account represents the net result of purchases and sales (new borrowing and repayments) of an asset (liability). We cannot therefore infer whether a larger than normal figure for, say, acquisition of company securities by other financial institutions is due to more purchases or fewer sales during the period.

However, despite these drawbacks there are still many interesting points that can be drawn from a study of a financial account. One fundamental thing that the accounts show is that those people who save in an economy are not the same as those people who invest in physical assets. The financial account thus demonstrates one of the reasons for the existence of financial institutions, which is to channel funds from savers to investors, and it shows the various routes by which the funds flow. This will be considered in more detail in the next chapter. The financial account, by setting the flows for each sector together in a consistent framework, also allows us to obtain a more complete picture of financial relationships when compared with looking at each sector's flows individually. For example, if we examine row 21.1 in the account for the third quarter of 1997 in table 1.13, we can see each sector's transactions in bank sterling deposits. Here we see that the net flows into bank sterling deposits over this quarter were positive, that is, more funds were deposited than withdrawn, hence the negative sign on the amount shown in the column for banks – an increase in liabilities for banks. Whilst all of the public sector, life assurance and pension funds, other financial institutions and ICC all made net deposits, net withdrawals were made by building societies, persons and the overseas sector. By looking down the column for life assurance and pension funds we can see that the principal investment by these institutions in this quarter was UK government securities.

Another interesting feature of the financial picture in the third quarter of 1997 is revealed in line 32. This shows that other financial institutions, primarily unit and investment trusts, were massively net sellers of overseas securities. Banks and ICC were net purchasers, although not to the same extent. The purchases of overseas securities by ICC is explained by the acquisitions of European companies by UK companies in that period. The financing of the purchase of overseas assets by other financial institutions can be seen by looking down the column for that sector. Thus we see that the purchase was mainly financed by the sale of miscellaneous overseas instruments.

This discussion of some of the features of the third quarter 1997 financial accounts matrix is intended to show that, bearing in mind the caveat on data deficiencies, some interesting insights into changing financial relationships can be obtained from a study of such accounts.

1.9   Conclusion

In this chapter we have started our examination of the role of a financial system in an economy, established some fundamental concepts of finance, have introduced data on wealth and financial transactions in the UK and shown the relationship between these. In the next chapter we build on this and examine further the role of a financial system in mediating between savers and investors before looking at how financial systems evolve.

Chapter 2

Financial intermediation and recent developments in the UK financial system

2.1 Introduction

In this chapter our primary aim is to describe the process of financial intermediation and in doing so we examine the arguments as to why we need financial institutions such as banks. We also examine the evolution of financial systems and in particular distinguish between the more market-oriented systems of the UK and US and the more bank-oriented systems of Germany and Japan. Finally we provide an overview of the tremendous changes that have taken place in the UK financial system over the last 20 years. This will provide a framework for the more specific discussion of events affecting financial institutions and markets which make up the remainder of this book.

2.2 The nature of financial intermediation

In developed economies, decisions to invest (in capital projects) are often taken separately from decisions to save. There are some exceptions to this: for example, firms which do not distribute all profits as dividends but retain some to finance investment are both saving and investing. However, even when saving and investment are carried out by the same economic agent, the timing of the decisions will often be different. Saving may precede the investment as sufficient funds are accumulated, or the saving may follow the investment as debts used to finance it are paid off. However, it is a general feature of developed economies that a high proportion of saving is not used immediately by the saver but is made available to investors elsewhere. In chapter 1, one of the roles of a financial system was described as the channelling of

29

Funds lent

Financial claim

Figure 2.1   *Direct financing*

funds from those economic agents with a financial surplus (lenders) to
those economic agents with a financial deficit (borrowers). Whilst most
borrowing is used to finance investment, this more precise statement
acknowledges that there will be some economic agents who borrow to
finance a deficit that has arisen not from investment but from an excess
of consumption over income.

A financial system essentially consists of financial markets and
financial institutions. In this section we examine the role of the financial
system, in particular financial institutions, in the process of channelling
funds from lenders to borrowers. To begin the analysis we return to our
simple economy, introduced in section 1.2, which consists of households
and firms. Assuming that households in aggregate are lenders and firms
in aggregate are borrowers, then the only way in which funds can flow
from lenders to borrowers is directly, as shown in figure 2.1.

In this simple economy, firms will finance some part of their investment by borrowing funds from households and in return households will
hold the financial claims issued by firms. Investment, which takes the
form of the purchase of physical assets such as buildings or machinery,
will generally be long term in nature and the borrower is likely to want
to repay the amount borrowed over a long period in line with the flow of
expected returns from the project. Further to this, investment returns are
likely to be uncertain. The firm making the investment may have
misjudged the market for the product, or the cost of producing the
product may be higher than anticipated. Both these factors would cause

returns to be less than expected. Furthermore, the purchased physical assets are generally highly specialised, making them difficult to sell, if problems occur, except at a loss. The claims that firms issue will have characteristics reflecting the nature of the investment project. They will seek to issue long-term claims to provide a reasonable prospect of the investment generating sufficient returns to repay the claim. The uncertainty of investment returns is likely to lead firms to seek to finance some part of the investment in the form of equity, where the claim can be remunerated according to the profitability of the investment.

Whilst some (wealthy) lenders will be happy to hold long-term, risky claims, it is likely that the majority of lenders will seek different characteristics in the claims they hold. By lending funds, the lender is indicating a willingness to give up some consumption now in return for greater consumption in the future. However, there are a great many uncertainties in life and many lenders will wish to retain discretion as to when that future consumption takes place. It is clear from this discussion that the requirements of borrowers and lenders are generally different. The claims issued by borrowers are likely to be long term and high risk whereas lenders are likely to prefer to hold claims which are more certain and short term. In addition, borrowers are likely to be seeking to borrow a sum of money greater than the sum that an individual lender will typically lend. In the absence of organised financial markets or financial institutions, as presented in figure 2.1, lending/borrowing will occur as a result of direct negotiation between two parties. The claims produced as a result of direct negotiation will be highly illiquid since it would be difficult to sell them in the absence of an organised market. There are also various types of cost involved in direct lending, which are:

(i)   search costs – the costs of searching out potential transactors, obtaining information about them and negotiating a contract;
(ii)   verification costs – lenders will incur costs in evaluating borrowing proposals;
(iii)   monitoring costs – lenders incur further costs, after the loan is made, from monitoring the actions of borrowers to ensure that the terms of the contract are met;
(iv)   enforcement costs – further costs arise should the borrower be unable to meet the commitments as promised and a solution must be worked out between the lender and borrower or other aspects of the contract enforced.

In addition to these transaction costs lenders are also faced with the problems arising out of asymmetric information. This refers to the situation where one party to a transaction has better information than the second party. In this case the borrower has more information about the potential returns and risks of the investment project for which funds are being lent than the lender. The existence of asymmetric information creates problems in the financial system both before a transaction is entered into, in evaluating borrowing proposals, and after, in monitoring and enforcing the loan contract.

2.2.1   *Asymmetric information: adverse selection and moral hazard*

The first problem created by the situation of asymmetric information is that of adverse selection. This is a problem at the search/verification stage of the transaction, when the lender is selecting a potential borrower. Adverse selection occurs when the potential borrowers who are the most likely to produce an adverse outcome are the ones who most actively seek out a loan and hence are most likely to be selected. Because adverse selection makes it more likely that loans will be made to borrowers who are likely to default, lenders may decide not to lend at all, even though there are borrowers who are good credit risks in the market.

To understand why adverse selection occurs, suppose you have two friends to whom you might make a loan. Your first friend, Sally, is a cautious person who borrows only when she has an investment project she is sure will generate a return that will safely pay off the loan. By contrast, your second friend, Anna, loves taking risks and has a scheme which she is sure will make her a lot of money. Unfortunately, as with most risky investments, there is a high probability that Anna will lose money from the investment and be unable to pay off the loan. Which of your friends is most likely to ask you for a loan? The answer is, of course, Anna, as she has a lot to gain if the investment does well.

If information were not asymmetric, in other words if you knew the likely risks and returns of the investment projects suggested by your friends, then you would not make a loan to Anna as you would know there is a good chance that you would not be repaid. However, given the existence of asymmetric information, you are more likely to lend to Anna than Sally because Anna is the friend who is more likely to ask you for a loan. Given the possibility of adverse selection you may decide not to lend to either of your friends. This will mean that Sally, who is good credit risk, would be denied finance for the times she has a worthwhile investment project.

A second problem that arises out of asymmetric information is moral hazard. This can occur after the loan has been made and is associated with the monitoring and enforcement stages. Moral hazard, in financial markets, is the risk that the borrower might engage in activities that are undesirable (immoral) from the lender's point of view because they make it less likely that the loan is repaid. The existence of moral hazard may make lenders less likely to make loans.

As an example of moral hazard suppose you have made a loan of £1,000 to another friend, Joe, who has asked you for the loan so he can purchase a computer and set himself up in business as a graphic designer. Once you have made the loan there is a risk that Joe will not use the money for what he claimed he was going to use it for, but instead use it to bet on the horses. If he bets on a 25–1 long shot and wins then he is able to repay the loan and keep £24,000 for himself. On the other hand, if he loses, which is likely as long shots do not often win races, then you do not get paid and Joe loses his reputation as a reliable friend. If Joe believes the gains from correctly betting (£24,000) are of more value than the cost (his reputation) if he bets incorrectly then Joe is more likely to place the bet with the borrowed funds. If you knew that Joe was likely to make the bet then you would prevent him doing so. However, it is difficult for you to monitor the activities of Joe once you have made the loan because information is asymmetric. The potential for moral hazard may make you reluctant to lend money.

Transaction costs and information asymmetries are important impediments to well functioning financial markets. One solution is the emergence of organised financial markets where tradable equity or debt (bond) financial instruments can be issued and acquired. Such markets are labelled capital markets as they allow firms to issue financial claims to enable them to raise finance to acquire capital (physical) assets. The existence of such markets overcomes some of the obstacles to lending/borrowing. In particular the ability to sell on claims in a market will enhance the liquidity of those claims to the lender and so encourage more lending to take place. A central feature of organised markets is the existence of specialised brokers who bring together buyers and sellers and so reduce search costs. However, there are still substantial transaction costs and high risks for the lender and the problems of adverse selection and moral hazard. As we will see in section 2.3.2 though, there are ways in which traded equity and debt contracts can be designed to minimise adverse selection and moral hazard, and financial intermediaries are able to reduce transaction costs and alleviate the problems of adverse selection and moral hazard. With the existence of financial intermediaries, small savers are able to lend money to financial intermediaries with lower transaction costs and in return hold the claims issued by those intermediaries where those claims will have characteristics such as high liquidity and low risk which are more attractive to savers. Financial intermediaries will use the funds to lend to borrowers

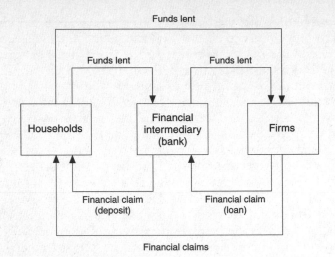

Figure 2.2   *Intermediated financing*

and thus hold the higher risk and longer-term claims issued by borrowers. This is illustrated in figure 2.2.

   The success of financial intermediaries, such as banks, is evidenced
by the fact that most external funds for non-financial businesses in the
UK are provided by banks – see figure 2.3.

   In the next section we examine the main reasons suggested to explain
why financial intermediaries exist.

2.3   What do financial intermediaries do?

Before considering the advantages of intermediated finance over direct
finance through organised markets, it is useful to observe that under
intermediated finance the chain of transactions between the firm and
ultimate lender is longer and this is likely to entail an additional element
of transaction costs. Any proposition that intermediated finance has
advantages over direct finance must be based on the premise that the
gains from intermediation outweigh the additional transaction costs.
There are two distinct explanations of the role of financial intermediaries and each of these is considered below.

2.3.1   *Banks as transformers*

An early account was provided by Gurley and Shaw (1960): financial
intermediaries exist to transform the primary securities issued by firms

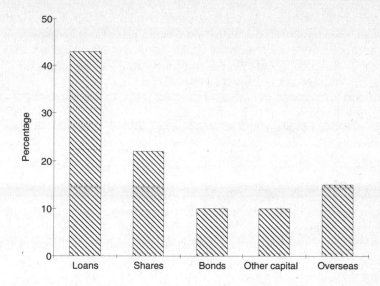

Figure 2.3 *Sources of external funds for UK non-financial firms for 1970–96. Loans are made up primarily of bank loans but include loans made by other financial institutions. Shares consist of issued ordinary shares. Bonds consist of debentures and preference shares. Other capital consists of mainly capital transfers and import credits. Overseas refers to capital funding originating outside the UK*

into the indirect securities desired by ultimate lenders. So an intermediary, such as a bank, will issue deposit claims which have the characteristics of small size, low risk and high liquidity and use a proportion of the funds raised to acquire the larger size, high-risk and illiquid claims issued by firms. The intermediary is undertaking three main transformations:

Maturity transformation
The liabilities of intermediaries, such as banks, are on average of a much shorter term than that of their assets. In fact, approximately half of UK retail banks' deposits are repayable on demand. Banks are said to be mismatching their balance sheets, or borrowing 'short' and lending 'long'. Mismatching exposes the intermediary to liquidity risk, which is the risk that it will have insufficient liquid funds to meet its commitments. Under normal circumstances only a small fraction of depositors demand repayment of deposits at a particular time and other depositors will be placing new deposits. It is therefore possible for a bank to estimate its liquidity needs and provide for it by holding some of its

assets in liquid form. However, if a large number of depositors demand repayment (i.e. a 'run' develops on the bank), perhaps because of concerns about the bank's solvency, the bank's ability to meet deposit withdrawals breaks down. Some of the strategies that banks use to manage liquidity risk are discussed in chapter 3.

Risk transformation
Financial intermediaries such as banks hold mainly loans in their asset portfolio which carry a higher risk of default than the deposits they issue to finance these loans. Banks are able to transform risky assets into virtually riskless deposits by:

(i)   minimising the risk of individual loans it takes on (i.e. by screen-
       ing out bad risks);
(ii)   diversifying risks (i.e. spreading risks by lending to different types
       of borrowers – this brings about a greater independence of loan
       risks);
(iii) pooling risks (i.e. having a large number of loans so that, as a
       consequence of the 'law of large numbers', the variability of losses
       is reduced);
(iv)   holding sufficient capital to meet any unexpected losses.

These techniques for managing this process of risk transformation are discussed in more detail in chapter 3.

Size transformation
It was noted above that lenders tend to want to lend smaller amounts of funds than the amounts which borrowers generally wish to borrow. Financial intermediaries are able to colleet together the small amounts made available by lenders and parcel these into the larger amounts required by borrowers.

The reason why we need financial intermediaries to undertake this transformation process is that there exist indivisibilities and/or economies of scale in lending/borrowing. For example, if an individual wanted to make a loan, to protect his investment he would probably have a contract drawn up by a lawyer where the terms of the loan are specified. The cost to the individual of having the contract drawn up may make it uneconomic to make the loan. However, a financial institution like a bank will be able to use a standard loan contract for a wide range of loans so the unit cost of the contract per loan is much smaller for the bank than for the individual. Thus financial institutions are able to take advantage of economies of scale to reduce transactions costs.

To illustrate more formally how financial intermediaries are able to reduce transaction costs, we denote the rate of interest as R and transaction costs as T_L and T_B for the lender and borrower, respectively (note that these costs are calculated as a percentage of the loan):

the net return for the lender $\quad R_L = R - T_L$
the net cost for the borrower $\quad R_B = R + T_B$
then $\qquad\qquad\qquad\qquad\quad R_B - R_L = T_B + T_L$

The introduction of an intermediary introduces a new element of cost, C, which we, for convenience, assume is paid by the borrower and is again expressed in percentage terms. Thus now:

$$R_L = R - T_L'$$
$$R_B = R + T_B' + C$$

where the prime indicates transaction costs after the introduction of the intermediary. Hence:

$$R_B - R_L = T_B' + T_L' + C$$

The gap between lending and borrowing rates will be lower and benefit both parties provided:

$$(T_B + T_L) - (T_B' + T_L') > C$$

That is, providing the intermediary has lowered transaction costs by more than its charge.

2.3.2 Banks reduce the problems arising out of asymmetric information

The second approach to explaining the existence of financial intermediaries views intermediaries as institutions that reduce or eliminate problems relating to asymmetric information in the lending/borrowing process. As we saw in section 2.2.1, lenders typically have less information than borrowers and as a consequence are faced with the problems of adverse selection and moral hazard. The problem of adverse selection can be solved by the production of more information on the circumstances of the borrower. One way this can be done is for private companies to collect and produce information which distinguishes good firms from bad firms and sell this information to lenders. In the US companies such as Standard and Poor's, and Moody's collect and publish information on firms' balance sheet positions and financial statements. This system of private production and sale of information does not completely solve the problem of adverse selection because of the free-rider problem. This problem occurs when people who do not pay for information take advantage of information that other people have paid for. So, if one person pays for information on a firm and then purchases directly the securities issued by that firm he may be observed by other investors who have not purchased the information but who also buy the same securities. If enough investors buy the securities the price will be bid up, thus negating the benefits to the original purchaser of the information. If this free-rider problem is known to investors then private firms will not be able to sell as much information, as the value of this information is limited by the free-rider problem.

However, financial intermediaries can help solve the adverse selection problem more fully. A financial institution, such as a bank, can develop an expertise in information production that enables it to select mainly good risks. One particular advantage that banks possess in this area is that they can gain information about potential borrowers from their transactions accounts held with the bank. If these potential borrowers route most transactions through their accounts, information is gained enabling the bank to build up a profile of a customer's suitability for credit and ability to repay loans. Such informational economies of scope provide one rationale for the joint packaging of payments and loan services (discussed in chapter 3). Because the bank lends to mainly good risks then it is more able to make a profit on its lending. An important element in the bank's ability to profit from information it produces is that it avoids the free-rider problem by mainly making private loans. A private loan is one that is not traded and therefore other investors are not able to observe the bank and bid up the price of the bank's loan to the point where little or no profit is made. The fact that the majority of the loans made by banks are non-traded is very important in their success in reducing the adverse selection problem in financial markets.

A bank is also able to reduce the adverse selection problem by asking the borrower to provide security (collateral) for the loan. Security is property provided by the borrower to the lender which, if the borrower defaults on the loan, can be used by the lender to reduce its losses. For example, with a mortgage loan made to enable a borrower to purchase a house, the house will be pledged as security. If the borrower fails to repay the full amount of the loan the house can be sold and the proceeds used to pay off the loan. The provision of security therefore guarantees that most of the loan will be repaid, thus reducing the problem of adverse selection for the lender.

The problem of moral hazard in financial markets was described in section 2.2.1 as the borrower engaging in undesirable activities after the loan is made which make it more likely the loan is not repaid. This can be reduced by banks through the use of restrictive covenants. A restrictive covenant is a provision written into a debt contract that restricts the borrower's activities. A restrictive covenant can be directed towards discouraging undesirable behaviour, for example by restricting the borrower to purchasing only particular items of equipment with the loaned funds. A restrictive covenant can also be used to encourage a borrower to undertake activities that make it more likely that a loan is repaid. For example, a mortgage loan may require a borrower to carry life assurance which pays off the loan in the event of the borrower dying. As a consequence of restrictive covenants, debt contracts are often complicated legal documents with various provisions which affect a borrower's behaviour. For restrictive covenants to work they clearly need to be monitored and enforced by the lender. This involves a cost and where the debt contract is traded the free-rider problem, discussed above, exists. If an investor knows that other investors are monitoring and enforcing restrictive covenants in debt securities (bonds) then he or she can free ride on their actions. If most bond holders do likewise then the likelihood is that not enough resources are devoted to monitoring and enforcement. This clearly increases moral hazard. However, because banks, as we saw above, provide non-traded loans, they are able to avoid the free-rider problem. Therefore a bank will receive the full benefits of monitoring and enforcement and is thus more likely to devote enough resources to this to reduce the moral hazard problem. The provision of security by the borrower will also enable the lender to exercise control over the borrower.

Lewis (1991) states that banks can therefore be viewed 'as "social accountants", specialising in the acquisition and dissemination of information, and "delegated monitors", who stay informed about developments inside borrowing enterprises and control their managers' behaviour'. Diamond (1984, 1996) also introduces the notion of banks as delegated monitors. He demonstrates that it is more efficient for lenders to delegate the monitoring of loans to banks. This is because, in general, many lenders are required to generate the funds required for one borrower and there are scale economies in monitoring, so it is more efficient to have one lender (the intermediary) monitor the borrower than many. This then prompts the question of who monitors the bank. Here Diamond shows that where the bank has a large number of loans and the loan portfolio is well diversified (thus making the individual loan risks more independent) then the costs to depositors in monitoring the bank (the delegation costs) are arbitrarily small. This is because where independent risks are pooled, that is, there are a large number of loans, you can rely upon the law of large numbers – as you increase the number of loans then the variability of losses reduces towards zero and actual defaults approach the expected level. If a bank can predict with greater certainty its actual loan losses then it can cover this by building a default premium into the interest rate charged to borrowers. So the bank is unlikely to become bankrupt and default on deposits if it has a large diversified loan portfolio. From the depositor's point of view there is little or no cost involved in monitoring the bank as bank deposits are virtually default free. Diamond therefore shows that banks, as financial intermediaries, perform an additional transformation from monitored debt into unmonitored debt.

2.4   Implications of financial intermediation

We have seen that financial intermediaries increase the amount of lending/saving in an economy by reducing the frictions that impede this process, in particular transaction costs and asymmetric information. As a consequence more funds will flow from lenders into productive investment. We can also examine the implications of the existence of financial intermediaries for individual lenders and borrowers using the Hirschleifer model (see e.g. Hirschleifer 1958). This is a two-period investment/consumption model and the initial assumptions of this model are:

(i)   two-period analysis;
(ii)   the existence of a perfect capital market, implying that:
    (a) the individual can borrow or lend what he or she wishes at the same ruling rate of interest,
    (b) there is perfect knowledge of the investment and borrowing opportunities open to the individual and
    (c) access to the capital market is costless;
(iii) there are no distorting taxes;
(iv)   the individual allocates consumption expenditure over the two periods so as to maximise utility;
(v)   investment opportunities are infinitely divisible.

The first important component of the analysis is the physical investment opportunities line (PIL) depicting the physical investment opportunities available to the firm/individual in period 0. These are ranked in descending order of profitability. This is shown in figure 2.4, where the vertical axis represents period 1 and the horizontal axis period 0. We assume for sake of ease of exposition that the individual has an initial endowment of goods equal to Y_0 and none in period 1. Hence any consumption in period 1 must be financed by saving goods in period 0

Figure 2.4   *Hirschleifer model: physical investment opportunities line (PIL)*

and investing them. Thus, point A represents a consumption of C_0, with $Y_0 - C_0$ being invested to produce consumption goods of C_1 for consumption in period 1. The slope of the PIL curve reflects diminishing returns to investment.

Consequently, given the amount of resources in period 0, Y_0, without a capital market or financial intermediaries the individual's consumption in period 1 is restricted to the proceeds from investment in period 0. Similarly any investment reduces the level of consumption in period 0. The optimum allocation of consumption between the two periods occurs at the familiar point of tangency between the PIL and the individual's indifference curve (i.e. point A in figure 2.5). At this point the marginal return on investment equals the individual's time preference as indicated by the slope of the indifference curve. Note the return is given by C_1 and the cost of the investment by $Y_0 - C_0$.

The introduction of a capital market or financial intermediaries changes the situation since the individual can borrow or lend so as to rearrange her or his investment opportunities. The borrowing/lending opportunities can be represented diagrammatically using the financial investment opportunities line (FIL), as shown in figure 2.6. The straight line represents the perfect capital market assumption that borrowing and lending can be achieved at the same rate of interest. The slope of the FIL is given by $-(1 + r)$ where r is the market rate of interest. The individual can move up and down the FIL; for example, investment of

Figure 2.5 *Hirschleifer model: optimal allocation of consumption between period 0 and period 1*

$0A$ funds in the financial market in period 0 would produce $0B$ in period $1\{0A(1 + r)\}$. Similarly investment of DA in the financial market in period 0 would produce $0E$ in period $1\{DA(1 + r)\}$.

The impact of the introduction of a capital market (financial intermediation) can be seen by combining the information given in figures 2.5 and 2.6 to arrive at figure 2.7. The individual can separate the two decisions (production and consumption) so that the following two conditions apply.

(i)   The present value of production is maximised at point A, where the marginal return on investment equals the capital market rate of interest, that is, where the PIL is tangential to the FIL furthest from the origin. Optimal production in the two periods is then C_0^* and C_1^*, respectively.

(ii)   Utility is maximised where the individual's time preference equals the capital market rate of interest. This occurs where the individual's indifference curve is tangential to the FIL so that the market rate of interest is also equal to the individual's time preference. This can occur by one of two means:

     (a)   Borrowing against further production to finance present consumption. This is illustrated in figure 2.7a, where $(C_0 - C_0^*)$ is borrowed in period 0, with consumption being C_0. In period 1

Figure 2.6   *Hirschleifer model: financial investment opportunities line (FIL)*

consumption is C_1, with $(C^*_1 - C_1)$ being the loan repayment.

(b)   Lending to finance future consumption. This is illustrated in figure 2.7b, where $(C^*_0 - C_0)$ is lent in period 0, with consumption being C_0. In period 1 consumption is C_1, with $(C_1 - C^*_1)$ being the proceeds of loan repayment.

Consequently utility has been increased by the introduction of a financial intermediary since the individual would have remained at point A without the intermediary, with consumption equal to C^*_0 and C^*_1 in the two periods, respectively; that is, the individual is on a higher or the original indifference curve following the introduction of an intermediary.

This analysis is only as good as its underlying assumptions. It is apparent that these are very (perhaps overly) restrictive. A perfect capital market is unlikely to occur in the real world for three reasons. First, in all markets borrowers pay a higher rate of interest than that earned by lenders. Hence the slopes of the FIL will differ for lenders and borrowers. Second, operators do not have perfect foresight and financial markets are characterised by a degree of uncertainty. Third, access to the capital markets is not costless. Furthermore, taxes do exist and consequently distortions are introduced into the raising of finance. Also, the assumption of a two-period analysis may appear to be restrictive but, in fact, is merely used to simplify the exposition. Similar

(a)

(b)

Figure 2.7   *Hirschleifer model: borrowing (a) or lending (b) to increase utility*

results could be obtained from multi-period analysis but would be more complicated to derive.

2.5   The future for financial intermediation

We have demonstrated that financial intermediaries have a role to play in financial markets because of the existence of frictions in markets or incompleteness of markets. It would appear that financial intermediaries have emerged as a response to transaction costs or asymmetric information. Some economists have argued (e.g. McCulloch 1981; Tobin

1984) that financial intermediaries are a transitory phase in an evolutionary process where the final phase is a complete set of markets embracing all commodities and all contingencies. Such markets are referred to as complete markets or Arrow–Debreu markets, following the Arrow–Debreu equilibrium model (for a theoretical exposition see Arrow and Hahn (1971) or for an introduction to the concepts of complete markets see Flood (1991)). Complete markets are characterised by negligible transaction costs. Complete markets would embrace futures markets, which allow trade in all commodities for delivery in the future, and option markets, which provide insurance against particular contingencies. The nature of futures and options markets is discussed in chapter 13. The existence of complete markets covering all commodities and contingencies is, of course, a theoretical construct. The question that is posed here is whether developments that lower transaction costs and alleviate the problems of asymmetric information in markets will lead to a decline in financial intermediation. There is evidence that large companies are moving away from intermediated finance through banks towards raising funds directly from capital markets. This phenomenon is referred to as dis-intermediation or securitisation and is discussed in chapter 12.

Diamond (1989, 1991) suggests that borrower reputation is important in the financing process. Where a borrower has no reputation then the problems of asymmetric information will mean that the borrower is likely to be dependent on banks for external finance. Once a borrower establishes a reputation (through, for example, a history of making good profits) the borrower is able to access the capital markets by issuing equity or debt claims. Reputation becomes a capital asset, so consequently firms are more likely to select safe rather than risky investments to protect that capital asset. The information provided by the firm's track record reduces the adverse selection and moral hazard problems for investors. It could also be argued that these companies are so large and well diversified that their debts may be considered to be of low risk.

2.6   Evolution of financial systems

The financial systems that have emerged in the major developed economies have some important differences in structure. The differences that exist, in particular the different relationships between the financial system and the corporate sector, have been suggested as one explanation for different economic performances of countries since the Second World War. We will examine this debate in chapter 16; however, to provide some background to this debate we consider here the relationship between the evolution of a financial system and the different phases of economic growth (see Rybczynski (1988) for further discussion).

In the early stages of the growth of an economy, that is, when an economy transforms itself from agrarian to industrial, it is banks which act as the main intermediary providing the external finance for the investment required for this restructuring. During this bank-oriented phase of the financial system, ownership of the productive resources of the economy is concentrated in few hands and there is little separation of ownership and control of these resources. As industrialisation continues it is usual for firms to obtain a larger proportion of their externally raised funds through the capital markets. This inevitably leads to a separation of ownership from control of firms, with ownership (i.e. holders of the equity claims issued by firms through the capital market) held by households both directly and increasingly indirectly through non-bank financial companies. The control of firms is delegated to professional managers subject to satisfactory performances of the company. In this market-oriented phase of the financial system the role of the banks in providing finance for firms is less important and generally passive. As industrialisation reaches a peak, there is greater restructuring of economic activity, that is, redirection of the resources in the economy through a change in the ownership and control of firms. This active restructuring takes place through the capital markets. As the economy moves into what has been termed the de-industrialisation phase, when the relative importance of the traditional manufacturing industries declines and the relative importance of service industries increases, there is a much greater level of economic restructuring. This places greater demands on the financial system, which, it is argued, moves into the securitised phase. The functions of the financial system expand under this phase so that enhanced capital and credit markets emerge along with markets for corporate control and venture capital. The financial system is more complete under the securitised phase and more importantly plays an active role in the restructuring of the economy. This restructuring takes place through the new markets in corporate control and venture capital. The market for corporate control is concerned with changing the ownership and control of existing firms and is increasingly carried out through the use of takeovers. Such takeovers are often hostile (i.e. the bid from the company proposing the takeover is opposed by the target company's management) but the takeover process may be seen as providing a discipline on companies, allowing control to be transferred from inefficient to efficient management – see chapter 16 for further discussion of this. The market for venture capital is concerned with the provision of finance to the new firms which emerge in this restructuring process.

The preceding description of the evolution of financial systems is very general and does not apply to all countries. The description is probably most applicable to the Anglo-Saxon economies of the US and the UK, with the transformation to a securitised financial system taking place earlier in the US. In contrast, countries such as Germany and Japan have continued to operate with a financial system which more closely represents the bank-oriented system.

2.6.1 *The Japanese and German financial systems*

An important feature of the Japanese economy is the *keiretsu,* which is a grouping of industrial firms with a core group of banks and other financial intermediaries. Many of the industrial firms will trade with each other. Linkages between the members of the group are enhanced by cross-shareholdings (i.e. each group member holds equity shares in the other members of the group). As banks in the group have equity ownership in the firms, this allows the banks to have membership on the firms' supervisory boards. The banks therefore have a close relationship with the firms in the *keiretsu* and the banks will favour these firms when it comes to making loans.

German banks also have close ties with industry through the *Hausbank* system. Banks hold shares in firms and, in addition, bank customers keep equity shares 'on deposit' at banks and give the bank proxies to vote with these shares. As a consequence, German banks have a controlling interest in many of the large firms and bank representatives sit on the boards of directors of these firms.

In countries like Germany and Japan, banks can and do act in an active way in industrial restructuring, providing risk capital (equity) to companies and then working closely with those companies. This close relationship also involves performance monitoring of the management of the company and where necessary banks may initiate a change in the management or ownership of companies. Such changes, in contrast to the market-oriented or securitised systems, are generally carried out without hostile confrontation. A long-term relationship is established between a bank and company in Germany and Japan and this gives the bank a number of advantages. In particular, banks have timely access to information and this helps the bank to monitor the firm more effectively. This enables a bank to reduce the adverse selection and moral hazard problems discussed in section 2.2.1.

The foregoing discussion of the evolution of financial systems presents a clear-cut distinction between bank-oriented and market-oriented or securitised systems. In recent years certain developments have blurred this distinction. As countries loosely associated with bank-oriented systems have moved into the de-industrialisation phase, the accompanying increased level of restructuring has tended to encourage a transition to more market-oriented or securitised financial systems. Countries experiencing such a transition are France and Italy. Also, companies in both Germany and Japan are now increasingly making greater use of capital markets, with a greater proportion of risk capital being provided by non-bank institutions. In addition, countries more strongly associated with bank-oriented systems have recently experienced hostile takeover activity, although the regulatory and institutional impediments to hostile takeovers in such countries suggest that such activity is unlikely to grow at a significant rate. Finally, although there are clearly advantages with a financial system where banks have a close relationship with the firms they provide capital to, this does not imply that banks in these countries do not make mistakes. The recent experiences in Japan illustrate this where deregulation of the banking system in the 1980s led to a boom in bank lending, with banks lending aggressively in the property market. When property values collapsed in the early 1990s, many banks were left holding massive amounts of bad loans. This has led to a number of banks failing including the tenth largest commercial bank in Japan, Hokkaido Takushoku, as well as Yamaichi Securities, in late 1997.

2.7   Recent developments in the UK financial system

There has been a tremendous change in the UK financial system over the last 20 years. The changes that have taken place can be analysed in a systematic way and in this section we provide a perspective on the main forces leading to change and the major changes that have taken place. This analysis, adapted from Llewellyn (1985, 1991), provides a framework for assessing and interpreting the more specific discussion of events in financial markets throughout the rest of this book.

Some of the main forces leading to change in any financial system are:

(i)   changes in the market environment,
(ii)   changes in the portfolio preferences of users of financial intermediation services,
(iii) changes in the preferences of and constraints on the providers of financial intermediation services.

The interaction of these forces produces financial innovation, which is essentially the development of new financial instruments and techniques of financial intermediation, and structural change in the financial system, with the appearance of new financial markets and changes in the organisation and behaviour of institutions. With this general framework in mind we can now examine the main changes in the UK financial system.

Over the postwar period up to the end of the 1960s the UK financial system was characterised by strict demarcation between the various types of financial institutions. So banks provided banking services and building societies provided housing finance services. As a consequence there was little competition between the different types of institution. There was also little competition within a particular financial market as, for example, banks and building societies operated cartels which set interest rates. Similarly within stock markets restrictive practices, in particular the existence of minimum non-negotiable commissions, had the effect of reducing competition. Towards the end of the 1960s the first competitive pressures were felt by banks as the relaxed requirement of entry into the City of London saw penetration by foreign banks into the UK banking system. In 1971, reform of the banking system, through a package of measures known as competition and credit control, led to the removal of the banking cartel and greater competition within the industry. However, most of the deregulation of the financial system has occurred since 1980, with the aim of introducing greater competition. Alongside this deregulation there has been a parallel trend to tighten up the prudential regulation of the system, with the aim of protecting the user of financial intermediation services. In 1980 controls on bank lending were abandoned, leaving banks free to expand into new areas and one area which was targeted was housing finance. Banks therefore entered into competition with building societies, which led to building societies abandoning their cartel arrangement, and, in 1986, to the Building Societies Act, which relaxed, to some extent, the constraints imposed on building societies. Also in 1986 the stock market underwent deregulation with a set of changes in trading arrangements known as Big Bang. As a consequence of these developments financial markets are much more competitive than they were at the start of the 1980s. Developments to protect users of financial intermediation services included the Banking Act of 1987, which tightened prudential regulation of banks following the collapse of the Johnson Matthey Bank in 1984, the Basle convergence accord of 1988, which introduced a new measure of capital adequacy of banks, which relates the capital held by banks to the risks they undertake, and the Financial Services Act of 1986, which introduced a new system of investor protection. Most of these regulatory measures have since been updated as regulators have attempted to 'keep up' with the rapid pace of change in financial markets

As described above, various forces in the financial system have led to both financial innovation and structural change. The main developments are now summarised.

2.7.1   *Financial conglomeration*

Deregulation and the greater competition it has produced have resulted in a steady erosion of the demarcation between the different types of financial institution. Financial institutions are seeking to reduce their dependence upon their traditional core business and diversifying into a wider range of products and services. One consequence of this is that function and institution are no longer closely aligned. Banks now provide a wide range of financial services in addition to their core business of intermediation and payments services. In the 1980s banks began providing mortgages and more recently have moved into life assurance and insurance business.

2.7.2   *Entry barriers are declining*

In retail financial markets the combined impact of new technology and the process of deconstruction has reduced barriers to entry into these markets. These developments are discussed in more detail in chapters 3 and 5. The mortgage market from the late 1980s onwards and retail banking from the mid-1990s have seen new entrants into these markets, making them more competitive. Insurance institutions and non-financial firms (such as supermarkets) have recently made tentative moves to establish a presence in retail banking.

2.7.3   *Growth of investment institutions*

Since 1980, the investment institutions (pension funds, life assurance companies, unit and investment trusts) have grown at a faster rate than banks and building societies (see table 2.1). The slower growth of banks

Table 2.1   *Growth of assets of UK financial institutions, 1980–96 (£billion)*

	1980	1984	1988	1992	1996	% growth (1980–96)
Banks[a]	117.4	271.4	401.8	552.1	817.1	700
Building societies	54.3	103.3	189.9	266.6	301.0	560
Unit and investment trusts	12.5	31.1	61.6	92.5	175.0	1,400
Life assurance companies	53.7	114.2	198.3	372.2	561.0	1,045
Pension funds	52.6	130.3	214.5	392.6	560.0	1,065

[a] Combined retail, merchant and other UK banks.
Source: CSO, *Financial Statistics*, various issues.

partly reflects a trend towards larger companies raising a greater proportion of external finance from capital markets and the greater role of off-balance-sheet business and other fee-paying business as banks have sought to diversify their income base (discussed further in chapter 4). The faster growth in the assets of pension funds and life assurance companies (as providers of personal pensions) partly reflects tax advantages for saving towards a pension. The growth in investment institutions' assets also reflects a move away from direct investment in equities and bonds by individuals towards indirect investment.

2.7.4   *Financial innovation*

The last 20 years have seen the development of new types of financial instruments, financial markets and techniques. One of the main innovations has been the development of financial derivatives, initially exchange traded but now also traded 'over the counter'. These include financial futures, options and swaps. These new instruments, discussed in detail in chapter 13, have emerged partly in response to volatility in financial markets and have widened the financial management and hedging techniques available to firms and financial institutions.

Another important development has been securitisation. A distinction needs to be made between primary and secondary securitisation. The former relates to borrowers bypassing lending institutions and raising finance directly from capital markets. Secondary securitisation is the

Table 2.2   *Gross domestic product and employment by industry, 1986–96 (as a percentage of total)*

	1986	*1988*	*1990*	*1992*	*1994*	*1996*
Gross domestic product						
Manufacturing	24.8	24.6	23.2	21.2	21.4	21.3
Financial services	21.7	22.4	23.9	24.9	26.2	25.6
Employment						
Manufacturing	23	22	21	19	18	18
Financial services	13	14	15	15	16	17

Financial services are defined as banking, finance, insurance, business services, renting and real estate services. This definition includes accounting and computing services and is therefore wider than the traditional perception of financial services. However, it is the narrowest category to which the data refer.
Source: CSO, *UK National Accounts*, 1997.

process whereby assets originally held on the balance sheet of a bank or building society are packaged and sold to a capital market institution which funds this purchase by issuing securities. In effect, secondary securitisation is the conversion of cash flows from a portfolio of assets (normally loans) into negotiable instruments which are secured on the underlying assets. The instruments are sold to investors. It is an increasingly used and flexible technique that allows lending institutions to increase the liquidity of the balance sheet and release capital that would normally be held against the loan. In the US in 1996, over two-thirds of residential mortgages and about half the credit card receivables were funded via securitisation programmes. Secondary securitisation by banks and building societies in the UK is growing (see chapter 4, section 4.2.1, for further discussion of this phenomenon).

2.7.5   *Growth of the UK financial services industry*

The financial services sector of the UK economy has grown substantially over the past 15 years. This growth has occurred in most developed countries, with the UK showing the greatest growth (see Davis 1996). This increase partly reflects the process of deregulation discussed above. The importance of financial services to the UK economy is illustrated in table 2.2, which shows the relative contribution to gross domestic product and employment by manufacturing and a widely defined (see note to table) financial services sector since 1986.

This provides support for the hypothesis that the UK economy has been going through a process of de-industrialisation, discussed in section 2.5 above, with a relative decline in the manufacturing sector and a relative growth in the services sector.

2.8   **Conclusion**

In this chapter we have described the process of financial intermediation and discussed the reasons why we need financial intermediaries. We have also set out, in broad terms, some of the tremendous changes in market structure and new innovations that have taken place in the UK financial system in recent years. In the rest of this book we examine in greater detail the changes to the various financial institutions and markets that make up the UK financial system, beginning with the banking industry.

Chapter 3

Retail banking

3.1 Introduction

In this chapter we examine the nature of retail banking as distinct from wholesale banking. Whilst such a distinction has in recent years become less relevant in practice as most retail banks also undertake wholesale business, we feel there is still some advantage to be gained from retail banking being considered separately from wholesale banking. The best way to approach this is to distinguish between banks and the retail banking industry. In the retail banking industry certain processes take place in order to supply retail banking services/products. Firms which specialise in these processes, called banks, have traditionally been the suppliers of these retail banking services/products. However, due to technological developments firms whose business is not predominantly banking are entering the retail banking industry. Banks have therefore lost their monopoly position in this industry but can use their core competencies to diversify into providing other services. As a consequence of these developments the retail banking industry is becoming increasingly characterised by a heterogeneous range of suppliers. In this chapter therefore we focus on retail banking, rather than retail banks, and begin by examining the nature of retail banking and recent developments in the industry. We then investigate the provision of payments services, one of the main services provided by the retail banking industry. Finally we discuss the risks inherent in retail banking, and the strategies adopted by firms to manage these risks. Wholesale banking is discussed in chapter 4.

3.2 Nature of retail banking in the UK

The traditional business of banking involves taking in deposits, which are then packaged and on-lent as loans. Retail banking refers to the

Table 3.1   *The combined balance sheet of UK retail banks at 31 December 1996*

Liabilities	£billion	Assets	£billion
Notes outstanding	2.7	Notes and coins	4.8
Total sterling deposits	467.8	Balances with the	
(of which, sight deposits)	(210.1)	Bank of England	1.7
		Market loans	102.1
		Total bills	12.2
		Repo bills	13.6
Foreign currency deposits	148.6	Investments	50.7
Items in suspense and		Advances	338.5
transmission plus capital			
and other funds	92.0		
		Other currency and	
		miscellaneous assets	186.5
		Banking Department lending	
		to central government	0.9
Total liabilities	711.0	Total assets	711.0

Source: *Bank of England Statistical Abstract*, 1997, table 3.4.

large-volume, low-value end of this business, where deposits are typically attracted from individuals and small businesses and loans are made to the same groups. This is in contrast to wholesale banking, where transactions are typically small volume but large value and customers are mainly medium/large companies and large organisations. In practice it is difficult to distinguish between retail and wholesale banks in the UK as many of the banks operating in the retail markets also operate, to some degree, in the wholesale markets. To operate as a bank in the UK a firm must be authorised by the Financial Services Authority (FSA) (up until June 1998, the Bank of England) as able to accept deposits in the UK. Once authorised, a bank's depositors are protected under the UK deposit protection scheme, discussed in chapter 18, and the bank is required to place 0.15 per cent of its eligible sterling liabilities in a non-interest-bearing account at the Bank of England. This has little relevance to any prudential assessment of the bank and is in effect a tax on banks, which is used to finance the various activities of the Bank of England.

By examining the combined balance sheet for retail banks in the UK (table 3.1) we can discern their main activities. Examining the liabilities side of retail banks' balance sheet, first we find the small item 'Notes outstanding', which refers to private bank notes issued by Scottish and Northern Ireland banks. The bulk of a bank's liabilities are deposits, accounting for 80 per cent of total retail bank liabilities, with 21 per cent of these deposits being in foreign currency. The majority of sterling deposits come from the UK private sector, that is, mainly individuals and firms. Of these sterling deposits about 45 per cent are sight deposits, which are defined as repayable on demand. This illustrates the extent to which banks rely upon demand debt rather than fixed-term debt to finance their assets. The other main liabilities are items in suspense and transmission, which refer for example to cheques drawn and in the course of collection, and capital and other funds, which refer mainly to banks' issued share capital, long-term debt and reserves. These latter capital funds are important items when it comes to assessing a bank's capital adequacy in relation to the risks it faces.

Turning now to the assets side of the balance sheet, we find a small item referring to balances with the Bank of England. This is mainly accounted for by the compulsory 'cash ratio' requirement whereby all authorised banks are required to hold 0.15 per cent of their eligible sterling liabilities, charged on those liabilities exceeding £400 million, in a non-interest-bearing account at the Bank of England. The cash balances held outside the Bank of England (notes and coins) account for roughly 0.7 per cent of total assets, which is a very low cash base. Additional liquidity is provided by market loans, which refer to short-term loans made through the money markets. Traditionally banks' market loans were 'call' or overnight loans to the discount houses. These loans are used to even out cash positions within the banking system. However, the retail banks' involvement in the inter-bank markets since 1971 has reduced the importance of this function and inter-bank loans now account for approximately 86 per cent of total market loans. Dealings between banks and the Bank of England, however, take place in order to smooth out shortages or surpluses of cash arising out of dealings between the banking system as a whole and non-banks as, clearly, the inter-bank market cannot perform this function. This is dealt with in more detail in chapter 10. Further liquidity is provided by the next item on the assets side, which is bills. These are mainly Treasury bills and bank bills eligible for rediscounting at the Bank of England via discount houses. The item of investments refers to retail banks' holdings of marketable securities. These are mainly government bonds or government guaranteed stocks and therefore have the characteristics of low default risk and marketability. The main assets of retail banks are sterling advances, which accounted for approximately 50 per cent of total assets or 65 per cent of sterling assets. Many of these advances are the traditional 'overdraft facility' made to business borrowers. However, since the mid-1970s banks have increasingly made term loans to businesses, with an average original term to maturity of around seven years. In addition, over the 1980s, following the removals of controls on bank lending, the banks have increasingly targeted customers in the personal sector with both long-term mortgage lending and unsecured term loans. The next items on the assets side of the retail banks' balance sheet are other currency and miscellaneous assets. Of the other currency assets, around 20 per cent is accounted for by advances, with the remainder being made up of mainly market loans and investments. Miscellaneous assets include the banks' physical assets, mainly premises and equipment, which provide the infrastructure of the business. The item repo claims refers to sale and repurchase agreements, where banks acquire balances through the operation of the new system of monetary control discussed in chapter 10. The final item is Banking Department lending to central government, which refers to the Banking Department of the Bank of England, which is included in the retail banks classification owing to its involvement in the clearing system. We consider the function of the Banking Department and the other functions of the Bank of England in chapter 17.

3.3   Recent changes in retail banking in the UK

To operate in the retail markets, banks have traditionally required an extensive branch network. However, technological developments, in particular the growth in automated teller machine (ATM) networks and telephone/postal banking, have enabled a new type of bank to emerge that does not need branches to conduct business. In the UK the pioneer was First Direct, which began in 1989 and is an operation of Midland Bank, one of the large clearing banks. By 1997 First Direct had around 650,000 customers and offered a full range of retail bank services from cheque accounts to personal loans. Most of the other established banks in the UK have followed the lead of Midland and started up a telephone/postal banking operation and most are also piloting schemes whereby customers can access the bank over a computer/modem link.

The traditional business of banking has been the provision of intermediation and payments services. Intermediation services, as we saw in chapter 2, involve the bank in issuing money-certain deposits and holding money-uncertain and non-marketable loan assets. Payments services are provided, as cheques drawn on bank deposits are accepted as a form of money. We saw in chapter 2 that banks exist either because they possess certain monopoly powers, in that they have a particular expertise not possessed by other firms, or they have a comparative advantage in the marketplace. In recent years banks have seen their monopoly position eroded as the kind of technological developments discussed above have lowered barriers to entry. The process of de-construction, discussed below, has also allowed firms to enter the industry by supplying just part of a banking service, and out-sourcing the other parts, again lowering entry costs. The consequence of these pressures is that banks now face greater competition in their traditional markets. Banks may also be losing some of their traditional comparative advantages in terms of possessing information advantage or having a cost advantage. The consequence of this is that banks are losing their comparative advantage over capital markets and so large companies are increasingly raising capital directly from markets. These developments impinge more directly on the wholesale end of banking and are dis-cussed in more detail in chapters 4 and 12.

Banks therefore are no longer monopoly suppliers of banking ser-vices. However, we need to be careful here to make the distinction between banks and banking. Banks are firms that are completely or predominantly in the business of supplying banking services, whereas banking is the industry supplying banking services. A good discussion of current and likely future developments in the banking industry is provided by Llewellyn (1996) and we summarise some of his arguments here.

In recent years the UK banking industry has seen the emergence of a number of non-banking firms supplying retail banking services. These new entrants fall into two categories:

(i)   *Supermarket banks*. For example, Sainsbury and Tesco, which are already in the retailing business, now offer retail bank services alongside other retail product lines and do so through an extensive branch network. At present the supermarket banks supply banking products in partnership with existing banks but in the future may decide to go it alone. Sainsbury's bank, for example, is authorised by the Bank of England to collect deposits.

(ii) *Other non-bank firms*. These are offering retail banking services using the telephone/postal service, that is without a branch net-work. Examples include insurance firms, such as Prudential and Scottish Widows, which have diversified into banking.

For new entrants to retail banking, both entry and exit costs are relatively low. For those firms operating a telephone banking service the costs of setting up a call centre are lower than the costs of establishing a branch network. For supermarket banks, the supermarkets already have in place an extensive branch network used for delivering other retail products. Exit barriers are also low because for most of the new entrants banking is only a relatively small part of their overall business and because the fixed costs of setting up the operation are relatively low. Another development which is also leading to lower entry costs is the process of deconstruction, described in box 3.1. This allows new entrants to focus on that part of the process that they have a comparative advantage in and to subcontract the other parts of the process to other firms which possess a comparative advantage (probably established banks). By subcontracting in this way new entrants can effectively buy into economies of scale without incurring high fixed costs. This again lowers both entry and exit barriers. One consequence of low entry and exit barriers is that the market for retail banking services is now more contestable (see chapter 5, box 5.1, for further discussion of contestable markets). A further development affecting the UK banking sector has been the conversion of many of the larger building societies into banks (see chapter 5 for discussion). These newly created banks, such as Halifax and Abbey National, are focused on the retail end of banking and plan to become retail financial conglomerates supplying banking, insurance and other financial services to the personal sector. As a consequence of all these developments there is now clearly excess capacity in the retail banking industry and further mergers are likely to bring about a consolidation of the industry.

What are the likely consequences of these developments? In terms of retail banking we are likely to see further differentiation between firms providing banking services. We will continue to see large financial conglomerates undertaking both retail and wholesale banking and undertaking most of the processes within the organisation. The banks that have converted from the building society sector and some of the new 'telephone' banks will develop further as retail conglomerates. We are also likely to see more specialist institutions offering some banking services or parts of banking processes. In summary the industry will become more heterogeneous.

The main implication of these developments for the established banks in the industry is that as they lose their comparative advantage in banking they are having to diversify into new activities. At the retail end of the industry one clear trend that has emerged is for banks to provide insurance services. 'Bancassurance' firms, where deposit taking and insurance are combined, are commonplace in Europe. It is an open question as to whether banks will diversify into non-financial business. Banks have developed certain core competencies that could be applied to other types of business. These competencies or areas of comparative advantage include:

Box 3.1 *Deconstruction of banking services*

The process of deconstruction refers to the decomposition of services or products into their component parts, thereby allowing the individual parts to be provided by separate firms. A good example of this is the provision of a mortgage loan. Recent financial innovation allows the components of this provision to be broken down into:

(i)   origination – the mortgage is brokered to a customer;
(ii)   administration – the paperwork is processed;
(iii) risk analysis – the credit worthiness of the borrower is assessed;
(iv)   funding – the finance is raised, the asset held on the balance sheet and capital allocated to the risk.

One firm may have a comparative advantage in, say, risk assessment whereas another firm may have a comparative advantage in origination. Also, a firm may originate the loan but may not be efficient in terms of funding it because of a capital constraint. It is becoming increasingly commonplace, in the US in particular, for banks to securitise their mortgage loans and issue subsequent securities on the capital market, thereby taking the loans off the balance sheet (this is discussed in more detail in chapter 4, section 4.2.1). The process of deconstruction lowers barriers to entry into the banking industry as firms can now enter the market without undertaking the whole process. They need to provide only that part of the process where they have a comparative advantage. A firm that originates the loan but does not wish to undertake the other parts of the process can subcontract (or out-source) these to other firms. Another firm may develop an expertise in risk assessment and take on only this part of the process from other firms.

By subcontracting, a small firm is able to buy into economies of scale which it could not achieve on its own because of the limited scale of its operation. We are likely to see the development of contract banking over the next few years as firms supply some parts of the process of a banking service and subcontract others. Therefore in the near future we are likely to see a spectrum of providers of retail banking ranging from, at one extreme, the very large banks providing most or all subcomponents of a wide range of services (i.e. both horizontally and vertically integrated) to, at the other extreme, the virtual bank which has an interface with customers, supplies a wide range of banking services but which subcontracts all the subcomponents of these services to other firms and just manages the contracts with these suppliers. A virtual bank supplying a wide range of services/products would be highly horizontally integrated but have low vertical integration. A virtual bank may sound unrealistic but out-sourcing is now very common in most manufacturing industries. Toyota for example supplies finished cars to its customers but subcontracts the production of many of the subcomponents. An example of a virtual firm is the typical supplier of personal computers, which buys in all the subcomponents and assembles to order.

(i)   information advantages – that is, information they possess about the financial affairs or lending risks associated with their customers – this information comes partly from the provision of payments services (see next section);
(ii)   risk analysis expertise;
(iii)   expertise in monitoring and enforcement of loan contracts;
(iv)   delivery capacity.

Therefore although established banks are likely to see some decline in their share of retail banking services in the new competitive industry, they are likely to compensate for this through diversification.

In the next section we examine the nature of the payments system in the UK and consider why it is that banks have traditionally combined payments with intermediation services.

3.4   Payments services

Banks until very recently have been the sole provider of payments services. A payments service is merely an accounting procedure whereby transfers of ownership of certain assets are carried out in settlement of debts incurred. Payments facilities generate a desire for instruments which:

(i)   serve as a medium of exchange enabling consumers to acquire goods;
(ii)   serve as a medium of payment to effect payment of the good acquired;
(iii)   act as a temporary store of purchasing power, since income receipts and payments are generally not synchronised.

As we saw in chapter 1, a commodity that takes on these three characteristics is termed money and any commodity can act in this role as long as it is generally accepted. In most developed economies the payments system that has evolved is based on government-issued paper money and cheques drawn on a bank deposit. The reasons for this are covered adequately in most texts on money and banking. What we propose to examine here are some recent developments in the UK payments system.

Recent financial innovation has made it possible to 'unbundle' the three functions of money so they can be separately carried out using different instruments. So, for example, a credit card may serve as the medium of exchange enabling goods to be purchased. A direct debit from a bank deposit account may then be used to effect payment at a later date and between the purchase and payment the funds used for payment may be held in a high-yielding account. Developments in technology, in particular in electronic funds transfer, are also bringing about changes in the payments system. The use of paper cheques is reducing as these new methods of payments are used. First, the debit card allows customers to make a payment directly from their bank account. The transfer of funds from customer to retailer takes place electronically. This transfer could be effected immediately or could be delayed, with batch transfers being made by the retailer. Regular electronic transfers of funds between accounts are now usually made through an automated clearing house debit. For example, most salaries are directly credited to employees' accounts this way and many customers use this facility to make regular utility bill payments. Developments which will become widespread in the near future include smart cards and Internet accounts. Smart cards, or stored-value cards, are prepaid cards the size of a debit or credit card. They contain an electronic chip which allows a customer to transfer money from an account on to the card. This transfer could take place from an ATM or specially equipped personal computer. The smart card can then be used for payment at a retailer's point-of-sale terminal. The retailer can then transfer accumulated balances to its account. Some UK banks have been running trials with smart cards and expect to introduce them more widely in the next couple of years. It is likely that the introduction of smart cards will reduce the amount of cash in use. Internet accounts allow a customer to undertake transactions over the Internet, for example to purchase a compact disk. The Internet retailer would electronically debit the customer's Internet account. If, to realise its value, this 'Internet cash' needs to be converted into traditional money, there is a role for banks. However, if Internet cash becomes a form of money in its own right then banks' role in the payments system will start to decline.

As we have noted above, payments services are generally provided together with portfolio services by an institution. This is because there are certain advantages in combining the two. The funds which are held in bank accounts before being used to finance purchases – although customers will attempt to keep these at a minimum as they can most likely obtain a higher return by lending them elsewhere – can in aggregate be used to on-lend profitably. Thus intermediation emerges as a byproduct of payments services. The profits from the intermediation services have generally been used to subsidise the costs of providing the payments service. Various schemes have been adopted by banks to enable the profits earned from the use of the idle balances of a customer to reduce or eliminate charges for the use of the payments service. For example, customers who kept a positive minimum and average account balance were then exempt from charges for payments services. Another method used was the calculation of implicit interest on a customer's idle balances, which was used to offset charges. The policy of deregulation of the financial system over the 1980s affected these arrangements. In particular, deregulation of the building societies – covered in chapter 5 – allowed them to set up deposit accounts with a chequebook facility. These accounts generally paid interest on the idle funds in the account whilst at the same time did not charge for the payments service. This additional competition for banks has induced them to introduce cheque accounts which either pay interest or involve no bank charges. De-regulation and the increased competition it brings have so far not led to the removal of cross-subsidisation whereby explicit rates of interest are paid on account balances but payments services are fully charged for (as suggested by Fama (1980), for example), but instead appears to have reduced the overall profitability of retail banking-type services.

The providers of payments services, though, obtain certain advantages which enable them to be more efficient in their intermediation operations. In particular, they will obtain valuable information about the financial circumstances of the customer. This enables them to judge whether it is suitable to extend that customer credit and once the loan is extended the transactions account can be used as a source of information in the monitoring process. Such specialised information, as we saw in chapter 2, provides part of the explanation for the existence of financial intermediaries. Also, the access to transaction details enables an institution to target other financial services at customers. These advantages therefore partly explain why institutions such as building societies have sought to introduce payments services.

3.5   Risks in retail banking

Banks, like all financial intermediaries, as we saw in chapter 2, are involved in managing risk. The principal risks that are managed by retail banks in the intermediation process are:

(i)   liquidity risk – this is a consequence of issuing liabilities which are largely payable on demand or at short notice whilst holding assets which have a longer term to maturity;

(ii)   asset risk – the risk that assets held by the bank may not be redeemable at their book value due to default, price risk or forced-sale risk.

Two additional sources of instability in the banking system stem first from the nature of the payments system and secondly from banks' increasing undertaking of business which involves contingent commitments. The payments system risk arises from the exposures created when funds are committed by a bank before final settlement. This is a feature of payment systems where settlement occurs at the end of the day. The last risk arises from transactions termed 'off balance sheet' as they do not appear on the balance sheet until the contingency arises. This is a feature of banking which relates more to the wholesale side, though it is relevant to retail banking to the extent that most retail banks also undertake wholesale business. We leave discussion of the nature of off-balance-sheet business and its implications for regulation until the next chapter.

In this section we examine first the nature of the two risks inherent in retail banking, identified above, and briefly examine the methods used by banks in their management. We also consider the nature of payments risk and recent moves by the Bank of England to tackle this problem.

3.5.1 *Liquidity risk*

Bank deposits can be withdrawn at call or very short notice, whereas a large proportion of a bank's assets are illiquid (advances typically make up 70 per cent of the assets of a retail bank). This practice of mis-matching or maturity transformation, discussed in chapter 2, exposes the bank to liquidity risk and as a consequence it is important that banks manage the inflow and outflow of their funds. The inflows and outflows of much of the funds passing through a bank are uncertain. Deposit inflows and outflows are largely uncertain and, on the assets side of the balance sheet, overdraft commitments introduce another element of uncertainty. The inflow and outflow of funds through a bank will be predictable to some extent on the basis of what has happened in the past. However, there will be a stochastic element to these flows and banks will have to structure their balance sheet in such a way that they can manage this uncertainty. A fundamental element in a bank's management of this uncertainty comes from the large scale of its operation and more importantly from a diversified base of deposit accounts. When a large number of uncertain net flows (mostly deposit accounts) are combined then a greater degree of predictability is achieved. The basic principle here is that it is better to have a large number of small accounts than a small number of large accounts. This reduces the uncertainty of the bank's cash flows but the remaining uncertainty still needs to be managed.

We will examine the requirements set out by the Bank of England to ensure that banks adequately cover this liquidity risk in chapter 18. What we concentrate on here are the two main strategies that banks can adopt to manage this liquidity problem.

Figure 3.1   *The reserve asset management approach to liquidity risk*

Reserve asset management
Figure 3.1 simply illustrates the reserve asset management approach to liquidity risk.

Inflows in the form of new deposits and loan repayments are added to the holdings of cash and liquid assets. Loan repayments will clearly be a more predictable element of cash inflows, determined by the loans made in the past, though the bank will have to allow for potential default on repayment of the loan. The outflows, in the form of deposit withdrawals and new loans made, will deplete the holdings of cash and liquid assets. The illiquid loan portfolio is protected from an unexpectedly large net outflow of funds by the holding of a buffer stock of cash and liquid assets. That is, the bank will hold cash and liquid assets at a level above that which is required to meet the expected volatility of cash flows.

The assets held in liquid form do not have to be comprised only of cash with a zero rate of interest, and a tiering or maturity ladder approach is generally adopted whereby some of the reserve assets held are short term and therefore easily realisable, such as callable or over-night deposits, and others are longer term and therefore less easy to realise but still liquid because of their marketability, such as bills, CDs, government securities, and so on. By holding these liquid assets rather than just cash the bank is obtaining at least some return on its funds. However, the return is still less than that it would obtain on its main earning asset, which is advances.

Liability management

Liability management involves relying on instruments bearing market rates of interest to fund activity. At its most general it involves determining a desired quantity of assets and then adjusting interest rates to attract in the desired level of deposits to fund this. This is in contrast to reserve asset management, where interest rates are held constant, at least in the short term, and the scale of the asset portfolio is adjusted in line with the quantity of deposits attracted at that rate. The form that liability management takes depends on the market for funds where existing deposits are drawn. If a bank is reliant on retail deposits then, leaving aside its ability to vary other characteristics of the deposits such as term, in order to attract new deposits it has to increase the interest rate on all deposits. This makes the marginal cost of the additional funds raised high. The existence of a market for deposits where the bank is effectively a price taker, so its borrowing does not lead to a rise in the interest rate, means the marginal cost of the funds raised is reduced. As we describe in chapter 10, the inter-bank market is such a market in the UK. Banks can therefore use the inter-bank market as a marginal source of funds and for the marginal use of funds, so that at the end of a working day if the bank has a shortage of funds it can borrow short term from the inter-bank market, or if the bank has a surplus of funds it can lend short term. The existence of an inter-bank market means that banks can raise additional funds at a lower marginal cost than raising interest rates across the board and also more quickly than from retail sources. As a consequence, retail banks in the UK have largely moved away from reserve asset management to liability management as a technique of managing liquidity risk. It has to be noted though that inter-bank markets are not perfect and that banks are not pure price takers in these markets. There is therefore some uncertainty about the quantity and price of funds raised through these markets and hence banks still require some level of reserve assets as a back-up. Note also that if there is a net shortage of funds in the banking system then banks have to look outside the inter-bank market to relieve this shortage.

3.5.2 *Asset risk*

The Bank of England (*Bank of England Quarterly Bulletin*, May 1980) identifies three ways in which a bank's assets are subject to the risk of a fall in value below that recorded in the balance sheet (their 'book value'). First, and most important in terms of the structure of the bank's assets, is the risk of default on the part of borrowers on the advances made by the bank. In chapter 2 we summarised some of the ways in which a bank can reduce credit risk.

As a first step a bank can minimise the risk of default on an individual advance by, for example, considering the use of the loaned funds and the financial circumstances of the borrower. Credit scoring plays an increasing role in selecting good risks in consumer lending. Under credit scoring a potential borrower is asked a standard set of questions relating to factors such as age, assets held, financial commitments and so on, and on the basis of the answers a score is calculated reflecting the credit risk of the person. The use of credit scoring has largely replaced judgement in determining whether to grant a loan and can easily be automated, so reducing the costs of acquiring information to judge a borrower's suitability. Another method of reducing risk for the lender is to require the borrower to provide security over the borrower's assets. In the event of the borrower defaulting the bank can sell the secured assets and recover part or all of the loan. A well known type of secured lending is mortgage lending, where the property is used as security. Second, a bank can increase the predictability of default by spreading its loan portfolio over many borrowers. This is known as pooling risks and requires the bank to make a large number of small loans rather than a small number of large loans. The bank can then rely on the law of large numbers to achieve a smaller variation in loan loss experience so that the actual loan loss will be very close to the average loan loss experience for that type of business. This outcome depends critically on the default risks across the loan portfolio being independent. To achieve this the bank needs to diversify its loans over different types of borrower. If, for example, a bank lends only to firms involved in the commercial property construction industry and there is a recession in that industry then the bank will suffer a high number of defaults (i.e. the default risks are not independent). If, however, the bank spreads its loans across firms in different industries and consumers then it is not as badly affected by a recession in one sector. Of course, if the whole economy goes into recession then it will incur a higher number of defaults. International diversification of loans may help to reduce this problem.

A second asset risk considered by the Bank of England is investment risk, which relates to capital-uncertain assets and refers to the risk of a price fall, thus reducing the value of the asset. The main capital-uncertain assets held by banks are government securities and if the general level of interest rates increases then the value of the bank's government securities will decline.

The final risk considered by the Bank of England is forced-sale risk, which refers to the risk that the realisable value of the asset may fall below its book value if the asset has to be sold at short notice.

A bank's exposure to these risks is an important consideration in determining its solvency and we consider this in detail in chapter 18, which examines regulation and prudential control of banks.

3.5.3 *Payments risk*

As we saw in section 3.3, a payments system provides for the transfer of funds between accounts at different institutions. In the UK, on an average day the payments systems process 16 million transactions with a total value of over £160 billion. We can separate payments systems into two types: wholesale and retail. Of the wholesale type, dealing with large-value, same-day, sterling transfers, the main system is the Clearing House Automated Payments System (CHAPS). CHAPS regularly processed daily payments of £100 billion through its 16 member banks in 1994. Of the retail payment systems, the cheque clearing and credit clearing systems deal with cheques and paper items, respectively. In addition, there is the Bankers' Automated Clearing Services (BACS), which is an electronic clearing house for items such as standing orders and direct debits.

CHAPS allows a bank to make guaranteed and irrevocable sterling credits to other banks in the system, either on its own account or on behalf of customers. At the end of the day, final debit and credit balances for each member bank are calculated and net settlements are made through settlement accounts held at the Bank of England. One type of risk that arises with this type of system is known as receiver risk. This arises when a system member provides funds to its customers, having received a payment instruction from another member but before final settlement. The receiving bank which has offered irrevocable funds to its customers is exposed to the sending bank until final settlement occurs at the end of the day. Those customers receiving funds before settlement may then initiate further transfers, creating additional obligations for their settlement banks. This may be repeated several times during a day, building up large exposures. If one of the settlement banks were to fail before final settlement the other members would be deprived of the money needed to fund their own payments. Thus a failure at one bank may lead to settlement failures at other banks and create a systemic crisis.

The solution to this problem is to move from end-of-day net settlement to real-time gross settlement (RTGS). This requires that all interbank transactions are recorded in the accounts of the central bank as they occur. It is then possible to structure the system so that a settlement bank receives an incoming payment instruction only after the payment has been settled by the central bank. Thus there is little scope for them to pass funds to their customers before final settlement. Such a system was implemented in the UK in the spring of 1996 (see *Bank of England Quarterly Bulletin*, May 1994, for further details of the system). The UK RTGS system is now being further developed to accommodate the euro (the proposed common currency for European Monetary Union – see chapter 15). The CHAPS–euro system will allow euro wholesale payments to be made between parties in the UK and cross-border from and to the UK through its link to TARGET (the RTGS system being developed in Europe).

3.6   Conclusion

In this chapter we have considered the changing nature of retail banking. As in most other areas of the financial services industry, technological developments are dramatically changing the methods of supplying services. These developments have lowered barriers to entry to the industry and we are now beginning to see a wider range of firms supplying retail banking services. Technology developments are also changing the nature of payments services, again lowering barriers to entry to the industry. To complete our picture of banking we turn in the next chapter to consider the nature of wholesale and international banking, where competition from markets has been powerful over the 1980s and 1990s.

Chapter 4

Wholesale and international banking

4.1   Introduction

In the last chapter we examined the nature of retail banking in the UK and noted that the distinction between this type of banking and wholesale banking has become increasingly blurred over recent years. To complete our discussion of banking we therefore turn in this chapter to examine the nature of wholesale banking. This type of banking can be further separated into domestic and international. We begin by examining the general nature of wholesale banking in section 4.2. This examination relates to activities which are captured on the balance sheet. An increasing amount of business of wholesale banks does not appear on the balance sheet and is termed off-balance-sheet business. We discuss the nature, causes and consequences of this type of business in section 4.3. In section 4.4 we discuss the nature of eurocurrency banking, which is now the most dominant form of international banking. Finally, in section 4.5 we consider the issue of sovereign lending, that is, lending by banks to sovereign countries. A boom in this type of lending over the 1970s led to consequences which blighted the international banking system over the 1980s, although recent initiatives appear to have provided a framework for a lasting solution.

Recent developments have reduced the international significance of British banks engaged in investment banking. Both Barclays and National Westminster have withdrawn from investment banking and this leaves the field to the major US banks and other European banks. Presumably this was because of their perception that size was to become more important in investment banking and that the groups were unwilling to allocate sufficient resources to this activity. The search for size in banking can be ascertained from the announcement in April 1998 of the merger between the two US banks Citicorp and Travelers Group.

This will create the largest company in the world, financial, commercial or industrial. Other recent mergers include Nations Bank and Bank America in April 1998 and Union Bank of Switzerland and the Swiss Banking Corporation in June 1998. Clearly, such mergers raise questions about the viability of the major UK banks and it may well be the case that mergers will occur within a British context.

4.2   Nature of wholesale banking

A large number of banks which operate in the UK do not come under the category of retail banks as defined in the last chapter. These banks are a heterogeneous group and the Bank of England, in its statistical analysis, separates them on the basis of the country where the headquarters are located and then, for the non-retail UK banks, further subdivides these to identify those operating as merchant banks. The breakdown of non-retail banks operating in the UK is as follows:

(i)   UK merchant banks – members of the British Merchant Bankers and Securities Houses Association (formerly the Accepting Houses Committee). Merchant banks have traditionally financed commerce and trade by the 'accepting' of bills. Their activities are now much broader and include direct lending to industry, underwriting new issues and providing advice on mergers, acquisitions, portfolio management, and so on.

(ii)   Other UK banks. This group captures all financial institutions registered as banks which are not included in the retail and merchant bank categories. As a consequence the activities of these institutions are diverse, ranging from small regional banks to finance houses, leasing companies and other specialised institutions, some of which are the subsidiaries of retail banks.

(iii)   US banks.

(iv)   Japanese banks.

(v)   Other overseas banks.

Most banks today are to some degree multi-product banks. As we noted in chapter 3, most retail banks also operate in the wholesale markets, but the converse is not true since the non-retail banks tend to operate solely or mainly in wholesale markets. We now examine the balance sheets of these different categories of wholesale banks, so as to identify some of the aspects of wholesale banking and in particular those features which distinguish it from retail banking. The sterling and foreign currency breakdown of the deposits of the different categories of banks is provided in table 4.1.

Table 4.1 *Sterling and foreign currency deposits of non-retail banks at end December 1996 (£million)*

	Sterling	Foreign currency	Sterling sight as a percentage of total sterling
UK merchant banks	23,440	13,317	21
Other UK banks	42,592	8,832	14
Japanese banks	29,728	149,465	7
US banks	26,234	121,450	26
Other overseas banks	159,623	533,958	14

Source: *Bank of England Statistical Abstract*, 1997, tables 3.5, 3.6, 3.7, 3.8, 3.10.

One salient feature of wholesale banking which contrasts with retail banking is the large size of deposits and loans and consequently the smaller number of depositors and borrowers. Minimum values for sterling deposits and loans are typically £250,000 and £500,000, respectively. The structure of the sterling deposits of these wholesale banks is also quite different from those of retail banks. For sterling deposits, the sight element is considerably lower for non-retail banks, with US banks showing the largest proportions at 26 per cent (see table 4.1), compared with 45 per cent for retail banks. This reflects the absence of these banks from retail banking. Approximately 22 per cent of sterling wholesale deposits are inter-bank (i.e. deposits of one UK bank placed with another bank – see chapter 10 for further discussion), the remainder being mainly time deposits from UK private companies and overseas companies and banks. For the foreign currency business a smaller proportion (approximately 10 per cent) originates from other UK banks, with by far the largest proportion originating from overseas customers and banks. One other feature of wholesale banking, indicated in table 4.1, is the greater extent of foreign currency business for both UK and overseas banks when compared with retail banks (where foreign currency deposits accounted for approximately 21 per cent of total liabilities). The overseas banks though, whilst engaging in a considerable amount of sterling wholesale business, are more heavily involved in foreign currency business. The reasons why overseas banks locate in the UK but deal mainly in foreign currencies are explored in section 4.4.

The assets held by non-retail banks are summarised in table 4.2, again broken down by type of bank. Non-retail banks, because the

Table 4.2   *Assets of non-retail banks operating in the UK at end December 1996 (£million)*

	Merchant banks	Other UK banks	Japanese banks	US banks	Overseas banks
Sterling					
Notes and coins and balances at the Bank of England	57	114	78	96	369
Market loans	8,194	9,561	11,758	8,819	64,646
Bills	35	160	46	6	1,183
Claims under repo agreements	5,079	230	2	1,333	9,277
Advances	7,988	38,702	15,932	12,478	66,187
Investments	4,672	3,437	1,871	1,739	17,419
Total sterling assets	26,025	52,204	29,687	24,471	159,081
Foreign currency[a]					
Market loans	5,811	6,778	105,210	70,567	311,900
Advances	4,706	1,789	34,237	41,884	136,650
Bills, investments etc.	5,142	3,645	12,311	17,487	116,374
Total foreign currency assets	15,659	12,212	151,758	129,938	564,924

[a] Selected foreign currency assets – some miscellaneous assets excluded.
Source: *Bank of England Statistical Abstract*, 1997, tables 3.5, 3.6, 3.7, 3.8, 3.10.

nature of their business is low volume, large value and hence unlikely to be conducted through cash transactions, require little in the way of cash balances. Much of the first item in table 4.2 is made up of the compulsory cash balance which the Bank of England requires of all banks. In terms of sterling assets, market loans are clearly important, with the main item here being inter-bank loans – the counterpart to inter-bank deposits. Compared with retail banks, a larger proportion of sterling assets of non-retail banks is accounted for by market loans. The item 'Claims under repo agreements' refers to balances acquired through the operation of the new system of monetary control discussed in chapter 10.

The extent to which overseas banks based in the UK have become involved in domestic UK activity is also revealed in table 4.2. Taken together, overseas banks accounted for 27 per cent of total sterling lending by way of advances to the UK private sector. A significant part of this lending was directed towards large construction projects, including the Canary Wharf development in the London Docklands and the Channel Tunnel. As is also the case for the liabilities side of the balance sheet, foreign currency assets form a significant proportion of total assets. Reference back to table 4.1 illustrates a fair degree of currency matching, since foreign currency assets for each category of bank are similar in total to foreign currency liabilities.

A common hypothesis about wholesale banks is that they aim to 'match' the term to maturity of their liabilities and assets. So, for example, a £100,000 three-month CD in its liability portfolio may be used to finance the purchase of a three-month commercial bill of value £100,000. Under this hypothesis wholesale banks are simply liquidity distributors or brokers of liquid assets and do not produce liquidity by undertaking maturity transformation. It is sometimes argued that wholesale banks cannot mismatch because, unlike retail banks, they typically have a small number of large-value deposits and therefore cannot rely on the law of large numbers effect which comes from having a large number of small-value deposits. This effect, as we saw in chapter 3, makes net withdrawals of deposits more predictable so that, it is claimed, in the face of uncertainty wholesale banks will aim to match the maturity of their assets with those of their liabilities. If wholesale banks are simply distributing liquidity then the justification for the existence of such banks is dependent solely on their ability to reduce the costs of liquidity distribution to a lower level than would exist if borrowers and lenders sought out each other directly. As we saw in chapter 2, banks can reduce costs in credit markets through specialisation, which enables them to achieve economies of scale in their lending and borrowing operations. However, unlike the normal type of financial intermediation described in chapter 2, there will be no reflection of the liquidity generated by the bank in its interest rate margin, as no liquidity is being generated. Of course this does not preclude other types of transformation, such as risk transformation.

We now turn to examine whether there is any evidence to support the hypothesis of matching by wholesale banks. The Bank of England has published the results of a survey of retail and non-retail banks operating in London, which show the maturity profiles of the aggregate asset and liability portfolios at the end of January 1987. These results (also presented in Lewis and Davis (1987)) are shown in table 4.3.

It should be noted that the figures in table 4.3 refer to business with non-banks, that is, the inter-bank positions are netted out, as these positions will be matched positions in aggregate. Whilst it is recognised that these figures refer to 1987, it is not thought that the overall position will have changed greatly since that date. The figures for business with

Table 4.3 *Maturity analysis of sterling and foreign currency business with non-bank customers of retail and wholesale banks in the UK as at end January 1987 (%)*

| | Sterling | | | | | | Foreign currency | | | |
| | Retail banks | | British non-retail banks | | Overseas banks | | All banks | | British banks | |
	A	L	A	L	A	L	A	L	A	L
0–7 days	3.54	83.51	13.98	52.83	12.64	41.29	11.96	38.15	11.11	47.95
8 days–1 month	3.49	7.89	3.09	18.74	12.75	21.97	11.00	23.97	8.20	20.70
1–3 months	6.18	6.28	6.27	15.61	15.35	20.88	13.71	18.15	10.21	17.19
3–6 months	5.01	1.00	6.19	4.36	5.69	5.16	9.33	6.87	7.86	6.71
6 months–1 year	5.91	0.67	10.42	4.70	7.20	4.03	6.09	2.68	6.61	2.29
1–3 years	10.21	0.24	18.11	1.83	12.65	2.37	13.11	2.02	15.20	1.74
Over 3 years	65.68	0.41	41.94	1.93	33.72	4.30	34.80	8.16	40.81	3.42

A = Assets.
L = Liabilities.
Source: Bank of England, *Sterling Business Analysed by Maturity and Sector*, March 1987; Bank of England, *Maturity Analysis by Sector of Liabilities and Claims in Foreign Currencies*, March 1987.

non-banks reveal considerable mismatching by wholesale banks, with the overwhelming majority of deposits having a maturity of under three months whilst a majority of assets have a maturity of over one year. The main features of this mismatching are:

(i)   similarity in the degree of maturity mismatching between sterling and foreign currency business;
(ii) wholesale banks whilst significantly mismatching appear do this to a lesser extent than retail banks – for example, for retail banks roughly 84 per cent of deposits fall in the category 0–7 days and 66 per cent of assets have a maturity of over three years, whereas for British merchant banks the figures are 53 per cent and 42 per cent, respectively;
(iii) UK wholesale banks appear to mismatch to a greater extent than overseas banks – in their operations in London.

This evidence therefore does not support the view that wholesale banks are only liquidity distributors but rather that they transform the maturity characteristic of the funds flowing through the institution, albeit to a lesser extent than retail banks. This result begs the question of how they are able to engage in maturity transformation and hence liquidity production for their non-bank customers when they do not have the advantage of the retail banks of the law of large numbers effect. That is, how do wholesale banks manage their liquidity risks? A related problem is that, given the small number of advances on the assets side of the balance sheet, there is less scope for pooling and diversifying default risks than with retail banking. The solution to the problem of liquidity risk is provided first by the practice of liability management, which, as we discussed in chapter 3, involves banks having access to inter-bank borrowings and other market-based deposits as an immediate source of funds to replace any shortfall in the event of maturing or withdrawn deposits. A second strategy, which has become increasingly available to banks since the mid-1980s, is the securitisation or marketisation of assets. This involves transforming previously illiquid assets such as mortgages into marketable instruments, which can then be sold on to a third party. This phenomenon is discussed in more detail under 'Asset-backed securitisation' below and is one aspect of the more general process of securitisation, which refers to the switch away from indirect, bank financing to direct financing through the capital markets observed since the mid-1980s (discussed in chapter 12). The solution to the problem of default risk has been for wholesale banks to form 'syndicates' to spread the default risk of a large loan over a number of banks. This is examined further in section 4.4.

The discussion of wholesale banking so far has focused on the activities which appear on the balance sheet. We now examine the growing phenomenon of off-balance-sheet business.

4.2.1   *Asset-backed securitisation*

An asset-backed security (ABS) is a tradable instrument supported by a pool of loans. The main type of ABS created in recent years is one based on a pool of residential mortgages. The creation of an ABS in the UK involves the bank removing some of its loans from its balance sheet and placing them with a special-purpose vehicle (SPV), which finances its holdings by selling ABSs to investors. This process, also known as securitisation, adds marketability to assets which would otherwise have very little liquidity. A detailed discussion of the ABS market in the UK can be found in Twinn (1994).

The first issue of an ABS was in the US during the 1970s. The first issue in the UK came in 1985 and the UK ABS market is now the second largest in the world. However, in the UK only a small proportion of lending has been securitised. The total issues by December 1996 had a principal of approximately £23 billion compared with a total amount lent by retail banks and building societies during 1996 of £580 billion. Nevertheless, the UK market is growing rapidly and the structure of lending is likely to change as a consequence. More recent securitisation exercises include two such deals by National Westminster. In March 1997, £1 billion worth of housing loans were converted into bonds. In the autumn of 1997 the same bank announced that it was restructuring £3 billion in corporate loans, selling them on to investors as securitised bonds. It was further reported in the *Financial Times* (4 August 1997) that the secondary market in Europe for loans was beginning to come to life. In the first quarter of 1997 the turnover in the market was £5 billion.

The main advantage of ABSs for the lender is that by removing assets from the balance sheet (provided the relevant risks are transferred to the investors) the institution frees up capital for other uses. Securitisation also allows an institution to concentrate on those aspects of the lending business in which it has a comparative advantage. Thus, for example, a small building society may feel it is more efficient at originating loans and so once the loans are obtained it can securitise the assets and sell them to institutions more efficient at securing the necessary funding. Another use of securitisation to a lender is that when it feels over-exposed to a particular sector or set of borrowers it can securitise part of its lending. The main attraction of ABSs to an investor is the margin they offer over other highly rated bonds. They also allow investors an opportunity to diversify their portfolios, increasing their exposure in areas to which they may not have direct access.

The common structure for an ABS issue in the UK is similar to the US 'pass through'. Here an originator separates suitable assets from its portfolio, normally assets of similar quality and repayment calendar. These assets are then sold to an SPV, thus providing a legal separation of the assets from the originator. The SPV then sells securities to investors to fund the purchase of the assets, which it holds in a trust on their behalf. The issued securities will normally have at least one credit rating in order to make them attractive to investors (see section 9.6). In addition, most issues have credit enhancement in order to boost the credit rating. A credit enhancement provides a degree of assurance to investors that the principal and coupon payments will be paid in a timely manner. Various methods of credit enhancement are used, with the most common, until recently, being an insurance contract. An ABS is normally issued as a floating-rate note (see chapter 12), paying the London inter-bank offer rate plus a margin.

As mentioned above, the UK ABS market is small but growing. Recently a wider range of assets than mortgages have been securitised. It is anticipated that as banks and building societies expand their lending and come up against capital constraints, ABS issues may be an attractive alternative to a capital issue if retained earnings cannot be accumulated quickly enough.

4.3   Off-balance-sheet business

Off-balance-sheet business refers to business undertaken by a bank which generates a contingent commitment and generally an income to the bank without the business being captured on the balance sheet under conventional accounting procedures. This type of business has long been undertaken by banks but grew rapidly in both volume and scope over the 1980s. In this section we examine the nature of off-balance-sheet business and the reasons for its growth in recent years. In order to consider the latter we broaden the picture to examine more generally the causes of financial innovation. Finally we examine some of the implications of off-balance-sheet business, in particular its implications for the regulation of banks.

4.3.1   *Types of off-balance-sheet business*

If we consider first of all the narrow definition of off-balance-sheet business, that is, activities giving rise to contingent commitments, then four broad areas can be identified.

(i)   *Loan commitments*. These cover any advance commitment by a
      bank to provide credit. Examples are: revolving lines of credit,
      where a bank provides a line of credit to which it is committed
      often for several years ahead; overdrafts, where a bank has agreed
      a facility but can withdraw it in certain circumstances; and note
      issuance facilities (see chapter 12), where the bank provides credit
      only in the event of others being unable to. Provision of these
      commitments generates a fee income for banks.
(ii) *Guarantees*. This involves a bank in underwriting the obligations
      of a third party, thus relieving the counterparty from having to
      assess the ability of the customer to meet the terms of the contract.
      Examples of such guarantees are acceptances, whereby the bank
      guarantees payment of a customer's liability to the holder of the
      debt, and performance bonds, which support the good name of a
      customer and her or his ability to perform under a particular
      contract. The bank receives a fee for providing such guarantees.
(iii) *Swap and hedging transactions*. These involve the bank in a
      transaction using one of the recently developed 'derivative' instru-
      ments such as swaps, forward contracts, options, financial futures,
      interest caps, collars, and so on. Many of these instruments are
      discussed further in chapters 11, 13 and 14. The transaction can be
      hedged (to neutralise a position exposure) or unhedged (left open
      to exposure).
(iv) *Securities underwriting*. Investment banks and merchant banks are
      involved in underwriting issues of securities, whereby they agree
      to buy a set amount of the securities which are not taken up in an
      issue. This guarantees the issuer that the whole of the issue is taken
      up and a fee is paid to the banks providing the underwriting
      service.

   All the above examples involve the bank in a commitment which may
or may not lead to a balance sheet entry in the future. There are a wide
range of other financial services provided by banks which generate fee
income and where the business does not lead to a balance sheet entry.
These include loan origination, trust and advice services, brokerage and
agency services and payments services such as the provision of credit
cards and cash management systems. The total income of a bank can be
roughly split into net interest income, that is, the margin between its
lending and borrowing rates, and fee or commission income. The
relative growth in fee or commission income and other non-interest
income (excluding capital gains from selling investments) since 1980
for Barclays Bank Group, shown in table 4.4, illustrates a general trend
for the UK clearing banks. The growth in importance of such income to

Table 4.4   *Fee or commission income as a percentage of net interest income for Barclays Bank Group, 1980–96*

1980	1982	1984	1986	1988	1990	1994	1996
29	34	41	45	52	64	84	84

Source: Barclays Bank annual report and accounts.

banks is illustrated by the fact that in 1996 it represented 84 per cent of the bank's net interest income as compared with only 29 per cent in 1980.

This relative growth in fee or commission income reflects both a growth in contingent commitment business and attempts by banks to diversify into related financial services such as selling insurance policies and securities trading. In the remainder of this section we concentrate on the nature of contingent commitment banking, which we call off-balance-sheet business whilst recognising that this term covers a wider range of activities.

4.3.2   *Nature of contingent commitment banking*

It is traditional to view a bank as a collection of assets and liabilities making up its balance sheet. We have already discussed in chapters 2 and 3 why banks engage in the traditional business of borrowing and lending, in terms of lenders delegating the collection and use of information to banks and sharing risks with banks, in return for a charge obtained from the interest rate spread. Banks are able to perform these services at a lower cost than ultimate lenders by specialising in collecting and skilfully using information about credit risks, thereby leading to a better selection of risks and, because of their size of operations, enabling them to pool and diversify risks more effectively. Lewis (1987) argues that banks perform similar information-gathering and risk-sharing roles when they undertake off-balance-sheet activities. For example, the establishment of a loan commitment, such as an overdraft, reduces the liquidity risk faced by the customer but exposes the bank to greater liquidity risk, which it is better able to bear through its size of operations and access to the wholesale markets. When a bank provides a guarantee of a customer's ability to meet her or his debts, as with a bill acceptance, then this leads to a lower interest rate being required by the market. When looked at from the lender's, or bill holder's, viewpoint the effect is akin to a depositor accepting a lower rate of interest from a bank because of the safety provided by the bank compared with holding a primary security. Other transformations of asset characteristics performed on the balance sheet have their equivalent off the balance sheet. Note issuance facilities provide an example of maturity transformation, where issues of short-term paper generate longer-term funding. When banks make available a syndicated loan, the borrower can negotiate the terms of the loan, including the interest rate basis, the currency and the date at which the loan is to be drawn down. All these choices can be made off balance sheet as well by means of currency swaps, interest rate basis swaps and financial futures contracts to alter draw down dates.

4.3.3   *Factors determining the growth in off-balance-sheet business*

The motives for banks' involvement in off-balance-sheet business are many. One motive indicated in the above discussion is the desire for the fee income that this type of business brings, thus diversifying the bank's income base. More generally banks have looked to diversify their operations and the liberalisation of financial services in most countries in recent years has allowed banks to expand into new areas of business. Whilst some of the contingent commitments described above have long been a feature of commercial banking, for example loan commitments and guarantees, the banks have in recent years found more innovative uses for such activities. Other parts of contingent commitment banking, such as swaps and options trading, represent more recent innovations; banks, rather than creating these, have encouraged their growth in use by being willing to run an unhedged position. Banks' involvement in financial innovation, and hence off-balance-sheet business, is related to the changing policy and economic environment and the changing preferences of users of the financial system. In order to examine these motives in more detail we now widen the discussion to consider the factors determining financial innovation.

As we saw in chapter 1, a financial instrument can be described by its underlying characteristics of liquidity, risk and so on. Financial innovation, as related to financial instruments, can be defined as the process of unbundling the characteristics and repackaging them to create new instruments. Indeed, recent developments have made it easier to unbundle and repackage the characteristics of an instrument even after it has been issued. For example, a ten-year, fixed-rate, dollar-denominated eurobond represents a particular package of characteristics. Any of these characteristics can be unpackaged and traded separately. The holder of the bond can swap the currency to yen or swap the fixed-interest stream to a floating rate. This example illustrates the fungibility of financial instruments compared with physical products.

Demand factors

The demand for financial innovation can be explained by reference to a number of factors, discussed below (see Bank for International Settlements (1986) for further discussion).

(i) *Changes in the financial environment.* Changes of policy regimes over the last 20 years have led to greater volatility of asset prices. In particular, the general move to floating exchange rates in the early 1970s after the breakdown of the Bretton Woods agreement and the adoption of monetary aggregates as intermediate policy targets have increased the scope for fluctuations in exchange rates and interest rates (see figures 14.1 and 14.2 for an illustration of this). The greater the volatility of asset prices and other prices, such as commodities, the greater is the uncertainty about future prices and hence the greater demand for instruments for hedging exchange rate and interest rate risk. We examine hedging strategies in greater detail in chapter 14.

(ii) *Greater perception of credit risks.* There was a deterioration in the credit standing of banks which had large exposures to the debts of less developed countries (LDCs) following the onset of the debt crisis in 1982 – discussed in section 4.5. One consequence of this was a desire by some banks to sell or swap some problem debts to diversify extreme exposures, and so a secondary market in LDC debt emerged (although not used to a significant extent to date). A further consequence of the decline in the credit standing of many banks was that investors were more wary of lending to banks and therefore were more willing to hold the direct securities of ultimate borrowers. In addition, large borrowers with good credit standing found they could obtain better terms by issuing their own securities through the capital markets rather than borrowing directly from banks. One result of this was some shift away from bank intermediation and towards capital market instruments as a source of financing – a process known as securitisation and further discussed in chapter 12. Banks, however, sought to benefit from this trend by securitising packages of their own loans so they could be sold on and by expanding their role in guaranteeing and underwriting securities issues so as to increase their fee income.

(iii) *Arbitrage opportunities in capital markets.* The existence of barriers, such as exchange controls, interest rate controls and reserve ratios, separating banking markets in different countries led to the development of eurocurrency banking. This in turn put pressure on domestic markets to lessen controls, thus eventually creating a global short-term money market. A similar process is occurring in the capital markets. Barriers separating capital markets have led to the emergence of eurobond and euronote markets (see chapter 12). However, the process of globalisation of capital markets is still incomplete, leaving banks to exploit arbitrage opportunities. The use of the swap transaction (see chapter 13) has enabled a borrower to raise funds in the capital market in which it has a comparative advantage and then swap the principal and interest on those funds to the currency in which it wishes to borrow. For example, a UK company which has a comparative advantage with its issues of sterling bonds but wanting to raise US dollars can issue a sterling eurobond and then swap with a US company wishing to raise sterling but with a comparative advantage in the issue of dollar bonds.

Supply factors

Two factors which have had a major influence on the supply of innovations have been increased regulatory pressures and developments in technology.

(i)   *Increased regulatory pressures.* One consequence of the deterioration in bank credits over the 1980s (see above) has been greater pressure from bank regulators for increased levels of capital in banking. The need to operate on higher capital ratios and the greater cost of raising additional capital due to their reduced credit standing led banks to pursue business that was not subject to capital adequacy controls, that is, off-balance-sheet business. Thus, banks actively contributed to the development and growth in use of instruments such as swaps, options, note issuance facilities and so on. Another consequence of increased capital pressures was, as noted above, the development of securitisation, whereby banks packaged up parts of their loan portfolio (e.g. mortgages) so that they could be sold on in markets.

(ii) *Technology.* Advances in computing, information processing and telecommunications technology have enabled more complex instruments to be designed and priced on a continuous basis. In particular, they have enabled the complex financial engineering of already issued financial products, as described above, to take place.

4.3.4   *Implications of the growth in off-balance-sheet business*

The growth in off-balance-sheet business has been largely the result of the interaction of the demand and supply factors described above. An important implication of this growth stems from one factor in particular, which is the desire of banks to escape capital adequacy controls. This has concerned the regulatory authorities, as banks have taken on risks which are not explicitly related to the bank's capital. These risks are similar to the risks faced by banks in their on-balance-sheet activities but are heightened by the greater uncertainty arising from the novelty of many of the instruments traded. Such risks include: first, liquidity risk, which is the risk of banks having insufficient funding to meet their obligations as they fall due; second, credit risk, which covers both the risk of default by a loan counterparty and the risk of a customer whose performance is guaranteed by the bank failing to deliver; third, position risk, which is concerned with exposure to adverse movements in interest rates and exchange rates (in relation to swap and hedging transactions, banks are exposed to position risk when they take up an unhedged position); and fourth, price risk. There was concern that banks may be underpricing new services in the sense that the income derived may not be sufficient to cover costs, including profit, over the long term. This fear was heightened by both keen competition, which could force prices down to uneconomic levels, and lack of experience of sufficient duration on which an assessment of the risks could be made.

Regulators have addressed the credit risk of off-balance-sheet transactions in their construction of a new risk–assets ratio (a capital ratio where the capital of a bank is related to the risk-adjusted value of its assets – see chapter 18). In the construction of this ratio, off-balance-sheet instruments are converted to a credit equivalent and then risk weighted along with the on-balance-sheet instruments. An illustration of banks' greater exposure to position risk as a consequence of the growth of off-balance-sheet business is provided by the case of Midland Montague, the investment banking arm of the Midland Bank Group. Their treasury operations in 1989 were positioned towards declining interest rates, which failed to materialise, and as a consequence the net interest income of the group was considerably reduced. A further risk of off-balance-sheet business is related to the novelty and complexity of the new instruments. This risk was highlighted in the swap market in 1989 when banks suffered sizeable losses following the ruling of the UK High Court that swap deals undertaken by local authorities, in excess of their underlying borrowing, were *ultra vires*. The banks which had entered into these swap arrangements had clearly not fully considered the risks arising from the special legal status of the local authorities. More recently, Union Bank of Switzerland confirmed losses of £80 million on its equity derivatives business in the first half of 1997 due, among other things, to an error in a computer model to price options. The collapse of Barings, discussed in section 14.6.2, provides another illustration of the problems with derivatives trading.

4.4   International banking

As we have indicated in section 4.2, much of the business of wholesale banks based in the UK is not concerned with domestic sterling borrowing and lending, but with borrowing and lending in foreign currencies. The Bank of England defines international banking as all banking transactions in foreign currency – both cross-border and with local residents – plus cross-border transactions in domestic currency. From this definition we can identify two distinct types of international banking. The first is traditional foreign banking, which, for UK-based banks, involves transactions in sterling with non-residents. The second type of international banking is termed eurocurrency banking, which, for UK-based banks, involves transactions in currencies other than sterling with both residents and non-residents. Traditionally the location of a bank determined the currency in which it would make loans, so to obtain dollar loans you would go to a US-based bank. Whilst such traditional foreign banking still exists, it has been largely replaced by eurocurrency banking, where the location of the bank is unrelated to the currency of its transactions.

4.4.1   *Eurocurrency banking*

In this section we first of all define the term 'eurocurrency' and then examine the reasons for the development and growth of eurocurrency markets, and their nature and operation. We then discuss eurocurrency lending before reaching a conclusion on the role of these markets in the international financial system.

Definition
A eurocurrency can be defined as a deposit or loan denominated in a currency other than that of the host country where the bank is physically located. Thus, for example, a deposit denominated in dollars placed with a bank located in London is a eurocurrency. In a similar manner, a deposit denominated in sterling placed with a bank located in Paris is a eurocurrency. Consequently the existence of eurocurrency markets permits the separation of location of the market and the currency and therefore political and currency risks. It is not surprising that the main currency employed in eurocurrency markets is the dollar (about 75 per cent of the total market), given the importance of the dollar in the international payments mechanism. Because of this dominant role, much of the following exposition will be in terms of the eurodollar market, though it can easily be extended to other currencies.

Table 4.5 *Eurobank A receives a payment of $1 million as a demand deposit: impact on the two sets of balance sheets ($million)*

	Liabilities	Assets
Consolidated US banking system		
US resident deposit	-1	0
Eurobank A demand deposit	+1	0
Net change	0	0
Eurobank A		
UK company time deposit	+1	+1
Net change	+1	+1

In order to demonstrate the operation of the eurodollar market we trace the effect of a series of hypothetical transactions on the balance sheets of both the consolidated US banking system and two eurobanks, designated A and B. Assume initially that a UK customer of eurobank A receives a payment of $1 million in respect of the sale of goods and he places this as a demand deposit with the bank. The impact of this on the two sets of balance sheets is shown in table 4.5.

Table 4.6 *Eurobank A places funds with eurobank B: impact on balance sheets ($million)*

	Liabilities	Assets
Consolidated US banking system		
Eurobank B demand deposit	+1	0
Eurobank A demand deposit	-1	0
Net change	0	0
Eurobank A		
Demand deposit with US bank	0	-1
Time deposit with eurobank B	0	+1
Net change	0	0
Eurobank B		
Time deposit with eurobank A	+1	0
Demand deposit with US bank	0	+1
Net change	+1	+1

Table 4.7 *Recorded changes to balance sheets if eurobank B lends $1 million to a customer ($million)*

	Liabilities	Assets
Consolidated US banking system		
Customer	+1	0
Eurobank B	-1	0
Net change	0	0
Eurobank B		
Demand deposit with US bank	0	-1
Loan to customer	0	+1
Net change	0	0

These changes represent the first round, with the customer lodging the receipt of dollars with his own bank as a time deposit. Suppose for sake of exposition that eurobank A has no immediate use for the funds, so they are placed in the market via a broker with eurobank B in the form of a time deposit earning a rate of interest higher than that paid to the bank's UK customer. The second-round impact of these changes on the various balance sheets is shown in table 4.6.

If eurobank B then lends the $1 million to a customer, the only changes recorded to the balance sheets would refer to the consolidated US banking system and eurobank B recording the change of ownership of the demand deposit and the loan. These would be as shown in table 4.7.

This completes the chain of transactions in our hypothetical example. Note these changes are simplified to the extent that we have assumed that the total sum, that is, the $1 million, has been moved around the system whereas in practice the various banks will have retained some portion as a reserve for their own protection. Secondly, we have not included the situation after the customer has used the loan. If this is paid to a US exporter for goods then the demand deposit at the US bank will have reverted back to a US resident and the chain completed. These caveats do not invalidate the general principle of the analysis. The points to note are that: no extra demand deposits have been created on the US banking system; and total eurodollar deposits are now $2 million (original customer with eurobank A, eurobank A with eurobank B), so that an extra $1 million deposit has been created by the operation of the eurobanks. This demonstrates the tiering in the eurocurrency markets, with the original demand deposit creating an additional deposit of

$1 million. In practice the quantity of extra deposits created would depend on the ratio of the reserves held by eurobanks in the form of deposits in banks within the US banking system against eurodollar deposits. Also illustrated by this example is the difference between gross and net measures of the size of the eurocurrency markets. The gross size is $2 million but the net size is $1 million dollars, that is, the gross size less the quantity of inter-bank lending.

Reasons for development and growth of eurocurrency markets
The interesting question posed is why did the market develop outside the US since, in our example, the original recipient of the deposit could have held it with a US bank rather than eurobank A. A number of reasons have been put forward. One suggestion is that the Eastern bloc countries wished to hold dollar deposits for international payment purposes but were reluctant to hold them in the US for fear that they could be 'blocked' in time of dispute. A second reason put forward is the existence of regulations in the US covering interest rates payable on deposits and capital flows.

Since their development in the early 1960s the markets have experienced a fast rate of growth. One of the main reasons for this is an advantage in terms of cost. As noted above, US banks were restricted in terms of interest rates that could be paid on bank deposits and this restraint became more onerous as interest rates rose worldwide. Furthermore, other regulations in the form of reserve requirements and deposit insurance raised the cost of banking in the US compared with a centre such as London where prudential control was more relaxed. Banks' costs were also lower in the eurocurrency markets since they operated as wholesale banks with no branch network. The effect of these cost advantages was that eurobanks could offer rates on deposits and charges on loans that were marginally more attractive than those relevant to similar transactions with banks located in the US. This raised the attractiveness of the eurocurrency markets and stimulated a fast rate of growth.

A second factor was the growth in international banking itself. This was stimulated by, first, the growth in world trade, necessitating a corresponding growth in the international payments system, and second, a growth of financial imbalances worldwide. In particular, the vast surpluses earned by members of the Organization of Petroleum Exporting Countries (OPEC) following oil price increases in the early 1970s were an important factor. OPEC members placed their surplus dollar revenue from the sale of oil with eurobanks. It is often claimed that the large US balance of payments deficits also aided the development of the market. The importance of this factor may be overestimated since, whilst it increased the total quantity of dollars, it does not explain why these dollar balances were held outside the US. The main reason for the continued growth of the market appears to be the cost advantage and it remains to be seen whether the market will continue to grow as quickly once the relative advantage of offshore centres is reduced following harmonisation of prudential regulation noted in chapter 18.

Nature of eurocurrency markets

We now briefly examine the general nature of the market. The first point to note is that it is a wholesale market with transactions typically of $1 million or more. As illustrated in our hypothetical example, the second point to note is that there is a significant volume of inter-bank lending, so that the gross size of the market is larger than the net size obtained when the inter-bank transactions are netted out. Interest rates are clearly related to those charged in domestic markets. Thus, the rate charged on dollar loans by banks situated in the US sets an upper limit to the rates charged for similar loans in the eurocurrency markets. Similarly, there is a relationship between the rates ruling in a particular location. Interest rate parity requires the following relationship to hold between rates on sterling in the domestic market and those on dollars in the London eurodollar market for transactions of similar maturity and risk, and so on:

Nominal rate of interest on sterling	=	Nominal rate of interest on eurodollars in London	=	Expected appreciation/ depreciation of the dollar versus sterling

Arbitrage will ensure that this relationship holds provided the market is efficient – see chapter 7 for a fuller discussion of this point.

The market is essentially a market for short-term deposits, with the average maturity of a deposit being in the region of three months. The main depositors and borrowers are governments, multinational corporations and banks from a wide range of countries, including the US. Lending appears on the other side of the bank's balance sheet. It is estimated by the Bank for International Settlements that at the end of 1989 approximately 80 per cent of outstanding gross international bank lending was of the eurocurrency type. The reasons for this dominance of eurocurrencies in international lending follow from those discussed above for the growth of the eurocurrency markets.

Eurocurrency lending

It is difficult to obtain separate figures for net eurocurrency lending, so the figures reported below refer to total international lending. The

Table 4.8   *Gross and net international lending, 1985–96 (figures in $billion adjusted to exclude estimated exchange rate effects)*

	1985	1986	1987	1988	1989	1990	1991	1992	1993	1994	1995	1996
Gross	297	657	760	511	807	714	-103	164	314	279	644	590
Net[a]	105	200	300	260	410	465	80	195	205	195	330	410

[a] Net figure excludes inter-bank lending but allows for banks' own use of external funds for domestic lending.
Source: *International Banking and Financial Market Developments*, Bank for International Settlements (various issues).

figures for the volume of new international lending from the mid-1980s to the mid-1990s are presented in table 4.8.

The net international lending figures exclude lending between banks and so provide us with a view of new international lending to companies, governments and government agencies. The eurocurrency part of this net international lending figure can be further separated into syndicated loans, which are large, long-term loans, and the rest, which are mainly shorter-term credits for financing trade and so on. The figures for international syndicated credits, which are mainly eurocurrency syndicated credits, are presented in table 4.9.

Eurocurrency loans and syndicated loans in particular were the method of financing the international imbalances of the 1970s following the oil price rises of 1973/74. Sovereign borrowers from the LDCs and the newly industrialising countries (NICs) in Latin America became important borrowers in this market. When the debt crisis broke in 1982 (see section 4.5) this had two main effects on the syndicated loan market. First, banks became reluctant to lend new money to LDCs and NICs unless forced to as part of a restructuring package of the International Monetary Fund (IMF) ('involuntary lending'). Second, those

Table 4.9   *International syndicated lending, 1981–96 (£billion)*

	1981	1983	1985	1987	1989	1991	1993	1995	1996
International syndicated credits	101	38	19	89	149	137	221	311	530

Source: Allen (1990) and Bank for International Settlements, annual reports (various).

banks with a high ratio of sovereign debt to capital found their credit rating reduced, which made raising funds in the capital markets more costly, leading to higher lending charges. One consequence of this was that highly rated borrowers found they could raise funds at lower cost through the international capital markets than through borrowing from banks. This led to the phenomenon known as securitisation, which is discussed in chapter 12. The overall effect of the debt crisis was to bring about a dramatic reduction in the volume of new syndicated lending, which continued until 1985. From 1986 to 1996 the market grew again, reversing the trend of the early 1980s which many commentators had predicted would continue. Most of the growth of syndicated credits since the late 1980s came from a greater use of this type of financing by industrial borrowers. By the early 1990s industrial borrowers accounted for over 80 per cent of total syndicated credits, compared with approximately 60 per cent in the early 1980s.

Syndicated loans are loans spread among many, sometimes over 100, banks. They are generally medium-term loans with maturities ranging from three to fifteen years, although the average maturity of new loans is around six to eight years. Interest rates on the loans are floating, with the interest rate related to a reference rate such as the London inter-bank offer rate (LIBOR), plus a margin representing risk and so on, and adjusted several times a year. Syndicated loans can be denominated in any currency although the US dollar is the most popular. Given the large number of banks involved in syndicated lending, it is natural that one bank will act as a 'lead' bank organising the arrangements of the loan. The lead bank will receive a fee for this service in addition to the normal interest rate charge.

There are a number of advantages for borrowers using the syndicated credits market compared with international capital markets. First, the loan provides a steady source of funds, unlike some of the short-term underwritten instruments of the euronote markets (considered in chapter 12). Second, borrowers can generally raise larger sums of money than through the capital markets. For example, a $13.6 billion credit was raised for Kohlberg Kravis Roberts for the leveraged takeover of RJR Nabisco in 1989. Third, deals can be arranged quickly. For example, in 1987 BP sought to raise a syndicated loan to finance its offer to purchase the remainder of the stock of Standard Oil. A consortium of banks, led by Morgan Guaranty, took just five days to arrange $15 billion, which was $10 billion more than BP actually required. The syndication of a loan across many banks also brings advantages compared with a loan from one bank, in that an individual bank in the syndicate will be less affected by a default. The lower risk implies that the cost of a syndicated loan should be lower.

The surge of corporate restructuring in the late 1980s using the vehicle of mergers and acquisitions, particularly in the US and UK, has been one of the driving forces behind the growth of syndicated lending. An increasing proportion of the financing of such activity has been debt, partly marketable debt in the US ('junk bonds') but largely loans raised through the method of syndicated lending. The advantage of syndicated loans in this activity is again the speed with which funds can be raised and the ability to raise these funds more discreetly than through the capital markets.

Another development in the syndicated credit market since the 1980s has been the emergence of a secondary market, in particular of LDC debt. This involves banks securitising the debt so that it can be sold on to a third party. The Basle agreement on capital adequacy (see chapter 18) means that banks have either to raise more capital or remove some assets from the balance sheet. A number of banks have chosen the latter course and this raises the prospect of the emergence of a general secondary market in syndicated credits. Allen (1990) states that this 'could be regarded as part of a more general process in the euromarkets, where in recent years innovation and securitisation have led to gradual dissolving of the boundaries between money, credit and capital markets'.

Consequences of eurocurrency markets

Finally in this section we consider the consequences of the development of the eurocurrency market. The market clearly carries out many of the facets of financial intermediation discussed in chapter 2. Maturity transformation is obviously present, with loans being of a longer term than deposits. Similarly, asset transformation is evidenced by the change of almost riskless deposits into more risky loans. This creates some dangers for the financial system given the interdependence of the operators within the market due to the presence of inter-bank lending built on a relatively small base of deposits held in US banks. Failure of one bank may have a large knock-on effect, creating problems for national supervisors of the domestic monetary system. In fact, as we have argued earlier for the parallel sterling markets, such operations may enjoy 'de facto' support since national supervisory authorities are loath to allow a major bank to default on its liabilities. There is also a concern arising from the overhang of sovereign lending financed by borrowing in the eurocurrency markets (see below). Furthermore, it is sometimes argued that the creation of such a large pool of acceptable currencies creates the potential for movement of funds in a manner that could lead to the destabilisation of exchange rates and the frustration of monetary policy.

A final concern has been expressed over the role of the eurocurrency markets in the propagation of inflation on a worldwide basis. It is sometimes argued that the creation of these markets has led to an expansion of the world money supply, which in turn leads to higher world inflation rates. However, an examination of the hypothetical examples at the outset of this section suggests that there was no expansion in the quantity of US dollars held at US banks but that secondary deposits were created in the manner of non-bank financial intermediaries building up credit on the base of bank deposits. This analogy suggests that the existence of the eurocurrency markets has permitted a growth of credit rather than the money supply per se, and as such may have increased the efficiency of the allocation of credit worldwide. This is also evidenced by the existence of syndicated lending, which permits the sharing of the risks of international lending amongst different banks from different locations.

In the next section we examine one of the consequences of the growth of international lending over the 1970s.

4.5   Sovereign lending crisis

In the 1960s and early 1970s most lending to developing countries was carried out by official institutions such as the World Bank and the IMF. This position changed, largely as a result of oil price increases between October 1973 and January 1974, which saw oil prices rise by over 400 per cent. These price increases were initiated by OPEC, a cartel whose member countries as a consequence experienced a dramatic increase in their foreign currency receipts. Oil-importing countries, however, experienced balance of payments deficits. Some of the developed countries were supported by direct capital flows from OPEC members; for example, $6 billion was placed in investments in the UK in the years shortly after the oil price rises. The oil-importing developing countries suffered the most problems, and those with access to the international financial markets generally chose to borrow to cover their balance of payments deficits in order to sustain growth. However, unlike the borrowing of the period prior to the oil price rises, developing countries turned increasingly to commercial banks. Developing countries were reluctant to borrow from the IMF because any funds provided were usually given as part of a reconstruction package which, because they were generally deflationary, were politically unpopular. The international agencies such as the IMF and the World Bank would in any event have been unable to support the scale of lending required, as the basis of their funding was the developed countries' governments, in particular the US, which were themselves experiencing problems. Since oil is priced in dollars, the commercial banks received a massive flow of liquid funds from the OPEC members in the form of eurodollar deposits and therefore had the ability to meet the developing countries' demands for funds. Much of this lending was to governments or was government guaranteed and was therefore termed sovereign lending. There was a widespread belief amongst the banking community that this lending was relatively safe, as countries could not go bankrupt. As a consequence any credit assessment was superficial and there was little monitoring by the banks as to the purpose to which the funds were put. Part of the blame for the crisis which came later can therefore be placed with the banks, which were imprudent in their lending. However, in mitigation, the banks were encouraged by Western governments to recycle the OPEC surpluses to offset the effects of higher oil prices on the world economy. Much of this lending was to the NICs of Latin America. The LDCs, particularly in the sub-Saharan region of Africa, generally did not have sufficient credit standing to gain access to loans from commercial banks.

To sum up this section, the developing countries borrowed heavily in dollars at floating rates of interest to finance balance of payments deficits (i.e. consumption) rather than investment. Consequently, adjustment to the higher oil prices was delayed and servicing the debt necessitated current-account balance of payment surpluses to earn the required dollars to meet the interest payments and repayment of principal.

There was little sign of problems resulting from this sovereign lending over the rest of the 1970s, partly because of negative real interest rates on the debt. Over the latter half of the 1970s though, the OPEC surpluses reduced as a result of dramatically increased imports.

In 1979, OPEC decided on a further sharp rise in the price of oil, which more than doubled the spot price, from $11 to $24 a barrel. Further increases also occurred in 1980. The response of the developed countries to this second round of oil price rises, however, was different. Around this time the governments elected in the UK, US and Germany adopted monetarist policies and so attempted to control inflation arising from higher oil prices by monetary restraint. This time there was no attempt to borrow and spend a way out of the problem. The policy of monetary restraint, however, contributed to a world recession, making it much more difficult for developing countries to expand exports to earn foreign currency. As part of the policy of monetary restraint, interest rates were increased, which led to a further deterioration in the debt-servicing capacity of the debtor countries. Thus, the combination of higher interest payments yet declining exports led to increased pressure on debtor countries. The first public sign of a crisis though did not occur

Table 4.10   *Net resource transfers to Latin America, 1981–85 ($billion)*

Year	Net capital inflow	Interest repayments and foreign profits	Net resource transfer
1981	49.1	27.8	21.3
1982	27.6	36.8	-9.2
1983	6.1	34.9	-28.8
1984	11.6	37.1	-25.5
1985	4.1	36.7	-32.6

Source: Inter American Development Bank.

until 1982, when Mexico, one of the leading borrowers and a country with proven reserves of oil which had achieved rapid economic growth in the previous four years, announced a moratorium on principal payments until the end of 1983. Pressure from the IMF on commercial banks with exposure to Mexico to provide new money prevented an actual default. However, the incident brought home to the international banking system the nature of the risks of sovereign debt.

The years between 1982 and 1985 have been termed the years of debt crisis management, with the IMF orchestrating commercial bank loan reschedulings along with 'concerted' lending packages. At the same time the debtor countries receiving help from the IMF were forced to accept politically unpopular austerity programmes. Whilst this period of management achieved stability for the international banking system, it did little to ease the problems faced by the debtor countries. Whilst there was some narrowing of the balance of payments positions for many debtor countries, this was at the expense of a sharp fall in investment and growth. Net resource transfers to Latin American countries over the period 1982 to 1985 were in fact away from these countries to the developed countries, as debtors paid back more than they received in new loans (table 4.10).

The next initiative came in 1985, when James Baker, the US Secretary to the Treasury, announced a new package which was aimed at improving economic growth in the debtor countries. With this package, additional funds were to be provided to finance supply-side reforms, such as encouraging inward investment, tax reform and the encouragement of competition in their economies. The Baker plan was aimed at 15 heavily indebted countries, mostly based in South America, with a total of $29 billion targeted over three years. Of this additional funding, $20 billion was to come from commercial banks and $9 billion from international agencies. However, as Sachs (1986) states, 'The Baker

Table 4.11 *UK banks' exposure to outstanding debt of Mexico, Argentina, Brazil and Venezuela, at end 1984, as a percentage of capital*

Bank	%
Barclays	62
Lloyds	165
Midland	205
National Westminster	73

Source: Estimate in Lever and Huhne (1985).

plan was significant not as a new policy, but rather an admission by the United States that the debt strategy up to 1985 had not generated adequate economic growth in the debtor countries'.

Whilst the commercial banks cautiously welcomed the Baker plan there were a number of problems identified. In particular, the smaller banks, which had already been withdrawing credit lines or writing off LDC loans since the crisis broke, were not anxious to increase their exposure again. This meant that the burden of new lending had to be taken up by the larger banks already heavily exposed. At the same time, these banks were being put under pressure by their central banks to increase capital ratios because of the greater risks. As the new lending under the Baker plan envisaged 'soft' terms, these new loans would likely be classified as high risk, thereby requiring greater capital backing. As a consequence, little new lending, from either official institutions or commercial banks, materialised. In addition, the supply-side reforms proved difficult to sustain and continuing high interest rates increased the pressure on debtor countries. To prevent defaults, banks were forced to agree to extensive rescheduling of the debt. Many debtor countries, faced with growing social problems and political unrest, began to impose conditions on the servicing of the debt. In March 1987, Brazil, the largest debtor country, declared a moratorium on interest payments on $68 billion of its outstanding foreign private sector debt. Against this background the commercial banks began to acknowledge the serious consequences of default. To illustrate the potential for insolvency of UK banks in the mid-1980s the exposure of the four main clearing banks to the four largest Latin American debtors, as a percentage of their capital base, is shown in table 4.11.

Citicorp became the first bank, in May 1987, to establish substantial reserves against poorly performing LDC debt. Other US banks with large exposures quickly followed the example of Citicorp. UK banks,

Table 4.12 *Exposure to debt and provisions for debt of the clearing banks,*
1987–89

	Provisions as % of exposure			Exposure to debt in 1989 (after deduction of provisions) as % of shareholders' funds
	1987	*1988*	*1989*	
Midland	29	33	50	80
Lloyds	34	34	72	50
Barclays	35	40	70	8
National Westminster	33	35	75	7

Source: published accounts.

led by National Westminster and under pressure from the Bank of
England and the stock market, which had started to mark down the price
of bank shares, also announced substantial provisions. Further substantial provisions were set aside in 1989 in response to a deterioration
in debt servicing by many debtor countries, discussed below. Whilst this
provisioning acknowledged the dangers of default of LDC debt, it did
not in itself help the debtor countries, as the provisions represented
funds set aside in case of default rather than any write-off of the debt.
The effect of the provisions was to improve substantially the financial
health of the banks, so that by the end of 1989 the four largest UK
clearing banks had exposure to LDC debt, after allowing for provisions,
of below 100 per cent of the core capital of the bank (table 4.12).

Over the latter half of the 1980s, a number of market-based solutions
were used by the banks to reduce their exposure to LDC debt. Three of
the solutions which have been often used are discussed below.

4.5.1 *Selling the debt in the secondary market in LDC debt*

A secondary market in LDC debt began in late 1983, and although much
of the activity in this market is inter-bank trading, with banks having the
aim of adjusting their portfolio of risks, it has also been used as a basis
for debt buy-backs by the debtor countries and as an intermediate stage
for debt–equity swaps (see below). The price of a country's debt in the
market does provide some indication of the current and future performance of the debt, and table 4.13 illustrates the generally deteriorating
position for the three main Latin American debtors over the latter half of
the 1980s, followed by an improvement in the early 1990s, the reasons
for which are discussed below.

Table 4.13   *Secondary market prices for selected LDC debt, 1986–92 (price in dollars of a $100 claim)*

Country	August 1986	April 1987	October 1987	March 1989	May 1990	December 1992
Argentina	66	60	34	17	76	63
Brazil	76	63	38	34	25	30
Mexico	56	59	47	41	46	59

Source: Sachs and Huizinga (1987), *Barclays Bank Review*, August 1990, and Clark (1993).

Table 4.14 shows the total returns on 'Brady' debt (see below) for the same three countries and it is obvious that the improved situation has continued.

The fact that a debtor's servicing record can influence the secondary market price of its debt introduces a moral hazard problem to the extent that any debt relief is tied to the secondary price of the debt, and debtor countries can 'engineer' a reduction in the price to obtain greater relief.

4.5.2   Debt–equity swap

This involves a debt denominated in a foreign currency being paid by the debtor in local currency, at an agreed discount, to the debt's face value. The bank then uses the local currency to invest in the debtor country, thereby acquiring a claim on a real asset, with the potential of capital gain as well as income return. For example, Midland Bank in 1989 swapped $63 million of debt owed by Chile for a $53 million investment in a Chilean copper mine. The discount in the swap was 16 per cent, which is better than the 35 per cent discount which would have resulted from selling through the secondary markct.

Table 4.14   *Total returns on Brady bonds, 1994–96 (1993 = 100)*

	1994	1995	1996
Argentina	78.79	102.49	128.10
Brazil	89.85	108.93	146.59
Mexico	70.6	96.02	118.23

Source: J. P. Morgan Web site (www.jpmorgan.com).

4.5.3   *Debt–debt swap*

This involves a bank exchanging the debt for bonds issued by the debtor country's government, where the bonds are issued either at a discount on the par value but with a market rate of interest or at par value with a lower than market rate of interest.

It has been estimated that, by 1989, the 15 countries targeted in the Baker plan had reduced their bank debt by 13 per cent using these and other methods. Despite some success in reducing debt burdens it was accepted that the debt burdens of debtor countries remained too high. A further initiative came in March 1989 in the form of a set of proposals announced by US Treasury Secretary Nicholas Brady. These proposals represented a shift from the earlier approaches to the debt problem in that they recognised the need for official backing of schemes designed to achieve voluntary reduction of market-based debt or debt service. However, the proposals also represent a continuation of the Baker approach in that participation is based on the pursuit of an IMF-approved economic adjustment programme and that new money is to be provided by the banks. Under these proposals debt relief is provided by the three methods described above. Official money to back the initiative is provided primarily from the IMF and World Bank but also from the governments of developed countries such as Japan. By 1994 eight Brady deals had been completed or agreed in principle. These were with Mexico, Costa Rica and the Philippines in 1989, Venezuela and Uruguay in 1990, Nigeria in 1991 and Argentina and Brazil in 1992. Brady deals completed since then have included two with east European countries, Poland and Bulgaria. A typical deal was that arranged with Mexico, covering $48.5 billion of its debt, where 88 per cent of the banks with exposure to Mexico opted for debt reduction (roughly half for bonds at a discount and half for bonds at par with a reduced interest rate), with only 12 per cent of banks opting to provide new money. The amount of new money provided fell well short of the amount targeted. This deal though has provided some help to Mexico, both directly in terms of a $1 billion reduction in interest payments per year (out of $8 billion in total) and more indirectly with the reduction in debt overhang increasing investor confidence, reducing domestic interest rates and increasing foreign direct investment and capital repatriation. The eight deals agreed up until 1994 did in fact reduce the value of debt service obligations by $65 billion, or just over one-third of the existing bank debt. The banks also obtained some benefit from the deal as the average secondary price of debtor countries' debt increased from approximately 40 cents in the dollar before 1989 to around 57 cents in the dollar in 1993, effectively

Table 4.15   *Net capital inflows to Brady-deal countries, 1990–96 ($billion)*

	1990	1991	1992	1993	1994	1995	1996
Mexico	8.4	25.1	27.0	33.8	15.7	-10.5	4.1
Costa Rica	-0.1	0.2	0.2	0.1	-0.1	0.3	n/a
Venezuela	-5.5	1.7	3.0	2.8	-3.6	-2.9	-1.7
Uruguay	-0.1	-0.4	-0.1	0.2	0.5	0.4	0.2
Nigeria	-4.2	-2.6	-7.8	-1.0	0.3	0.8	-3.6
Philippines	2.1	2.9	3.2	3.3	5.1	5.3	n/a
Argentina	-5.9	0.2	6.9	10.4	9.2	0.3	7.5
Brazil	-5.4	-4.9	5.9	7.6	8.0	2.9	n/a

n/a = not available.
Source: IMF, *International Financial Statistics*, February 1998.

boosting the value of the residual debt left on the balance sheets of banks. The secondary market price of many of the Latin American debtor countries' debt continued to rise from 1994 to 1996, as evidenced by the increase in returns on bonds issued by these countries under a Brady deal (see table 14.14). Another indicator of the improving financial position of debtor countries has been the tremendous increase in private capital flows into those countries, particularly those that have agreed a Brady deal. Table 4.15 shows a satisfactory trend for most Brady-deal countries in net capital flows made up of direct and portfolio investment through equity and bond markets and repatriation of flight capital. Significant exceptions to this general statement occur in the cases of Mexico (1995), Venezuela (1994–96) and Nigeria over virtually the whole period. These exceptions are no doubt due to political cir-cumstances. Despite the positive developments following the Brady initiative, significant problems still remain for the debtor countries. Despite the permanent improvements in debtor countries' positions, debt service obligations remain heavy and whilst re-entry to the private capital markets is helpful, the key to long-term recovery is improvement in the real economy, which occurs more slowly than improvement in the financial economy. The debtor countries were also helped since 1990 by significant reductions in US interest rates. The LIBOR for US deposits, to which most loan contracts were linked before the Brady deals, declined by about 500 basis points between 1990 and 1993, and has increased only slightly since 1993. Those countries that agreed a deal early on obtained interest savings on that portion of their debt that was left at floating rates. Countries agreeing later will have obtained much larger interest savings. Indeed, the relationship between the decline in international interest rates and the improvement in secondary market prices has been found to be very strong (see Dooley *et al.* 1994) and thus a reversal of these interest rates may bring back debt servicing problems.

4.6   Conclusion

In this chapter we have examined the nature of wholesale banking in general and its international dimension in particular. Attention has also been focused on two developments concerning the wholesale banking sector, namely off-balance-sheet business and the sovereign lending problem. As we have noted in this chapter, the former development has implications for the way banks are regulated and we consider this issue further in chapter 18. The problems that have arisen out of sovereign lending appear to have been mitigated since the latter part of the 1980s, in the sense that large defaults on the debt will not now threaten the solvency of the main banks involved. The position of the debtor countries, though much improved for those that have agreed Brady deals, remains vulnerable to an upturn in international interest rates.

Chapter 5

Building societies and finance houses

5.1 Introduction

In this chapter we examine two other deposit-taking institutions, namely building societies and finance houses. In view of their greater importance in the financial system and the recent significant changes affecting them, the major proportion of this chapter is directed towards the building societies.

The building societies have traditionally been mutually owned, specialist financial institutions, borrowing from the personal sector and lending back to the personal sector in the form of a mortgage to finance house purchase. Up until the beginning of the 1980s they enjoyed a virtual monopoly in the mortgage market. On the borrowing side, although experiencing some external competition for personal sector deposits from banks and National Savings, there was little internal competition between different building societies owing to a cartel arrangement on the setting of interest rates. Over the 1980s, however, building societies experienced a considerable degree of change as various liberalisation measures stimulated competition in the mortgage and personal savings markets. The Building Societies Act 1986 allowed for progressive deregulation of the products that building societies can offer on both sides of the balance sheet. The specialist institutions became, as a consequence of these changes, more able to emulate banks as general providers of financial services. The 1986 Act also provides a procedure for a society to transfer from mutual to company (i.e. bank) status. The Abbey National was the first to follow this route, in 1989. A wave of conversions and bank takeovers of building societies then took place between 1995 and 1998, resulting in nine of the top ten building societies in 1995 losing their mutual status. A further Building Societies Act in 1997 aims to stem this loss from the mutual sector by taking

101

regulation of the remaining building societies in the direction of a more permissive regime and away from the prescriptive framework of the 1986 Act.

In this chapter, after providing a brief history of building societies (section 5.2), we concentrate on an examination of the pressures for change and the actual changes that have taken place in building society activity over the 1980s and early 1990s (sections 5.3 to 5.6). Finally, in section 5.7, we provide a brief survey of finance houses.

5.2   History of the building society movement

The first building societies were founded in the late eighteenth century. These early societies were set up by a group of around 20 to 30 people who contributed on a weekly basis to a fund which financed the purchase of land and the building of houses. These early societies were known as terminating societies, because when all the contributing members had been housed the society terminated. The next stage came with the development of permanent societies, which increasingly borrowed from those who did not wish to buy a house and lent to those who both financed the construction of new homes and purchased existing homes. By 1912 approximately half the building societies were of this permanent type and no new terminating societies have been formed since 1953.

Another characteristic of a building society is that it is a mutual organisation. This means it is owned by its members, principally its depositors and borrowers. A key difference then between the mutual organisation and a public limited company (p.l.c.) is that for a mutual the customers are themselves the owners of the firm whereas for the p.l.c. there is a separation of the two.

Up until the early 1980s there was little change in the activities of building societies, which had a specialist role involving intermediation within the personal sector, borrowing in the form of deposits and lending in the form of a mortgage to finance house purchase. Nevertheless, since that date the structure of the industry has significantly changed in two respects. First, the branch networks of the societies have expanded; and second, the concentration of building societies has increased. This is illustrated in table 5.1.

The 2,286 building societies in existence at the beginning of the century were in the main small in size and operated over a limited local area. The inter-war period saw the beginning of branching, as societies sought to expand their catchment area for personal savings. Expansion of the building societies' branch networks appears though to have come to an end over the last half of the 1980s. Concentration of the building

Table 5.1   *Changes to the structure of the building society industry, 1900–96*

Year	Number of societies	Number of branches
1900	2,286	n/a
1920	1,271	n/a
1940	952	640
1960	726	985
1980	273	5,684
1884	190	6,816
1988	131	6,912
1992	105	5,765
1996	88	4,613

n/a Not available.
Note: figures for branches for 1940 and 1960 are estimates.
Source: *Housing Finance*, 1997.

society sector has proceeded at a rapid pace since 1960, with the majority of mergers between societies taking the form of a smaller society transferring its engagement to a larger society. These developments were accompanied by a large expansion of the business of building societies, as evidenced by the figures shown in table 5.2 for the level of personal sector deposits with the banking sector and total shares and deposits of building societies.[1] The figures terminate at the end of 1988, to exclude the complications caused by the transfer of Abbey National from building society to bank status.

The figures in table 5.2 illustrate the success of building societies in the competition for personal sector deposits compared with banks. We consider this competition in more detail in the next section. What we are concerned with here is the controversy which arose as to whether the growth of building society deposits adversely affected the banks to any extent. The traditional argument followed the rationale that since building societies maintain their own deposits with the banking sector, the growth of building society deposits did not entail deposit losses for the banking sector, but rather a change in ownership. A second argument put forward noted that the societies lent exclusively on mortgages whereas banks conducted little mortgage lending and hence there was

---

1   The main account at building societies is the share account (opening a share account confers part ownership in the society). The other kind of account is the deposit account, which does not confer ownership rights. Total shares refers to the total of share accounts and deposit accounts.

Table 5.2   *Stocks of personal sector savings held with banks and building societies, 1963–88 (£million)*

	Bank deposits[a]	Building society deposits[b]	Ratio of a to b
1963	6,232	4,057	0.65
1965	7,210	5,211	0.72
1970	10,036	10,194	1.02
1975	19,206	22,748	1.18
1980	36,598	50,002	1.37
1985	61,488	104,922	1.71
1988	94,129	152,700	1.62

Source: CSO, *Financial Statistics*, various issues.

little competition between these two classes of institution on the assets side of the balance sheet.

The first argument is of an extremely dubious nature. To the extent that building societies keep reserves in the form of public sector debt (see table 5.6 for further details), funds are lost to the banks in precisely the same manner as any other open market sale of government securities. The second argument is certainly no longer true. As we discuss in the next section, banks have become extremely active lenders in the mortgage market since the early 1980s. Even more significant is the fact that the traditional argument ignored the effect of competition on the terms under which banks raised deposits. Increased competition for retail deposits must have raised to some extent the cost to banks of obtaining such deposits. These costs could arise, apart from the direct impact on interest rates, in a variety of ways, including reversion to Saturday opening, innovative time deposit schemes and reduction of charges on the operation of current accounts. Building societies' entry into the wholesale money markets – discussed in the next section – has also increased the demand for wholesale funds, which must have again raised to some extent the cost of funds for banks in this market.

5.3   Competitive pressures on building societies

Building societies have experienced greater competition in both their funding and lending activities since the end of the 1970s. As noted above, the main competitors to building societies in the personal sector savings market have been banks in particular and, to a lesser extent,

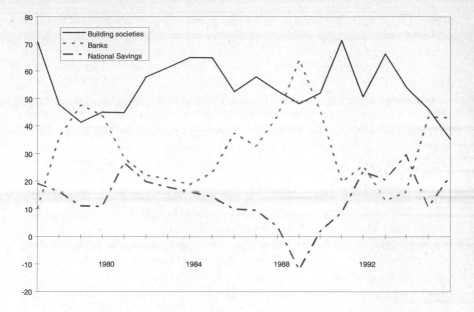

Figure 5.1   *Competition for personal sector liquid assets, 1977–96 (%).*
Source: CSO, Financial Statistics, *various issues*

National Savings, although since the mid-1980s building society deposits have also come under competition from equity instruments following a number of privatisation issues, the growth of unit trusts and the growth in equity prices. Figure 5.1 illustrates the competition for personal sector liquid assets since 1977.

Over much of the 1970s the building societies faced little competition from other institutions for personal sector deposits. As we saw in chapter 3, the banks changed the balance of their funding from the retail market towards the wholesale market over the 1970s. Banks, however, did make an adjustment to this balance at the end of the 1970s and targeted personal savings for a few years. This was repeated in the late 1980s and mid-1990s, illustrating the ability of banks to move between the retail and wholesale markets for funding, according to relative availability and cost of funds. A further reason for banks targeting the personal savings market is that they view retail funding as a base for selling other retail financial services. A more specific reason for the greater competition though was the decision to put banks and building societies on the same footing in terms of deducting tax from depositors' interest at source at a composite rate of 25.25 per cent from April 1985 (abolished for both banks and building societies from April 1991). It was believed that the effect of quoting bank interest rates net of tax rather than gross would be to make their uncompetitiveness more obvious. In response to these pressures banks introduced high-interest deposit accounts similar to the building societies' short-notice and instant-access accounts. Later in the 1980s banks offered high-interest cheque accounts and more recently cheque accounts free of bank charges. As a consequence banks have regained some of the share of personal sector liquid asset holdings they had lost to building societies. Further competitive pressures on building societies' funding has come from the government at times of high public borrowing in the early 1980s and 1990s, when greater emphasis was placed on funding the public sector borrowing requirement (PSBR) through National Savings.

Up until the early 1970s the majority of the building societies' funding came from the ordinary share account. Building societies then introduced, in 1973, term accounts, which offered a guaranteed differential over the ordinary share rate in exchange for the depositor leaving the deposit untouched for a certain length of time. Term accounts were generally for two years up to five years. These accounts grew very rapidly over the 1970s and by 1982 accounted for just over 23 per cent of building society personal sector funding. The next main innovation from building societies came in the early 1980s, in response to the greater competition described above, with the introduction of the short-notice account and later the instant-access account, where a higher rate of interest than the ordinary share rate is paid in exchange for a short period of notice or some minimum level of deposit. By the end of 1989, these short-notice and instant-access deposits accounted for just over 83 per cent of the total of personal sector deposits with building societies.

Another major development in building society funding since the mid-1980s is the greater volume of funds raised from wholesale sources. A series of changes in the taxation position of building societies from 1983 allowed them to pay interest gross of tax on various wholesale instruments, thereby making the issue of such instruments more appealing to investors and hence making wholesale funding a more viable proposition for building societies. The Building Societies Act 1986 placed an upper limit on wholesale funding of 20 per cent although this was raised to 40 per cent in 1988 and then 50 per cent in 1994 following representations from building societies. The percentage breakdown of retail and wholesale funding for building societies is shown in table 5.3.

The largely floating-rate assets (mortgages) of societies means that they would prefer to hold wholesale floating-rate liabilities (a breakdown of the main wholesale instruments issued by building societies is provided in table 5.6). Therefore the most attractive eurobond for

Table 5.3 *Breakdown of building society funding, 1982–96 (%)*

Year	Retail funds	Wholesale funds
1982	100	0
1984	98	2
1986	90	10
1988	86	14
1990	81	19
1992	80	20
1994	63	37
1996	67	33

Source: *Housing Finance*, 1997.

societies (in cost terms as well) has been the floating-rate note (see chapter 12 for further discussion). These issues have largely been eurosterling floating-rate notes. Since March 1986, though, societies have been able to enter into interest rate swaps and so have started raising funds through the fixed-rate note market. The ability of societies to enter into currency swaps since the beginning of 1987 has added further flexibility, allowing societies to raise wholesale funds in a variety of currencies.

Access to the wholesale markets has allowed societies to practise liability management (see chapter 3). As with banks, which switched to liability management over the 1970s, societies have been able to reduce the level of liquid assets they hold – see section 5.6 below.

On the lending side, the building societies had a virtual monopoly on mortgage lending over the 1970s and accounted for some 82 per cent of the outstanding stock of mortgages at the end of 1979. Over the 1970s banks, although involved to a limited extent in mortgage lending, were restricted by direct controls on their lending which impinged most directly on their lending to the personal sector. Building societies, as mutual organisations, were not profit maximisers but instead attempted to reconcile the conflicting demands of borrowers for low interest rates and savers for high interest rates by maintaining a relatively stable path for interest rates over time. This was made possible by the cartel arrangement which existed whereby the Building Societies Association (BSA) recommended rates of interest to be charged to borrowers and savers. Such an institutional structure minimised the role played by interest rates in equilibrating supply and demand for mortgages. The stickiness of rates offered by building societies on shares and deposits meant that at times the rates were uncompetitive, thus reducing inflows

Rate of interest (%)

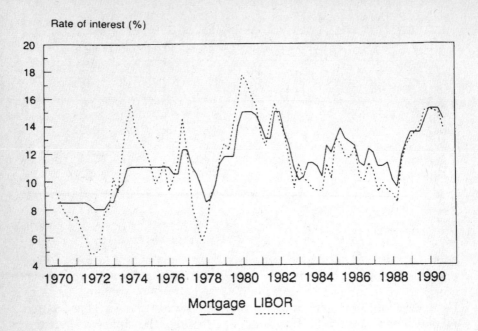

Mortgage LIBOR

Figure 5.2 *Mortgage interest rates compared with LIBOR, 1970–92. Source: CSO*, Financial Statistics, *various issues*

(see figure 5.2). This shortage of funds for lending that occurred at times could be made up by the societies running down liquid asset stocks.

However, this provided only a temporary solution and, given that societies would not raise interest rates to reduce the demand for mort-gages, other means of rationing were pursued. These included queues and changes in lending arrangements. The latter generally took the form of lowering either the ratio of loan to the borrower's income or the ratio of loan to the value of the associated property. Another criticism of the cartel arrangement was that the rates of interest set were designed to protect the smaller, less efficient societies. This had the effect of allowing the larger societies to operate on margins which would not occur in a competitive environment and therefore provided no incentive for them to cut costs, so that the industry as a whole operated at a higher cost. However, a defence of the cartel that was often made was that because the mortgage rate was often kept below market rates, the cartel kept the cost of borrowing low (although at the expense of savers).

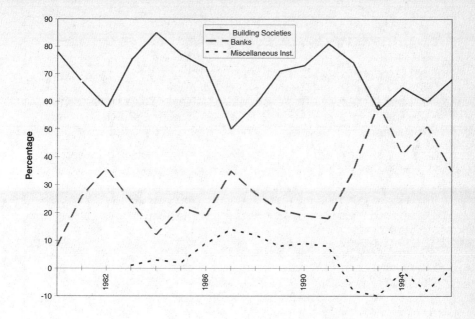

Figure 5.3 *Share of net new mortgage lending, 1980–96 (%). A negative value indicates that repayments exceed lending. Source:* Housing Finance, *1997*

The market structure just described began to break down shortly after the start of the 1980s. In mid-1980, direct controls on bank lending (known as the 'corset') were lifted and the banks immediately strove to develop new areas of business. In particular they entered the mortgage market (see figure 5.3) and by 1982 they had achieved a market share of new mortgage lending of 36 per cent. After this initial expansion bank mortgage lending slowed down, though picked up in the 1990s, reaching a peak of 59 per cent in 1993 despite a depressed mortgage market. This illustrates that banks can enter and leave the mortgage market freely as factors such as demand and relative profitability change (box 5.1).

5.4   Consequences of the competitive pressures

Greater competition in the mortgage market and retail deposit markets has had a number of consequences. First of all it has made societies

Box 5.1   *Contestability of the mortgage market*

One consequence of the increase in competition in the mortgage market and process innovation (i.e. new ways of delivering products) is that the mortgage market now largely conforms to a contestable market. A contestable market (see Baumol (1982) for further discussion) requires two conditions:

(i) costs of entry into the market are low – in particular, a prospective entrant should be able to compete on the same (or lower) cost base than an incumbent;

(ii) costs of exit from the market are low – this requires any fixed costs incurred to be recoverable or be used to deliver other products/ services.

If a market is contestable then new firms will enter it when there are supernormal profits and leave when these supernormal profits disappear. This strategy is sometimes referred to as 'hit and run'.

In the mortgage market, entry costs are now low because of the development of technology and the emergence of 'telephone banking'. Credit scoring has reduced the time it takes to assess risks and process a mortgage application. New entrants based on telephone delivery (with no branch networks to support) will be able to operate on fixed costs that are lower than those of incumbents. Exit costs are low because the fixed costs of establishing a telephone-based operation are low and because such an operation can be switched into delivering other financial products such as car or home insurance. The banks have also been able to move into and out of the mortgage market at different times as their fixed costs (mainly branch networks) are used to deliver a wide range of financial products/ services.

more sensitive to interest rate changes, which in turn has led to the breakdown in the cartel arrangement between societies, precipitated by the decision of Abbey National to leave the cartel in September 1983. The BSA recommendation of rates came to an end in October 1983, although the BSA continued to advise rates until November 1984. The greater competition in the mortgage market and the breakdown of the cartel led to both a greater availability of mortgage funds and price clearing in the market and therefore to an end to non-price rationing. Mortgage rates now move more in line with money-market interest rates and for much of the 1980s and 1990s were above them (see figure 5.2). This induced entry into the market by specialist mortgage lenders,

Table 5.4 *The stock of dwellings in the UK: distribution by tenure (as a percentage of total), 1960–94*

	1960	1970	1980	1990	1994
Owner occupied	42.0	50.0	56.1	65.8	66.2
Rented from local authority or new town corporation	26.6	30.4	31.1	21.9	19.4
Rented from private owners	31.4	19.6	12.7	12.3	13.8

Source: *Housing Finance*, 1997.

which are funded completely from wholesale sources (the miscellaneous institutions in figure 5.3). A rapid expansion in mortgage lending therefore occurred over the 1980s and this is reflected in the growth of home ownership, illustrated in table 5.4.

Whilst the main explanation of the growth in home ownership, particularly over the 1980s, is likely to be the greater availability of mortgage funding, other factors include the policy of tax relief on mortgage interest payments, the sale of council houses and the decline of the private rented housing stock.

The buoyancy in the mortgage market has also led to lending insti-tutions, particularly building societies, extending the type of lending. Traditionally, mortgages have been predominantly in the form of first advances for the purchase of a house. In the latter part of the 1980s, second mortgages and further advances, not directly connected with home improvements, have been available. It is now relatively easy for owner-occupiers to withdraw cash from the equity built up in their property, without moving house, simply by increasing the debt on the property. This led to a rapid growth in equity withdrawal in the late 1980s as house prices increased at a rapid rate. Equity withdrawal is defined as the difference between the net increase in the stock of loans for house purchase and the private sector's net expenditure on additions to the stock of owner-occupied housing, including improvements.

Estimates of equity withdrawal are provided in table 5.5. Whilst these may exaggerate the position because of the likely under-recording of housing improvement expenditure, there is still likely to have been a growing leakage of funds from housing into consumption expenditure over the 1980s, contributing to the consumption boom in the latter half of that decade. The fall in house prices in the early to mid-1990s with the consequent fall in equity built up in houses is likely to have slowed down this process.

Table 5.5   *Equity withdrawal by the personal sector, 1980–88 (£million)*

Year	Net loans for house purchase	Private sector net investment in housing[a]	Equity withdrawal
1980	7,368	5,952	1,416
1981	9,483	6,353	3,130
1982	14,127	7,606	6,520
1983	14,520	6,887	7,633
1984	17,030	7,888	9,142
1985	19,032	8,926	10,106
1986	26,979	10,640	16,339
1987	29,521	12,456	17,065
1988	40,834	16,171	24,663

[a]Private sector residential fixed investment + council house sales – government capital grants to the private sector for housing purposes.
Source: Miles (1989).

The greater competition faced by building societies led the government to recognise that new legislation was required to enable them to compete with other financial institutions on a more equal basis. In 1981 the BSA established the Nature of a Building Society Working Group, under the chairmanship of John Spalding, who was the chief general manager of the Halifax Building Society. This led to a report in 1983 entitled *The Future Constitution and Powers of Building Societies*. The two key proposals of this report were:

(i)   that the mutual status of building societies should continue but that a procedure should be established whereby a society could convert to p.l.c. status;
(ii)   that societies should be permitted to undertake a wider range of business, but which should be related to the mainstream business.

After a period of consultation the BSA published its final proposals in February 1984 in a report entitled *New Legislation for Building Societies*. In July 1984, the government published its proposals in a green paper, *Building Societies: A New Framework*. This largely followed the proposals put forward by the BSA. This finally led to the publication of the Building Societies Bill, which received Royal Assent in 1986 with most of its provisions taking effect from 1 January 1987.

Box 5.2 *Categories of additional retail financial services permitted under the Building Societies Act 1986*

(i) Banking services –
   • money transmission (including providing chequebook accounts),
   • credit cards,
   • unsecured lending (up to a maximum – see text),
   • foreign currency services.
(ii) Investment services –
   • manage investments,
   • establish personal equity plans,
   • operate a stock broking service,
   • provide investment advice.
(iii) Insurance services –
   • underwrite insurance,
   • provide insurance.

Under the Building Societies Act and subsequent revisions, societies are permitted to offer additional services, which fall into the categories of retail financial or land related. Examples of additional services under the former category are listed in box 5.2.

Under the category of land-related services are services relating to the acquisition, development, management or disposal of land primarily for residential purposes, in particular the provision of estate agency services, conveyancing and estates management.

A further provision under the Act allows a society to convert from mutual status to p.l.c. status. A society following this route ceases to be a building society and effectively becomes a bank. Therefore as part of the conversion procedure the society would have to obtain approval from the Bank of England. A building society that converts is afforded protection from takeover for five years. The Act also allows societies to operate in the other member states of the European Union (EU). Finally the Act introduced a new supervisory body for building societies, namely the Building Societies Commission. In 1998 the new super-regulator, the Financial Services Authority, takes over the role of supervising building societies.

5.5 After the Act

The new services which societies have most actively taken up are in the category of banking services. In general though it is only the larger societies which have the capital and the size of operations to enter into competition with banks. The Nationwide Anglia was the first society to offer, in the spring of 1987, an interest-bearing current account with chequing facilities, called the Flex Account. The other large building societies now also offer similar current account services. Most of the larger societies have also introduced a credit card although the credit card market has been saturated since the end of the 1980s. Most societies offer an ATM service through the Link network. The Link network comprised approximately 14,000 machines in 1997 compared with approximately 16,000 operated by the banks (there is some overlap between these networks as some of the smaller banks' machines are also part of the Link network). A further development in 1990 was the expansion into banking services by the National and Provincial Building Society through the acquisition of Girobank.

A second, and less successful, area of expansion by the larger building societies was into estate agency operations. These societies saw estate agencies as an additional channel for the distribution of their mortgages. However, this expansion occurred in the final stages of a housing boom, so that when the market went into depression in the early 1990s an excess capacity in estate agency operations was revealed and most agency chains have made substantial losses. This has prompted a number of societies to sell their estate agency businesses, generally at a significant loss.

The smaller societies, not having sufficient capital to diversify into banking services, have in the main concentrated on their traditional business of savings and mortgages. Merger activity continues as some societies have attempted to achieve a size which will allow them to take advantage of more of the diversification possibilities provided by the Act. Some smaller societies have diversified into specialist services allowed under the Act that do not require such a large amount of capital. For example, some have set up a subsidiary to handle mortgage administration for other new lenders such as foreign banks.

For one building society, the Abbey National, the Building Societies Act was perceived as not going far enough in removing restrictions. In July 1989 it became the first building society to take advantage of the relevant provision in the Act and convert to p.l.c. status. There are two main advantages to converting to p.l.c. status. First, it provides an escape from restrictions imposed on building societies. For example, building societies are not permitted to undertake corporate banking and there are limits on the extent of unsecured lending they can carry out (see below). International operations for building societies are still limited to EU countries. Secondly, it is argued that societies need to convert in order to obtain additional capital, which they may use to diversify more quickly.

The act of conversion itself leads to an injection of capital from the new shareholders and, by increasing the primary capital of the company, enables other forms of capital to be increased commensurately.

After the incorporation of Abbey National there was a gap of five years before the next major development, which was the transfer of business of the Cheltenham and Gloucester Building Society to Lloyds Bank (effectively a bank takeover of a building society). Since then there has been a wave of conversions and takeovers resulting in most of the top ten building societies at the start of 1995 losing mutual status. Building societies that converted between 1995 and 1997 are the Halifax (after a merger with the Leeds), Alliance and Leicester, Northern Rock and Woolwich. Building societies that have been acquired by banks are the Bristol and West, and Birmingham Midshires (in 1998). In 1997 the Nationwide, the largest remaining building society, came under pressure at its annual general meeting to introduce a proposal for members to vote on conversion. This was defeated but pressure remains on the remaining larger building societies to convert to p.l.c. status. These pressures are accentuated by two factors:

(i) Upon conversion, members obtain a share of the capital of the building society. Taking the Halifax conversion as an example, capital was paid out in the form of shares with some basic pay-out to all members plus a variable pay-out to depositors relating to the size of the deposit. The capital of the society will have been built up over a long period of time. So the current generation of owners is effectively receiving a subsidy from all previous generations of owners.

(ii) It is easy for a person to become a member of a building society. To qualify as a depositing member receiving a share of the capital of the Halifax, the minimum deposit required was £100.

The wave of conversions has prompted a debate on whether the mutual organisation is no longer appropriate to the more competitive retail financial services sector. The arguments for and against the mutual organisation are presented in box 5.3.

The government in 1994 addressed some of the concerns of building societies about the restrictive nature of the building society regulatory framework by:

(i) increasing the limit on wholesale funding from 40 per cent to 50 per cent;

(ii) allowing societies to establish subsidiaries to make unsecured loans to businesses;

Box 5.3   *Advantages and disadvantages of the mutual organisation*

Mutual organisations, like building societies, have a fundamental advantage over p.l.c.s, which is the absence of external capital which needs to be serviced. This enables the building society to follow one of two strategies:

(i)   maintain a wider interest margin than is necessary and build up reserves through high profits;
(ii) maintain a low (but sustainable) interest margin and increase market share.

During the 1980s building societies chose to adopt strategy (i), probably to obtain advantages that come with large reserves such as security, better credit rating and so on. As reserves were built up the implicit value to owners also built up, yet owners were unable to release this value. In the absence of a secondary market in mutual ownership stakes, the only feasible way a member of a building society is able to release such value is to vote for conversion. A building society could adopt strategy (ii) and provide benefits to members through a higher interest rate to depositors and a lower interest rate paid by borrowers (compared with p.l.c. retail financial firms). Some building societies that have chosen to remain mutual have explicitly adopted such a strategy. In order to convince members of the benefits of mutuality a building society needs to demonstrate its margin advantage and, in addition, find ways, other than conversion to p.l.c. status, to release some of the accumulated reserves to members (one possibility is for a society to operate with a margin that generates a loss for a period of time).

However, there are a number of weaknesses with the mutual organisation:

(i)   There are potential agency costs deriving from weak member control. Agency costs arise in any form of organisation where there is a separation of decision making and ownership. Potential conflicts of interest arise between managers and owners because of incomplete contracts. It is impossible to devise contracts for managers that specify courses of action for all future circumstances. Managers must inevitably have discretion which, of course, could be abused. It is argued that these agency costs are more severe for a mutual, compared with a p.l.c., because owners have less influence on managers. This is a result of:
      • a very diverse shareholding, that is, a large number of small shareholders;
      • an absence of large shareholders who have an incentive to monitor and control;
      • the absence of performance-related shareholdings for managers.
(ii) The absence of tradable ownership rights means that managers are not subject to capital market discipline through the effect of dissatisfied owners selling shares, forcing down the share price. In addition there is no takeover threat.

Although there are clear agency costs for the mutual, in practice there is no evidence that they have adversely affected the efficiency and performance of building societies.

(iii) giving societies the right to wholly own general insurance companies which offer housing-related products such as building and
contents insurance.

Further reform has come with the Building Societies Act 1997. This
changed the regulatory regime for building societies away from the
prescriptive framework introduced by the 1986 Act, where everything is
prevented unless powers are granted to allow an activity, to a permissive
regime where everything is allowed unless specifically prohibited. This
should make it easier for a building society to diversify more easily
within the retail financial sector. The second major change introduced
by the 1997 Act is that it removes the five-year protection from takeover
for building societies that have converted to p.l.c. status if they launch a
hostile bid on any other company. This provision is designed to protect
the remaining smaller mutual building societies from takeover.

5.6   The balance sheet of building societies

We now turn to examine some of the effects of the changes previously
described as revealed by the aggregate balance sheet position of building
societies at the end of 1996 (table 5.6).

The balance between wholesale and retail funding for building societies has been discussed in section 5.3. The other part of liabilities is
made up of the societies' capital, which is mainly reserves. As building
societies are mutual organisations, owned by their depositors and borrowers, they do not make profits on their operations in the sense of an
amount available for distribution to shareholders. Any surplus that is
made on their operations is added to reserves. Specific capital adequacy
requirements for building societies have been introduced by the Building Societies Commission. These requirements set down a separate
capital ratio for each category of asset as well as for off-balance-sheet
items (see chapter 4 for further discussion of off-balance-sheet items).
The capital ratios for each category held by a society are then aggre-
gated and the desired capital ratio is this aggregate plus a margin of at
least 0.5 per cent.

On the assets side of the balance sheet the first seven items make up
societies' liquid assets. Up until the Building Societies Act 1986,
societies were required to operate with a minimum of 7 per cent of their
assets in liquid form. The Act abolished this minimum requirement and
instead stated that societies should keep sufficient assets in a form which
enables them to meet liabilities as they fall due. However, a maximum
level of liquid assets was set by the Act at $33^1/_3$ per cent. With the ability
to raise up to 50 per cent of deposits from wholesale sources, building

Table 5.6   *Building societies' balance sheet at end 1996 (£million)*

Liabilities		Assets	
Retail shares and deposits	212,825	Cash	400
Wholesale funds:		Sterling and foreign	
CDs	8,412	currency bank deposits	31,415
Term deposits and		Bank bills	328
commercial paper	25,199	Building society CDs	1,912
Bank borrowing	3,561	UK government stocks	6,311
Bonds	11,190	Other public sector debt	589
Foreign currency	8,770	Other liquid assets	11,335
Total wholesale funds	50,431	Total liquid assets	51,352 (17%)
Other liabilities and		Commercial assets:	
reserves	28,200	Class 1	219,119 (89%)
		Class 2	9,530 (4%)
		Class 3	16,852 (7%)
		Total commercial assets	245,501
		Other assets	4,322
Total liabilities	301,185	Total assets	301,185

Source: CSO, *Financial Statistics*, 1997.

societies are now more able to practise liability management – see chapter 3 for a discussion of this concept – and as a consequence there is less need to hold a large cushion of liquid assets. An adjustment has therefore occurred so that, in 1982, building societies' liquid assets amounted to approximately 20 per cent of total assets whilst at the end of 1996 this had declined to 17 per cent. The composition of building societies' liquid assets portfolio has also changed since the 1980s; in particular, there has been a decline in holdings of government securities and an increase in holdings of short-term deposits and CDs. Part of the explanation for this is a change in the interpretation of the law regarding capital gains in 1984 which led to societies being taxed at the normal corporate rate whereas previously gains had generally been tax free. A further reason is that the greater volatility of societies' retail inflows in the latter half of the 1980s as a result of greater competition from banks and equities led societies to prefer short-term rather than long-term assets.

Building societies' commercial assets are divided into three classes by the Act. Broadly speaking, class 1 assets are first mortgage loans to owner-occupiers of residential property, class 2 assets are other loans secured on property and class 3 are unsecured loans, investment in residential property and investments in subsidiaries and associates. Initially the limits for these three classes of commercial assets were set so that not less than 90 per cent of assets had to be in class 1 and not more than 5 per cent in class 3. In addition, smaller societies were prohibited from owning certain class 3 assets. Following representations from societies these limits were reviewed and are now set at a 25 per cent maximum for class 2 and class 3 assets combined, with a maximum of 15 per cent in class 3.

The introduction of class 3 unsecured lending allowed societies to offer credit cards and cheque accounts with overdraft facilities. At the end of 1996 building societies in aggregate were well below the prescribed limits, with class 2 lending at 4 per cent and class 3 lending at 7 per cent.

5.7   The finance houses

Finance houses (or non-bank credit companies) comprise a rather heterogeneous group of financial institutions, which includes subsidiaries of UK banks and overseas financial institutions and several independent institutions. Their activities are specialised and they account for a very small proportion of total lending by financial institutions. At the end of

Table 5.7   *Non-bank credit companies' balance sheet at end 1996 (£million)*

Liabilities		Assets	
Commercial bills	1,345	Cash and balances with banks	262
Bank loans	5,880	CDs	7
Loans from other			
financial institutions	1,196	Other current assets	965
Other UK loans	207	Finance leases	1,213
Overseas loans	28	Loans and advances to:	
Other current liabilities	506	UK companies	3,442
Capital	8,237	UK persons	12,522
		Other financial assets	28
		Physical assets	202
Total liabilities	18,641	Total assets	18,641

Source: CSO, *Financial Statistics*, 1997.

1996 they had total assets of £18.6 billion, compared with £300 billion for building societies. The combined balance sheet for finance houses at the end of 1996 is shown in table 5.7.

Table 5.7 reveals the nature of the business of these institutions. The majority of their funding is by way of loans from banks and other financial institutions. On the asset side, their main business is the provision of instalment credit, with the majority of this going to the personal sector. Finance companies also provide a significant amount of finance to companies in terms of instalment loans as well as through leasing and factoring. Leasing involves the finance company (the lessor) purchasing a physical asset which is subsequently leased out to a firm (the lessee) in return for a series of rental payments over a term which usually approximates its economic life. As the lessee is in the same position as if the asset had been purchased outright then finance leases are equivalent to raising a loan. Factoring involves a finance company taking over all or some of the debts owed to a company. The purchase price represents less than the book value of the debts and the gap represents the profit, including a risk element, for the finance company. As far as the company whose debts have been taken over is concerned, the gap is equivalent to the interest on an equivalent loan, with the benefit being an immediate acquisition of funds as compared with the delay before debts are normally paid.

This brief survey illustrates the nature of finance houses acting as financial intermediaries by obtaining funds mainly from banks, and therefore ultimately individuals and companies, and lending to individuals and companies. These institutions undertake a transformation of the characteristics of the funds as they pass through the institution. The transformation of risk is evident from the risky nature of their main lending activity, that is, consumer credit, as compared with the perceived nature of their liabilities. This transformation is of course reflected in the relatively high interest charges on their instalment loans.

5.8   Conclusion

In this chapter we have concentrated our attention on the significant changes that have taken place in building society activity since 1980. These changes were brought about largely by deregulation of the banking sector in 1980, which led to greater competition between banks and building societies on both sides of the balance sheet. This led to the breakdown in the building society cartel on interest rate setting and a virtual end to non-price rationing in the mortgage market. In fact the mortgage market now largely conforms to the proposition of a contestable market. The Building Societies Act 1986 enabled building

Table 5.8 *Percentage of owner occupation in the industrialised world*

Ireland	81
Norway	79
Greece	77
Spain	76
New Zealand	74
Australia	73
Finland	68
UK	68
Italy	67
Belgium	65
Luxembourg	64
Canada	63
US	63
Japan	61
Portugal	58
Austria	55
Sweden	55
France	54
Denmark	51
Netherlands	45
Germany	38
Switzerland	30

Source: *Observer* newspaper, 15 January 1995,
from Council of Mortgage Lenders.

societies to diversify their activities and so compete more effectively in the new environment. However, they were still largely confined to the provision of retail services and housing finance in particular. Further reforms of building society regulations in the 1990s have allowed societies even more scope for diversification. However, a number of large societies have chosen to escape the restrictions still imposed on building societies and convert to bank status. Others have been the subject of a bank takeover. As some life assurance companies have sought to convert from mutual to p.l.c. status and several of the larger remaining building societies are under pressure to convert by some members it would appear that the future of the mutual organisation in the UK financial services sector is under threat. We show in this chapter that the mutual organisation does have an advantage over the p.l.c. and if this is used appropriately it may serve to ensure the survival of such organisations.

As restrictions on societies have been relaxed, the demarcation between banks and the larger building societies has become blurred and
the distinctive nature of building societies has, to some extent, been lost.
Whether a role remains in the medium term for a distinct specialist
institution providing housing finance is therefore an open question. A
related issue commented upon in this chapter is that building societies
are facing a significant degree of competition in their traditional business of mortgage lending. Furthermore, there has been some doubt
expressed as to whether the rate of home ownership, illustrated in table
5.4, will continue to grow as rapidly as it has done in recent years, with
the consequence that the demand for mortgages may not grow as
rapidly. However, although population growth is expected to slow down
in the late 1990s, the slowdown in the rate of household formation is
likely to be much less marked, assuming incomes and rents continue to
grow at recent rates. The long-run outlook for home ownership and
hence mortgage demand may therefore not be as gloomy as some have
predicted. Further support for this view is provided by the figures shown
in table 5.8, which indicates that the proportion of home ownership is
lower in the UK than in a number of other industrialised countries. This
suggests that owner occupation may not have reached saturation point.

Chapter 6

Investment institutions

6.1 Introduction

The investment institutions are a class of financial intermediary which enable small investors to participate in collective investment funds. These institutions pool together a large number of small-value contributions into a fund which is used to finance the acquisition of a diversified portfolio of assets. The small investor thus obtains the benefit of the lower risks that come from a large, diversified portfolio at a lower outlay than would be required if investing directly. Such indirect investment in capital market instruments has long since replaced direct investment by individuals, so that investment institutions now dominate the capital markets. This is illustrated in table 6.1, which shows the sectoral holdings of UK gilts and equities for 1996. This type of financial institution contrasts with deposit-taking institutions such as

Table 6.1   *Investment institutions' holdings of UK equities and gilts, 1996*

	Percentage of total holdings at market value	
	Equity	Gilts
Persons	19.4	4.2
Pension funds and insurance companies	54.5	54.3
Other financial companies	7.3	21.7
Overseas	16.6	18.5
Other	2.2	1.3
Total	100.0	100.0

Source: CSO, *Financial Statistics*, 1998, table 2A, and Bank of England, *Gilts and the Gilt-Market Review 1996–7*.

Table 6.2   *Assets of investment institutions for selected years (£billion)*

	1982	1984	1986	1988	1990	1993	1995	1996	% growth 1982–96
Pension funds	83.6	130.3	190.5	214.5	302.7	463.9	508.6	559.6	569.4
Life assurance companies	79.9	114.2	158.6	198.3	232.3	412.9	494.7	561.2	602.4
Investment trusts	10.1	15.2	20.5	19.3	20.3	39.4	44.1	51.4	408.9
Unit trusts	7.8	15.1	32.1	41.6	41.6	89.5	107.1	129.7	1562.8
Total	181.4	274.8	401.7	473.7	596.9	1005.7	1154.5	1301.9	617.7

Source: CSO, *Financial Statistics*, various issues.

banks and building societies principally in the nature of its liabilities. Investment institutions, unlike deposit-taking institutions, have long-term liabilities and this is reflected in the nature of their asset portfolios. In the next section we examine the different types of investment institution and the growth of these institutions in recent years. The remainder of this chapter is concerned with the nature of the activities of the different types of investment institution.

We also include an appendix which provides an introduction to Lloyd's insurance market. This topic lies outside the main thrust of this text but is of sufficient interest to warrant some discussion.

6.2 Types of investment institution

There are five main types of investment institution:

(i) pension funds,
(ii) life assurance companies,
(iii) investment trusts,
(iv) unit trusts,
(v) open-ended investment companies.

The last came into existence only in 1997, and we do not include the category of general insurance companies in the class of investment institutions for reasons which we outline in the next section.

At the end of 1996 the combined assets of these four types of institution were £1,301.9 billion. This compares with total assets for building societies of £301 billion and £1,546 billion for all banks reporting to the Bank of England. As we noted in chapter 2, investment institutions have shown rapid growth in recent years and this is illustrated in table 6.2.

Of the investment institutions, unit trusts have shown the most rapid growth over the period covered by table 6.2, albeit from a low base. The two largest investment institutions, namely pension funds and life assurance companies, have achieved the roughly the same rate of growth over this period. We examine the reasons for the growth of these different institutions in later sections. First of all we discuss the nature of general insurance and in particular the reasons why we do not consider it to be an investment intermediary.

6.3 General insurance

The Insurance Companies Act 1982 separated the business of insurance companies into two categories: general insurance and long-term

Table 6.3   *Assets of general insurance companies at end 1996*

Asset	£million
Short term (net)	5,934
UK government securities	16,797
Local authority	54
UK ordinary shares	13,677
Other UK company securities	3,958
Overseas securities	13,366
Unit trusts	383
Loans and mortgages	1,265
Property	2,344
Other	37,071
Total	94,849

Source: CSO, *Financial Statistics*, November 1997, table 5.2A.

business. The former category encompasses a wide variety of business, all of which is concerned with providing insurance against specific contingencies, for example fire, accident and theft. Such insurance is provided over a fixed period of time, generally one year. The general insurance companies hold funds, or reserves, to enable them to meet claims on the insurance policies they have issued. As most of these policies are effective for one year and claims are usually made very soon after the event giving rise to the claim, general insurance companies' liabilities are mostly short term. Even where claims take a number of years to settle, a reserve is maintained to cover possible payments. The short-term nature of their liabilities is partly reflected in the assets making up the funds of general insurance companies – see table 6.3.

The majority of the long-term assets of general insurance companies are marketable and so can be called on at short notice, but they also provide a return to compensate for any underwriting loss – a common situation in the competitive general insurance industry where premium income is less than claims and the shortfall has to be found out of earnings on investments. However, we are concerned in this chapter (and this book) with financial intermediaries, which, as we described in chapter 2, channel funds from savers through to investors. The premium income which flows into general insurance companies is essentially a payment for a consumption service (indemnity against loss) and therefore cannot really be classified as savings. Also, whilst general insurance companies hold financial assets, these are more a byproduct than a central feature of their business. We therefore conclude that general insurance companies are not strictly financial intermediaries and we do not consider them further in this chapter.

6.4 Nature of the liabilities of pension funds and life assurance companies

6.4.1 *Life assurance companies*

The long-term, or life assurance, business of insurance companies can be separated into four broad categories.

(i) *Term assurance*

A term assurance policy provides insurance cover, for a specified period, against the risk of death during that period. If the insured survives the specified period then no payment is made. These term policies, which can be characterised as pure insurance policies, do not provide large sums for investment.

(ii) *Whole-of-life policies and endowment policies*

With a whole-of-life type of policy the insurance company pays a capital sum on the death of the person assured, whenever that event occurs. With an endowment policy a capital sum is paid out at the end of some specified term or earlier if the assured dies within the term. Both these types of policies provide cover against premature death and provide a vehicle for savings. The premiums for both will be higher than for term assurance because the company is committed to paying out a capital sum at some point in time. As a consequence the life insurance company has to accumulate a substantial fund out of which payments can be made as they fall due. Both these types of policies may be 'without profits', in which case the money value of the benefit is fixed in advance, or 'with profits', where a minimum sum assured may be augmented by bonuses declared by the company. These bonuses will be related to the performance of the fund over the life of the policy and so the 'with profits' policies have the effect of transferring some of the risk of building up sufficient benefits to the policyholder when compared with 'without profits' policies. In some cases a policy may be 'unit linked', where the premiums paid are used to purchase units in a chosen unit trust and the final payment is then dependent on the performance of that trust.

The role of endowment policies has been recently subject to criticism on two counts. First, there is the level of commission paid to the

insurance sales person at the time of initial sale of the policy. These
initial costs incurred by the insurance company have caused such
policies to have a low 'surrender' value, that is, the price the insurance
company will pay the policyholder on cancellation of the policy in
respect of payments already made on the policy. This problem is mainly
in respect of the early years of a policy, when such commission charges
are large relative to payments on the policy. Companies are required to
be more open now and commission payments have to be disclosed to the
potential policy purchaser. The second criticism concerns the use of
endowment policies with respect to house purchase, whereby the capital
sum is paid directly to the mortgage company on maturity of the policy.
As indicated earlier in this section, such policies can be with or without
profits. Originally the policy value was fixed so as to be equal to the
mortgage debt on maturity so that any profits connected with the policy
provided a windfall gain to the policyholder. However, the practice
arose of assuming profit levels and taking out a policy which matched
the mortgage debt only if the assumed profits were actually achieved.
Consequently if the profits attached to the policy were less than the
assumed level when the mortgage expired, the policyholder was left
with a shortfall which had to be met from her or his own pocket. In
some cases the mortgagee was unable to make the required payments.

(iii) *Annuities*
Annuities generally involve a policyholder paying an initial lump sum
which is used by the insurance company to provide an agreed income
until death. In this case the insurance company will immediately create
a fund which is then run down as payments are made to the policyholder.

(iv) *Personal pensions*
These are discussed below.

6.4.2   *Pension fund liabilities*

Pension provision in the UK comes from three basic sources: the state
scheme, an occupational scheme and a personal pension. These sources
are often denominated tier 1, tier 2 and tier 3, respectively. The state
scheme consists of a first component of a flat-rate pension, paid since
1925, and a second component, which is earnings related. We examine
recent developments in the provision of state pensions later in this
section. Occupational pensions are provided by employers in both the
public and private sector. It is these pension schemes which involve the
build-up of an investment fund and which form the pension funds we

refer to in this chapter. Personal pensions are pensions tailored to an individual's requirements and until recently were provided only by life assurance companies. As a consequence such pensions are counted as part of life assurance business. Recent reforms, outlined later in this section, have, however, widened the range of institutions which can provide personal pensions.

There are two basic types of occupational pension scheme: the unfunded or pay-as-you-go scheme and the funded scheme. Many of the public sector schemes are unfunded schemes, whereby the costs of providing benefits are met out of current contributions. In such schemes, therefore, there is no build-up of an investment fund and little impact on the capital markets. All the state pensions are run on an unfunded basis, with benefits provided out of the general revenue of the government. The occupational schemes of the Civil Service, the National Health Service, teachers, police and other parts of the public sector are also unfunded, although in some instances a notional fund is maintained. The public sector industries and local authorities, however, run funded schemes. The disadvantage of unfunded schemes is that if the number of contributing members declines or the number of people receiving bene-fits increases relative to contributors (due, for example, to medical advances leading to longevity, decline in birth rate, early retirement, etc.) then the burden on contributors can become excessive. The burden of unfunded schemes is likely to become extremely onerous in the beginning of the next century. This is often referred to as the 'demo-graphic time bomb'. This danger is particularly important since most unfunded schemes refer to government employees and therefore the cost will be borne by the taxpayer.

However, the UK is recognised as one of the few major economies which does not face a serious long-term problem of pension payments. The present value of net public pension liabilities is estimated at 5 per cent of GDP compared with over 100 per cent in Japan, Germany and France. There are two principal reasons for this:

(i)   the basic state pension has been held constant in real terms since 1980 (it is currently about 15 per cent of average earnings),
(ii) there is a second-tier State Earnings-Related Pension Scheme (SERPS) but only 17 per cent of employees belong to it – most employees belong to funded private occupational schemes.

There is also a risk with occupational unfunded schemes that the company may be wound up, thus making the pensions provided by the company insecure. In the private sector it is therefore the funded pension scheme which is the norm. With the funded scheme, the

Table 6.4 *Growth of life assurance and pension funds, 1986–96 (£billion)*

	1986	1987	1988	1989	1990	1991	1992	1993	1994	1995	1996	Total
Net receipts[a]	18.7	20.2	20.6	28.1	27.8	28.9	28.4	29.5	28.4	33.0	44.2	289.1
Revaluations[b]	39.2	3.7	19.3	28.4	25.0	32.1	40.6	158.5	-78.9	109.5	61.3	399.5

[a] Contributions of employers + life assurance premiums + investment income of funds + current grants from governments – pension and other benefits – transfers to other pension schemes – administrative costs. These are net receipts of funded schemes only.
[b] Changes in personal sector holdings of equity in life assurance and pension funds – net receipts. The figure for revaluations may therefore also include any unidentified transactions.
Source: CSO, *National Income Accounts*, 1997, table 4.10 for net receipts, and *Financial Statistics*, 1998, table 9.1J, for personal sector holdings of equity in life assurance and pension funds.

contributions of working members, along with in most cases the contributions of employers, are paid into a fund which is invested to yield income and capital gain, out of which benefits are paid. With most funded schemes, benefits are determined by a contributing member's length of service and final salary upon retirement.

6.4.3 *Growth of pension funds and life assurance companies*

We noted in section 6.2 that the assets of pension funds and life assurance companies have increased in value at a rapid rate over the 1980s and 1990s. In this section we examine the reasons for this growth. First of all we analyse the nature of the growth of these institutions by separating their growth into two categories: net receipts, and changes in price of the assets held (revaluations). Details are shown in table 6.4.

It is clear from table 6.4 that revaluations of assets held by the funds have accounted for a slightly larger proportion of the growth in funds over the whole period. This is explained by the strong growth in equity prices (company shares making up a substantial part of the funds' total asset portfolio, as we shall discover in the next section) both in the UK and overseas over this period. This revaluation effect is strong in 1986, 1992, 1993 and 1995 but almost disappears in 1987 as a result of the stock market crash. In 1994, the revaluation effect was strongly negative because of a decline in stock market prices in that year. It should be remembered, however, that wealth figures, from which revaluations are obtained, are notoriously difficult to measure, so the aggregate for the whole period is likely to be more accurate than the figures for individual years. The steady growth in net receipts throughout the period reflects the strong performance of the assets held by the funds feeding through into investment income in the form of dividends, interest and rent.

The contractual nature of premiums for life policies and contributions for pension schemes provides stability for the funds. Most life policies and pension schemes are paid into over a period of many years and, as we have noted above, there are penalties involved in cashing in life policies in the first few years after commencement. Life policies as a vehicle for long-term savings were encouraged up to 1984 by the existence of tax relief on premiums, at 15 per cent. A further development was the introduction of mortgage interest relief at source (MIRAS) in 1982, which gave a boost to endowment policies linked to mortgages (i.e. only the interest is paid on the mortgage over the term it is taken out for, with the maturing endowment policy used to pay back the capital sum at the end of the term). Building societies have been active in selling endowment mortgages, in order to earn commissions, and the strong marketing of endowment mortgages continued after 1984 when the ending of tax relief increased the costs of this type of mortgage relative to the straight repayment mortgage. We have already indicated potential problems with the use of endowment policies as a vehicle for house purchase.

Another boost for insurance companies has come from the recent changes in the state pension system (described below) which have made personal pensions more attractive. As noted above, insurance companies had a monopoly in this type of pension scheme until recently and, despite attempts to broaden the range of providers, are still the main source.

The important factors explaining the growth of pension funds over the last 20 years are related to government policies. The first of these is the taxation treatment of 'approved' occupational pension schemes. The contributions of both employers and employees are deductible from taxable income. In the 1997 July budget, the advance corporation tax credit was abolished for most tax-exempt investors. This is a credit representing the tax paid by companies on the dividends they distribute. Up until July 1997, pension funds were able to claim this tax back from the Exchequer. It is estimated that the removal of this source of tax benefit for pension funds has reduced their income by about £5 billion per annum. Finally the benefits payable by a fund are subject to the pensioners' rate of personal income tax, except for any lump sum paid up to a set limit, which is tax exempt. Such fiscal privilege has un-doubtedly had a positive impact on the growth of occupational funds.

Government policies with regard to the state pension have also had an effect on occupational schemes. In 1978 the government introduced the SERPS, which provided greater benefits than the second-tier state earnings-related scheme it replaced. At the same time tougher minimum requirements on benefits paid out by occupational schemes were laid down if employers were to contract out of the state scheme. Most schemes in fact chose to contract out, which in many cases meant that benefits had to be raised. It has been estimated though that, in 1988, approximately 13 million people were contracted into SERPS and were not in an occupational scheme. After a review of social policy in the mid-1980s, the government argued that with increasing longevity and a declining birth rate the burden on the working population in supporting pensioners when SERPS matured early in the twenty-first century would become intolerable. As a consequence SERPS was reformed and the central feature of the new pension arrangements, which came into force in April 1988, was to transfer the responsibility for pension provision from the state to the private sector. To achieve such a transfer, first, benefits available from SERPS were curtailed in order to provide an incentive to take out a private pension or join an occupational scheme and, second, the procedures for contracting out of SERPS were made easier and financial incentives were provided to individuals to take up a personal pension and to employers to start up occupational schemes. The monopoly on provision of personal pensions held by insurance companies was also removed to allow other financial institutions such as banks and building societies to become providers. The aim here was to encourage competition in provision. Such developments are likely to lead to an expansion of both personal pensions and occupational funds. At the time of writing (early 1998) the operation of the welfare state is being scrutinised by the new Labour government. One aspect of this critical examination is a consideration of the provision of pensions, particularly in view of the demographic time bomb referred too earlier. It is quite likely that more of the burden of the provision of pensions will be passed on to the individual, thus leading to increased demand (with an element of compulsion?) for personal pension arrangements (i.e. tier 3).

One consequence of the competition in selling pensions in the past was that, in some cases, customers were sold pensions which were not appropriate to the individual circumstances of the customer. This situation is being unravelled at the moment and it is likely that compensation will be paid to quite a large number of the purchasers of pension schemes. Estimates of the total compensation likely to be paid are in excess of £2.5 billion. The issue has still not been resolved and it is estimated that there are still 650,000 priority cases due for completion by the end of 1998. The industry watchdog, the Personal Investment Authority (PIA) (see chapter 18 for a discussion of the role of the PIA in the financial regulatory system and changes to the system currently being envisaged), had set a target of 90 per cent of the most urgent cases to be cleared up by the end of 1997. Some companies have failed to meet this target and face substantial fines for their failure. Attention is now being directed towards medium-priority cases, which are to be cleared up by the end of 1998.

6.5 Portfolio investment of pension funds and life assurance companies

The portfolio investment of both life assurance companies and pension funds is determined by the nature of their liabilities and the return and availability of the various types of financial asset. In the previous section we noted that the liabilities of both life assurance companies and pension funds are long term. In evidence to the Wilson committee in 1977, the life assurance companies stated the objectives of their investment strategy as being to maximise return, subject to risk, within an asset structure that takes the term structure of their liabilities into account. A particular risk faced by life assurance companies is that when a contract is written, certain sums are guaranteed to be paid in the future and these sums exceed the value of the premiums over the life of the contract. For example, in the case of an endowment policy, a guaranteed sum is assured at the outset. This sum will have been determined by reference to actuarial calculations about mortality and a prediction of likely returns on investment of the premiums. There is therefore a risk that outcomes of mortality, investment returns and so on may prove worse than the life assurance company's assumptions. In order to protect itself against such a risk the life assurance company can 'match' the term structure of its assets and liabilities. In this situation the assets should have a given yield which should be at least equal to the investment returns assumed in the calculation of the sum assured. The ideal type of asset for matching purposes is the UK government (gilt-edged) security. As we saw in chapter 1, this asset possesses the characteristics of safety, known term to maturity, fixed interest rate and known redemption value if held to maturity. By carefully selecting gilts with terms to maturity which match the term to maturity of its liabilities, a life assurance company can protect itself against changes in invest-ment returns and so be in a position to meet its contractual requirements. However, there are several disadvantages with this strategy of matching. First, life assurance companies also write 'with profits' policies and the holders of these policies will expect bonuses to be paid. To achieve the returns necessary to pay bonuses, life assurance companies will need to hold some proportion of their asset portfolio in assets which yield higher returns than gilts. Indeed, competition between life assurance companies will encourage them to hold high-yielding assets such as equities. Second, there is a practical constraint to life assurance companies holding portfolios constructed only of gilts, which is that there are insufficient quantities of gilts across the range of maturities required for matching. However, the matching strategy provides a benchmark for life assurance companies in that the further away the fund is from a fully matched position, the greater the risk for the company of not meeting its contractual requirements.

The liabilities of pension funds, whilst being long term, are also different in nature to those of life assurance companies, as in most cases benefits to be paid out are not known with certainty. As we noted in the last section, the benefits of most occupational pension schemes are related to the final salary of the contributor, which is not known in advance. Wage inflation complicates matters further as it increases the benefits to be paid by the fund, which has been accumulated from lower contributions over past periods. Index linking of final benefits, which

Table 6.5 *Asset portfolio of life assurance companies and pension funds at end 1996 (%)*

	Life assurance companies	Pension funds
Short term	4.8	4.5
UK government securities	16.4	10.8
(of which index linked)[a]	(11.6)	(47.9)
UK local authority	0.2	0.1
UK ordinary shares	41.2	50.0
Other UK company securities	6.7	1.2
Overseas securities	12.4	17.2
Unit trusts	7.9	3.8
Property, loans, mortgages	8.5	4.9
Other	1.5	7.4
Debtors	0.4	0.2

[a] Percentage of holdings of gilts not total assets.
Column totals may not sum to 100 due to rounding errors.
Source: CSO, *Financial Statistics*, November 1997, tables 5.1A and 5.1B.

occurs with some schemes, provides an additional uncertainty. As a consequence, the concept of matching is less relevant to pension funds. A greater consideration is to achieve returns in excess of the rate of inflation. Hence pension funds will look to hold assets which, over the long term, yield positive real returns. Examples of such assets are equities and property. Index-linked gilts, introduced in the early 1980s, provide a benchmark in this regard.

We now turn to examine the actual investments made by life assurance companies and pension funds over the 1980s and early 1990s. We consider first the actual holdings of the main categories of assets for the two institutions at the end of 1996. We then examine the investment strategies of the institutions over the recent past as revealed by net investment of cash flows, which represent the conscious investment decisions of the institutions.

The figures in table 6.5 reveal that life assurance companies held a greater proportion of their portfolio as UK government securities than did pension funds. This follows from the discussion above where we noted that the principle of matching is more relevant to life assurance companies. Pension funds have placed greater emphasis on index-linked gilts, which make up a larger proportion of their total holdings of gilts compared with life assurance companies. Index-linked gilts are perhaps more relevant to pension funds, as we noted above. Whilst equities are

Table 6.6 *Investment of life assurance companies' and pension funds' net receipts, 1987–96 (percentage of total)*

	1987	1988	1989	1990	1991	1992	1993	1994	1995	1996
Life assurance companies										
Short term	13.9	8.0	5.6	35.7	4.5	11.3	-2.8	-3.1	7.6	16.3
UK government securities	10.0	9.4	-5.7	-4.6	13.1	46.6	29.3	30.5	25.5	32.3
UK ordinary shares	46.0	36.9	17.5	32.5	33.3	14.1	39.6	35.2	15.0	21.8
Other UK company securities	10.7	16.4	16.7	8.5	12.9	13.4	11.9	12.6	9.3	7.6
Unit trusts			13.9	0.5	4.6	-0.3	7.0	3.8	2.4	1.7
Local authority			0.0	-0.5	0.1	0.0	0.3	1.3	0.2	0.1
Overseas securities	0.4	8.5	24.3	17.3	21.5	5.8	10.6	13.6	13.5	11.8
Property	7.3	10.8	7.2	6.0	6.6	3.1	1.8	10.7	0.9	1.9
Loans and mortgages	7.1	9.0	13.0	2.4	0.6	2.4	-0.9	-4.1	1.7	-1.0
Other	4.5	1.1	15.2	2.3	2.7	2.8	2.8	-0.1	13.8	12.3
Debtors net of creditors			2.3	0.0	0.0	0.8	0.3	-0.4	-9.7	-4.7
Pension funds										
Short term	36.9	14.6	23.5	17.0	-48.9	0.4	36.6	34.0	49.8	37.3
UK government securities	-21.3	-13.7	-32.9	-19.9	-18.4	35.6	39.6	146.9	104.8	52.9
UK ordinary shares	81.0	50.5	4.0	59.0	66.1	7.3	-23.3	6.5	-87.9	-60.5
Other UK company securities	4.5	5.9	10.5	3.7	9.8	0.0	-5.2	-2.2	3.0	–1.0
Unit trusts			3.5	0.6	1.8	9.9	11.0	10.8	39.6	31.5
Local authority			-0.2	-0.2	0.0	0.0	0.4	0.2	0.1	0.0
Overseas securities	-0.7	28.7	81.6	48.5	73.1	7.6	25.8	-78.0	-20.8	33.6
Property	1.5	2.8	0.7	-3.6	3.7	13.8	5.3	-2.0	-0.7	-3.2
Loans and mortgages			0.0	-0.2	0.0	-0.9	-0.1	-4.1	2.1	0.0
Other	4.5	11.4	9.3	5.7	12.7	31.0	9.5	-12.5	9.1	9.4
Debtors net of creditors			0.0	-10.8	0.0	-4.6	0.3	0.4	0.9	0.0

Column totals may not sum to 100 due to rounding errors.
Source: CSO, *Financial Statistics*, November 1997, tables 5.1A and 5.1B, and related earlier tables.

the main asset held by both life assurance companies and pension funds, they make up a greater proportion of the portfolio of pension funds. This reflects the greater requirement on the part of pension funds to achieve positive real returns. When we take into account overseas securities, which are mainly ordinary shares of overseas listed companies, then the proportion of equities held by pension funds is approximately 70 per cent of the portfolio. Another asset which generally yields positive real returns over the long term is property. Surprisingly, life assurance companies have been more active investors in property than pension funds, with the latter concentrating their investment attentions mainly on equities in recent years. We can observe this more clearly by examination of each institution's cash flow investment over the period 1987 to 1996, which is summarised in table 6.6.

The figures in table 6.6 reveal the importance of UK equity investment for both types of institution, which had taken advantage of the rising equity market in the 1980s and 1990s (see figure 8.4).

For life assurance companies the figures portray a picture of allocation of funds to UK company securities over the whole period. The position for pension funds is more variable, with a particularly large proportion of funds being allocated to UK company securities in 1987 and a withdrawal of funds over 1993–96. The stock market crash of 1987 has brought about a slowdown in equity investment, although the proportion of investment directed towards equities in the year after the crash was in fact greater than the proportion in the first five years of the decade. The popularity of equities for institutions is mainly explained by the fact that the real return (i.e. nominal return less the rate of inflation) on UK equities averaged approximately 13 per cent per year over the 1980s (compared with 1 per cent over the 1970s). The attractiveness of equities also partly explains the decline in investment in UK government securities by both types of institution over the 1980s. The real return on gilts averaged at about 8 per cent per year over this period. The dramatic fall in investment in gilts in 1986–88 by pension funds also reflects the decision by the authorities to buy back gilts following budget surpluses (see chapter 9 for further discussion). The position was reversed for both life assurance companies and pension funds over 1992–96. This was no doubt due to both the decline in the rate of inflation making fixed-interest securities more attractive, and the return to budget deficit increasing the supply of gilts. Property investment by both types of institution also declined over the 1980s as property returns slowed over this period. The real return on property was, on average, approximately 4 per cent per year over the 1980s. The slump in property values towards the end of the decade resulted in property investment virtually ceasing for pension funds and a net sale of such assets during the period 1993–96.

Investment in overseas securities was high in the early 1980s as the institutions sought to restructure their portfolios following the removal of exchange controls in 1979. A second increase in investment in overseas securities occurred in the middle of the decade as institutions sought to take advantage of the worldwide boom in equity prices. As was the case for domestic equities, the stock market crash of 1987 led to a dramatic slowdown in investment in overseas securities and some repatriation of funds by UK institutions. Following a recovery in world stock markets in 1988, investment in overseas securities picked up again. The purchase of overseas securities was more pronounced in the case of pension funds than for life assurance companies but fell off dramatically in 1994–95.

A final comment on investment strategies concerns the variable inflows into short-term assets. Investment institutions have relatively low liquidity requirements and although short-term assets provide some return, this is generally lower than the main assets held by these institutions. Short-term assets therefore represent a depository for funds awaiting investment in the main earning assets. High investment in short-term assets generally implies uncertainty about the future returns on the main earning assets. Thus, for example, we note high investment in short-term assets in 1987, particularly by pension funds, reflecting a slowdown in equity investment in the final quarter following the stock market crash and an increase in receipts following the buy-back of gilts by the authorities. The same feature is apparent for the years 1993–96.

We now turn to an examination of the future investment behaviour of pension funds. During the early 1990s two major scandals hit the pension fund industry. In 1991, the directors of Belling, the UK cooker manufacturer, acting in their capacity as trustees of the company pension scheme, purchased a Belling subsidiary for the scheme using £5.5 million of pension assets. In addition, they borrowed £2.1 million from the company pension fund. These cash injections were designed to salvage the ailing Belling company. However, Belling went into liquidation in 1992 and the liquidators valued the subsidiary at £2.5 million. As a consequence, Belling pension scheme members suffered a considerable loss of money from their fund (*Financial Times*, 25 and 26 June 1994). This, however, pales into insignificance when compared with the disappearance of £440 million from pension funds controlled by the late Robert Maxwell. As a result of the Maxwell deficit, the government set up the Goode committee to review the legal and general environment of pension funds. Following receipt of the report the Pensions Act 1995 went on to the statute books, becoming law in 1997. This Act introduced many new provisions for governance of pension funds, including setting out the composition and responsibilities of the trustees of a pension fund. A pensions regulator, termed the Occupational Pensions Regulatory Authority, has also been established. Some criticism has been made about the effectiveness of this new authority since it has an annual budget of only £8 million and a core staff of some 75.

Two key areas of the Act concerning investment are the statement of investment principle (SIP) and the minimum funding requirement (MFR). All fund trustees must produce an SIP, which lays out the rationale and assumptions underlying the investment strategy to be followed by the fund. This statement must be reviewed annually. The introduction of the MFR is designed to increase the security of the benefits of members of specified schemes where members receive a pension based on the individual's final salary level. The sponsors of the pension are required to publish, annually, the level of funding against the scheme's liabilities. Remedial measures must be taken if the ratio drops below 100 per cent. Funds have five years to remedy the situation but if the ratio has dropped below 90 per cent then the situation must be remedied within one year. The latest date for complying with the MFR regulation is 2007.

6.6 Unit trusts and investment trusts

Unit trusts and investment trusts are institutions which allow individuals or companies to purchase a stake in a larger and more diversified portfolio than they would normally be able to hold directly and at the same time to obtain the benefits of a sophisticated portfolio management service.

A unit trust is a fund to which individuals and companies may contribute in order to obtain a share in the returns generated by the fund. The institution is legally constituted as a trust, where a trustee acts as guardian of the assets on behalf of the beneficial owners and a separate management company is responsible for investment decisions. The terms and conditions governing these investment decisions are specified in the trust deed under which the institution operates. The trustee company is generally a bank or insurance company.

The industry of fund management underwent diversification over the 1980s and many institutions, including retail banks, merchant banks, stockbrokers and insurance companies, have become more involved. At the end of the decade insurance companies accounted for the largest share of ownership of unit trust management companies.

A contributor to a unit trust purchases 'units' at a price which reflects the aggregate value of the trust's net assets divided by the number of units outstanding. The funds are termed 'open ended', which means that the fund can expand by issuing new units at the same value as existing units at that point in time, or it may contract, through unit holders selling back their units to the fund at the prevailing price. There is no secondary market in units, with all sales and purchases of units being made with the trust managers, although another intermediary may act as agent to the transaction. The price at which an investor purchases units is known as the offer price and the price at which he or she sells them back to the trust is known as the bid price. To determine these prices the trustee will request the investment manager to value the assets held at bid or offer price. The price of units is then calculated by adding to the offer price stamp duty, stockbroker's commission and managers' charges (including VAT). With managers' charges typically in the region of 5 per cent and a dealing spread (the difference between the bid and offer prices on the underlying assets) of 2 per cent then the difference between unit offer and bid prices can be around 9 per cent. The prices of most units are calculated daily and the changing prices therefore reflect the changing prices of the underlying assets. The calculation of bid and offer prices just described represents a maximum spread. The quoted spread is normally much lower as fund managers do not always have to buy or sell the underlying securities when they are buying and selling units but match a certain proportion of buying and selling orders. The quoted price will therefore lie within the maximum calculated spread so that during periods of net sales of units the quoted offer price will be at the calculated offer price, with the quoted bid price at a higher price than the calculated bid price. Conversely, during periods of net re-demption of units, the quoted bid price will be equal to the calculated bid price, with the quoted offer price lower than the calculated offer price.

Traditionally the price at which the unit trust managers have trans-acted with investors has been the price related to the last valuation – known as historical or backward pricing. An alternative method, known as forward pricing, means that units are sold at prices that prevail at the valuation (a few hours after the order is processed). The Department of Trade and Industry has recently implemented new rules that give unit trust managers the choice of pricing on a forward or backward basis, with the investor being informed of the chosen method. The advantage of forward pricing is that investors are sold units at (almost) current rather than historical prices. The disadvantage is that investors do not know the transaction price when the order is made.

We noted in section 6.2 that unit trusts have grown rapidly over the 1980s and at the end of 1996 had assets of just over £129.7 billion. They can invest in a wide variety of assets including bank deposits, UK and overseas company shares and government securities. As we can observe

Table 6.7   *Investments held by unit trusts at end 1996 (%)*

Short-term securities	3.0
UK government securities	2.1
UK company securities	55.9
Other sterling assets	0.2
Overseas company securities	37.5
Other overseas securities	1.3

Column totals may not sum to 100 due to rounding errors.
Source: CSO, *Financial Statistics*, November 1997, table 5.2D.

from table 6.7, the main asset held is company shares, both UK and overseas.

In contrast to unit trusts, investment trusts are p.l.c.s whose business is the investment of funds in financial assets. Investment trusts raise their finance like any other company, through the issue of shares and debentures, by retaining income and so on. Therefore if an investor wishes to acquire an interest in an investment trust he or she must acquire its shares either by subscribing to a new issue or by purchasing the shares on the stock market. These shares can be sold on to a third party through the stock market.

The investments held by the investment trust industry are summarised in table 6.8. Ordinary shares make up the overwhelming majority of securities held. Overseas shares form a larger proportion of total equity holdings of investment trusts than of unit trusts.

The existence of borrowed funds, as opposed to equity, in the capital structure of an investment trust means that if the value of the underlying securities fluctuates there is a 'gearing' effect on the value of the shares issued by the trust. To illustrate this effect we will consider a simple

Table 6.8   *Investments held by investment trusts at end 1996 (%)*

Short-term securities	2.7
UK government securities	2.8
UK company securities	50.3
Other sterling assets	1.1
Overseas company securities	41.5
Other overseas securities	1.5

Column totals may not sum to 100 due to rounding errors.
Source: CSO, *Financial Statistics*, November 1997, table 5.2C.

example of an investment trust which has a capital structure comprising £8 million in shareholders' equity claims, attributable to 4 million issued shares, and £2 million of outstanding debt. The total value of funds invested by the trust is therefore £10 million, which we assume is invested only in ordinary shares. The net asset value (NAV) per share (the value of assets less debt divided by the number of issued shares) is thus £2. Now if the value of the investment trust asset portfolio were to double to £20 million then the NAV per share would increase to £4.50. Therefore a 100 per cent increase in the value of assets held has led to an increase in the NAV per share of 125 per cent. The gearing effect of course can work to the detriment of shareholders when the assets of the investment trust fall in value. There is also a gearing effect on the income to be distributed to shareholders resulting from a change in the net income (before interest) derived from the investment trust's asset portfolio. Whilst the gearing effect is always of benefit to shareholders, in terms of NAV of their shares, in a rising stock market, the effect from income generation will be of benefit only if the return from utilising the borrowed funds is greater than the interest cost. The actual gearing of investment trusts in aggregate in recent years has been relatively modest, averaging around 8 per cent.

A particular curiosity of investment trusts is that the share price of most of them is at a significant discount to the NAV per share. The price of shares is of course determined by demand and so the existence of a discount would imply that demand for the investment trust's shares is lower than the demand for its portfolio of shares bought independently. We noted in section 6.2 that investment trusts have not grown as rapidly as unit trusts over the 1980s. This lower demand for the services of investment trusts may be because, unlike unit trusts, investment trusts cannot advertise themselves through the media. Another factor which discourages investors may be the greater risk of the investment, which comes from the gearing effect. The existence of a discount makes investment trusts vulnerable to takeover, especially when a trust owns an appreciable stake in a target company. The potential bidder can acquire up to 30 per cent of the trust and therefore the shares owned by it at a discount. The full bid for the remainder will have to reflect the NAV. An example of such a process includes, in 1979, Lonhro's agreed acquisition of the Scottish and Universal Trust, which held 10.29 per cent of the shares in House of Fraser, which Lonhro went on to bid for.

6.6.1   *Open-ended investment trusts*

A shakeup in the UK investment industry is likely to occur in the near future. Early in 1997 the introduction of a new type of investment fund received official approval. This type of fund is termed an 'open-ended investment company' (OEIC). The fund will operate in a manner similar to that of a unit trust since it can expand or contract as investors pay money into the fund – hence the term 'open-ended'. However, an OEIC is a company and can be listed on the Stock Exchange. One salient difference from investment trusts is the fact that the shares will reflect the value of the fund and will therefore not trade at a discount or premium. Furthermore, the shares will have a single price rather than the separate buying and selling prices indicated for unit trusts. It is rather early to comment on the current position of OEICs in view of their recent introduction but a radical shift in cooperative asset holding may come about for two reasons. First, a number of fund managers are understood to be considering transferring from unit trusts to the new institutions. Second, competition from OEICs will attract new funds at the expense of unit and possibly investment trusts.

6.7   The performance of institutional investors

Rising equity markets around the world over most of the 1980s and 1990s resulted in historically high performances, with regard to returns, by UK fund managers. The discussion that follows examines the nature of this performance over the 1980s and 1990s.

Average annual returns on pension fund investments over the 1980s were 19.5 per cent, which compares favourably with average inflation and wage inflation, over the same period, of 6.9 per cent and 9.5 per cent, respectively. The figure for wage inflation represents a form of target return for those pension funds where benefits are linked to final salary. This performance over the 1980s contrasts strongly with performance over the 1970s, where pension fund investment returns underperformed wage inflation by, on average, approximately 6 per cent per year. The consequence of this was that pension fund actuarial deficits had to be met by higher contributions from employers. The considerably higher investment income over the 1980s and 1990s resulted in actuarial surpluses for many funds, which allowed companies to take 'contribution holidays'.

The investment performance by pension funds over the 1980s and 1990s was largely a consequence of rising equity markets, which, as we noted in section 6.5, were tapped by funds which invested most of their cash flows into equities. The diversification into overseas equities, where growth has at times been stronger in particular markets than in the UK, has also been a contributory factor. However, the diversification into overseas equities has not been as successful as it could have been, as evidenced by a failure of funds to match closely the index in overseas equity markets. The return on UK equities achieved by institutional investors was on average 23.2 per cent per year over the 1980s, compared with a 23.6 per cent return on the Financial Times Stock Exchange Index of 100 leading shares (FT-SE 100) – a close match after taking costs into account. In contrast there was underperformance of the indexes in the US by, on average, 3.6 per cent and in Japan by, on average, 2.5 per cent. The underperformance has continued to occur and performance measurers WM report that over the period 1986–96 managed funds achieved an annual return of 13.9 per cent against 14.2 cent for the FT-SE 100 (*Financial Times*, 8 October 1997). This underperformance has led to consideration by fund managers of index-tracking funds. These are funds which are constructed according to a chosen index, with the shares making up that index included in the fund according to the weightings in the index. Such an index has the advantage of low transaction costs, as shares are bought and sold only to keep the fund in line with the index. Depending on how well the index has been tracked, this type of passive management yields returns in line with returns on the index. Index funds were first established in the US and have become increasingly popular in the UK in recent years as direct sellers of index-linked unit trusts, such as Virgin Direct, have promoted such funds. It has been estimated that about 16 per cent of UK pension funds are now of the index-tracking type (*Financial Times*, 8 October 1997) and that 15 per cent of retail sales of unit trusts are index-tracking funds (*Daily Telegraph*, 8 October 1997).

A final comment concerning fund management relates to the way the performance of managers is assessed. Performance of fund management is conventionally assessed on quarterly. This is not to say that managers are hired and fired on such a timescale but it is argued that subtle pressures may be introduced. Such pressures may lead managers to focus on short-term objectives. If a hostile takeover attempt is made and a fund manager holds shares in the target company in her or his portfolio then it is argued that the manager may accept the offer to boost short-term performance. We consider the general debate about 'short termism' in more detail in chapter 16.

6.8   Conclusion

In chapter 2 we noted the significant growth of assets held by investment institutions in recent years when compared with the growth of assets held by the deposit-taking institutions. In this chapter we have shown that the principal reason for this is that the main assets held by investment institutions are equities, which achieved substantial returns, in terms of both income and capital gain, over the 1980s and 1990s.

Other reasons suggested to explain the growth of investment institutions relate to government policy and include tax-privileged contributions to pension funds and changes in the state pension scheme which have encouraged private provision.

We have indicated the nature of legislation which is designed to prevent future pension fund scandals. It is also interesting to note that some large firms are giving up in-house pension fund management teams and contracting the business to outside professional fund managers. This is just one example of the current tendency for firms to concentrate on their core business and to contract out peripheral business. We also noted the criticisms that have been levied against the life assurance industry. The scale of the problem is indicated by a survey by actuaries AKG, who reported that 20 per cent of pension policies and 15 per cent of life assurance policies sold in 1992 were terminated within the first year (*Financial Times*, 3 January 1995). It is also believed that industry-wide compensation for mis-selling of pensions could amount to between £2 billion and £2.7 billion.

We have now completed our discussion of financial institutions and so in the next section of this book we turn our attention to financial markets.

Appendix. Lloyd's of London

This appendix has been mainly contributed by Professor Peter Franklin, Bass Leisure Dean, Nottingham Business School, Nottingham Trent University.

Introduction

Lloyd's of London is a unique institution. Based in architecturally distinct, high-tech, state-of-the-art premises in the heart of the City of London, Lloyd's sources its worldwide insurance business by operating through international insurance brokers accredited to Lloyd's and by being capitalised partly by wealthy individuals known as 'names' and, more recently, partly by corporate institutions. In recent years the latter component has become more important.

Historically, the unique structure of Lloyd's has been a source of competitive advantage and a base for continuing curiosity about the potential longevity of a worldwide business which depends significantly on private capital. Before we look at recent and prospective developments at Lloyd's, it is sensible to understand the role of names within Lloyd's and then go on to outline some of the underlying business transactions which distinguish Lloyd's from other non-life insurers.

Names

Names are wealthy individuals who are recruited to Lloyd's to provide the capital which supports the underwriting activities of the Lloyd's insurance market. Lloyd's names are introduced by a members' agent. The principal role of a members' agent is first to advise its members (i.e. its names) on the choice of Lloyd's syndicates which operate within the market and secondly to administer the names' Lloyd's affairs.

Names normally join a number of different underwriting syndicates, each of which specialises in different sorts of risks. Each of these syndicates is managed by a managing agent and the profits or losses made by the syndicate are shared among the names in proportion to the names' shares in the syndicate. Names are required to accept the principle of unlimited liability, so that if an underwriting member (i.e. name) sustains a substantial underwriting loss, the member is liable to meet these losses from other (i.e. non-Lloyd's) assets.

Following substantial losses incurred by some syndicates, the efficacy of an insurance market entirely dependent on wealthy individuals' capital has again become an issue, and in 1994 Lloyd's admitted corporate capital for the first time.[1] Corporate capital has given Lloyd's a welcome opportunity to increase its overall underwriting capacity; it has also enhanced Lloyd's overall capital adequacy. In 1998 corporate capital represented 60 per cent of total underwriting capacity.[2]

In the meantime, Lloyd's has had to deal with the difficult situation caused by the past losses incurred by some syndicates. Whilst names are required to assume unlimited liability, in practice Lloyd's has generally not caused underwriting members to declare bankruptcy. Indeed, Lloyd's has set up a hardship fund to help members who have been particularly badly affected. This action, and others outlined later in this appendix, aims to give confidence to past, current and future names in the potential benefits of being an underwriting member at Lloyd's.

Having looked at the capital base supporting the Lloyd's insurance market, it is now appropriate to look at some of the fundamental business and financial transactions which characterise the operations of the market.

Underwriting: the fundamental transaction

At Lloyd's, underwriting involves an exchange between two parties: one a professional underwriter who acts on behalf of her or his names or corporate members; the other a Lloyd's broker who acts on behalf of the insured.

In simple terms we can imagine an insurance broker being instructed by a manufacturing group to obtain buildings insurance for its factories and offices. Acting on behalf of the insured, the duty of the broker is to obtain the best cover possible at least cost, and as a result the broker will need to search the insurance market to find one or more underwriters who are willing to accept the implied risks.

Being a broker accredited by Lloyd's gives the broker a greater number of prospective underwriters to choose from. Not only can the broker approach non-life insurance companies (such as Eagle Star or General Accident), but as a Lloyd's broker the risk can now be offered to Lloyd's underwriters. Indeed, the Lloyd's broker may well come to the initial view that Lloyd's is most likely to offer the best deal; alternatively, the broker may judge that it is essential that Lloyd's is seen to take the lead in the market, and set the premium rate.

So, going back to our simulation, the Lloyd's broker enters the Underwriting Room at Lloyd's and approaches one of the underwriters known to have expertise in buildings insurance for factories and offices. The underwriter interrogates the broker about the details of the prospective liability, including any specific terms and conditions, and makes three judgements:

(i)   whether or not to accept the risk,
(ii) and if so, what proportion,
(iii) at what premium rate.

The fundamental insurance transaction, therefore, is an agreement between the Lloyd's broker and the underwriter about:

(i)   the details, terms and conditions relating to the insurance policy,
(ii) the premium rate,
(iii) the proportion of the risk accepted by the underwriter.

Assuming the first underwriter takes only a small fraction of the overall risk, the process and agreement reached between the broker and the first underwriter is replicated with others. The broker therefore moves from the 'leading' underwriter to a second and a third and so on until 100 per cent cover has been obtained for the risk.

The financial transaction

With the risk now covered, the next transaction is a financial one. The broker is now committed to forward the premiums he or she has agreed; the underwriters are committed to accept the risk and, in return for the premium payments, authorise the issuing of an insurance policy to the insured through the broker.

This relatively simple financial transaction masks significant changes in the assets and liabilities of the parties associated with the transaction. These changes are outlined in table 1.

Table 1   *Changes in the assets and liabilities of the participants in the insurance transaction*

Insured	Broker	Underwriter/name
Impact on liabilities		
The insured company has covered its property risks	The broker assumes the costs of placing the business with an underwriter	The underwriter has now assumed the risk and is liable in the event a claim is incurred
Impact on assets		
A premium payment has been made and as a result the company's financial assets have reduced	To offset costs, the broker receives commission from the underwriter for the business placed	The underwriter receives a premium payment (net of commission and reinsurance) which is added to existing insurance funds

As table 1 indicates, the insurance transaction has the net effect that the underwriter's balance sheet changes such that both liabilities and assets increase.

Asset portfolio management, Lloyd's and financial intermediation

So far we have seen two transactions: one an insurance transaction; the second a financial one. This exchange of money for insurance cover, however, has one other effect: the alteration of the underwriter's assets and liabilities, and by extension, the continuing change in their asset portfolios.

Asset portfolio management is consequently an integral feature of the day-to-day operations of Lloyd's underwriters. In practice, asset portfolio management is delegated to the agents who manage an underwriting member's (i.e. names) Lloyd's business. These managing agents act on behalf of names, crediting premiums and, in profitable times, disbursing profits.[3] Lloyd's advisers perform a similar function on behalf of corporate members. Managing agents therefore play an important if secondary role, and by managing the funds attributable to names act as a specialised form of financial intermediary.[4] As is well documented, substantial losses were incurred by a number of syndicates in the late 1980s and early 1990s leading to doubts over the stewardship of the syndicate managing agents.

Some Lloyd's members have felt sufficiently aggrieved to begin legal proceedings against the Society of Lloyd's itself, seeking to annul their underwriting obligations on the grounds of negligent or fraudulent misrepresentations alleged to have been made by the Society through its agents. Others are pursuing legal action against managing agents, claiming compensation for underwriting liabilities which, they allege, would not have been incurred but for the negligent actions of the agents.[5] On its behalf, Lloyd's is endeavouring to reach a settlement outside the courts by agreement with the names, and simultaneously Lloyd's is 'ring fencing' past losses so as to protect future investors from incurring liabilities attributable to past losses. In fact a recovery plan was debated in 1996 which was agreed only after the market made a £3.2 billion settlement to compensate the names for their losses. As a result, a new company called Equitas was set up in September 1996. This took charge of more than £11 billion of the old liabilities incurred up to and including 1992, by reinsuring them. Equitas is not authorised to write new business and will therefore reduce over time as its liabilities reduce. Legal disputes are still running – particularly in the US – but it is hoped that the situation will be resolved in the near future.

Lloyd's business

Lloyd's business is split into four main areas. The breakdown for 1996 is as follows:

Marine (20.5 per cent)
This can range from insuring yachts to super-tankers and their cargo to offshore drilling rigs. Over 13 per cent of the world's marine business is placed at Lloyd's.

Non-marine (51.4 per cent)
An enormous range of risks comes under this category including fire, windstorm (e.g. hurricanes), earthquake, theft, product liability and disease.

Aviation (10.9 per cent)
Lloyd's writes over 25 per cent of the world's aviation business.

Motor (17.2 per cent)
Lloyd's motor underwriters are the largest insurers of private motor vehicles in the UK. Lloyd's will stand ready to insure unusual and high-value vehicles and non-standard risks.

Concluding remarks

In this short exposition it is not possible to deal fully with the rich
texture of life at Lloyd's, nor to give a satisfactory or entirely justified
view about its future potential. Yet, as a final observation, one of the
enduring features of Lloyd's is its very endurance: its ability to survive
unimagined and unexpected geological, political, technical and social
shocks. One would be a fool to write off Lloyd's future. However, it
needs to reform further in preparation for the next century.[6]

It would appear that recent reforms, particularly the formation of
Equitas and the introduction of corporate capital, have proved successful. The society has announced profits for the years 1993, 1994 and
1995 and profits are projected for 1996 and 1997. It would seem,
therefore, that the worst of the troubles facing Lloyd's have been
overcome.

Notes

1   In Lloyd's *Global Results 1993,* published in 1994. The report indicates that at
     the beginning of 1994, there were 17,256 names and just 95 corporate members.
2   In Lloyd's *Global Results 1997,* published in 1998. The report shows that
     corporate capital in 1998 provided £6,119 million of underwriting capacity out of
     a total of £10,168 million (the remaining capacity being provided by 'names').
     This represents an increase in capacity from the low of £8,878 million in 1993
     but is lower than the peak of £11,382 in 1991. The number of corporate members
     in 1998 was 435.
3   Profits arise from two sources. Underwriting profits arise from the difference
     between claims and premiums. They are supplemented by any investment income
     earned from the financial assets held by Lloyd's or the members' agents acting on
     behalf of Lloyd's names.
4   Strict and limiting regulations govern the composition and balance of the asset
     portfolios which the managing agents control. As a consequence, the scope of
     financial intermediation is much more limited than (say) for a merchant bank
     advising a personal client.
5   *A Guide to Corporate Membership,* Lloyd's of London, September 1993, pages
     97 and 98
6   The *Post Magazine* of 26 May 1994 reported that if returned to power at the next
     general election, the Labour Party 'would bring Lloyd's under full statutory
     control' rather than regulation via the Lloyd's Act of 1982. Under the new
     regulatory arrangements being introduced at the current time (April 1998) regu-
     lation and prudential control of Lloyd's will pass to the FSA.

Chapter 7

Financial markets: introduction

7.1   Introduction

With this chapter we begin our look at the main financial markets making up the UK financial system. All of the markets we consider in subsequent chapters are located in London and, although they serve the domestic economy, a substantial amount of transactions through these markets are international. In the case of markets such as foreign exchange (see chapter 11) and eurosecurities (chapter 12) the majority of transactions conducted through London are for non-UK residents. We therefore begin this chapter by considering the importance of London as an international financial centre and some of the reasons for this. We then turn to consider in sections 7.3 and 7.4 some general issues relating to the nature of financial markets, including types of trading systems and types of trading activity. We then finish this chapter with a discussion of the nature of an efficient financial market.

7.2   London as an international financial centre

Three international centres dominate the financial scene. These are New York, London and Tokyo. The main exception to the dominance of the so-called golden triangle which these three centres make up lies within the sphere of exchange-traded futures and options, where Chicago dominates. We now outline the position of London in the various international financial markets.

7.2.1   *Derivatives*

During 1989 the major markets in Chicago (the Chicago Board of Trade and the Chicago Mercantile Exchange) accounted for 65 per cent of

151

total world trade in these increasingly used financial instruments. At this time London and the rest of Europe attracted 6.25 per cent and 7.14 per cent, respectively. It is, however, pertinent to note that the US share is decreasing and by 1997 the Chicago exchanges together accounted for just 33 per cent of total world trade. This compares with around 16 per cent through London (the largest centre in Europe) and 16.5 per cent for the rest of Europe.

London is also the world's leading centre for over-the-counter (OTC) derivatives activity. The 1995 Bank for International Settlements (BIS) survey found London accounted for 27 per cent of activity, with New York, the second largest centre, accounting for 20 per cent. Paris and Frankfurt accounted for 8 per cent and 5 per cent of global OTC derivatives business, respectively (Bank for International Settlements 1996).

7.2.2   Banking

London has long been a major international banking centre and has developed since the 1960s as a eurocurrency banking centre. At the beginning of the 1980s, London was by far the largest international banking centre in the world, accounting for 27 per cent of total international lending. Table 7.1 shows that by the end of the 1980s the figure had declined to just over 19 per cent and London had lost its dominance to Japan, which accounted for 21.5 per cent. However, in the early 1990s Japanese banks began withdrawing from international banking

Table 7.1   *International banking: analysis by centre, 1980–93 (% of total international claims outstanding)*

	December 1980	December 1985	September 1989	December 1993
Belgium	4.2	3.8	3.2	4.2
Luxembourg	6.7	4.1	4.0	6.6
France	10.8	7.1	6.4	10.3
Germany	5.5	3.2	3.7	8.9
Switzerland	4.5	6.4	5.5	7.2
UK	27.0	25.4	19.3	21.1
Japan	5.0	10.8	21.5	18.4
US	13.4	13.3	9.4	10.9

Source: *Bank of England Quarterly Bulletin*, various issues.

Table 7.2 *International banks in London: share of international lending through London, 1975–93 (%)*

	End 1975	End 1989	End 1993
US	38	13	9
Japan	13	35	23
UK	22	17	18
Other European	6	22	25
Other overseas	22	13	25

Source: *Bank of England Quarterly Bulletin*, various issues.

following a decline in Japanese stock markets, which reduced the capital of the banks, and a decline in Japanese property prices, which reduced profits. Thus, by the end of 1996 the positions of London and Japan in the ranking of international banking had reversed, with London having a share of 18 per cent, Japan as second largest, taking 14 per cent, and the US in third place with 8 per cent. The UK accounted for over 30 per cent of such lending in European countries. In fact, the UK is responsible for more cross-border lending than Germany and France combined.

The 1980s saw a marked increase in Japanese international banking conducted through both Tokyo and its overseas establishments in London, the US and elsewhere. This growth largely reflected the growth in Japanese international trade and investment. London, in fact, is the most important centre for Japanese banks outside of Japan. The decline in Japanese banks' international lending, referred to above, is therefore reflected in the decline in Japanese bank lending through London in the early 1990s – see table 7.2.

The US banks were the dominant international banks in London over the 1960s and 1970s. However, over the 1980s and early 1990s they experienced a decline in their share of total international lending, both generally and through London. This partly reflects a retrenchment by US banks, to concentrate on domestic business, following the sovereign debt crisis, which broke in 1982. However, whilst the on-balance-sheet business of US banks operating in London has declined, these banks continue to be the main players in international off-balance-sheet activities, such as foreign exchange dealing and swaps. The other main source of growth of international banks based in London is other European banks, particularly German banks, which in 1993 accounted for 16 per cent of international lending through London.

The dominance of London in international banking is reflected in the fact that, at the end of 1993, 521 foreign banks were established in London. This compared with 340 in New York, 170 in France and 150 in Germany. By the end of 1996 the number of foreign banks in London had increased to 560. This included 35 new European banks, which had established a presence in London over 1995–96 despite the continuing uncertainty over the UK's position on European Economic and Monetary Union (EMU). In addition, there were 173 securities houses established in London, underlining London's lead not only in securities transactions (discussed below) but also in investment banking.

7.2.3   *Foreign exchange*

The London foreign exchange market is the largest in the world. This was confirmed in the BIS 1995 survey. London accounted for 30 per cent of global foreign exchange business with New York, the next largest centre, accounting for 16 per cent of business. More than half of foreign exchange business done in European countries is done in London. Average net daily turnover in London is six times greater than that in Frankfurt and eight times that in Paris.

7.2.4   *Equities*

Whilst only the third largest equity market (after New York and Tokyo), London's importance as an international centre for equity dealing is evidenced by the fact that there are more foreign companies listed on the London Stock Exchange (LSE) and turnover in foreign company equities is larger than on any other world equity market. In 1997, 65 per cent of all foreign equity trading carried out on national exchanges was done through the LSE.

7.2.5   *International bonds*

Given its importance in international banking business and foreign exchange dealing, it is not surprising that London is one of the major centres for dealing in eurocurrencies and eurobonds. An indication of London's dominance of the secondary trading of eurobonds is given by the fact that 80 out of 114 dealers reporting daily or weekly prices to the International Securities Markets Association (ISMA) were located in London. Estimates for 1994 suggest that London accounts for 60 per cent of primary eurobond syndication and 75 per cent of secondary market trading.

7.2.6 *Fund management*

London is second only to Tokyo for the management of institutional equities. According to a survey in 1996 by Technimetrics, an investment research company, more than $1,638 billion of institutional equities were managed in Tokyo, compared with $1,218 billion in London. The next largest European centre was Zurich, with $423 billion in equities under management. Edinburgh was ranked as the fifteenth largest fund management centre, with institutional equity holdings of $132 billion (Bank of England 1997).

7.2.7 *Reasons for London's importance*

The emergence of London as an international financial centre can be explained with reference to a number of factors. The first is the time zone factor, with London occupying a position mid-way between the western and eastern time zones, which allows financial trading to take place 24 hours a day, with business switching between the three major financial centres of New York, Tokyo and London. However, this does not explain why London rather than another European centre developed. London has a long tradition of international business, arising from the development of the Empire and the accompanying international trade. International financial institutions have been attracted to London be-cause of the existence of a number of features. These include a suitable pool of experienced and skilled labour, relatively light restrictions on access to financial markets, a tax regime which is not hostile to financial innovation, the absence of exchange controls since 1979, relatively light reserve requirements, a stable political regime and the English language. This last factor is an important consideration for US institutions setting up a European base. A more detailed discussion is provided by Davis and Latter (1989) and Davis (1990), with the latter paper examining the development of international financial centres from a more theoretical perspective.

The growing concentration of financial firms in London due to these factors will have attracted to London new firms, which are likely to have been the more innovative financial institutions, at the forefront of the development of new instruments and techniques. This in turn will have reinforced the importance of London as a financial centre. The impor-tance of financial services to the UK economy was noted in chapter 2, table 2.2. The UK's finance, banking, insurance and financial auxiliary services account for 8 per cent of GDP and 5 per cent of employment. Using a wider definition (as in table 2.2) which includes financial business and professional services, such as accountancy, consultancy, computing and legal services, the contribution is 26 per cent of GDP and 17 per cent of total employment. In 1996, the UK financial sector was the largest net contributor to the UK's balance-of-payments current account, with net overseas earnings exceeding £22 billion.

All the markets mentioned above are both global and 'wholesale' markets and deal only in large-value transactions between both domestic and foreign institutions. The retail markets are linked to these markets via banks and other financial institutions. Thus, for example, a private individual buying foreign currency for a holiday would go along to a high street bank, which would have obtained the currency originally on the London foreign exchange market. The markets are also organised in the sense that trading there requires operators to conform to rules specified within a 'rule book' and/or those imposed by the supervisory authority. These markets, together with the financial institutions which use the markets, are known colloquially as 'the City'. In the next section we examine in more detail the nature of markets.

7.3   The nature of markets

In the past, it was easy to define a market according to the geographical location where deals were made; for example, a stock exchange was a building where interested traders could meet and strike bargains. In many cases the growth of screen-based information systems has changed all this. This has removed the need to meet fellow traders and deals can be made over the telephone or on the screen itself. Up to now this has not been true of all markets since, for example, the largest financial futures exchanges have tended to maintain the 'open outcry' system of trading, although this is changing, as discussed below. This raises the question of how to define an organised market, since asset prices are now publicly available via the payment of a subscription to an information system (the pricing function is said to be 'transparent'). Three core functions can be identified. First, there is the price discovery system, whereby demand for and supply of the particular asset are brought together to determine the equilibrium price. The trading rules of the market determine how this function is to be carried out. The second core function is the surveillance function, through which the public can be guaranteed as far as possible that any deal is fair. The market is, in effect, giving its stamp of approval. This latter function is also ensured through the trading rules by such means as regulations concerning disclosure, settlement and so on. Third, an organised market provides either a meeting place where, or a network through which, interested parties can be brought into contact with each other. The problem for the organised market is that both the first two functions are in the nature of public goods. Consequently there is little to stop individuals extracting the information and dealing on their own account (i.e. 'piggy-backing').

Markets can be characterised in a number of ways. First, a distinction can be drawn between continuous and batch markets. In a continuous market, as the name suggests, buyers and sellers are in continuous contact with each other throughout the period the market is open and deals can be concluded at any time. On the other hand, in a batch market, orders for purchases and sales are accumulated and are executed together at particular times.

A second distinction can be made between auction and dealers' markets (sometimes these two market types are called 'order-driven' and 'quote-driven' markets, respectively). Futures markets are examples of auction markets, where an 'open outcry' system is used for dealers to strike individual bargains between each other. Open outcry is characterised by the presence of traders in close physical proximity, in a trading pit, who must verbally or otherwise publicly announce their bids and offers. To execute a trade, a trader must establish eye contact with the trader bidding or offering and say 'sold'. At any given time only the best bid and offer price are valid for execution. Another feature of the open outcry system is the presence of a type of trader known as a local. Local traders are members of the exchange but have limited capital compared with the institutional members. Locals will trade primarily for their own personal account and generally trade by taking small, short-horizon (e.g. seconds or minutes) positions. The role of locals is important in this type of market and this is reflected in the fact that they generally account for more than 50 per cent of total trading volume in the market. The existence of locals means that customer orders arriving in a trading pit usually find a two-sided market that can accommodate their trades immediately. Thus, locals provide liquidity in the market.

In the case of the dealers' markets, market makers exist and they guarantee to operate throughout the time the market is open. They publicise two prices for an asset throughout the market. The first is known as the 'bid' price and refers to the price at which the market maker is prepared to buy the asset. The second and higher price is termed the 'ask' price and is the price at which the market maker is prepared to sell the relevant asset. The gap between the two prices is known as the 'bid–ask spread' (or more simply the 'spread') and provides funds to meet the market maker's operating costs and the provision of profits. Normally there is some slight variation between quotes by different market makers and the spread between the highest bid price and the lowest ask price is termed the 'market touch'. This provides an indication of the liquidity of the market. A market is said to be 'tight' if prices are close to the true market value for small transactions and 'deep' if this applies to large transactions. Thus, for example, a market for which the bid–ask spread is small for large and medium transactions but widens substantially for small transactions would be said to be deep but not tight.

A final attribute of a market is termed 'immediacy', which is the speed with which a proposed transaction can be completed. In the case of continuous dealers' markets, immediacy is present provided the dealers do not suspend trading for any reason.

7.3.1   *Electronic trading*

A growing number of stock and futures exchanges use electronic trading systems. In this section we compare the main features of electronic trading with more traditional trading systems and identify some of the reasons for this trend towards adopting electronic trading.

The LSE in October 1997 introduced an electronic order book for trading in shares making up the FT-SE 100. The 'old' quote-driven trading system of deals struck with market makers over the telephone will continue alongside electronic trading for non-standard trading of FT-SE 100 shares and trading of all other shares listed on the LSE. The electronic system (SETS – see section 8.4.5) currently accounts for around 40 per cent of the trading of FT-SE 100 shares and there are plans to extend this system for trading the top 250 shares listed.

The London International Financial Futures and Options Exchange (LIFFE), currently using open outcry for trading during normal trading hours, has also announced plans to begin trading individual share options on an electronic system from November 1998 and plans to allow for futures contracts to be traded on this system a year later. A number of other futures exchanges are considering plans to move from open outcry to electronic trading, such as the Sydney Futures Exchange. So the question posed by these developments is what is motivating this move by exchanges to adopt electronic trading platforms?

An electronic matching system is made up of a set of computer terminals connected via high-speed communication links to a central host computer. Bids and offers are entered into a remote terminal and sent to the host computer, which queues them according to price and for bids/offers at the same price, according to time received by the host. Only the host computer has complete information on the market. A trader will see only the best bid or offer. All trades take place through the host, which automatically executes an order.

Open outcry systems are still popular in derivatives trading although as noted above an increasing number of exchanges are automated or planning to move to automated systems and, in addition, those exchanges which are open outcry provide for automated trading outside normal trading hours – see chapter 13 for further discussion.

A number of studies, for example Massimb and Phelps (1993) and Sarkar and Tozzi (1998), have examined the relative merits of open outcry and electronic matching systems. There are two important measures of a trading system's effectiveness: liquidity and cost. The general result from these studies is that electronic matching improves the operational efficiency of the market in terms of customer order delivery, accurate record keeping and so on, and operates at a lower cost, as evidenced by a narrower spread between bid and offer rates. As an example, the German Futures Exchange (Deutsche Terminbörse; DTB) and LIFFE both trade the Bund futures contract (a contract on the German government bond) but the DTB uses an electronic trading system and LIFFE is (currently) open outcry. In 1997 the cost of a round trip for the Bund (i.e. the buying and selling of one contract) on the DTB was $0.66 compared with $1.50 on LIFFE. However, the open outcry market has a number of advantages; in particular, it offers greater liquidity. High liquidity is important when executing large orders or complex orders where it is important that the trade has minimal impact on the price. As noted above, locals supply liquidity on open outcry markets. The existence of locals is partly dependent on their ability to observe other traders in the marketplace. This allows a trader to identify when another trader has a large buy or sell position and thus infer the future trading behaviour of that trader. This is not possible using electronic trading systems. However, a further advantage of electronic trading is the ability to have remote trading. It is possible for a trader with an appropriate connection to the host computer to be located anywhere, even in another country. The DTB has been particularly successful in promoting remote trading and in November 1997, 65 of its 171 members were remote traders.

So there are advantages with both electronic trading and floor trading. As noted above, the trend is towards electronic trading, which suggests that cost advantages and the ability to have remote trading outweigh the disadvantages of this type of system. As electronic trading systems become more sophisticated it is likely that some of the disadvantages of current systems can be overcome.

Financial markets provide opportunities for many different types of activity and we now consider three specialist activities, namely hedging, speculation and arbitrage.

7.4   Hedging, speculation and arbitrage

These techniques originally developed in the commodity markets and we shall use a hypothetical example of the sale/purchase of grain in the following discussion to illustrate their role.

The term 'hedging' refers to the purchase of a financial instrument or portfolio of instruments in order to insure against a possible reduction in wealth caused by unforeseen economic fluctuations. For example, a producer of grain may wish to hedge against a fall in the price of grain over some future period. One method of achieving such a hedge is to find a party who wishes to hedge against the opposite risk, that of a price rise. One example of such a person would be a bread producer who wishes to avoid a rise in price of future purchases of grain. The two parties can then agree on the price of grain for future delivery and this removes the risk of adverse price changes for both parties. This type of transaction would take place in a futures market, where trade is highly organised. Such markets exist for all major commodities traded and for many financial assets, including foreign currency, short-term deposits, bonds and equities. At this stage it is worth emphasising that both traders have gained certainty of price rather than made a profit. For example, if the price of grain does fall the purchaser has foregone profits which would have been obtained if he or she had deferred purchasing grain until later. The converse would apply in the case of a price rise.

A second hedging possibility for the grain producer is to transfer the risk to a party who is less risk averse than the hedger. Such a party is a speculator who would purchase (or sell goods) for later resale (or purchase) in the hope of profiting from any intervening price changes. In this example, the speculator would purchase the grain at a set price for delivery in the future (the 'futures' price) in the expectation that the market price at that time (the future 'spot' price) had risen above the purchase price. If speculators make accurate forecasts they improve the efficiency of markets. They buy when prices are perceived to be low and sell when prices are perceived to be high, thus evening out price fluctuations. However, inexpert speculators (and in some instances rational speculators) can destabilise markets – for further discussion see Newberry (1989). Speculative activity is prevalent in all the major commodity and financial markets.

An arbitrage opportunity is an investment strategy that, in a particular situation, guarantees a positive pay-off with no possibility of a negative pay-off occurring. Thus, arbitrage takes advantage of price or yield differentials in different markets (geographically or over time) in a riskless transaction. A simple example of an arbitrage transaction would be to borrow at one rate and lend at a higher fixed rate of interest when there was virtually no risk of default. Given the growth of information technology such differentials would not be expected to exist for any significant period of time, since the action of arbitrageurs serves to eliminate them.

7.5 The efficient markets hypothesis

At this stage it is also useful to examine in general terms the nature of the term 'efficiency' as applied to markets. Efficiency can take three meanings: operational efficiency, allocative efficiency and informational efficiency. The first type of efficiency is concerned with whether the market operates at the lowest level of cost or whether excessive resources are allocated to the operation of the market. In this connection it is likely that absence of price competition and the presence of cartels will lead to economic inefficiency. This is one of the motives behind the drive to liberalise financial markets seen in recent years. The second facet refers to the role of the market in the allocation of resources. The third aspect deals with the question of whether market prices reflect all available information. The 'efficient markets hypothesis' is restricted to this narrow and technical meaning of the term efficiency but it is, however, worth noting that it would be difficult to conceive how allocative efficiency is possible if informational efficiency is not present.

If market efficiency is present anywhere, it is likely to be in the context of some financial markets. This is so for a number of reasons. First, financial assets are akin to durable assets in the sense that they are not purchased for immediate consumption. In fact, as we noted in chapter 1, they are purchased because of both the running yield or return they offer and, probably what is more important, the expectation of a capital gain, which may occur due to price change. Second, continuous trading is a feature of financial markets and in many cases this is international rather than just national continuous trading. Consequently prices are free to move to eliminate any imbalance between demand and supply. It may be expected that, given these two features, dealing between sophisticated traders would force financial asset prices to reflect all available information. There will be clearly some dispersion in the interpretation of information but, on average, the market will arrive at the 'correct' view.

The idea of market efficiency embodies two components. First, the belief that an equilibrium market price exists. Second, the actual observed market price of the asset will adjust to this equilibrium price quickly. Two predictions follow from these observations:

(i)   prices will alter only if new information is received on the market –
        this is technically known as 'news';
(ii)   since all information within the designated information set is
        reflected in the price, all knowable above-normal profits will have
        been eliminated by trading, or 'arbitrage' in the technical jargon.

The second prediction carries with it the belief that trying to outperform
the market by forecasting is not worthwhile because the market price
will contain an accurate prediction in the light of current conditions. The
qualification concerning above-normal profits is particularly important.
Trading on financial markets is risky and, unless it is assumed that
operators are risk neutral or indifferent to the degree of risk, it is natural
to assume that a relatively high level of profit is necessary to induce
them to enter the market. However, it is very difficult to quantify a
precise numerical value for this element of profit necessary to compensate for the high degree of risk (or 'risk premium' as it is called in
the literature), so that the 'efficiency' of the financial markets is still a
controversial issue.

A formal definition of the 'efficient markets hypothesis' is that a
specific market may be termed efficient if the prices of the assets traded
on that market instantaneously reflect all available information. Fama
(1970) neatly defines three types of empirical test of market efficiency
defined according to the extent of the information set available:

(i)   weak efficiency – in this category the asset price is tested to see
        whether it reflects fully the information concerned in the history of
        both the price and volume of trading of that asset;
(ii)   semi-strong efficiency – in this instance the asset price is required
        to reflect fully all publicly available information; the information
        set here would include all reports and statistics available in the
        media;
(iii)   strong efficiency – this embodies the requirement that the asset
        price should reflect all information, whether publicly available or
        not; this category would include all privileged (inside) information.

In a further article, Fama (1991) modified the categories of efficiency
tests. Instead of tests of weak efficiency, he used the title 'test for return
predictability'. This would include not only tests based on the past
performance of the variable but also tests based on any form of forecasting and as such includes some tests previously included under the
heading of semi-strong tests. For the second category, Fama proposes
the title 'event studies' and for the third category 'tests for private
information'. This categorisation seems more suitable for some markets

(e.g. stock exchanges) than others (e.g. foreign exchanges) because of the extensive use in studies of those markets of both pricing models to forecast stock prices and dividends and the effect of events such as stock splits, dividends and exchange listing on the value of a firm. Clearly, these categories are interdependent. Thus, a market which is strongly efficient must also satisfy the semi-strong and weak tests. Similarly, a market which satisfies the semi-strong test must also satisfy the weak test. It is unlikely that any market will fully satisfy the requirements of efficiency on all occasions but, conversely, it is difficult to conceive of a market which is perfectly inefficient – that is, a market in which asset prices never reflect any available information! Consequently the important question is whether markets approximate efficiency for all practical purposes.

Empirical testing of the efficient markets hypothesis is fraught with problems. Normally at least two hypotheses coexist in any such test: first, that expectations are formed in the manner prescribed in the particular test and are used to arrive at the information set; and second, that the market uses these expectations in an efficient way in the price-setting process. Thus, failure to find support for the efficient markets hypothesis may be due to failure of either (or both) of the sub-hypotheses. This is referred to as the dual hypothesis problem. A further difficulty arises because we observe price data at discrete periods, generally at the end of the day, which is the trading price reported most often in the media. The assumption underlying most empirical work is that the process of arbitrage has been completed during the trading period, so that the end-of-trading price reflects all the information in the prescribed test.

The plan of the rest of this section on financial markets is as follows. In chapters 8 and 9 we discuss the equity and bond markets before proceeding in chapter 10 to examine the money markets. In chapters 11 to 13 we examine the foreign exchange market, the international financial markets based in London and the traded options and financial futures market, respectively. In chapter 14 we finish the section with a discussion of how these markets may be used to manage risk. Generally in each chapter we not only describe the institutional detail but also the extent to which the market concerned conforms to the efficient markets hypothesis.

Chapter 8

The market for equities

8.1   Introduction

The market for equities is part of the capital market, which refers to the market for long-term finance, as distinct from the money markets, which are markets for short-term funds. Clearly, this distinction is difficult to draw at the margin but the normal convention is to treat funds raised with an original maturity of greater than one year as capital funds. In principle the capital market can be divided into two segments: the primary market, where new capital is raised, and the secondary market, where existing securities are sold and bought. Again, this distinction is blurred since new capital can be raised via a stock exchange and existing securities sold on the same market. Furthermore, the existence of a secondary market is necessary to support the primary market since an essential prop to the market for long-term capital is the existence of a market where these long-term claims can be sold if the holder needs to obtain liquidity. A further distinction can be made between private sector finance and public sector finance. We can also distinguish between fixed-interest securities and equities. In this chapter we discuss the equity market and in chapter 9 the market for fixed-interest securities.

We begin by examining in section 8.2 some general issues relating to the raising of long-term finance by private firms. In section 8.3 we focus on the primary market for equity issues followed in section 8.4 by the secondary market, where equity securities are traded. We then examine in section 8.5 the nature of and causes of the global stock market crash of October 1987. In section 8.6 we consider the degree to which stock markets conform to the efficient markets hypothesis. Our conclusions are presented in section 8.7.

8.2 The primary capital market

At the outset of this section it is worth examining the ways in which private firms can raise long-term finance. The main methods in recent years have been the following:

(i)   internal funds;
(ii)   long-term bank loans;
(iii)   issues of equities;
(iv)   issues of fixed-interest securities;
(v)   finance from official sources.

An important source of finance to firms comes from the profits they have attained from trading but have not distributed to shareholders in the form of dividends. This is referred to as internal funds. All the other sources of capital in the list above are referred to as external sources of finance. We have discussed the nature of bank loans in chapters 1 and 2, so no further comment will be made in this section other than to draw the reader's attention to the importance of this source of finance. Equities are discussed below. Fixed-interest securities are referred to as bonds and the nature of the corporate bond market is discussed in chapter 9. Finally it is possible for firms to obtain government assistance, for example the award of investment grants in connection with the regional selective assistance policy of the UK government.

8.2.1 *Nature and valuation of equities*

An equity security refers, in the UK, to a share issued by a company (in the US an equity security is referred to as a stock). A share represents ownership in the firm that issued the security. A shareholder owns a percentage interest in the issuing firm. A shareholder can earn a return either through an increase in the price of the share or through a payment of dividends by the firm. The firm though is under no obligation to pay dividends. Shares have no maturity date and they confer the right of residual claimant on the shareholder. That means that a shareholder has a claim on all assets and income left over after all other claimants have been satisfied. Most shareholders have the right to vote at the annual general meeting of the company.

There are two type of shares, ordinary or preference (in the US, common stock and preferred stock). The main differences between them are that preference shares receive a fixed dividend and preference shareholders have priority over the claims of ordinary shareholders, but after that of fixed-interest security holders. Finally, ordinary share issues far exceed issues of preference shares.

The value of an ordinary share can be valued in the same way that any asset is valued, that is, it is the present value of the future stream of cash flows received by the holder. The future cash flows that the holder of an ordinary share might receive are future dividends and the price the share will sell for in the future. The future price of the share, however, is itself the present value of the dividends that follow and a share price even further into the future. Taken to an extreme, the current price of a share is the simply the present value of the future dividend payments to infinity. Hence:

$$P_0 = D_1/(1 + i) + D_2/(1 + i)^2 + D_3/(1 + i)^3 + \dots + D_\infty/(1 + i)^\infty \quad (8.1)$$

where P_0 = price of share at time 0 (present); D_n = dividend paid at time n; i = discount rate.

Equation 8.1 provides us with an accurate measure of the price of an ordinary share; however, it is not a very useful method for computing the price as we do not know the future dividend payments. If we assume that dividends increase at a constant rate then equation 8.1 can be rewritten as:

$$P_0 = D_1/(i - g) \quad\quad\quad\quad\quad\quad\quad\quad\quad\quad\quad\quad (8.2)$$

where P_0, i and D_1 are as before and g is the expected constant dividend growth rate. Equation 8.2 is known as the Gordon growth model and it is appropriate to use this for valuing an ordinary share when dividends are expected to follow a constant growth pattern in the future.

For example, suppose that you want to estimate the price of a share where the next dividend payment is expected to be £0.50 per share, the discount rate is estimated to be 10 per cent and dividends are expected to grow at a rate of 5 per cent per year. Applying the Gordon growth model, we find:

$$P_0 = £0.50/(0.10 - 0.05) = £10.00$$

Thus the share should sell for £10.

8.2.2 *Financing patterns of UK firms*

Figure 8.1 shows the pattern of finance raised by UK non-financial firms over the period 1963–96. A few explanatory remarks concerning figure 8.1 are necessary. First, the statistics available combine issues of debentures and preference shares. We noted above that preference shares pay a fixed rate of dividend and therefore the security has similarities to

Figure 8.1   *Pattern of finance raised by UK non-financial firms, 1963–96*

a debenture. Second, the item marked 'Other capital' comprises mainly capital transfers and import credits. Third, the item 'Other loans' refers to instalment credit received and loans from financial institutions other than banks and from the public sector.

Figure 8.1 illustrates the changes in the relative importance of the various components over time. Over the whole period the importance of internal funds as opposed to external funds is patently obvious, approximately 62 per cent of total funds raised being generated from within companies. It is interesting to note though that the proportion of internal funds has shown a steady decline since the 1970s. Of the external funds raised, bank loans are the most important component for most of the period. In the seven years from 1990 to 1996 the share of bank loans has, however, shown a dramatic decline compared with previous years. The reason for this was that from 1991 to 1994, when the UK economy was in recession and just coming out of recession, companies were net repayers of bank loans. The figures for 1995 and 1996 show that the share of bank loans, as a proportion of total capital raised, is back to its normal level of around 13 per cent. Issues of ordinary shares contributed only 6 per cent of total funds over the period, although this figure was significantly higher in the later part of the period compared with the 1970s, and indeed reached an average of over 10 per cent in the 1990s, as firms took advantage of the rising equities market. However, this figure includes shares issued to finance takeovers, so the additional or new corporate finance raised by firms through equity issues during this period was considerably smaller and was, in fact, negative during the period 1970 to 1985 (Mayer and Alexander 1990). Debentures and preference shares showed a large drop from 1973 until the end of the 1980s, owing no doubt to the rises in the rate of interest to levels not experienced before. As firms became accustomed to these levels, issues of debentures and preference shares picked up again. Note also the rising importance of overseas funding towards the end of the period. The overall trend, therefore, revealed by figure 8.1 is a greater use of external finance by firms since the 1970s, with greater use made of share and debenture issues, particularly in the 1990s.

8.3   The primary market for private sector securities

New issues of private sector securities, which include ordinary shares, preference shares and debentures, can be made by firms whose securities are already quoted on the LSE or by those companies seeking a listing on it. In this latter case companies must meet a list of requirements concerning financial status and past trading record. The main requirements are that companies must have a three-year trading record, the expected value of the shares after issue must exceed £700,000 and 25 per cent of the share capital must be held by the public. There are currently over 2,000 UK companies listed on the LSE and the average capitalisation for a listed UK company was £158 million in 1997. The LSE itself is the competent authority for listing in the UK and has the responsibility for regulating companies that are admitted to the official list. In particular, after admission to the LSE, a company must comply with the LSE's continuing obligations. These set out rules regarding conduct of listed firms, in particular, rules relating to the disclosure of information to the market.

Companies that want access to the stock market but do not meet the requirements for an official listing can join the Alternative Investment Market (AIM), which opened on 19 June 1995. AIM replaced the Unlisted Stock Market and there are no restrictions on entry relating to length of trading period or size of company. A nominated adviser, who is approved by the LSE, is responsible for deciding whether a company is suitable for the market. A nominated adviser is usually a bank or stockbroker. The adviser is also responsible for ensuring that the firm's affairs are in order and that its documentation has been adequately prepared. The applicant will also be required to find a minimum of one market maker prepared to deal in its shares. Similar to the requirements for inclusion in the official list, the applicant will be required to provide price-sensitive information to the market (including unaudited interim accounts), which will be disseminated in the normal manner. The aim of the new market is to facilitate raising of finance by small companies whilst still maintaining a satisfactory degree of investor protection.

Every new issue will involve a sponsor, whose main role is to assess the company's suitability for a listing and prepare the company for it. The sponsor may be a merchant bank or stockbroker. Where a merchant bank is appointed as sponsor the firm may need to appoint a stockbroker as well, which, in these days of financial conglomerates, may be part of the same company. The broker's responsibility is to advise on timing and pricing of the issue. The merchant bank/broker may act as a principal by buying the shares from the company and then disposing of them on its own account, or it may act as an agent. Even in the latter case, some risk is involved since the bank/broker normally provides a guarantee that a specified sum will be raised. In order to spread this risk of a failure to sell the whole issue to the public, the bank/broker will normally arrange for the issue to be 'underwritten'. This involves an institution guaranteeing that the whole issue will be sold at the price indicated. If the issue is taken up by the public the underwriter has no further liability. If, on the other hand, only part of the issue is sold to the public (i.e. is 'partly subscribed'), the underwriter will purchase the remainder of the issue herself or himself. In return for this service the underwriter will obtain a commission on the issue in the region of 1 to 2 per cent of the capital raised. In the case of rights issues (i.e. of further shares in a listed company – see below), the new shares are generally offered to existing shareholders at a discount of around 15 per cent of the market price and the charge for underwriting appears, for the last 30 years or so, to have been fixed at 2 per cent irrespective of the quality of the issuer and has, therefore, attracted the attention of the Office of Fair Trading (OFT). The OFT investigated the underwriting of equity issues on two occasions in 1995 and 1996 and found little evidence of competition in underwriting or a willingness of companies to use deep discounted issues to avoid underwriting fees altogether. As a consequence the OFT referred the matter to the Monopolies and Mergers Commission in November 1997; its report had not been published at the time of writing. The main underwriters of new issues are the long-term investment institutions, that is, the insurance companies, the pension funds and investment trusts.

The main methods for new issues are the following:

(i) *Placings*. The issuing house purchases the securities from the issuer and places the shares with investors. Normal prudence dictates that the major proportion of these placings will be re-placed with further investors, who are generally the long-term investment institutions. Initial public offerings up to £25 million may be placed entirely with clients of the sponsor subject to a minimum of 5 per cent being placed with at least one independent market maker. For offers between £25 million and £50 million (defined as medium-size offers), up to 75 per cent of the offer may be placed with the sponsoring broker's clients. At least 5 per cent of the shares being placed direct must be offered to two independent market makers of the shares concerned. All offers greater than £50 million must be made by way of an offer for sale. In this case, a sponsor will be permitted to place or underwrite 50 per cent of the issue with its clients. As in the case of medium-size offers, there must be at least two independent market makers and they must be offered at least 5 per cent of the shares placed or underwritten.

(ii) *Offers for sale by tender.* In this case the public is invited to purchase shares at any price over a publicised minimum. A single so-called 'striking price' is established at which it is believed that the issue will be fully subscribed and all tenders at that or a higher price will receive an allotment at this striking price irrespective of whether the tender was at a higher price or not. This system of allocation is called a 'common price tender'.

(iii) *Offers for sale.* Here the issuing house purchases the whole issue at a specified price and then offers the issue for sale to the general public.

(iv) *Offers for sale by subscription.* This method is a variation of (iii), whereby the company rather than the issuing house offers the shares to the public.

For companies whose shares are already quoted on the LSE, further issues of equity are made by means of a 'rights issue' (i.e. a secondary issue). Existing shareholders have the right to purchase additional shares in proportion to their existing holdings at a fixed price. The price is normally at a discount to that currently quoted on the LSE so that the issuing price is unlikely to be higher than the price quoted on the LSE at the time of the issue due to price fluctuations. The shareholder does not have to take up the rights issue and may, in fact, sell the right. If it so wishes, the issuing company may avoid the need for the issue to be underwritten by making the right at a large discount compared with the current market price (at a 'deep' discount) so as to make the offer attractive. Such rights issues must be approved by the shareholders and protection for existing shareholders against dilution of their holdings is afforded by the Companies Act 1985 and LSE rules. These are termed preemption requirements. As part of the reorganisation following 'Big Bang' (discussed later in this chapter), the LSE decided to withdraw the preemption rights requirement for listed companies. Other methods of raising equity finance, in particular a placing, are now more common for secondary issues, as funds are more speedily obtained than for rights issues. However, shareholders must give approval for this at the company's annual general meeting. The LSE has followed this path mainly because it wished to reduce the possibility that new member firms would bypass the London market and issue securities through other world capital markets.

The method of issue adopted by an individual firm will depend on the costs involved relative to the total funds being raised. These costs include administrative expenses, advertising and, in the case of an issue by a company new to the LSE, any discount on the nominal price of the share. Placing is generally the cheapest method as there is no need for widespread advertising. As a consequence the placing is the most frequently used method of obtaining a listing and is particularly geared towards smaller companies. The main disadvantage with a placing is that the resulting shareholder spread is more limited.

8.4   The secondary market for private securities

The LSE as well as being the market for primary private sector capital issues is also the market for secondary trading of both private sector securities and public sector debt (gilt-edged securities – discussed in

Figure 8.2   *Turnover on the London Stock Exchange – gilts and company securities, 1976–96*

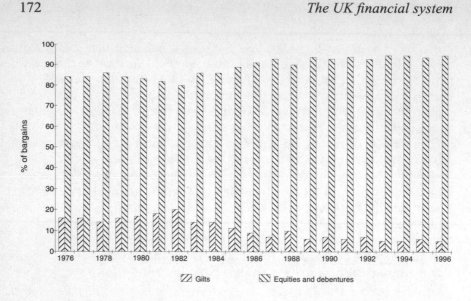

Figure 8.3   *Number of transactions on the London Stock Exchange – gilts and company securities, 1976–96*

more detail in chapter 9). Figure 8.2 shows that in terms of turnover, trading in gilt-edged securities is the main component, although this declined over the 1980s and early 1990s. Figure 8.3 shows that whilst the percentage of turnover attributable to gilt trading is higher than that for equities and debentures, the number of trades (bargains) is proportionally lower for gilts. This implies that the average size of order is much larger for gilts than equities.

In chapter 7 we saw that London is an international financial centre and the LSE reflects this. Table 8.1 shows that London is the third largest stock market in the world in terms of both market value of domestic equity and total turnover (i.e. domestic and foreign), and the largest in Europe. However, it is, by far, the largest stock market in the world in terms of foreign company turnover.

8.4.1   *Changes in trading arrangements: Big Bang*

The arrangements at the LSE were subject to a fundamental change on 27 October 1986, the so-called 'Big Bang'. Prior to this date the LSE was subject to a number of restrictive practices. Three in particular were important. First, there was single capacity, since the market makers in shares, termed jobbers, were able to deal only on their own account. All contact with the jobbers was to be conducted via stockbrokers who, in

Table 8.1   *Comparison of major world stock exchanges at end 1997*

Exchange	Market value of domestic equity (£billion)	Number of companies		1997 turnover (£billion)	
		Domestic	Foreign	Domestic	Foreign
New York	5,436	2,691	356	2,266	295
Tokyo	1,287	1,805	60	497	0.7
London	1,251	2,465	526	524	722
NASDAQ[a]	1,033	5,033	454	2,552	117
Germany	502	700	n/a	600	28
Paris	411	744	193	239	5
Toronto	358	1,362	58	188	0.3
Switzerland	348	216	212	297	45

[a] National Association of Securities Dealers' automated quotations system.
Source: London Stock Exchange, *Quality of Markets Review*, 1998.

turn, were unable to deal in shares. In other words, stockbrokers were purely agents acting as intermediaries between the ultimate customer and the jobber. Second, a cartel arrangement applied whereby minimum commissions were fixed for all trades, irrespective of size. Third, ownership of brokers and jobbers was restricted to private partnerships until 1969. In that year brokers and jobbers were permitted to form p.l.c.s and further relaxation occurred in 1971 when ownership of corporate members could be held by outside members but subject to the severe restraint that no one shareholder could hold more than 10 per cent of the capital of a single firm. Economic theory predicts that cartels have the effect of raising members' income and consequently it is certain that the minimum commission arrangement raised dealing costs. On the other hand, it was suggested that it protected the interest of the public since there was no conflict of interest because the market makers could not deal directly with the public and brokers could not deal in shares. Thus, each party had no motive to act against the interests of the public.

There were two separate motives for change. First, after 1979, the Conservative government was interested in increasing the degree of competition throughout the economy. This resulted in a referral of the LSE rule book to the Restrictive Trade Practices Court in 1979. Within this motive was, perhaps, the feeling that the government was providing excessive commission incomes on dealings in gilts. Second, the LSE was losing business following the abolition of controls on movements of capital for UK residents in 1979. Share dealings have become dominated to an increasing extent by the institutions. These are the agents most likely to suffer from minimum prices since their deals would be of a large size. A significant development at this time was the growth of American deposit receipts (ADRs). US financial institutions purchased blocks of shares in UK companies and then issued titles to the underlying shares which were traded on the New York Stock Exchange. Costs of trading were lower in New York, which had experienced its equivalent to Big Bang ('May Day') in 1975. Consequently large dealings in UK shares tended to move to New York at the expense of London.

Agreement was reached in 1983 between the LSE and the government which led to the dropping of the referral to the Court. Three important components of the agreement were:

(i)   the abolition of minimum commissions,
(ii) the permission of dual capacity,
(iii) relaxation of the rules of outside ownership.

With regard to point (ii), there is now a single form of institution called a broker-dealer, who can either operate on her or his own account or as an agent for another institution/person. Within this category there is a subset who are registered to act as market makers or dealers. These market makers may specialise in a particular group of shares. Restraints operate where broker-dealers who are not market makers are acting as an agent, inasmuch as they can deal on their own account or match an order with another client only if they can show that they can execute the order at a superior price than by going to a market maker. Similarly, market makers can act as an agent only if they can deal at a price at least as good as that which could be obtained from another market maker.

The three components of the agreement were closely interconnected. Abolition of minimum commissions would place the income of brokers under great pressure, so that they would be likely to seek alternative sources of income. One such source would be market making. Second, dealing is a high-risk industry and new sources of capital would be needed in view of the likely fall in incomes. Thus, outside interests were permitted to own 100 per cent of the share capital of single-member firms as from 1 March 1986. This led to a scramble to buy up firms and to form financial conglomerates.

Along with changes brought about by 'Big Bang', a screen information system, SEAQ, described below, was introduced, so that the old 'face-to-face' discussions between LSE members were quickly eliminated. What effect did these change have on share dealing? First, the level of commissions fell on deals. In February 1987 the *Bank of*

Figure 8.4   *Changes in the value of the FT-SE 100 Index, 1985–95*

England Quarterly Bulletin suggested that, for an equity deal in the region of £10,000 to £1 million, commission rates fell from 0.4 per cent to 0.2 per cent. Larger falls were reported in larger deals, with the largest fall being obtained in deals carried out by the institutions, which have conducted a large part of their business net of commission. It also appeared that commissions on small transactions did not rise to any great extent and might have actually fallen slightly. The evidence also suggested that the market touch had fallen for beta and gamma shares and remained the roughly same for alpha shares. (Alpha, beta and gamma refer to categories of shares based on trading activity, with alpha shares being the most actively traded; note that this categorisation was ended in 1991 – see below.) There was also anecdotal evidence that the touch did not widen significantly for larger quotes; in other words the market is deeper than before.

As would be expected from the elementary theory of demand and supply, lower prices stimulated demand and increased turnover was observed on both the listed and unlisted markets immediately after Big Bang. Increases of the order of 20 per cent were obtained and this, together with the trend increase in share prices experienced during the early months of 1987, enabled profitable trading to continue. Reference to figure 8.2 demonstrates the dramatic growth in turnover in the years after 1986. However, this situation did not last for any length of time and substantial falls in share prices occurred on a global basis during October 1987. This is demonstrated in figure 8.4.

The graph reveals a steady rise in the share index from 1985 to the middle of 1987, when the dramatic fall in prices occurred. It is also noticeable that the rise in the index was particularly pronounced during the early months of 1987. As is demonstrated in figure 8.2, the fall in prices was accompanied by a decrease in the volume of turnover, resulting in a dramatic loss in profitability for the broker-dealers. In fact this decrease in trading was far more pronounced in the number of transactions than in turnover. As noted above, the larger orders were subject to falls in commission rates and this enhanced the general loss of profitability in the market. In other words there was large-scale excess capacity, which led to some firms giving up market making altogether. Following Big Bang there were some 32 domestic equity market makers but by 1990 this had fallen to 26 firms. Reductions in capacity also came from other firms restricting their market-making activities.

8.4.2 *Pre- and post-trade transparency*

The price information is distributed through the Stock Exchange Automated Quotations System (SEAQ), which supports two market segments, domestic and international. Quoted prices are indicated to the market via an information service provider such as Reuters. The former categorisation of domestic shares (alpha, beta, gamma and delta) has been abolished and, from January 1991, shares have been allocated to bands according to their 'normal market size' (NMS), based on market turnover. A well informed equity market requires public disclosure of information relevant to the pricing of shares. This information includes such items as price quotations, prices at which deals are made, and trade volumes, in addition to general macroeconomic information and specific information relating to individual companies. The technical term for the presence of such information in the market is 'transparency'. Transparency can be subdivided into two categories, pre-trade and post-trade. Pre-trade transparency is provided by SEAQ price quotations and the requirement for companies to provide the market with relevant information. The requirement for post-trade transparency is met through the publication of details of the prices at which deals have been made. Deals for all shares with a NMS greater than 2,000 shares must be reported to the system within three minutes of the trade taking place, provided the transaction is less than six times the NMS of that share. A delay of 60 minutes is allowed before reporting in the case of deals greater than six times the NMS of that share. A third reporting class occurs in the case of 'block deals' between market makers. These are defined as trades greater than 75 times the NMS of that share. In this case notification must be carried out after five days or after the market maker has offset 90 per cent of the trade (whichever is the earlier). Note that the LSE monitors closely the unwinding of the block trade. All 'agency crosses' (in-house deals) must be reported, irrespective of the NMS of the equity concerned. A further example of the lack of transparency concerns the permission of market makers to avoid disclosure of the quantity of any given stock owned by them. Normally, disclosure is required by an investor who owns more than 3 per cent of the total shares in one company.

The justification of the delay in reporting large trades is based on the view that details concerning the large trades provides competitors with information on which to base their strategies. Thus, for example, knowledge that there was a large seller in the market following a block trade may lead to a fall in prices and hence losses for the market maker. A further query with respect to delayed publication of trade details concerns the impact of the lack of information on derivatives exchanges, since the derivative price may not reflect accurately the price of the underlying shares. This may be driving derivative trade away from London to Continental exchanges. The question of delayed reporting was the subject of investigation by both the Securities and Investment Board and the OFT.

The LSE also operates a screen-based market for shares which is restricted to market makers; this is termed the inter-dealer broker (IDB) market. Transactions for this market executed on IDB screens are also disclosed.

The analogous system for leading international stocks which are traded by international market makers operating in London is the SEAQ International. Reporting of transactions are less onerous in this market, which, given the degree of international competition, seems reasonable.

Illiquid stocks have presented a problem to the LSE since the fall in trading volume consequent upon the 1987 stock market crash. 'The bottom 50% of listed stocks (about 1200 issues) represent just 1.2% of LSE turnover' (Securities and Investment Board 1994). This makes it difficult to devise a trading structure which meets the needs of both the market makers and potential buyers and sellers and in particular the LSE's requirement for the existence of at least two market makers. The LSE has attempted to deal with this problem through the creation of the Stock Exchange Alternative Trading Service (SEATS). This is a combination of a 'bulletin' service with permission for there to be a single trader or market maker. The market maker is required to make continuous two-way prices (i.e. for purchase and sale of shares). Investors will also be able to post on the bulletin orders to buy or sell stocks. The market maker is obliged, on trading, to fulfil orders on the bulletin which are at the same price or at better prices than those at which it is proposing to trade. At the same time brokers must show proposed trades to a market maker before matching orders within their office. This will permit the market maker and investors to have the first chance of meeting the order.

8.4.3   *Settlement*

A new rolling settlement was introduced in July 1994 whereby each day's transactions are to be settled five (formerly ten) business days after the transactions take place (a so-called T+5 rule). It is intended that the rolling settlement should move eventually to T+3. In addition a new settlement system, CREST, was introduced in July 1996, replacing Talisman. This system was designed by the Bank of England following a failed attempt by the LSE to develop a paperless share transfer system, named Taurus. Ownership of CREST has been handed over to an independent company, Crestco. Under CREST, share transfers are carried out using an electronic book-entry system. This eliminates from share trading the need for paper certificates and should lead to a reduction in costs and an improvement in settlement arrangements. However, whilst the bulk of trades will not involve share certificates, some investors who rarely trade are permitted to retain the use of certificates.

8.4.4   *Competition*

Stock exchanges are subject to ever-increasing competition. There is a considerable degree of actual and potential competition with the LSE in dealing in both UK and foreign equities from such channels as:

(i)   ADRs traded on US exchanges. US financial institutions purchase blocks of shares in UK companies and then issue titles to the underlying shares which are traded on the New York Stock Exchange and the National Association of Securities Dealers' Automated Quotations System (NASDAQ), an electronic securities exchange. Large investment institutions may choose to trade UK shares this way if there are cost advantages.

(ii)   OTC dealing in equities between institutions.

(iii) Equity and equity derivative indexes (both exchange traded and OTC). Futures and option contracts on LSE indexes, as well as options on individual shares, can be traded on LIFFE (see chapter 13 for a full description of these instruments) as well as OTC.

Trading equity derivatives allows investors to gain exposure to the equity market without actually trading on the LSE.

(iv) Tradepoint. This is an electronic order-matching exchange that permits both dealers and professional investors with an electronic link to trade around 1,200 UK equities. Tradepoint is commercially operated and is a recognised investment exchange under the Financial Services Act 1986 and began trading in September 1995. Its turnover in 1997 was less than 1 per cent of the volume of the LSE; therefore it is not a serious competitor at present.

(v) Other European exchanges. The LSE has been successful in attracting listings of foreign shares and for many years was able to attract business that would normally be transacted through overseas exchanges. Other European exchanges, in particular the French and German bourses, have competed intensely with London in the 1990s to win back business. Table 8.1 showed that London is still the largest exchange in Europe in terms of foreign company turnover, but the French and German exchanges have recently won back from London some business in trading their own domestic shares.

8.4.5   *Change to electronic trading*

As discussed in section 8.4.1 above, the LSE, following Big Bang, was a continuous dealers' market using screens to display prices but not for actual trading. Such a market is termed 'quote-driven' since market makers registered with the LSE indicate firm quotes for buying and selling specific securities up to a specific size. As we saw in chapter 7, the main alternative to a quote-driven market is an 'order-driven auction market'. The rules applying to auction markets are quite different from those applying to quote-driven markets. There is the complete absence of market makers indicating firm prices at which they are prepared to deal. In the case of order-driven markets, orders are executed on the basis of price and time. Consequently orders at the best price will be executed first. The price is kept near the equilibrium price by a steady flow of orders. Deviations from the perceived equilibrium price will stimulate offsetting intervention by speculators. In recent years most of the major stock markets in Europe have moved over to electronic order-driven systems. To maintain its competitive position, the LSE moved to an order-driven system in October 1997 for the trading of shares making up the FT-SE 100 index. The order-driven system is known as the Stock Exchange Automatic Trading System (SETS).

A broker will normally route an order to SETS and the order will be matched automatically by the system. Two types of order are possible:

'limit' and 'market fill' (or 'at best') orders. In the former case the deal takes place only at a price indicated as the limit. So, if there is a suitable matching order on the order book then the order is executed immediately. Otherwise the order will wait until suitable matching orders come along. In the latter (market fill) case the deal takes place at the best price displayed in the market at that time. So, a 'sell' order will be matched with the highest available buying price. Likewise, a 'buy' order would be matched with the highest available selling price.

Not all orders for FT-SE 100 shares will be executed through the order book. Large trades, which are defined as eight times the NMS, can be executed through a worked principal agreement, which occurs off the order book. Also, where an order is relatively small (currently defined as £5,000) or will not be settled within the standard five-day settlement period then it will not be channelled through the order book. Instead a broker will conduct the trade through a retail service provider (playing a similar role to a market maker). Retail service providers will still be required to execute the trade at the best price that would have been available had the trade been conducted through the order book.

So the LSE now operates a hybrid trading system. A large number of trades of FT-SE 100 shares are routed through an electronic order book. The LSE claimed in a press release in March 1998 that 40 per cent of trades in FT-SE 100 shares are routed through SETS but that 75 per cent of trades are conducted at order book prices (but this includes business conducted off the order book). Trades in non-FT-SE 100 shares continue to be conducted through the quote-driven system.

8.5   The global stock market crash of October 1987

There is no consensus concerning the reasons for the dramatic fall in stock market prices which began on Monday 19 October 1987 ('Black Monday') when the New York Stock Exchange suffered a drop of 22.6 per cent (its largest ever in a single day), which quickly spread to most exchanges around the world, including London. Four possible causes have been suggested.

First, there was uncertainty over the international payments situation. Recent years had seen persistent balance-of-payments disequilibria. The US and the UK had experienced large deficits, which had been matched by large surpluses obtained by Japan and Germany. At the same time corrective measures for the US federal budget deficit seemed to be proving inadequate. Perhaps the perception of the serious nature of these problems was enhanced by the continued problem of sovereign debt (see chapter 4). It could be argued therefore that bad US trade figures on the Thursday before the crash provided the trigger for the fall in stock prices. Two problems remain with this approach. First, the worldwide nature of the crash across a wide number of exchanges in different countries seems to be out of keeping with the weight of news. On the other hand a look at the fundamentals suggests that share prices should be sensitive to changes in expectations. We have seen in section 8.2 above that the value of a share can be calculated using the Gordon growth model – equation 8.2 is reproduced here, but note that we do not know the next dividend payment, so this is represented by the investor's expectation of the next dividend $E_t D_t$, where E_t is the expectations operator:

$$\text{Current price} = E_t D_t / (i - g) \tag{8.2}$$

Note that equation 8.2 requires the discount rate (i) to be larger than the expected growth rate of dividends (g). If values of £0.30 for forecast of dividends and 8 per cent and 6 per cent for the discount rate and dividend growth rate, respectively, are assumed, then the share value will be £15. If the expected growth rate of dividends falls to 5 per cent, the price of each share falls to £10. This explanation would, therefore, require investors to revise downwards their expected rate of growth of dividends (or equivalently the forecast of dividends) or to revise upwards the required rate of discount in the light of uncertainty about future events due to the international financial problems. A problem with this approach is that survey evidence in the US suggested that investors regarded the equity market as being overvalued before the crash. This evidence was, however, collected after the crash and may be tainted with wisdom after the event.

The second potential cause for the crash has been identified with 'speculative bubbles'. The basis of the belief in the existence of speculative bubbles is that rises in share prices induce expectations that the price will rise even further. This has been dubbed 'the greater fool theory' in the sense that each purchaser believes that he or she will find an even bigger fool who will buy the equity at a higher price, which, by definition, is not related to the fundamentals. This cause implies market failure in the sense that shares become increasingly overvalued until the bubble bursts at a particular point in time for what may seem a trivial reason. Examination of the time pattern of the share price index in figure 8.4 shows the index increasing at a fast rate throughout the early months of 1987 and this might be taken as casual support for the 'speculative bubble' hypothesis. However, existence of speculative bubbles would require that sequences of price changes are related but Santoni (1987) presents evidence that this requirement was absent from daily data for the US for the period 2 January 1986 to 25 August 1987. Two tests were applied to the Dow-Jones index for this period, one based on an examination of the autocorrelation coefficients and one based on runs of positive and negative changes. Neither of these tests supported the rejection of the hypothesis that the data conformed to a random walk.

The third possible cause lies in the belief that there may have been a temporary market failure triggered by an initial price decline. Suggested causes of this failure include:

(i)   value-insensitive trading due to automatic computer trading,
(ii) false price signals resulting from the abnormally heavy trading observed,
(iii) the absence of countervailing price-sensitive market traders acting from a viewpoint of the fundamentals.

It could be argued that the heavy price falls themselves induced a change in market expectations which then validated the new, lower prices. It may also be argued that the growth of high-speed communications and trading mechanisms increased the possibility of such crises and this led to a demand for the introduction of circuit breakers in markets. These would have the effect of suspending trading when prices fall (or rise) beyond a specific amount during the day. For example, in October 1997 the New York Stock Exchange introduced circuit breakers, so that if the Dow Jones Industrial Average stock index declines by 250 points below the previous day's closing price, the Exchange prohibits trading for one hour. The idea is that a 'cooling-off' period may restore calmer conditions during the subsequent trading period. Two problems arise with such proposals. First, if traders wish to trade, they may well do so off the market. Second, is it appropriate to suspend trading just at the time when the public has a strong desire to trade?

A fourth reason for the crash, suggested by the Brady Commission (1988), concerns the use of the futures market to obtain portfolio insurance. Discussion of the futures market takes place in chapter 13 but it is possible to outline here the main thread of the argument. If it were possible to enter into a series of put options (i.e. the right to sell all the securities in a portfolio at predetermined prices) then the risks of adverse price changes would be reduced. Portfolio insurance replicates this position by taking a simultaneous position in a risky portfolio and a synthetic put option by shifting funds from the risky portfolio into a safe liquid asset on the basis of the Black/Scholes option pricing model. This involves selling shares when prices are falling and, if used by sufficient operators, will increase the volatility of prices on the market. In the US, portfolio insurers bought and sold futures contracts on a share index rather than the shares themselves. This has the obvious advantage of lower cost since it would be difficult, and therefore costly, to carry out the alternative of entering into contracts to purchase or sell shares across the whole range of securities in a share price index. A second facet of the argument concerns the practice of arbitraging between shares making up the index and the relevant futures contract. For example, if the futures contract falls below the share price by a sufficient amount then it is possible to make a profit by purchasing the futures contract and selling the shares making up the index. Clearly, the futures price discount must be sufficiently large to offset the transactions costs. During the week preceding the crash, portfolio insurers were selling futures heavily and this induced index arbitrage purchasing futures and selling shares. It appears that at certain critical times the volume of this trading accounted for up to 66 per cent of transactions. In addition, the underlying techniques of portfolio insurance are well known on the market so that other operators could identify when insurers were likely to sell securities. This would lead them to try to sell in advance of the insurers in the hope of buying stock back later at the lower price induced by the sales of the insurers.

It is claimed that the volume of sales on the futures market was so large on the Monday and Tuesday of the crash that index arbitrageurs were unable to absorb the pressure by purchasing futures, but the falling futures price still provided a guide as to the likely price of the shares making up the market, thus inducing more sales and price falls.

The causes of the crash are still controversial and we are unable to come to any firm conclusion. We now move on to consider the empirical evidence concerning the efficiency of the stock market.

8.6   The stock markets and the efficient markets hypothesis

In this section we briefly survey the literature on the informational efficiency of the stock market. As the literature on this topic is extensive, some degree of selection is inevitable. We therefore concentrate on representative studies. At this stage we would, however, like to stress the practical importance of the efficient markets hypothesis. If the stock market conforms to the efficient markets hypothesis, then forecasting future movements in share prices is not likely to be worth the effort involved because the market price reflects all available information. Thus, on average it will not be possible to outperform the market consistently. The caveat applying to this statement is that of risk aversion and it may be that the operator's degree of risk aversion is less than that ruling in the market.

Most early studies tended to support the hypothesis that the LSE was efficient. Using Fama's (1991) categorisation we discuss the efficiency of the LSE under the headings of return predictability, event studies and private information.

8.6.1 *Return predictability*

One interesting approach to considering predictability of stock returns is to examine the role filter rules. Basically a filter rule is an automatic instruction to buy a stock after it rises x per cent above a recent trough and sell again after it falls y per cent below a recent peak. The object of the rule is to identify cycles from which it is hoped to make profits. The size of x and y (which may be the same) is determined empirically from past data. If the two filters are small a large number of transactions will be undertaken. This increases cost but at the same time, hopefully, identifies profitable trading opportunities. Thus, there is a trade-off between costs and the identification of potential for profit. An early study by Alexander (1954) suggested that filter rules did offer scope for obtaining profits above those realised from a buy and hold strategy. These conclusions were modified in the light of biases in the original study. A subsequent study, by Fama and Blume (1966), investigated the profitability of a wide range of filters for the 30 individual securities in the Dow-Jones index. The period involved was between 1957 and 1962 and the total number of observations ranged between 1,200 and 1,700 per share. After taking commissions into account, filter rules failed to provide as profitable a strategy as that obtained from buying and holding the securities.

If profits can be made by studying past behaviour, it would be expected that daily share prices would exhibit a degree of serial correlation. Serial correlation would be positively signed if a change one day is followed by a change in the same direction the following day. Filter rules should pick up such changes. However, it may be that changes in one direction would be followed by changes in the opposite direction the following day; that is, price reversal takes place. Filter rules would not pick up such changes but an examination of the degree of serial correlation would detect such price movements. In fact, most studies of serial correlation of daily changes in security prices have failed to reveal many significant coefficients (e.g. Fama 1965).

8.6.2 *Event studies*

Event studies examine the behaviour of share prices following an announcement of an event such as a merger or profits warning (or for that matter an announcement of increased profits). One problem with such studies is the dual hypothesis problem mentioned in chapter 7 (section 7.5). Generally, event studies require a model to explain the share price and ascertain whether the actual price diverges from the theoretical price. Two examples of event studies are free from this restraint. These are 'stock splits' and 'stock dividends'. In the former case the shares are split into smaller units – say shares of £5 nominal value instead of £10 each. The resulting nominal value of capital remains unchanged but it is represented by a larger number of shares denominated in proportionately smaller value (50 per cent in the example quoted above). Stock dividends occur where dividends are paid in shares instead of cash. In both cases the underlying value of the company remains unchanged. Consequently the aggregate value of the firm should remain unchanged. In fact the empirical evidence supports this view (e.g. Fama *et al*. 1969). This perhaps represents the 'cleanest' information concerning the efficiency of stock markets.

8.6.3   *Private information*

On the other hand, there is alternative evidence of some forecasters being able to 'beat' the market. First, regarding predictive evidence, Dimson and Marsh (1984) describe a study covering 3,364 share one-year horizon forecasts by a number of brokers for a large UK investment institution during the calendar years 1981 and 1982. They found that acting on these forecasts produced profitable trading. Similarly Bjerring *et al*. (1983) examined the profitability of the recommendations of a Canadian brokerage house for forecasts involving both US and Canadian stocks. After allowing for transaction costs Bjerring *et al*. calculated that an investor who followed the recommended list would make 9.3 per cent more than those who bought and held the market. Finally, Value Line in the US categorises stocks according to the expected performance over the next 12 months. The prediction of Value Line is good – see for example Stickel (1985) – enabling above-market returns to be obtained. These forecasts suggest either that the analysts have information not fully incorporated into the share price (insider information) or confirm that they are good forecasters compared with other market forecasters.

Other evidence against the efficient markets hypothesis as applied to the stock market comes from two different sources: the volatility of the prices of stocks; and the so-called anomaly literature.

The first attack on the efficient markets hypothesis came from the observed volatility of share price changes. This work is particularly associated with Shiller (e.g. 1981). Shiller studied the aggregate dividends and earnings of the Standard and Poor index from 1871 to 1979. This information was used to calculate what the price of the index should be if investors possessed perfect foresight. The actual value of the index was more volatile and this led Shiller to conclude that the market was excessively volatile, which could be explained only by irrational behaviour of the operators. The method involved may be illustrated quite easily with reference to a single share. Define the perfect foresight market value (V^*) as:

$$V^*_t = \Sigma \delta^{t+k} D_{t+k} \tag{8.3}$$

where $\delta = 1/(1 + R)$ is the discount factor. D represent dividends and R is the constant real rate of return.

The rational expected value of V^*_t is equal to the observed value V_t plus a random uncorrelated error term e_t, that is:

$$V^*_t = V_t + e_t$$

This leads to the variance bound:

$$\text{Var}(V^*) > \text{Var}(V) \tag{8.4}$$

However, it has been argued (see Kleidon 1986) that it is inappropriate to use time series data from one economy to construct variance bounds and that the correct method would be to derive cross-section statistics for expectations and realisations from identical economies.

The second criticism involves the anomaly literature discovering that prices vary according to an unusual pattern. Typical examples are the fact that returns measured from the close of Friday to the close of Monday are typically negative over a wide range of securities (see e.g. Gibbons and Hess 1980). Blume and Friend (1974) showed that there were large differences between the returns on large firms and those on small firms and these differences were not explainable by models of security pricing. It was also noticed that the majority of these differences occurred in January (Keim 1986). These anomalies are difficult to explain within the context of acceptance of the efficient markets hypothesis.

The efficiency of the stock market is still an open question but a growing volume of evidence may point to a refutation of this hypothesis in its extreme form. The question of whether this evidence is sufficient to claim that the LSE does not approximate an efficient market remains a question of judgement.

8.7   Conclusion

In this chapter we have focused on the market in London for equities. We have shown that only a small proportion of new finance is raised by way of new issues of equities and the major source of finance for UK firms is the ploughing back of profits. We have also discussed the competitive pressures on the LSE that led to a fundamental change in trading arrangements for the secondary market in 1986. This introduced the system of market makers providing firm quotes on a continuous basis. This system served the LSE well for a number of years. However, competitive pressures from European exchanges forced it to re-examine its trading arrangements and as a consequence a hybrid trading system has emerged whereby most trades in FT-SE 100 shares are traded through an electronic order book whilst trading in remaining shares takes place through market makers. It is too early to comment on the success of the switch to electronic trading. The trend throughout the world, however, is towards electronic order matching. Finally, the extent to which the equities market conforms to the efficient markets hypothesis was examined and we were unable to reach an unambiguous conclusion in one direction or the other.

Chapter 9

Interest rates and the bond market

9.1   Introduction

In this chapter the main foci of discussion are the bond market (in particular the market for gilt-edged securities) and the term structure of interest rates. We have linked these two topics together because the discussion of the term structure of interest rates is mainly conducted in the context of government securities. As an introduction, in section 9.2 we briefly discuss the reasons why different securities have different interest rates. In section 9.3 we survey the differing theories of the level of interest rates. In section 9.4 we examine the general nature of bonds followed in section 9.5 by a look at the market for UK government securities (gilt-edged market) in terms of new issues, secondary market trading and the recent innovations of gilt repos and gilt strips. In section 9.6 we briefly examine the nature of corporate bonds and credit ratings. In the final section we examine the term structure of interest rates or why interest rates on securities vary according their term to maturity. In particular we discuss the three main theories which explain the term structure and review some of the evidence relating to these theories.

9.2   The structure of interest rates

Two interest rates are quoted in the press. The lower figure represents the rate at which funds are accepted on deposit (the 'bid' rate) and the higher figure the rate at which the institution is prepared to lend out funds (the 'offer' rate). At the outset of the discussion it is necessary to emphasise that interest rates on different securities differ for a number of reasons, in particular:

(i)   the risk of default,
(ii)   the cost of administering the security,

Table 9.1   *Selected one-month money market rates (offer rates)*

Treasury bills	Bank bills	Sterling CDs
$7^1/_4$	$7^9/_{32}$	$7^7/_{16}$

Source: *Financial Times*, 'London money market rates', 6 March 1998.

(iii) tax arrangements,
(iv) the term of the security.

Discussion of the relationship between interest rates and the term of a security is carried out in section 9.7. Clearly, the risk of default is an important determinant of the difference between interest rates charged to different borrowers. Market arbitrage should equalise the risk-adjusted rate of return rather than the actual rate itself. The role of risk can be illustrated with reference to the structure of rates for one-month securities on the London money markets at close of trading on 5 March 1998, shown in table 9.1. It can be seen that these short rates rise slightly as the risk of default (almost non-existent on the first security) increases.

Later in this chapter we investigate the market for bonds, both government-issued and corporate-issued bonds. The default risk associated with government bonds is virtually non-existent (as with Treasury bills in table 9.1) as the government can always increase taxes or print money to pay off its obligations. The return on these bonds is therefore termed the risk-free return. The return on corporate bonds will generally be higher than on UK government-issued bonds as investors perceive a greater risk of default. The difference between the risk-free return and the rate of interest on securities with default risk is termed the risk premium, and this indicates how much additional interest must be paid so that an investor is willing to hold the risky security.

The other factors are fairly easily dealt with. Very small loans at, say, pawnbrokers incur not only a high risk but are also costly to administer, with the result that the interest rate charges involved are also high. Tax arrangements differ between financial securities, with some being tax exempt and others bearing taxes at the normal rates. Clearly, it would be anticipated that the rates charged would differ in such circumstances.

A final distinction must be made between nominal and real rates of interest. The nominal rate is the rate paid on the loan or security whereas the real rate is the rate paid after making allowance for inflation. The relation between these two rates is shown below:

$$(1 + R) = (1 + i)(1 + E\Delta p) \tag{9.1}$$

where R is the nominal rate and i is the real rate (both rates applying to a single period) and $E\Delta p$ is the rate of inflation expected during the period to maturity.

Simplifying equation 9.1 produces:

$$R = i + E\Delta p + iE\Delta p \tag{9.2}$$

Since the last term on the right-hand side is the product of two decimals, which are both likely to be small, the relationship may be approximated by:

$$R = i + E\Delta p \tag{9.2a}$$

Equation 9.2a is the normal formula used to link the real rate of interest and the nominal rate (often called the Fisher equation). Market efficiency suggests that short-term, nominal rates of interest for differing maturities should therefore be a function of both the real rate for the relevant maturity and the level of inflation expected during the maturity of the security. We return to this topic in the next chapter, in section 10.5.

9.3   The level of interest rates

The level of interest rates can be considered to be an index or some average value around which individual interest rates vary according to the factors discussed above. This is the approach taken in basic macro-economic textbooks which discuss the determination of 'the' rate of interest via IS and LM curves. In this connection two distinct theories can be discerned: the monetary approach, and loanable funds theory.

The monetary (not monetarist) approach explains the level of interest rates in terms of the demand for and supply of money. Typically, money demand equations depend on factors such as real income, rate(s) of interest on money (this may be implicit or a convenience yield) and alternative assets and possibly inflation, and incorporate some form of dynamic adjustment to the desired long-run equilibrium. Money supply is normally specified to depend on a variety of rates of interest, such as those paid on deposits and earned on bank loans, and the monetary base. Non-domestic factors can be allowed for by the inclusion of foreign rates of interest in both the demand and supply functions. The equilibrium rate of interest then follows from the equality of the demand for and the supply of money. In terms of the economy as a whole these are of course only the proximate determinants of the level of interest rates because the levels of real income and other explanatory variables will themselves be determined within the context of a simultaneous model, at the same time as the interest rate. Notice this explanation is in terms of stocks. Increases in the rate of interest can be due to either an increased demand for money or a reduction in the supply of money.

In contrast, the loanable funds approach emphasises flows in the form of the demand and supply of credit by the various sectors, including the overseas sector. In turn, savings come from the financial surpluses of the various sectors in the form of excess of income over expenditure. The main sources of savings come from personal savings and retained profits by firms. At times, however, the overseas sector provides credit by way of balance-of-payments capital inflows. Borrowings are required to finance either consumption or investment expenditure. For ease of exposition in the following narrative we shall assume that borrowing to finance consumption expenditure can be considered as negative saving and that all borrowings are made for the purpose of financing investment. Links to the monetary sector are introduced via increases in the money supply being representative of an additional source of credit but provided by the banks. Similarly, increases in the demand for money (technically known as hoarding) are akin to a demand for loanable funds. Hence the supply of loanable funds can be defined to be the sum of saving (S) plus increases in the money supply (ΔM) whereas the demand for loanable funds is specified as investment (I) plus increased demand for money (ΔH). Thus, the equilibrium rate of interest is determined by the equality of the demand and supply schedules for loanable funds, that is, where:

$$I + \Delta H = S + \Delta M \tag{9.3}$$

It is argued that both investment and saving are functions of the rate of interest, with savings increasing and investment declining as the domestic rate of interest rises. The allocation of savings to and borrowings from overseas as opposed to domestic sources will depend on the relative levels of domestic and foreign rates after taking into consideration the prospects of exchange rate changes during the period of the loan. The other two components may in the main reflect changes in taste (hoarding) and government policy and so can be considered as an addition to the interest rate components. However, this is not a vital assumption since, if anything, the money supply is likely to increase and hoarding to decrease as domestic interest rates rise, in the same manner as savings and investment.

Equilibrium in the credit market is demonstrated in figure 9.1. Increases in the rate of interest can, according to this approach, be

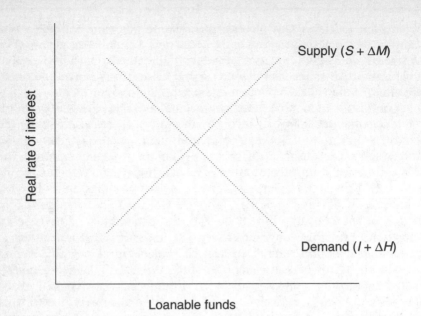

Figure 9.1   *Real rate of interest as a function of the supply of loanable funds*

caused by an increase in the demand (i.e. a shift in the demand curve to the right) for loanable funds attributable to increased investment or hoarding or a reduction in the supply (i.e. a shift in the supply curve to the left) due to reduced saving or a reduction in the money supply. A rise in the foreign rate of interest (given expectations of future interest rate changes) would also cause a rise in domestic rates through a reduction in supply of, and an increase in demand for, domestic loanable funds. It should be noted that this explanation of the level of interest rates emphasises real factors, such as productivity determining investment opportunities and saving as a function of thrift, so that the rate of interest is the real rate.

Although the two theories have a different rationale, they are consistent with each other to a considerable degree. First, long-run equilibrium requires that both:

(i)   savings equal investment (using the broad definitions adopted in this section);
(ii)   changes in the money supply equal changes in the demand for money.

Second, the predictions of the two theories are the same following, for example, an increase in the quantity of money. Similarly, an increase in investment will raise the rate of interest directly in the case of the loanable funds theory and indirectly in the case of the liquidity preference (i.e. monetary) theory via the resulting increase in income raising the demand for money. A possible reconciliation is that the liquidity preference theory applies mainly to the short run, where for example factors in the money market are predominant, whereas the loanable funds theory is more relevant to the long run, where agents have sufficient time to adjust their expenditure and financing plans.

9.4 Nature and valuation of bonds

In the UK, fixed-interest securities, or bonds as they are more commonly referred to, are issued by the government (gilt-edged securities) or companies. The main issuer of bonds in the UK is the government. What we briefly examine here is the nature and valuation of these securities. They are long-term securities, with an original maturity of over one year, although normally the original maturity is well above one year and can be over 20 years. They pay a fixed rate of interest, at set intervals until maturity, called a coupon. For UK gilt-edged securities the interval is every six months. Another characteristic of a bond is its par value, which refers to the price at which the bond is redeemed at maturity. In the UK the par value is £100. This is not necessarily the price at which the bond is issued – they may be issued at a discount or premium to the par value. As with equity securities, discussed in chapter 8, the value of a bond is calculated as the present value of the stream of future cash flows generated by the security. These cash flows are the regular (known) coupon payments plus the (known) redemption value payable on the maturity date. Thus the value of a bond can be found using the following expression:

$$P_0 = C_1/(1 + i) + C_2/(1 + i)^2 + C_3/(1 + i)^3 + \dots$$
$$+ C_n/(1 + i)^n + M_n/(1 + i)^n \qquad (9.4)$$

where P_0 is the price of the fixed-interest security at time 0 (the present); C_n is the fixed-interest (coupon) payment at time n; M is the redemption value of the security; i is the discount rate.

To take an example, Treasury 7% 2001 is a UK government-issued bond which pays £7 per annum to its holder and has a maturity date of 2001, at which time the holder of the bond will be paid the redemption value, which is £100. If we assume that there are three years left to maturity and the interest is paid annually (in fact UK gilts pay interest semi-annually but we ignore this to simplify the analysis[1]), then given a discount rate of 10 per cent and using expression 9.4, the value of the bond is:

$$P = 7/(1.10) + 7/(1.10)^2 + 7/(1.10)^3 + 100/(1.10)^3$$
$$P = £92.54$$

Thus a fair price to pay for the bond is £92.54. This does not mean the price in the market will be £92.54 as other factors affecting supply and demand for the bond may lead the price to diverge from its fair price.

9.5   The market for UK government bonds (gilt-edged securities)

In this section we examine the reasons why the UK government issues bonds, the methods of issue of these bonds and the market for trading the bonds after they have been issued.

9.5.1   *The government's borrowing requirement*

The central government requires finance to meet the surplus of its expenditure over revenue and to meet the cost of refinancing debt as it matures. Further funds may be necessary to cover the cost of inter-vention in the foreign exchange markets. If the government intervenes to push the exchange rate down, this entails the selling of sterling on the foreign exchange markets in return for convertible currency reserves. Thus, finance has to be raised over and above that required for purely domestic purposes. In contrast, intervention to push the exchange rate up involves the loss of convertible currency reserves and a gain of sterling finance, thus reducing the amount of finance that needs to be raised for purely domestic purposes. Consequently, even if the central government is in fiscal balance during any one year, new issues of debt may be necessary to refinance maturing existing debt and to finance intervention

---

1   The formula for bonds where the coupon is paid more frequently is:
$$P_0 = (C_1/f)/(1 + i/f) + (C_2/f)/(1 + i/f)^{2f} + (C_3/f)/(1 + i/f)^{3f} + \dots$$
$$+ (C_n/f)/(1 + i/f)^{nf} + M_n/(1 + i/f)^{nf}$$
where the symbols are as defined before save f, which is the frequency of payment and the Cs, which are the annual coupon payments. Thus for the example quoted above with the coupon paid half yearly the value of the bond is:
$$P = 3.5/(1.05) + 3.5/(1 + 0.05)^2 + 3.5/(1 + 0.05)^3 + 3.5/(1 + 0.05)^4 +$$
$$3.5/(1 + 0.05)^5 + 3.5/(1 + 0.05)^6 + 100/(1 + 0.05)^6$$
$$= £92.4; \text{ i.e. almost approximately the annual compounding in this case.}$$

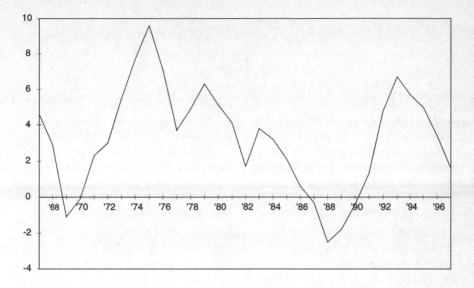

Figure 9.2 *UK PSBR as a percentage of GDP, 1967–97. Source: Bank of England,* Gilts and the Gilt-Market Review 1996–7

in the foreign exchange market though, of course, this last component may be negative. Any finance that may be necessary is obtained through the issue of new securities of a variety of types and maturities including:

(i) bonds, termed gilt-edged securities,
(ii) non-marketable debt such as National Savings and tax reserve certificates,
(iii) Treasury bills.

Most government debt issues, by value, are in the form of gilt-edged securities. Figure 9.2 shows the PSBR over the period 1967 to 1997 expressed as a percentage of GDP. This ratio therefore shows the financial deficit of the public sector in relation to the output of the economy. Note that one of the Maastricht criteria that had to be satisfied before a country could enter stage 3 of EMU is for the government budget deficit to GDP ratio to be less than 3 per cent (see chapter 15).

One feature of figure 9.2 is the move into budget surplus in the period 1987–90. Some of this surplus was due to the revenue achieved from the sale of assets through the policy of privatisation but the remainder is due to a positive fiscal balance. The surplus meant that the markets tended to be short of funds, causing upward pressure on interest rates. As we discuss in chapter 10, this forced the Bank of England to intervene in the discount market by purchasing commercial bills of exchange, thus providing extra funds for the discount market. The other side of this coin was of course the bill mountain, that is, the stock of commercial bills held by the Bank of England as a result of purchases in the market. The early 1990s saw the UK economy in recession, with a consequent rise in the PSBR as tax revenues fell and welfare spending increased. As the economy has grown again since 1993 the PSBR as a percentage of GDP has fallen to the extent that by the end of 1997 the ratio was 1.6 per cent, which is below that required for entry into the single currency. Ironically though the UK government announced in late 1997 that it would not enter the single currency at its starting date of January 1999.

Turning now to the various methods of raising finance, we have already discussed the nature of Treasury bills in chapter 1. These are money market instruments, normally with a three-month maturity, issued by the government. They are an instrument traditionally used by the Bank of England for managing its operations in the money markets and do not contribute in a significant way to financing the government's deficit. Sales of non-marketable debt are achieved by varying the returns on National Savings from time to time, according to prevailing interest rate conditions. In addition, major innovations are made, though very infrequently. Such innovations include the introduction of premium bonds and index-linked National Savings. In the next section we consider the issue of gilt-edged securities, which are the main instrument for funding the government's debt.

9.5.2   Gilt-edged securities market: new issues

The management of government debt has traditionally been undertaken by the Bank of England. However, from April 1998 this role was transferred to the Debt Management Office, an agency of the Treasury. This transfer coincides with the government's decision to give the responsibility for setting short-term interest rates to the Bank of England. The reasons cited by the government to explain this transfer of debt management responsibility are:

(i)   inside information – the gilts market may charge a premium if debt management is believed to be open to influence from inside information on interest rate decisions to the detriment of private investors;

(ii) possible conflict of interest – monetary policy considerations may have had an influence on debt management policy.

Despite a change in responsibility for debt management there has been no significant change in policy arising out of the change.

Gilt-edge securities can be separated into two main categories: conventional and index-linked. Conventional issues are standard issues of gilts paying a fixed-rate coupon. Index-linked gilts are securities whose coupon and redemption value are adjusted to account for movement in the retail price index, with a time lag of eight months. They therefore provide a hedge against inflation. The cost, to investors, of providing this hedge is a lower nominal coupon payment compared with conventional gilts.

The main method for the issue of conventional gilts is through regular auctions. In 1997 all conventional issues were through the auction method. With this method all stock is sold to the highest bidders and the issue is not underwritten. Occasionally the Bank of England has supplied conventional gilts to the market as a tap stock. With this method the Bank would take some stock on to its own books and then sell this over a period of time in its dealings with gilt-edged market makers (GEMMs) – see section 9.5.3. This is a flexible method of issue allowing the issue to sold to the market at times when there is a demand for it. For index-linked gilts the only method of issue in 1997 was the tap issue; however, at the time of writing (spring 1998) consultation is under way on whether to move to an index-linked auction programme.

9.5.3 *Gilt-edged securities: the secondary market*

Major changes in the market for gilts occurred in October 1986 at the same time as changes to the market for UK equities (Big Bang), discussed in chapter 8. Prior to Big Bang there were eight gilt-edged jobbers, of whom two accounted for 75 per cent of the turnover. The new system of trading created an institution known as a GEMM, who acts in a dual capacity as market maker and broker. GEMMs have an obligation to communicate, on demand, to other market participants continuous and effective bid–ask prices for a wide range of gilts in any trading conditions. GEMMs have a direct dealing arrangement with the Bank of England in gilts such that the Bank will bid to buy gilts from the GEMMs at prices of its own choosing and will respond to bids for gilts from the GEMMs at its discretion. GEMMs are expected to participate actively in the gilts issue process, in particular by bidding competitively at auctions. In return for these obligations GEMMs are given special facilities not available to other gilt market participants. One such facility is that the GEMMs have sole access to the IDB mechanism. The essential purpose of the IDBs is to enable the market makers to unwind their stock positions as and when required without

Table 9.2   *Sectoral holding of gilts, end December 1996 (£billion)*

	Holdings	%
Public sector		
local authorities	0.1	0.1
public corporations	2.0	0.7
Financial companies and institutions		
banks	20.9	7.5
building societies	9.0	3.2
life assurers	92.0	32.8
pension funds	60.5	21.5
other financial institutions	30.8	11.0
Industrial and commercial companies	1.7	0.6
Persons	11.9	4.2
Overseas	51.9	18.5
Total	280.8	100.0

Source: Bank of England, *Gilts and the Gilt Market Review 1996–7.*

trading directly with each other whenever they wish this dealing to be anonymous. A further important support to the market making function is provided by stock exchange money brokers, who both lend stock to the GEMMs and also money generated from their equity lending operations at rates which are competitive with those in the money market. From March 1997 GEMMs are no longer required to be separately capitalised and most GEMMs have assimilated their businesses into group-wide securities trading operations, enabling them to benefit from lower regulatory capital requirements. At the end of 1997 there were 17 GEMMs.

The total nominal value of gilt-edged stock outstanding at the end of 1997 was £295 billion in nominal terms. The market holdings of gilts were made up of approximately 34 per cent 0–7 years of outstanding maturity, 27 per cent 7–15 years, 15 per cent 15 years and above, 20 per cent index-linked stock and 0.7 per cent undated stock. The estimated sectoral holdings of gilts for the end of 1996 are given in table 9.2. This shows that the main holders of gilts are the investment institutions, in particular life assurance funds. The reasons for this are discussed in chapter 6.

9.5.4 *The gilt repo market*

A major new innovation occurred in the gilts market in January 1996 when a gilts repo market was introduced. Repo stands for 'sale and repurchase agreement', where one party sells securities to another party for cash, with an agreement to repurchase those securities at an agreed future date and price. In effect it is a way of borrowing securities, with the seller (or borrower) obtaining better terms than would normally be obtained if they simply borrowed cash. On the other side of the transaction, the buyer of the repo (i.e. the lender of money) should be less concerned about the possibility of default by the borrower since, if default does occur, the lender has the security. Repos then are a form of secured borrowing, or lending.

The introduction of a repo market has allowed repo activity to be widened beyond the existing GEMMs. This has allowed all market operators to adopt a wider range of trading strategies. A common use of the gilt repo is to finance long positions in gilts. By undertaking a purchase of gilts and at the same time repoing that stock (usually repoing it to the seller) an investor can simultaneously take on and finance a long position in the market. Investors can therefore obtain exposure to the market with minimal financing costs. Another strategy made possible by repos is to 'short' the market – selling stock that is not owned. By making trading more flexible it is hoped that the liquidity of the gilt market is enhanced, so increasing the attractiveness of gilts to investors. There is some evidence to suggest that liquidity in the gilt market has improved, with firms able to transact larger deals than previously without moving market rates or spreads against them. The resulting increased demand for gilts should lead to the additional benefit of lower funding costs for the government by several basis points. It is estimated that a reduction in yields of one basis point will eventually lead to an annual reduction in public spending of £25 million.

There are no formal market makers in gilt repos and although GEMMs are active in the market there were at the end of 1997 an additional 20 institutions, mostly banks and securities houses, which quoted repo rates on request. The repo rate is the rate of interest on the cash extended under the agreement. At this early stage of the market's development the activity is concentrated at the very short end of the maturity spectrum, with around 90 per cent of trading at overnight to one week's maturity. However, trades of up to three months are now common and some trading at six months' maturity is taking place. The gilt repo market has developed alongside the existing unsecured money markets, offering an alternative liquid form of funds. By November 1997 the amount of gilt repo outstanding was £72 billion compared with

£100 billion for sterling CDs. It is estimated that about half of all overnight transactions in the sterling money markets is accounted for by gilt repos. Since March 1997 gilt repos have been used in the Bank of England's daily money market operations. This is considered in more detail in chapter 10, section 10.4.

9.5.5   *The gilt strips market*

Another innovation occurred in December 1997 when a facility for 'stripping' gilt-edged securities was introduced. Stripping is the process of separating a conventional coupon-bearing gilt into its constituent interest and principal payments, so they can be separately held or traded as zero-coupon bonds. For example, a two-year gilt (which consists of four semi-annually paid coupons and one payment of principal at the maturity date) could be separated into five zero-coupon bonds. So, after stripping, the coupon payment payable after six months would become a six-month maturity zero-coupon bond, the coupon payment payable after 12 months would become a 12-month maturity zero-coupon bond, and so on. Note that a zero-coupon bond is a bond that pays no coupon payment and its only cash payment is the one paid on maturity of the bond.

Gilt strips, created through the official gilt strips facility, remain direct obligations of the UK government. The advantage to investors of zero-coupon bonds is that they provide a much simpler cash flow structure, which can be used to match liability cash flows more precisely. Not all gilts are strippable and at the end of 1997 eight strippable stocks existed amounting to 30 per cent of total conventional stocks in issue. It is also possible to reconstitute a coupon-bearing gilt from the constituent strips. Both stripping and reconstitution take place through GEMMs.

This completes our discussion of the gilt-edged market and we now turn to examine briefly the corporate bond market and the importance of credit ratings in this market.

9.6   The corporate bond market and credit ratings

Gilt-edged securities are perceived by investors as having virtually zero risk of default as the UK government is the guarantor and is very unlikely to default. Bonds issued by the governments of developing countries are likely to have a higher associated risk of default, as are issues of bonds by companies. The main domestic issuers of sterling bonds other than gilts are UK companies and local authorities. The volume of issues has been variable over the last 20 years and reference to figure 8.1 will give some idea of the magnitude of recent issues. A wide variety of bonds exist. The typical bond offers a fixed return each year (i.e. the coupon) and has a fixed date for redemption. The bond indenture is a contract that states the lender's rights and privileges and the borrower's obligations. Most UK-issued bonds are secured either by specific assets of the issuer or by a floating charge against the issuer's assets, so that in the case of bankruptcy the proceeds from the sale of those assets accrue to the bond holders. Secured bonds in the UK are termed debentures and a mortgage debenture would be a bond secured on specific land or buildings. Bonds that are not secured are termed unsecured loan stock. Other bonds carry what is termed a negative pledge, which commits the company to refrain from subsequently issuing bonds which carry greater security or preference in the event of default by the company. Some bonds also carry the right to convert into equity of the company at specific dates and terms. These are called convertibles.

The risk of default clearly differs for different borrowers and so the returns demanded by investors to induce them to hold bonds will also vary. Investors can obtain information on the likelihood of default or delayed payment of a security from the rating assigned by a credit ratings agency. Originally these ratings were applied solely to corporate bond issues but over recent years coverage has extended to a wide variety of debt instruments: local authority bonds, asset-backed securities, medium-term note programmes (see chapter 12), commercial paper programmes and bank CDs. The main rating agencies are the US-based Moody's Investors Service, and Standard and Poor's (S&P), although many smaller, more specialised agencies have emerged in recent years. Most agencies use their own system of symbols to rank securities according to risk of default. For example, for S&P the highest-quality ranking is AAA and the lowest is D, with a further 19 grades between these two extremes. A distinction is usually made between investment-grade ratings and speculative-grade ratings, with bonds graded BBB or above under the S&P system designated as investment grade. Generally the rating agency charges a fee to the issuer related to the size and type of the issue. Increasingly regulators, particularly in the US, have used the ratings applied to bonds and other debt instruments to simplify their prudential control of financial institutions. For example, the Basle Committee on Bank Supervision proposed in its 1993 market risk guidelines that internationally active commercial banks dealing in securities should hold extra capital against their non-investment-grade bonds.

Table 9.3   *Spreads between corporate bonds and US Treasury bonds, 1973–87 (averages)*

Rating	Basis points
AAA	43
AA	73
A	99
BBB	166
BB	299
B	404
CCC	724

Source: Cantor and Packer (1994).

Given the growth in the credit ratings industry and the increasing reliance being placed on the ratings they produce, it is important to consider their reliability. One study of the reliability of credit ratings, by Cantor and Packer (1994), found that the two main agencies referred to above do a reasonable job of assessing relative credit risks, so that lower-rated bonds were found to default more frequently than higher-rated bonds. However, they also found that assessments of absolute credit risks have been less reliable, as default probabilities associated with specific rankings have drifted over time. This latter result suggests that the use of a specific grade as a cut-off to determine which securities are investment-grade securities, and therefore should be assigned less capital for prudential purposes, is suspect. Cantor and Packer also report the fact that for US corporate bonds the yields are closely related to the rating grade. Table 4 from their article is reproduced as table 9.3 to illustrate this point. Clearly, the yield increases as the credit rating falls and this helps explain why companies are prepared to pay fees to credit rating agencies for this service. However, an important caveat is necessary. The figures in the table do not prove that there is any causal relationship between credit ratings and yields; in other words, the credit ratings may not provide any information in addition to that contained in market prices. It may be that the market had assimilated the available information and produced results similar to those derived by the credit rating agencies.

9.7   The term structure of interest rates

We have seen, in section 9.2, how risk can influence interest rates. Another factor that influences the interest rate on a security is its term to maturity. Securities with identical risk characteristics may have different interest rates because the time remaining to maturity is different. A plot of the yields on securities with differing terms to maturity but the same risk and other characteristics is called a yield curve. First of all we need to define the term yield to maturity as the return on security which is held to maturity. Thus, if we take as an example a three-year bond, redeemable at par (£100) and returning a coupon of £X paid once a year and with a current market price of £V, then solving equation 9.4 for R provides the yield to maturity on that bond:

$$V = X/(1 + R) + X/(1 + R)^2 + X/(1 + R)^3 + 100/(1 + R)^3$$

Notice in this example that we are assuming the interest received is immediately reinvested in the security. The term structure then refers to the differences in yields to maturity on securities, which are identical except for the outstanding (not initial) maturity. The yield curve itself is a representation of the term structure in a graphical form.

It is difficult to find examples of securities identical in all respects save for the outstanding term to maturity, with one major exception. This is for government securities, where the risk of default is virtually zero but more crucially is the same on all issues. For example, the UK government has approximately 80 different issues of gilt-edged securities (at the end of 1997) with similar terms, although differences do occur (e.g. index-linked, undated stock, etc.). Thus, the quantity of different stocks issued is sufficient to derive yield curves. This contrasts with issue of bonds by companies although, in principle, their debt issues would be subject to the same term structure plus a risk premium, which might vary over time, and between different companies. Figure 9.3 depicts some of the patterns of yield curves which have been observed over time. However, it should be noted that yield curves almost always slope upwards.

Consequently any credible theory of the term structure must be able to explain a variety of patterns of yield curves but also explain why the usual pattern is upward sloping. Three theories have been put forward to explain the term structure of interest rates: the expectations theory; the preferred market habitat theory; and the market segmentation theory. We now consider each of these theories in turn.

9.7.1 *The expectations theory of the term structure*

The expectations theory explains the term structure of interest rates as being a function of rates of interest expected to exist in the future. Thus, for example, if short-term interest rates were expected to rise, it would

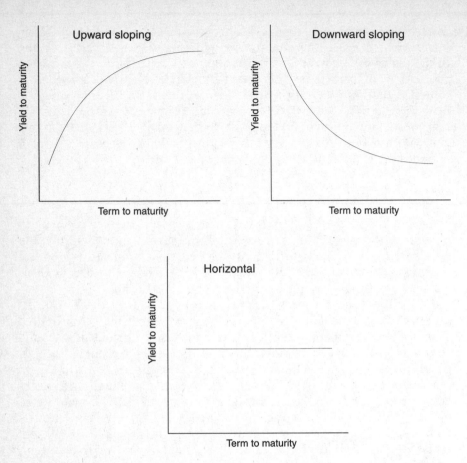

Figure 9.3   *Observed yield curve shapes*

be reasonable to assume that long-term rates encompassing the period of those future short-term rates would be higher than current short-term rates. According to this theory, arbitrage ensures that the return for holding different securities for a specific period will be the same irrespective of their outstanding maturity. This is the basis of the expectations theory and in the following paragraphs we critically examine this theory. We make the following preliminary assumptions:

(i)   agents possess perfect foresight, so they know all current and future interest rates;
(ii)   a perfect capital market exists;

(iii) interest is paid once a year and is immediately reinvested in the same bonds;

(iv) two classes of bonds only are available –
    (a) a one-year bond,
    (b) a three-year bond,
both of which are issued at par;

(v) the investor has a holding period of three years, that is, he or she wishes to invest funds for three years.

Assumptions (iii) to (v) are merely simplifying assumptions to facilitate the exposition. Assumption (i) is clearly unrealistic and is made as a temporary aid to the explanation and will be relaxed later in this section. The second assumption is one normally made in the analysis and implies the absence of transaction costs, a spread between buying and selling prices and so on. It is a useful approximation to the truth as long as it is realised that the resulting predictions are likely to be less precise in practice.

Investors then have a choice of investment strategies. They can either buy a three-year bond or alternatively buy a sequence of one-year bonds, reinvesting the proceeds as the first two bonds mature. The choice of which strategy to follow will depend on which offers the higher return. Consequently arbitrage and market clearing will force the yields on the two strategies to be equal. For example, if the yield on the three-year bond is higher then agents will buy three-year bonds at the expense of one-year bonds. This raises the yield on one-year bonds (lowers the price) and lowers the yield (raises the price) on three-year bonds. The converse would apply if the yield on one-year bonds was higher than that on three-year bonds. Thus, given the assumptions made, market clearing ensures that:

$$(1 + {}_tR_3)^3 = (1 + {}_tR_1)(1 + {}_{t+1}R_1)(1 + {}_{t+2}R_1) \qquad (9.5)$$

where the first subscript applied to R refers to the time to which the interest rate pertains (i.e. t represents year 1, $t + 1$ represents year 2, etc.) and the second subscript the time period of the rate (e.g. 1 is the one-year rate and 3 the three-year rate). The term on the left-hand side represents the return from purchasing a three-year bond at time t and that on the right-hand side the return from investing in a succession of one-year bonds for three years. Consequently the three-year rate can be expressed as the geometric average of the current and subsequent one-year rates. Note also that we have ignored the redemption of the bonds at the end of year 3 because the sum obtained would be the same in both cases.

Patently, the assumption of perfect foresight is absurd if applied to the real world and must therefore be relaxed. This entails replacing the known future rates with their expected values, denoted as $E_{t\ t+1}R_1$ and so on. The first subscript (t) refers to the time period at which expectations are formed and the second subscript the time period over which the rate is to hold. At this stage we introduce another assumption at the same time as relaxing that of perfect foresight. This is the assumption that the agents are risk neutral, that is, they are indifferent to risk due to the uncertainty of the future interest rate (not default) and motivated solely by the return on the security. In this case market equilibrium would for all practical purposes be the same as that given perfect certainty but with the expected values replacing the perfect foresight variables, and would therefore be represented by:

$$(1 + {}_tR_3)^3 = (1 + {}_tR_1)(1 + E_{t\ t+1}R_1)(1 + E_{t\ t+2}R_1) \tag{9.5a}$$

So now the three-year rate is the geometric average of the known one-year rate and the expected future one-year rates. More generally, any long-term rate can be decomposed into a series of short-term rates and for the one-period rates (R) the equilibrium condition can be shown as:

$$(1 + {}_tR_n)^n = (1 + {}_tR_1)(1 + E_{t\ t+1}R_1)(1 + E_{t\ t+2}R_1) \ldots$$
$$(1 + E_{t\ t+n-1}R_1) \tag{9.6}$$

Solving for R_n gives:

$$R_n = \{(1 + {}_tR_1)(1 + E_{t\ t+1}R_1)(1 + E_{t\ t+2}R_1) \ldots$$
$$(1 + E_{t\ t+n-1}R_1)\}^{1/n} - 1 \tag{9.7}$$

showing that the long-term rate will be the geometric average of the current known and future expected short-term rates into which it can be decomposed. This result is perfectly general and is not restricted to the one-period rates used for the above demonstration.

We now look at the predictions of the expectations theory. First, the shape of the yield curve reflects expectations of future interest rates. Thus, if interest rates are expected to rise in the future, the yield curve will slope upwards, whereas if they are expected to fall, a downward-sloping yield curve will be observed. The second prediction follows from this dependence on expectations of future interest rate movements. The relative supply of securities with different maturities will not affect the yield curve. This has implications for government policy. If the expectations theory is correct, it is irrelevant, in terms of the impact on the economy, whether the authorities intervene at the short or long end of the market. Arbitrage will cause the shape of the yield curve to remain the same in either case, since the long rates will retain the same relationship to short-term rates given by expectations. Arbitrage will also ensure that inflation expectations are incorporated into the term structure via their impact on current and expected short-term rates. Finally, external effects would also be included via the interest rate parity condition applying to the various term rates.

The expectations theory is open to a number of objections. First, over long periods of time upward-sloping yield curves are more commonly observed in the markets than other shapes. Whilst it is certainly true that interest rates have tended to rise since the 1950s, this is unlikely to be sufficient to account for the general preponderance of upward-sloping yield curves. It is likely that some other factor has also been at work. The second source of criticism is that the degree of forecasting ability credited to market operators is to say the least excessive. Is it really credible to assume the existence of agents able to forecast future movements of interest rates for a large number of years ahead? The third objection arises in connection with forecasting difficulties. The existence of uncertainty regarding future movements in interest rates casts doubts on the appropriateness of the assumption of risk neutrality. Casual observation of portfolios suggests diversification, rather than concentration of asset holdings in areas where the highest expected mean returns exist, as would be suggested by the dominance of risk-neutral operators. Similar to the third objection is the problem of the potential existence of diverse expectations which, according to the expectations theory, would suggest an infinite amount of dealing between operators. The problem of the existence of diverse expectations can be accommodated by appealing to pragmatic considerations such as transaction costs or limitations on borrowing, which, in practice, prevent unlimited dealing between operators.

We now turn to an examination of the preferred market habitat theory, which meets these objections to some extent.

9.7.2 *The preferred market habitat theory of the term structure*

The preferred market habitat theory assumes that market operators are in fact risk averse, that is, they are unwilling to incur extra risk without some extra reward in the form of a premium. Given that the risks on long-term securities are greater than those on short-term securities, it would be expected that long-term rates would be higher than short-term rates; that is, the yield curve would normally slope upwards. This does not imply that expectations of future rates are irrelevant and, as we shall see in the following explanation, these expectations will be incorporated into the yield curve.

It is believed that there is a difference between the preferences of lenders and borrowers. Lenders will prefer to hold short-term securities so that they can liquidate their loans more easily in the event of cash shortages. In contrast borrowers prefer to borrow long term so as to obtain greater security of funding. This is another illustration of the conflicting requirements of lenders and borrowers encountered generally in direct financing (see chapter 2). This divergence of preferences is reinforced as far as the lenders are concerned since long-term lending involves a greater degree of risk, as the future is uncertain and the market prices of long-term securities fluctuate more than those of short-term securities. Note the risk that we are considering is not one of default since the securities are identical in this respect by assumption. The logical consequence of these points is that lenders demand, and borrowers are prepared to pay, a risk premium for long-term lending over the rates for short-term lending. The risk premium is also likely to rise as the term of lending increases and may vary over time according to the degree of uncertainty present. The important point is that the risk premium is unlikely to be constant. Hence a risk premium (L) is introduced into the market clearing equilibrium discussed earlier, so that agents will enter arbitrage arrangements only if the gain is greater than the risk premium. This means that the long-term rate will be greater than the geometric average of the current actual and future expected short-term rates. More formally the equilibrium condition described by equation 9.6 has to be replaced by:

$$(1 + {}_tR_n)^n = (1 + {}_tR_1 + L_1)(1 + E_{t\,t+1}R_1 + L_2)(1 + E_{t\,t+2}R_1 + L_3) \dots$$
$$(1 + E_{t\,t+n-1}R_1 + L_n) \tag{9.8}$$

where $L_n > L_{n-1} > \dots L_1$.

Similarly, solving for R_n, it is necessary to replace equation 9.7 with:

$$R_n = \{(1 + {}_tR_1 + L_1)(1 + E_{t\,t+1}R_1 + L_2)(1 + E_{t\,t+2}R_1 + L_3) \dots$$
$$(1 + E_{t\,t+n-1}R_1 + L_n)\}^{1/n} - 1 \tag{9.9}$$

Note that in this theory expectations still play an important role but their impact is modified by the existence of a risk premium. This leads to the prediction that the normal shape of the yield curve will be upward sloping owing to the existence of the risk premium but that downward-sloping yield curves will be observed in instances when the expected fall in interest rates is sufficient to offset the risk premium. Debts of the various maturities are no longer perfect substitutes for each other, so that changing the relative supply of debt with different maturities will, according to this theory, alter the term structure and the shape of the yield curve.

Moving from postulating that debts with different maturities are imperfect substitutes to the belief that no substitution at all is possible leads to the market segmentation theory.

9.7.3 *Market segmentation theory of the term structure*

The essence of this approach to the explanation of the term structure is that there are completely separate markets for debt of different maturities. Substitution between these markets is not possible, which explains the title of market segmentation. This leads to the prediction that the shape of the yield curve reflects the differing demand and supply conditions in the various markets. It is quite plausible to see the bond market as segmented, with investment institutions such as pension funds and the life assurance companies preferring to operate at the long-term end, and with banks and building societies, for which liquidity is more critical, preferring to operate at the short-term end.

In this extreme form it is easy to be critical of the view that no substitution is possible. For example, if it is felt that long-term rates are more attractive than short-term returns, it is not necessary for, say, five-year bonds to be substituted for three-month Treasury bills. All that is necessary is that portfolios go longer so that, say, five-year debt is substituted for four-year bonds in one portfolio and, say, two-year bonds for one-year bonds in another. Substitution over small but overlapping segments of the maturity spectrum means substitution over the whole spectrum. A ripple effect will occur so that in the end the more attractive (in terms of yield) longer-term debt has been substituted for shorter-term debt across portfolios in total until equilibrium is restored.

We have completed our review of the theory of the term structure and now move on to examine briefly the relevant empirical evidence.

9.7.4 *Empirical evidence on the term structure*

Early empirical studies tended to favour the expectations theory. For example, Modigliani and Shiller (1973), building on earlier work by Modigliani and Sutch (1966), approached the problem of testing the role of expectations in the term structure by obtaining forecasts of short-term rates and then examining how well these forecasts explained the term structure in conjunction with a risk premium. Forecasts of future rates were based on averages of past observed nominal rates and inflation, on the grounds that the expected nominal rate could be considered to be the sum of expected real rate and the expected rate of inflation. The estimating equations were quite satisfactory, with a high degree of explanatory power and well determined coefficients. Further support for the role of expectations was obtained by Meiselman (1962), who, using an error correction model, found firm evidence of correlation between forecasting errors and the changes in the expected one-year rates implied by the expectations hypothesis. The way these are derived can easily be seen by assuming a two-year holding period and the existence of only one-year and two-year bonds. In this case, according to the expectations hypothesis, market clearing would require that:

$$(1 + {}_tR_2)^2 = (1 + {}_tR_1)(1 + E_{t\,t+1}R_1) \tag{9.10}$$

The expected short rate implied by the expectations theory can then be obtained by solving for $E_{t\,t+1}R_1$ from equation 9.10 to obtain:

$$1 + E_{t\,t+1}R_1 = (1 + {}_tR_2)^2/(1 + {}_tR_1) \tag{9.11}$$

Further evidence supporting the role of expectations in the determination of the term structure came indirectly from the difficulty in identifying any role for supply-side effects in the form of alterations in the available quantities of securities with differing maturities (see for example Malkiel (1966) for the US and Goodhart and Gowland (1977) for the UK). Possibly the apparent absence of these effects can be attributed to the authorities supplying debt with maturities which compensate for any changes in relative yields.

Subsequently, however, the role of expectations in the determination of the term structure has come under attack from two sources. First, similar to our discussion of excess volatility in chapter 8, section 8.4, with reference to the stock market, the volatility of long rates seems excessive (see for example Shiller 1979). The second line of attack concerns the behaviour of short-term rates. Sargent (1972) noted that short rates exhibit a high degree of first-order correlation, so that estimation of equations of the form:

$$R_t = b + R_{t-1} \tag{9.12}$$

produces estimates of b greater than 0.8 and often not significantly different from unity, thus implying a random walk. This information should be incorporated into expectations of future short-term interest rates but evidence by Sargent (1972) for the US and Goodhart and Gowland (1977) for the UK suggests that the revision of expected rates is less than that implied by the observed historical autoregressive properties. This characteristic has more destructive implications for the expectations theory of the term structure. Since long rates underpredict changes in short rates, any movement in short rates would alter the slope of the yield curve. Thus, for example, an increase in short-term rates would produce less than appropriate changes in long rates, so that the slope of the yield curve would tend to decrease (assuming that it was upward sloping for purposes of exposition) or even become negative if the change in short rates was sufficiently large. Goodhart (1989) points out that on balance the long rate has tended to fall when the yield curve is upward sloping and rise when it is downward sloping. In the case of a major fall in short rates this also has the implication that operators could profit from selling long-term bonds since it is likely that long rates will rise (i.e. bond prices fall) in the future. Evidence by Mankiw and Summers (1984) suggests this directional failure is also matched by an inability of the term structure to predict future short-term rates of interest.

This survey of the empirical evidence has of necessity been brief and we have merely tried to identify the important strands of the literature. For further detail the reader is referred to Goodhart (1989) and the original studies. Nevertheless, we have covered sufficient ground to indicate the main areas of controversy and to draw the conclusion yet again that the efficiency of yet another financial market, in this case the bond market, is an open question.

Chapter 10

The sterling money markets

10.1 Introduction

The sterling money markets located in London are markets for short-term funds and consequently provide facilities for economic units to adjust their cash position quickly. The rationale for their existence is that receipts of and payments in cash are not generally synchronised. Quite large cash balances are needed if these variations in payments made and received are to be accommodated. The problem here is that cash holdings provide either no or a very low return, so that the opportunity cost of holding large working balances is quite high. If on the other hand markets exist which can, at short notice and with low transaction costs, absorb surplus cash and also provide facilities for borrowing, then agents can economise on cash holdings and earn a higher rate of return on the deposits made in the money markets. Thus, cash positions can be adjusted by placing funds on deposit in the money markets when cash balances are temporarily too high and withdrawing or borrowing funds when the balance is too low. The success of this strategy depends on the existence of well functioning markets which can offer facilities for such transactions by catering for short-term deposits or lending without large fluctuations in rates of interest. This is particularly true of the banks themselves, which keep their working balances at the Bank of England and no interest is paid on these balances. Therefore the banks have a clear incentive to reduce these balances to the absolute minimum.

Sections 10.2 and 10.3 of this chapter review the assets traded in the money and other markets. The Bank of England's operation of monetary policy is reviewed in section 10.4 before proceeding to a brief review of the extent to which short-term rates of interest incorporate inflation expectations, in section 10.5. The institutional detail covering the banks

212

is discussed in chapters 3 and 4 and the reader may find it necessary to refer to these chapters in order to appreciate the following analysis.

10.2 Assets traded on the money markets

Since the money markets are concerned with short-term funds it is only natural to expect that the assets traded on such markets will also be of a short-term nature. Such assets can be neatly divided into two categories, namely securities quoted at par and securities quoted on a discount basis.

10.2.1 *Securities quoted at par*

The first category includes money market deposits (MMDs) (e.g. inter-bank deposits) and negotiable CDs. The minimum size of transaction for MMDs is usually £500,000 and the deposits are non-negotiable. Deposits can be made for a variety of periods from a minimum of overnight, but are mainly for maturities of less than three months. CDs are negotiable certificates confirming that a deposit has been made with a UK office of a UK or foreign bank and, since 1983, with certain large building societies. Issues in London can be denominated in either dollars or sterling, with the latter market being the larger. They are issued in multiples of £10,000 from a minimum of £50,000 and are usually for a maturity of between three months and five years. The key advantage of a CD as distinct from a straight deposit for the holder is that it is negotiable, that is, the holder can liquidate the loan should a need for the funds arise. Consequently the rate of interest on CDs is normally slightly lower than that on MMDs for the same maturity (see table 10.1 for details).

The return on an MMD is straightforward to calculate and is given by the following formula:[1]

$$r = P \times i(n/365) \tag{10.1}$$

where r = the rate of return, P = the par value of the deposit, i = the annualised rate of interest on the deposit and n = number of days to maturity.

---

1   Note in the UK the financial year is assumed to consist of 365 days. This is not always the case and in some countries (e.g. in the US) it is assumed to consist of 360 days.

For example, the return on a deposit of £1,000,000 bearing an annual rate of interest of 6 per cent and a maturity of 91 days would provide the following return to the holder:

$$r = 1,000,000 \times 0.06(91/365) = £14,958.90$$

Clearly the end value of the deposit is $P + r = 1,014,958.90$.

The formula for the calculation of the return on a CD is more complicated because allowance must be made for the fact that the security can be traded on the secondary market. The relevant formula is:

$$r = \{(P/MP) \times [1 + i(nim/365)] - 1\}(365/nrm) \qquad (10.2)$$

where r is the annualised rate of return on the CD, MP is the current market price of the CD, nim is the number of days for which the CD was issued, nrm is the number of days remaining to maturity and P and i are as defined for equation 10.1.

For example, a £50,000 91-day CD with a fixed rate of interest of 7 per cent per annum purchased in the market for £50,500 with 61 days remaining to maturity would provide the following return:

$$r = \{(50,000/50,500) \times [1 + 0.07(91/365)] - 1\}(365/61)$$
$$= 0.044 \text{ or } 4.4 \text{ per cent}$$

Solving formula 10.2 for MP gives the market price of the CD:

$$MP = P \times \{1 + i(nim/365)\}/[1 + r(nrm/365)] \qquad (10.3)$$

In this case r measures the rate of return required on the security. Using the same example given above but solving for MP gives:

$$MP = £50,000 \times \{1 + 0.7(91/365)\}/[1 + 0.044(61/365)]$$
$$= \text{approximately } £50,500$$

10.2.2 *Securities quoted on a discount basis*

Bills of exchange
Securities issued on a discount basis include bills of exchange and commercial paper. The nature of a bill of exchange was discussed in chapter 1. The various types of bills are as follows.

(i)   *Treasury bills*. These are issued by the Treasury. The normal initial maturity is 91 days. Some issues are for longer periods and the vast majority are in sterling.

(ii) *Commercial bills*. These are issued by commercial undertakings and consequently involve a higher degree of risk of default than Treasury bills and, therefore, a higher rate of return. Within the broad category of commercial bills further distinctions can be made according to the degree of risk of default. Some bills can be drawn on or 'accepted' by banks (see chapter 4 for a discussion of acceptance) and this will entail a lower rate of return (or discount) than other commercial bills. Some bills, issued by specified banks regarded as of high standing, are denoted as eligible for discount at the Bank of England in its money market operations (see section 10.4 for a discussion of this topic). These will command an even lower rate of discount than commercial bills without this cachet.

(iii) *Local authority bills*. These bills are issued by local authorities with a maturity up to six months.

Commercial paper

In 1986 the powers conferred on the Treasury by the Banking Act of the same year to remove specified transactions from the definition of deposit taking were exercised. This relaxation permitted the issue of short-term sterling debt. Further relaxations occurred in 1987 and more fundamentally in 1990. This last revision permitted an extension to five years of the maximum permissible maturity of the paper issued under this facility. Paper issued with an original maturity of up to and including one year is termed 'commercial paper', whereas issues with an original maturity exceeding one year but less than five years are called 'medium-term notes'. It is only the first category which really forms part of the money markets. Thus commercial paper is a short-term financial instrument, similar to a promissory note. It is a general unsecured financial instrument with a maturity typically between seven days and three months. Commercial paper contrasts with bills of exchange since it is the liability of the issuer only, whereas bills are obligations of the drawer and the accepting house, except when issued by the Treasury, banks and building societies.

Issues can be in sterling or other currencies. Sterling issues can be made by companies with net assets valued in excess of £25 million. In addition, they must have shares and debt listed on the LSE or on the unlisted securities market. In the case of issues by non-resident companies, the qualification is that similar criteria have to be met on an 'authorised' stock exchange in the country where the company is located. Authorisation in this case entails recognition and approval by the LSE. Issues can also be made by financial institutions. Although not a legal requirement, issues are normally restricted to investment-grade ratings (see chapter 9 for a discussion of bond rating).

Valuation of securities quoted on a discount basis
The valuation of securities quoted on a discount basis is obtained using the present value formula quoted in chapter 1 for the valuation of bonds. In this case there is a single pay-off for a portion of a year, so that the formula becomes:

$$MP = P/\{1 + r(nrm/365)\} \tag{10.4}$$

with *MP*, *P*, *r* and *nrm* as defined earlier.

For example, a £50,000 Treasury bill due in 40 days' time with a rate of interest on comparable securities equal to 4 per cent per annum is valued at:

$$MP = £50,000/\{1 + 0.04(40/365)\} = £49,781.78$$

Alternatively, given the market price the return could be calculated by the following formula:

$$r = \{(P - MP)/MP\}(365/nrm) \tag{10.5}$$

or in the above example:

$$r = \{(50,000 - 49,781.78)/49,781.78\}(365/40)$$
$$= 0.04 \text{ or } 4 \text{ per cent per annum.}$$

Repos
The nature of the repo was discussed in chapter 9, so in this chapter we will restrict the discussion to the valuation of a repo. It should be noted that most repos are of a short-term nature so that they are instruments used primarily in the money market rather than capital market instruments. Note that the security being repo'd can be a long-term security, such as a gilt, whilst the repo is a short-term instrument. Quotes are usually made on a yield basis using the formula appropriate to the market concerned. For example, consider a Treasury bill repo. The Bank of England agrees to buy a £100,000 bill with an outstanding maturity of 60 days for £99,346.76 and resell the bill to the purchaser in 10 days' time for £99,455.04. The repo rate on this transaction is then:

$$r = \{(99,455.04 - 99,346.76)/99,346.76\}(365/10)$$
$$= 0.03978 \text{ or } 3.98 \text{ per cent per annum.}$$

Table 10.1   *London money rates, 16 April 1998*

	Three-month spread
Inter-bank sterling	$7^{17}/_{32} - 7^{13}/_{32}$
Sterling CDs	$7^{15}/_{32} - 7^{13}/_{32}$
Treasury bills	$7^5/_{16} - 7^3/_{16}$
Bank mills	$7^5/_{16} - 7^1/_4$
Local authority deposits	$7^{15}/_{32} - 7^{13}/_{32}$

Source: *Financial Times*, companies and markets, 17 April 1998, p. 31.

10.2.3   *Relative rates of interest in the various markets*

Table 10.1 is an extract from the *Financial Times* companies and markets report for 17 April 1998. The original table contains a number of maturities but, for the sake of ease of exposition, we comment only on that for three months. From table 10.1, we can see that a bank can deposit (lend) in the inter-bank market for three months at an annual rate of $7^{13}/_{32}$ per cent. Similarly the bank could raise funds (i.e. borrow) in the inter-bank market at an annual rate of $7^{17}/_{32}$ per cent. Turning now to the CD market, CDs can be sold at a price yielding a return of $7^{15}/_{32}$ per cent per annum and bought for a price yielding $7^{13}/_{32}$ per cent per annum. This implies that the selling price for the holder is less than the buying price (see formula 10.3) and, in other words, suggests that the bank's buying rate is less than its selling rate. Note also that the mid-point of the CD rates is slightly less than that of the sterling inter-bank deposits. The figure for Treasury bills shows a rate slightly lower than that for CDs, indicating the greater liquidity of that instrument.

10.3   The London sterling money markets

The London money markets are 'wholesale' markets with transactions typically for amounts considerably in excess of £500,000. There are no particular central locations where members meet face to face and most of the business is conducted via the telephone or even by personal visits. In many cases brokers act as intermediaries, bringing depositors and borrowers together. In March 1997, the Bank of England announced that it was changing the methods by which it operated in the money markets. The old traditional discount market has disappeared and the Bank has in its money market operations both broadened the range of institutions with which it will trade as well as widened the type of debt traded. We

Table 10.2   *London sterling money markets*

	Size (£billion)
The traditional discount market	26.7
The local authority market	1.5
The inter-bank market	97.7
CD market	107.9
Finance house deposit market	4.8
Commercial paper market	7.6

The size of a market is not an unambiguous concept and the statistics have been derived as follows:

Discount market – total borrowed funds by the discount houses at end of February 1997 (CSO, *Financial Statistics*, November 1997, table 4.2d).

Local authority market – total stock of temporary money at end March 1997 (CSO, *Financial Statistics*, November 1997, table 1.3b).

Inter-bank market – total sterling time deposits of banks held with UK banks at end February 1997 (CSO, *Financial Statistics*, November 1997, table 4.2c).

CD market – total of sterling CDs issued by banks plus CD issues by building societies at end February 1997 (CSO, *Financial Statistics*, November 1997, tables 4.2c and 4.3a).

Finance house deposit market – total short-term funds obtained by non-bank credit companies from the banks at end December 1996 (CSO, *Financial Statistics*, November 1997, table 5.2b).

show in table 10.2 the main London money markets, together with an estimate of their size just prior to the introduction of the new system.

The longest established market is the traditional discount market (discussed in section 10.4), with the markets developing alongside the discount market over the last 30 years being termed parallel or complementary money markets. The most recent development is the commercial paper money market.

Although in the above classification we have distinguished between different markets, we would like to emphasise that these are all closely interrelated, with the same institutions operating in many of the markets. Interest rates will vary only slightly between the various markets because of the slightly differing intrinsic characteristics of the instruments involved. For example, as noted earlier, inter-bank deposits will command a small premium over CD interest rates for comparable maturity terms because of their greater degree of liquidity. Similarly, deposits with differing terms will also attract differing rates of interest, as will deposits with institutions of lower credit worthiness. Nevertheless, these differences are likely to be fairly minor so that arbitrage will ensure that the interest rates in the various markets will tend to move together, as they reflect a similar trading environment. The basic similarity between these markets is that they all cater for short-term funds.

10.3.1 *Parallel money markets*

There are a number of general points about the structure of parallel or complementary markets that are worth making before the more detailed discussion of the various markets themselves.

(i)   Lending is not secured in the manner discussed above for the traditional discount market.

(ii)   There is no direct intervention by the Bank of England in these markets, so the discount and the gilt repo markets are the sole channels used by the Bank of England to enforce its short-term interest rate policy. Consequently interest rates in these markets move freely to reflect the underlying forces of supply and demand.

(iii) There are strong links between all the markets (both parallel and the discount). The same operators are involved to a considerable extent and arbitrage will ensure that interest rates move in a similar manner in all the markets.

(iv)   There is no formal lender of last resort standing behind these markets in the manner that the Bank provides borrowing facilities for the discount houses. On the other hand, our discussion of the responsibility of the Bank of England to preserve the stability of financial markets in chapter 17 suggests that the Bank would be extremely loath to countenance the failure of any major monetary institution. This proviso suggests that this distinction between the discount and parallel money markets was already superficial prior to the introduction of the new arrangements discussed in the previous section.

(v)   Much of the volume of transactions in these markets is routed via brokers, who act as intermediaries between the ultimate borrowers and lenders.

We now turn to an examination of these markets. The discussion on each market is much briefer than that of the discount market in the following section. This does not mean that these markets are less important to the operation of the UK financial system but rather that they possess a relatively simple structure.

The first market we wish to discuss is the local authority money market. The requirement of local authorities to raise short-term finance arises from the different timing of their receipts and payment. Finance can be raised in a variety of ways. The first method is through the issue of bonds, normally for maturities of one to five years. The second method is through the issue of bills. Normally these are offered for tender and possess maturities of up to six months. The third method of interest in this discussion is by way of what is called temporary money. These are deposits with local authorities for varying periods up to one year but, in fact, the average maturity is for a much shorter time, with the greater proportion of deposits being for less than seven days. The minimum size of deposit is £100,000 and the deposits are non-negotiable. The sources of the deposits are monetary institutions (roughly 50 per cent), large industrial and commercial companies and overseas institutions.

The inter-bank market, as its name suggests, is a market for unsecured lending between different banks. The market grew rapidly during the 1960s when the international banks, newly located in London, extended their inter-bank lending practice from foreign currencies to sterling deposit. In fact the market now is considerably broader than just between banks (both retail and wholesale) as depositors include large industrial and commercial companies, international institutions, discount houses and other financial institutions. Borrowing in the inter-bank market provides an indication to the banks of the marginal cost of raising new funds, so that one rate in particular, the LIBOR, is widely used as a basis for calculating charges on loans with variable interest rates. In addition, their own lending rates are sensitive to movements in this rate.

This market provides a means for banks to balance their inflow of deposits with the demand for loans (see discussion of liability management in chapter 3). Thus, for example, a bank with a new deposit and no foreseeable immediate demand for a loan can make a deposit in the inter-bank market and earn a rate of interest. Similarly, a bank with a demand for a loan from a customer and no new deposit to hand can raise the necessary deposit in the market. In this way the market serves a smoothing function in a manner similar to that described for the discount market. A second function of the market is the provision of facilities for non-banks to make deposits for short periods as part of their cash management techniques. The third function provided by the market is that it enables less well known banks to raise finance by borrowing in the inter-bank market rather than direct from customers. As a final comment it should be noted that the existence of inter-bank lending increases the connecting links between banks and raises the potential risk of systemic failure following the collapse of one institution.

A third parallel money market is the secondary market in CDs. The advantage of CDs over sterling money market deposits depends critically on the existence of a secondary market in which existing CDs can be bought and sold. The market makers in this secondary market are the discount houses.

The fourth market to be considered is the market for finance house deposits. This is smaller than the other markets considered so far and refers to the raising of funds by finance houses, which, in turn, use the funds for the finance of consumer credit, leasing, block discounting and factoring. Many of the institutions concerned are now classified as banks, which tends to blur the distinction between this and the inter-bank market. Many of the deposits come from banks and other financial institutions but deposits are also made by industrial and commercial companies.

The sterling commercial paper market represents a recent development in the sterling money markets. In its present form it dates from 1986 though an inter-company market for short-term deposits existed in the 1970s. In terms of world markets for commercial paper, the US is the largest. The BIS reported that at the end of 1996 outstanding issues in the US amounted to approximately $800 billion, compared with only $7.6 billion in the UK. In fact the BIS has estimated that the US market accounted for just over 90 per cent of total world outstanding issues (Bank for International Settlements 1997). The recent growth in issues of commercial paper represents the general move towards securitisation. This can be attributed to a number of factors, such as financial liberalisation, and the move by banks and financial institutions towards fee-earning operations as distinct from direct lending.

The Bank of England permitted the use of authorised intermediaries to manage the issue of commercial paper and the standard way of issuing such debt is to make issues via a lead bank or security house, which will manage the whole programme. The functions of the lead manager include making arrangements for the issue and redemption of the debt, offering advice on the issue and arranging the placing of the debt with other dealers. Issues are in large denominations and an indication of the size of issues can be obtained by noting that the average size of outstanding debt is £27 million (November 1994) though, of course, there will be large variations around the mean. At the moment there also appears to be no secondary market although, in some cases, the dealers are prepared to buy paper back before its maturity. Given the short-term nature of the debt generally issued, it is probably true to say that there is little need for a secondary market for the sale of existing commercial paper.

This market offers new scope for the raising of money by industrial and commercial companies. It is difficult at this stage to comment on

Table 10.3   *Value of sterling paper, 1986–96 (£billion)*

	Commercial paper	Medium-term notes
1986	0.5	
1987	2.1	
1988	3.3	
1989	3.5	
1990	3.8	0.4
1991	3.7	1.0
1992	3.9	3.3
1993	5.5	7.9
1994	6.1	11.7
1995	6.4	15.8
1996	7.5	20.6

Source: *Bank of England Statistical Abstract*, 1997, tables 17.1 and 17.2.

the cost of raising finance through the issue of commercial paper because of the wide variety of issuers. The market also offers a short-term outlet for industrial and commercial firms to place surplus funds. The development of the commercial paper market contributed to the relaxation of the formerly close relationships between banks and their customers. Business came to be conducted on a transactional basis, where the paper was placed with financial institutions offering the lowest cost for the particular service. In addition, competition between institutions led to low rewards for dealers in the market. Nevertheless, this market has seen a fast rate of growth, as can be seen from the details shown in table 10.3, particularly in the case of medium-term sterling notes.

10.4   The Bank of England's money market operations

The main operators in the traditional discount market were:

(i)   the Bank of England (hereafter termed the Bank),
(ii)   the commercial banks,
(iii) the discount houses.

As we will see below, the main impact of the changes introduced in 1997 were to increase the range both of counterparties, from just the discount houses noted in (iii) above, and of instruments through which

Table 10.4 *Overnight interest rate volatility in selected countries, 1988–91 (mean absolute deviation in basis points)*

	1988	1989	1990	1991	Average
Germany	15.7	18.2	13.6	13.4	15.2
Japan	8.7	8.5	7.1	8.4	8.2
UK	50.4	32.9	14.8	25.3	30.9
US	12.3	11.9	12.3	21.1	14.4

Source: Kasman (1992).

intervention is conducted. Counterparties now also include banks, building societies and security firms, and the Bank now deals in repos in gilts as well as Treasury bills and eligible bank bills (for details of the gilt repo market see chapter 9). Additionally, in 1997 some changes were made to the facilities for late assistance to the market.

It was claimed that the previous system, whereby most of the Bank's open market operations were conducted through the discount houses, led to excess volatility of overnight interest rates. In fact Kasman (1992) investigated the variability of overnight interest rates in a number of centres and the unambiguous result was that the volatility of such rates was higher in the UK than in other centres. Summary results are shown in table 10.4. Similarly, the intra-day volatility of the rates also appeared to be quite high. One source of disposing of excess or acquiring additional balances so as to meet targets is the overnight market. Hence excess volatility in this market will increase the risk and cost to operators, and this must lead to a widening (however slight) of bands by market makers in the money markets in general.

By broadening the scope of the Bank's daily operations, it is anticipated that the new arrangements will increase the degree of competition and efficiency of the sterling money markets as well as leading to further integration of gilt-edged and money markets. The sheer volume of instruments available – the Bank estimates the existence of approximately £250 billion of gilts, which can be traded in the repo market, as against £20 billion of available bills (*Bank of England Quarterly Bulletin*, February 1997) – should also reduce the degree of overnight volatility of interest rates. Finally it is interesting to note that the move towards intervention in the gilt repo market brings the UK into line with general European practice, which would facilitate joining the single currency in the future should it be desired to do so.

We now turn to discussing in more detail the mechanics of the Bank's open market operations in the sterling money markets. Normally there are wide imbalances between receipts by and payments to the government, which would have consequences for short-term interest rates according to whether there was a shortage or surplus of funds in the market. The precise mechanism by which the shortages/surpluses occur is discussed below. The object of the Bank's daily money market operations is to enforce its short-term interest rate policy. This will entail evening out the flow of funds either at existing rates of interest or at a rate of the Bank's choosing. Banks which hold settlement balances (i.e. balances used for settling transactions with other banks) with the Bank are called settlement banks. The majority of banks hold settlement balances with settlement banks rather than the Bank, so that the ultimate impact of shortages/surpluses falls on the settlement banks. The settlement banks are required to achieve a positive balance on their settlement balances at the Bank at the end of the day though, in practice, they are likely to aim for holdings slightly more than the bare minimum given the uncertainty regarding the future volume of transactions during the day. The settlement banks can use the discount houses to offset daily fluctuations in their individual balances at the Bank. This is achieved by making deposits at the discount houses, with such loans being secured by collateral security in the form of asset titles. Under the new system the banks and other authorised counterparties can also engage in repo transactions directly with the Bank so as to ensure that sufficient funds are available to prevent the settlement banks' accounts from being overdrawn. In this way the Bank is the marginal supplier of liquidity to the banking system.

In order to understand the nature of the Bank's operations in the money market it is necessary to describe the background of the impact of payments to and by the central government on the settlement banks' cash position. Any payment by the central government to other sectors increases these banks' balances at the Bank. Conversely any payment to the central government by any other sector has the effect of reducing the settlement banks' balances at the Bank. Generally there is a shortage of funds (i.e. payments to central government exceed payments by it) and such shortages arise from three sources:

(i)   Exchequer transactions, that is, those necessary to finance a central government budget deficit after sales of long-term debt (a budget surplus leads to an excess supply of funds);

(ii) maturing assistance, such as loans to the discount houses and the Bank's holdings of commercial bills – in this case funds pass to the central government as the debt is repaid; this item has been a major component of the total market shortage in recent years, and note this drain would not occur if the Bank purchased only central government rather than commercial securities;

(iii) increases in the volume of notes and coins in circulation – increased holdings of notes and coins involve a payment to the Bank for them.

The daily totals of these payments are both very large and also fluctuate widely. Part of this impact is netted out as some commercial banks will be withdrawing funds from the market whereas others will be lending additional funds, but overall it is likely to lead to market imbalances which are both large and difficult to predict. For example, the *Financial Times* (money market report, 24 November 1994) noted that on 23 November 1994 'the Bank of England cleared a £600 million daily shortage in UK money markets'. The size of the shortage can become extremely large in certain circumstances. For example, the defence of a specific exchange rate will lead to a large volume of payments to the government as sterling is exchanged for exchange reserves.

The impact of any shortage/surplus is seen in the sterling money markets. The Bank will deal, that is, undertake open market operations, through repo transactions in gilts, marketable government foreign currency debt and eligible bills (Treasury, eligible local authority and eligible bank bills). The term 'eligible' refers to bills which are of sufficient quality so that the Bank will accept them in its daily market operations. The Bank will also purchase eligible bills outright. In the case of shortages of funds (typically the case) in the market the Bank will buy bills (Treasury bills, eligible bank bills and local authority bills) from the discount houses and also engage in repo or make loans to them. Conversely, in the case of surpluses it would sell Treasury bills. The bills are categorised into the following bands according to their outstanding maturity:

band 1   1–14 days;
band 2   15–33 days;
band 3   34–63 days;
band 4   64–91 days.

Intervention is mainly at the short end of the maturity spectrum, that is, in bands 1 and 2, with an average maturity of intervention in practice of around 14 days. This has the result that a very small variation in the price of a bill will lead to a significant change in the annual rate of interest. Intervention through the repo market will also involve maturities of around 14 days.

Each morning at 9.45 a.m. the Bank indicates its forecast of the daily shortage via financial news screens such as Reuters and Telerate. This prediction will be amended in the light of new information received by the Bank. Normally the Bank conducts two daily open market operations, at 12.00 noon and 2.30 p.m., but provision is made for an early trading session at 9.45 a.m. if warranted by the forecast of the size of that day's shortage. Intervention is normally at a fixed rate but the Bank reserves the right to operate on a variable-rate tender basis. If this right is to be exercised the market operators will be advised accordingly. A special late repo facility is available for the settlement banks between 3.50 and 3.55 p.m. to provide for cover against unforeseen contingencies. This facility provides for overnight liquidity.

The early 1990s saw a move towards RTGS between banks for wholesale transactions (see chapter 3 for a discussion of RTGS). This means that individual payments/receipts between banks will be settled immediately instead of being netted out at the end of the day. Given the large size of such transactions, this increases the risk of an individual bank being short of funds at the Bank, so that its balance there would be negative at the close of the banking day. This poses the danger that intra-day credit could extend to overnight credit, which could affect monetary conditions. Consequently, whilst, as noted above, the Bank will provide overnight credit, this is carried out at a penal rate unless the shortage was due to a misleading forecast of the size of the day's overall shortage. The penalty rate is fixed at 1 per cent above base rate (or the highest overnight rate, whichever is the higher) plus an additional 0.5 per cent for each time a particular bank has used the facility during the previous three months. The use of the penalty rate provides a strong incentive for banks to avoid use of this facility.

Prior to the introduction of the new system in March 1997, the banks used the discount market as the primary mechanism to even out their cash position. In terms of the attributes discussed in chapter 1, deposits with the discount houses are liquid, short term, capital certain and virtually free of default risk. As they earned a rate of return, they offered the perfect medium for banks to carry their first reserves against any cash shortages. Since the greater proportion of the deposits made with the discount houses originated from the banks themselves, the discount houses could themselves be considered almost as 'arm's length' departments of the banks. They borrowed funds from the banks, purchased short-term monetary assets and sold such assets to the banks. They operated to make a market in Treasury bills and eligible bank and local authority bills. They underwrote the Treasury bill tender (see chapter 9) and operated facilities to borrow and lend gilt-edged stock through money brokers. As an assistance to the provision of these facilities, the discount houses used to have a special direct dealing relationship with the Bank which involved the purchase and sale of bills to the Bank and also borrowing facilities. Clearly the new arrangements, whereby banks can deal directly with the Bank, will impinge on the privileged position of the discount houses. One discount house, Union, has already announced plans to close its trading operations. Other discount houses are likely to merge with their parent banks, though it is estimated that the discount houses account for some 40–45 per cent of dealing in the gilt repo market and this offers them alternative trading potential. In order to allow the discount houses time to restructure their operations, the Bank has indicated that, for a two-year transition period, they can maintain a special late repo facility with the Bank. At the time of writing (spring 1998) it is too early to forecast what the position of the discount houses will be in two years' time.

10.5   Short-term interest rates and inflation

It may be considered difficult to apply tests of market efficiency to markets for short-term deposits given the degree of intervention by the authorities. However, one interesting question was raised by Fama (1975) concerning the role of inflationary expectations in the setting of short-term rates of interest. Equation 9.2a is reproduced below for the sake of convenience:

$$R_t = i_t + E\Delta p_{t+1} \qquad\qquad (9.2a)$$

where R is the nominal rate of interest, i is the real rate and $E\Delta p$ refers to the expected rate of inflation. Equation (9.2a) (the 'Fisher' hypothesis) has often been tested by running a regression of the general form:

$$R_t = \alpha + \beta E_t \Delta p_{t+1} \qquad\qquad (10.6)$$

Comparing equation 10.6 with equation 9.2a reveals the explicit assumption made that the real rate, i, is a constant. An estimated value for β of unity supports the existence of complete adjustment of the nominal rate to inflation expectations – often called the strong Fisher hypothesis. A value between zero and unity supports the weak Fisher hypothesis, that inflation expectations have some role to play in the determination of short-term rates of interest but are not completely anticipated. Early evidence failed to support the view that the markets were incorporating efficient forecasts of inflation in the setting of interest rates. Various reasons were suggested, including poor price data and faulty representation of the inflation series – normally carried out by a distributed lag of past price changes.

Using US data, Fama (1975) tested whether the nominal interest rate acted as a good predictor of inflation by transforming equation 10.6 to obtain:

$$\Delta p_t = \beta' R_t - \alpha' \tag{10.7}$$

where $\alpha' = 1/\alpha$ and $\beta' = 1/\beta$.

Fama found support for the strong Fisher hypothesis since the estimate of β' was not significantly different from unity. This result was criticised by a number of investigators. The first criticism was that it was possible to obtain alternative estimators of the future rate of inflation using time series analysis and, when compared with the predictions from the rate of interest, it was found that these provided additional information. This suggested that the market's setting of short-term rates of interest failed to take into account all available information concerning future rates of inflation. The second approach followed the inclusion of additional variables on the right-hand side of equation 10.7, and it was found that these improved the fit of the equation, thus implying an improvement in the forecasts of future inflation. Fama (1977) conceded that these criticisms were correct but argued that the improvements were very small quantitatively, so that his initial result was largely intact.

Demery and Duck (1978) carried out a similar analysis based on UK data and also found support for the Fisher hypothesis but, in this case, the weak version. They concluded that nominal rates of interest rise as expectations of inflation rise but that, even in the long run, they probably fail to adjust fully for the increase in expectations of future inflation.

Chapter 11

The foreign exchange market

11.1 Introduction

In this chapter we first of all examine, in section 11.2, the nature of exchange rates and this is followed by a discussion of the determination of exchange rates in section 11.3. In sections 11.4 and 11.5 we explore the nature of the foreign exchange market (the 'forex') and the types of business carried out on the market. Finally we briefly summarise the empirical evidence concerning the efficiency of the forex in section 11.6.

11.2 The nature of exchange rates

The first step in our analysis is to clarify certain concepts with respect to the exchange rate. There are two ways in which exchange rates can be quoted. First, it is possible to define the exchange rate in terms of units of foreign currency per unit of domestic currency, for example $1.5 per £1 – this is known as the 'indirect' quotation. Equivalently we could say the price of $1 is £0.67, that is, in terms of units of domestic currency per unit of foreign currency – this method is known as the 'direct' quotation. It is the custom in the UK to use the first method (i.e. the indirect quotation of exchange rates) of defining the exchange rate whereas in the rest of the world it is more usual to use the second method (i.e. direct quotation). We shall use the normal UK method in the rest of the text. In fact the rate we have been discussing, that is, the rate quoted in the financial media and determined in the foreign exchange markets, is termed the 'nominal' exchange rate. In practice many commercial decisions are made with respect to the 'real' exchange rate, that is, the nominal exchange rate adjusted for the relative prices of the countries concerned. This can be specified algebraically as:

$$S^R_{t} = S_t^*(P/P^F)_t \tag{11.1}$$

where S^R is the real exchange rate, S is the nominal exchange rate (units of foreign currency per unit of domestic currency) and P and P^F are indices of domestic and foreign prices, respectively. One further clarification of exchange rate definitions is appropriate. We have so far discussed exchange rates in terms of two countries and these are called 'bilateral' rates. If it is desired to measure the average level of the exchange rate against a range of representative currencies, it is necessary to construct an index of the exchange rate valued against a representative basket of currencies with weights attached to the relevant bilateral rates based on their importance in trade with the country concerned. The IMF has developed a model for calculating effective exchange rates termed the 'multilateral exchange rate model'.

11.3   Determination of exchange rates

It is also useful as a prelude to the consideration of the foreign exchange markets to summarise current theories concerning the determination of exchange rates. It is an area of great controversy and it will not therefore be a great surprise to the reader to learn that there is no single theory which commands a wide degree of acceptance. All agree that, in the absence of intervention by the authorities, the exchange rate is determined by the demand and supply of currencies on the market, but there is little agreement on the factors underlying the forces of demand and supply. There are basically four main models, which differ from each other to a greater or lesser degree.

The first, the simple monetary model, assumes flexible prices and combines the purchasing power parity (PPP – see below) view of exchange rates with a simple quantity theory. Consequently changes in the exchange rate in the case of flexible exchange rates or in the balance of payments given fixed rates are attributable to differences in the rate of monetary expansion in the two countries involved.

In contrast, the second model, commonly designated the Mundell–Flemming model, assumes fixed prices. In a regime of floating exchange rates, balance-of-payments equilibrium is obtained through the sum of the current and capital accounts being zero. A zero balance on the current account is not required even in the long run and the offsetting balance on the capital account is achieved via the equilibrium rate of interest which clears the domestic goods and money markets. In the case of the fixed exchange rate regime, balance-of-payments equilibrium is achieved through changes in official reserves caused by intervention by the authorities in the foreign exchange markets.

The third model, the Dornbusch model, is an amalgam of the previous two models. Financial markets are supposed to clear instantaneously, that is, prices are perfectly flexible. This contrasts with the goods markets, where prices are sticky. This results in the well known prediction that the exchange rate overshoots the long-run equilibrium level following a shock. The long-run equilibrium level is, however, consistent with the predictions of the simple monetary theory discussed earlier.

The fourth model is the portfolio balance model, which widens the choice of assets available rather than concentrating simply on money. Consequently the exchange rate arises from the determination of equilibrium portfolios and any shock will change the desired composition of the portfolio and therefore the equilibrium returns, including that on foreign assets, which includes expected exchange rate changes. A good detailed account of exchange rate determination is given in Copeland (1994).

Foreign exchange markets are about arbitrage and this process is likely to establish certain relationships between bilateral rates. First, it would be expected that prices in domestic or foreign currency of traded commodities would be the same whether priced in domestic or foreign currency. This is PPP. Second, it would also be expected that returns on financial investment in different international centres would be the same after allowing for potential exchange rate changes. This is called 'interest rate parity' (IRP). Third is the relationship which may be expected to exist between interest rate differentials between two countries and the respective real rates of interest and expected inflation (i.e. the international Fisher relation). We now discuss these three propositions in more detail.

11.3.1 *Purchasing power parity*

The modern doctrine of PPP is due to the work of the Swedish economist Gustav Cassel, though in fact it can be traced back to David Ricardo. The basis for the analysis is the 'law of one price'. Suppose a car sold in the UK for £10,000 and the identical model sold in the US for $15,000. Clearly, abstracting from transport costs, the equilibrium exchange rate is $1.5 per £1. At any other exchange rate arbitrage is possible. Thus, for example, if the exchange rate was $1 = £1, then the car could be purchased for £10,000 in the UK and transported to the US and sold for $15,000, earning a nice profit. Because cars were being purchased in the UK and sold to the US, this would set up an increased demand for pounds on the market (or equivalently an increased supply of dollars) thus causing the pound to appreciate (or equivalently the dollar to depreciate). This arbitrage would be possible until the exchange rate equalled \$1.5 per £1. The converse process would occur if the dollar/sterling exchange rate exceeded \$1.5 per £1. PPP extends this relationship (i.e. the law of one price) from a single identical good to bundles of internationally traded goods. PPP also comes in two forms, absolute PPP and relative PPP. Absolute PPP contends that the bilateral exchange rate will depend on the relative prices in domestic currency of goods in the two countries. More formally:

$$S^{\text{PPP}} = P^{\text{F}}/P \tag{11.2}$$

where S^{PPP} is the PPP exchange rate (units of foreign currency per unit of domestic currency) and P and P^{F} are domestic and foreign price indices, as before. Relative PPP is a weaker concept and portrays the bilateral exchange rate changing in line with the difference between the inflation rates of the two countries concerned. More formally:

$$\Delta S^{\text{PPP}} = \Delta P^{\text{F}} - \Delta P \tag{11.3}$$

where ΔP^{F} and ΔP refer to the percentage rates of inflation in the two countries. Thus, for example, if inflation in the UK is expected to be 5 per cent and in the US 2 per cent (both per annum) the exchange rate would be expected to depreciate at the rate of 3 per cent per annum. Given that arbitrage in goods takes time, it would be expected that an efficient market would cause the market exchange rate to tend to PPP over time rather than at each instant. We review the evidence concerning PPP in section 11.6.

11.3.2 *Interest rate parity*

The second relationship, IRP, concerns movements of capital between financial centres. It would be expected that the total expected return in each centre would be the same or otherwise opportunities for profitable arbitrage would exist. To illustrate this point, let us suppose that the arbitrageur starts by holding sterling; the one-period return from assets in sterling ($P^{£}$) is simply $(1 + R^{£})$ where $R^{£}$ is the relevant interest rate on sterling securities. In contrast, the one-period return from assets denoted in foreign currency (say dollars for illustrative purposes) may be defined as:

$$P^{\$} = S_t(1 + R^{\$})/(E_t S_{t+1}) \tag{11.4}$$

where the time periods are consistent and $R^{\$}$ represents the one-period nominal rate of interest on dollar securities and $E_t S_{t+1}$ is the spot rate (\$

per £1) expected to exist at the end of the single period. Thus, the equation represents a spot purchase of dollars at the rate of S_t, the subsequent purchase of a dollar security yielding a rate of interest equal to $R^\$$ during the period t to $t + 1$ and the subsequent repurchase of sterling at period $t + 1$ expected to be at the spot rate $E_t S_{t+1}$. Arbitrage would be expected to ensure that $P^£ = P^\$$, otherwise opportunities for profitable arbitrage would exist and capital flows would remove the incentive for arbitrage. For example, if the return in New York was higher than that in London, funds would flow from London to New York, thus causing the sterling spot rate (S_t) to depreciate (or equivalently the dollar to appreciate) and the rate of interest in New York to depreciate. Both of these phenomena would reduce the return in New York, so eliminating the differences in return between the two centres.

Equation 11.4 can be modified by substituting the forward rate (F_t) for the expected spot rate so that all rates (both interest and exchange rates) are known with certainty at time t. Hence equation 11.4 is rewritten as:

$$P^\$ = S_t(1 + R^\$)/F_t \qquad (11.5)$$

where F is the forward rate ($ per £1).

To illustrate this calculation, consider the following constellation of closing rates on 16 April 1998 as reported in the *Financial Times* currencies and money report dated 17 April.[1] $S_t = 1.6924$; F_t (for 12 months) $= 1.6668$ and the eurodollar rate of interest for 12 months $=$ 5.75 per cent per annum. Hence the return from the eurodollar investment would be: $1.6924(1 + 0.0575)/1.6668 = 1.0737$, making a return of 7.4 per cent.

Again, arbitrage should ensure that $P^£ = P^\$$. In fact on the day the 12-month rate of interest on eurosterling was 7.4 per cent.

In this case IRP is termed covered interest parity because forward cover has been taken out against future movements in the exchange rate (see section 11.5 for a full discussion of forward and spot rates). The previous type of IRP, when no forward cover is taken out, is termed

---

1   Note we are working from the midpoints (see section 11.5 for an explanation of this term) and the period is for one year to simplify the mathematics. Also note that the forward rate is for delivery in 12 months' time and the interest rates are quoted on an annual basis. This is what is meant by the statement 'where the time periods are consistent'. The same calculations would apply for different time periods but would require the interest rates to be adjusted from an annual basis, e.g. for three months divided by 4.

uncovered interest rate parity. The efficient markets hypothesis implies that the returns in the two centres should be equal, so that both types of IRP should exist in the foreign exchange market. The evidence for the existence of this type of efficiency will also be examined in section 11.6.

11.3.3 *The international Fisher relation*

The domestic Fisher equation was summarised in equation 9.1, which is reproduced below for convenience:

$$(1 + R) = (1 + i)(1 + E\Delta p) \tag{9.1}$$

where R is the nominal rate and i is the real rate (both rates applying to a single period) and $E\Delta p$ is the rate of inflation expected during the period to maturity. A similar relationship could be applied to a foreign country, say the US, such that:

$$(1 + R^\$) = (1 + i^\$)(1 + E\Delta p^\$) \tag{9.1a}$$

where $ indicates the corresponding US variable.

Dividing (9.1a) by (9.1) produces:

$$\frac{(1 + R^\$)}{(1 + R)} = \frac{(1 + i^\$)(1 + E\Delta p^\$)}{(1 + i)(1 + E\Delta p)} \tag{11.6}$$

Equation 11.6 may be approximated by:

$$R^\$ - R = (i^\$ - i) + (E\Delta p^\$ - E\Delta p) \tag{11.6a}$$

In other words the nominal interest rate differential between two countries will equal the sum of the gaps between the respective real rates and the expected inflation differentials.

11.4 Nature of the forex

In this section we review the nature of the London foreign exchange (forex) market. Much of the quantitative detail concerning the institutional framework about the forex is derived from Bank of England surveys of the operators within the market carried out in March 1986, April 1989, April 1992 and April 1995. These were carried out at the same time as other central banks' surveys and were reported in the *Bank of England Quarterly Bulletin* of September 1986, November 1989, November 1992 and November 1995, respectively. As a result of the information derived from the 1995 surveys, the BIS estimated that the total global foreign exchange turnover (net of all double counting) amounted to a staggering US$1,190 billion per day (*Bank of England Quarterly Bulletin*, November 1995).

The UK forex is located in London and there is no significant market for foreign exchange elsewhere in the UK. Retail transactions are of course carried out by local financial institutions but these institutions ultimately obtain their currency mainly from transactions on the London forex.[2] London continues to be the largest centre worldwide for foreign exchange dealing and the average dealing turnover was estimated by the Bank of England to be about US$464 billion per day in 1995. This compares with figures of US$90, US$187 and US$300 billion per day in 1986, 1989 and 1992, respectively. Other large centres were New York, Tokyo, Singapore and Hong Kong, where average daily turnovers in US$billion were 244, 161, 105.4 and 90.2, respectively, in 1995. Closely behind were Switzerland ($86.5 billion per day), Germany ($76.2 billion per day) and France ($58.0 billion per day). It is interesting to note that the gap between London and New York and Tokyo has widened considerably, since the corresponding figures for the 1992 surveys for New York and Tokyo were $192 billion and $128 billion per day, respectively. The magnitude of these flows indicates that the trading in currency in London is far greater than that warranted by trade flows[3] into and from the UK, thus demonstrating the importance of London as a world financial market. A second feature revealed by the surveys is the very fast rate of growth in the volume of transactions. This far outweighs the growth of physical trade and no doubt is a reflection of the liberalisation of capital markets and, in particular, a general relaxation of capital controls.

The dollar is the main vehicle of exchange on the London forex and the bulk of the trading consists of sterling/US dollar (11.5 per cent) and

2   One example of the retail business is 'tourist rates' quoted in the press. Compared with the rates quoted in the wholesale market, tourist rates are generally both higher and command a wider spread between the bid and offer rate (see section 11.5 for a discussion of the bid/offer spread). This is partly due to the smaller denomination of the transaction. A second possible reason is that the retail market comprises operators who are likely to have a lower level of knowledge of rates charged elsewhere than the wholesale market operators.

3   This is also true of the market in general. The average daily turnover of US$1,190 billion per day far exceeds the average daily level of trade payments. This indicates the important role of capital movements in the forex.

US dollar/Deutschmark (21.5 per cent). The combined figure for these two types of transactions dropped from 41 per cent of total transactions in 1989 to 33 per cent in 1995. The figures for US dollar/yen trading rose from 12.3 per cent of total transactions in 1992 to 17 per cent in 1995. Nevertheless, trading not involving the US dollar (termed 'cross-currency') also grew, from 16 per cent in 1992 to 19.6 per cent in 1995 (from only 3 and 9 per cent in 1986 and 1989, respectively) and about 16 per cent of this business involved sterling/Deutschmark transactions (the corresponding figure for 1992 was 30 per cent, indicating a widening of the currencies traded in the cross-currency market).

The surveys also showed that the business on the London forex was more diversified than elsewhere. For example, in Tokyo 76 per cent (67 per cent in 1992) of the business was between the yen and US dollar and in New York 64 per cent (74 per cent in 1992) of the business was between the US dollar and the four major currencies (Deutschmark, yen, sterling and the Swiss franc) as compared with 55 per cent in London (59 per cent in 1992).

The market is a continuous dealers' market and there are four types of operators within it:

(i)   *Market makers*. These are mainly the major banks, who agree to buy and sell currencies on a continuous basis. Although the detail may be finalised using other means, such as the telephone, trading is carried out via quotes on screens, so there is no building serving as a market meeting place. The gap between the bid and ask prices reflects the market maker's margin to cover costs and make a profit. Profits will also accrue from taking a view of the future course of exchange rates, that is, speculation. The market maker carries a stock of currencies and he or she is the operator who incurs the risk of unanticipated changes in exchange rates. Business in the market is quite widely dispersed since 10 of the 301 principals in the Bank of England 1995 survey covered only 44 per cent of the reported business (43 per cent in 1992 and 35 per cent in 1989, so there is some slight evidence of a drift towards a greater degree of concentration).

(ii) *Brokers*. These are institutions which act as intermediaries. They act as agents seeking out bargains and do not trade on their own account. The total share of business passing through brokers amounted to 35 per cent of the total in 1995. The corresponding figures for 1992, 1989 and 1986 were 34 per cent, 38 per cent and 43 per cent, respectively. Although it would appear that there is little change in the position between 1992 and 1995, this is not quite true. Five percentage points of the total passed through electronic brokers as distinct from traditional voice brokers, so there is continuing evidence of a declining share of total business passing through brokers. It is believed that this trend has continued since April 1995 and that use of the traditional voice broker has declined further. The contrasting figures for the US showed 13 per cent of the principals' foreign exchange business passing through electronic brokers and 24 per cent through voice brokers

(iii) *The Bank of England.* Apart from its role of supervising the market, the Bank will, as is true of other central banks, intervene in the foreign exchange markets to influence the exchange rate. Intervention is normally carried out via a broker, with the identity of the Bank being kept secret.

(iv) *Customers.* Customers for foreign exchange transactions on the forex are large companies and other financial institutions. The proportion of turnover reported to have been accounted for between market makers and their customers rose from 9 per cent in 1986, 15 per cent in 1989 (9 per cent with other financial institutions and 6 per cent with non-financial institutions) and 23 per cent in 1992 (14 per cent with other financial institutions and 9 per cent with non-financial institutions) to 25 per cent of total turnover in 1995 (18 per cent with other financial institutions and 7 per cent with non-financial institutions).

11.5 Nature of forex business

Two types of cash market transactions can be distinguished:

(i)   spot transactions,
(ii) forward transactions.

Discussion of derivative transactions are reserved until chapter 13.

Spot transactions are required to be settled within two working days of the agreement. These fell as a proportion of total turnover from 1986 to 1995 (73 per cent to 41 per cent) whereas the proportion of forward transactions showed an increase from 27 to 60 per cent over the same period. In the following discussion we will use the dollar/sterling rate for illustrative purposes. Market makers quote two rates. The lower rate represents the rate or price at which they are prepared to buy sterling in exchange for US dollars (or, of course, sell dollars in return for sterling). The higher rate is the rate at which they are prepared to sell sterling in return for US dollars (or equivalently buy dollars in exchange for sterling). For example, the *Financial Times* in the currency market report section on 9 July 1998 gave, amongst other information, the following for the US 'pound spot – forward against the pound' for 8 July:

(i)   closing midpoint, 1.6372;
(ii)   bid–offer spread, 368–376.

The spot quotation shows the best closing sterling midpoint rate, that is, the average of the buying and selling. On this day the spread was given by 1.6368 to 1.6376 so that market makers would buy pounds from the seller at the rate of $1.6368 for each pound. Conversely they would be prepared to sell sterling at the rate of $1.6376 per £1. The bid–offer spread quoted above indicates this range in shortened form, by omitting the 1.6 from the full quote.

Forward transactions represent an agreement to purchase the currency at a later date but at a price agreed now. An outright forward transaction occurs where there is an agreement to purchase/sell a currency forward without any corresponding agreement to resell/repurchase that currency at a later date. A margin may be required by the seller of the forward contract but some market makers merely require the purchaser to hold cash in a deposit account with them. As evidenced by the Bank of England 1995 survey, the bulk of such forward contracts were for maturities up to seven days (42 percentage points out of the 60 per cent of total market turnover comprising forward contracts). Seventeen percentage points represented maturities greater than seven days but up to one year, with the remaining 1 per cent being for maturities more than one year. In some instances the trader will not be certain when the precise payment is required and he or she can, in such circumstances, arrange for an option forward contract, which enables the trader to purchase (or sell) the currency at an agreed rate within a specified time period rather than on a particular date. A further type of forward contract is a 'swap', either a spot purchase against a forward sale (or vice versa) or a purchase and sale of currencies forward for different dates. This type of contract formed the major component of the forward transactions (52 percentage points out of the total of 60 per cent).

The forward rates at the end of trading on 8 July 1998 were shown in the same currency market report as $1.6345 for delivery in one month's time, $1.6286 in three months' time and $1.6405 in one year's time. Also quoted is the percentage gap between the spot and forward rates (i.e. [spot rate – forward rate]/spot rate) at an annualised rate; for example, for the three-month forward rate 2.1 per cent, calculated as $4[100\{(1.6372 - 1.6286)/1.6372]\}$.[4]

4   The multiplication by 4 is to convert the figure to an annual basis.

11.6   The efficiency of the foreign exchange market

The question of whether the foreign exchange market is efficient (in the informational sense) is one of considerable importance for the end customer of the market. If arbitrage between sophisticated traders produces prices which do reflect instantaneously all available information, then forecasting by end customers is not a worthwhile exercise since the market has already processed the available information. In this section we provide a brief survey of the current literature on market efficiency with respect to the foreign exchange markets. This research is ongoing and the interested reader is recommended to examine the original literature. A particularly good survey is contained in Taylor (1995).

We first of all consider the evidence concerning the existence or otherwise of PPP. Efficiency with respect to PPP is different from the types of efficiency so far examined because it involves a time element. Arbitrage in goods is not instantaneous as is the case in arbitrage in financial instruments. Hence PPP would be expected to apply in the long run (unspecified period) but not in the short run. The empirical literature on this subject is, to say the least, voluminous. It is therefore possible in this text to present only the main themes of the various studies – see Copeland (1994), Pilbeam (1992) and Taylor (1995) for further discussion and references. The main conclusions from the literature are as follows:

(i)   The evidence concerning the existence of PPP is ambiguous. Some studies find support, others do not. Evidence is more supportive of the existence of PPP in the long run rather than the short run. It is also true that more recent studies find quite strong support for PPP in the long run.
(ii) Evidence is more supportive of PPP for traded than non-traded goods.
(iii) The exchange rate is more volatile than national price levels. This is contrary to PPP.
(iv) Graphical presentation of bilateral exchange rates demonstrates periods of prolonged departure from PPP but also a tendency to fluctuate around the PPP level.

Reverting back to Fama's (1970) classification of types of efficiency (see chapter 7), we first of all deal with the weak tests. One type of study concerning the weak efficiency of the foreign exchange markets relates to filter rules. As noted in chapter 7, the nature of a filter rule is to buy the currency if the price rises x per cent above a recent trough and sell the currency if it falls y per cent below a recent peak. The object of the rule is to identify upturns and downturns other than small fluctuations and the values of x and y are set by the speculator in the light of previous experience of the series. Clearly, the smaller are x and y the greater will be the number of profitable opportunities identified but also the greater the cost of the transactions, which will offset and perhaps eliminate the profits obtained. On the other hand, large values for x and y will reduce the transaction costs but miss some profitable opportunities. Two major studies of the profitability of filter rules were carried out by Dooley and Shafer (1976) and Logue and Sweeney (1977). Both these studies identified profits above a 'buy and hold' strategy but losses were incurred in some periods. This raises the question whether these profits were the reward for incurring risk of exchange rate losses. Also, there is a fundamental problem with this type of study concerning whether the profitable filter rules derived in such studies are genuinely 'ex ante', that is, represent trading opportunities open to traders. In any case one can argue that if a profitable filter rule were identified traders would use the rule and the resulting arbitrage would eliminate the profits. Taylor (1986) examined time series analysis methods of forecasting the sterling/dollar exchange rate using daily observations for the period 1974 to 1982. He again found some improvement of the forecasts over predictions by market prices but the improvement was quite small.

One type of semi-strong test of market efficiency arises from covered interest arbitrage establishing IRP (see equation 11.5 and related discussion). This hypothesis has been tested by a number of researchers, including Frenkel and Levich (1975, 1977) and Taylor (1987). In general, Frenkel and Levich, using end-of-day data, found that profits were not available from covered interest arbitrage in the eurocurrency markets after taking into consideration transaction costs. In the case of domestic centres some profits were available but these could perhaps be accounted for by the greater risks involved, such as actual or potential controls on capital movements. Taylor, using high-frequency data (i.e. observations of actual rates during the day), found some departures from IRP during times of turbulence on the foreign exchange markets but that in general IRP held. Further casual evidence arises from the fact that many banks define the forward rate by solving equation 11.5 for F_t given the spot rate and appropriate rates of interest. The quotation indicated above from the *Financial Times* is derived in this manner.

A second type of semi-strong test involves testing for 'speculative' efficiency. Given the existence of risk-neutral speculators, the expected (ex ante) return in different centres should be the same if the market is efficient. The linchpin for testing speculative efficiency is the uncovered IRP condition, which states that:

$$\Delta E_t s_{t+k} = R_t^* - R_t \tag{11.7}$$

where $E_t \Delta s_{t+k}$ is the expected change in the spot rate between time t and $t + k$ with the expectation formed at time t (s represents price of foreign currency per unit of domestic currency in logarithms) and R represents the interest rate appropriate for period t to $t + k$. The asterisk denotes the foreign rate of interest.

To illustrate this condition, consider what would happen if this equality did not hold taking, as an example, the UK as the domestic country and the US as the foreign country. Hence the exchange rate is quoted in the form of dollars per pound. If $R_t^£ > R_t^\$$ (with the super-scripts £ and $ representing the domestic (UK) and foreign (US) rates of interest) then the pound is expected to depreciate (i.e. $\Delta E_t s_{t+k} < 0$) by the same amount so that the return in the two countries is the same. If $\Delta E_t s_{t+k} < R_t^\$ - R_t^£$ then the return in the UK will be greater than that in the US so that the resulting arbitrage (i.e. funds flowing to the UK) should eliminate this gap. The converse would occur if $\Delta E_t s_{t+k} > R_t^\$ - R_t^£$. Note that this condition critically depends on the existence of risk-neutral speculators and would be vitiated if a risk premium was neces-sary to compensate speculators for taking risky positions in the forex. Equating the return in the overseas centre with that in the domestic centre using equation 11.5 we obtain:

$$(1 + R_t^£) = S_t (1 + R_t^\$) / F_t \tag{11.8}$$

Taking logarithms and noting that the logarithm of $(1 + a$ small decimal$)$ is approximately equal to the original number and rearranging gives:

$$s_t - f_t = R_t^£ - R_t^\$ \text{ or equivalently}$$

$$f_t - s_t = R_t^\$ - R_t^£ \tag{11.9}$$

where the lower-case letters denote logarithms.

Substituting equation 11.9 into equation 11.7 and noting that, with rational expectations, the gap between the expected change and actual change will differ only by a random forecast error term with a mean of zero:

$$\Delta s_{t+k} = f_t - s_t + \varepsilon_t \tag{11.10}$$

This can be estimated by the regression equation:

$$\Delta s_{t+k} = \alpha + \beta(f_t - s_t) + \varepsilon_t \tag{11.11}$$

Equation 11.11 will be equivalent to equation 11.10 only if $\alpha = 0$ and $\beta = 1$. Empirical studies over a number of currencies with differing time periods have failed to validate this requirement (see e.g. Fama 1984). In fact most studies derive an estimate of β nearer -1. Thus the joint hypothesis of risk neutrality and speculative efficiency is decisively rejected.

In a similar manner we can evaluate the forecasting ability of the forward exchange rate. If we assume again that speculators are risk neutral, then their sole motivation will be to attain profits. If the forward rate for the dollar against the pound is below the level they expect at the end of the period in question, then they will buy sterling forward and sell the sterling spot on the maturity of the agreement. If their expectations are correct they will obtain a profit denominated in dollars. Conversely, if the risk-neutral speculators expect a lower spot rate as compared with the relevant forward rate, then they will sell sterling forward and buy spot later to cover the forward contract. Obviously if the exchange rate moves in the reverse direction to that expected, then the speculators will make a loss and the assumption of risk neutrality infers that they are not deterred from their attempt to take advantage of potential profits by the chance of a loss. Hence, given the existence of risk-neutral speculators, the forward rate should provide a good prediction of the spot rate in the future. More formally:

$$F_t = E_t S_{t+k} \tag{11.12}$$

where F_t is the forward rate observed at time t for the delivery of currency at time $t + k$ and $E_t S_{t+k}$ is the expected spot rate at time $t + k$ with the expectation formed at time t.

It is possible to test equation 11.12 by running regressions of the form:

$$S_{t+k} = \alpha + \beta F_t \tag{11.13}$$

If the forward rate is an unbiased predictor of the spot rate, it is necessary that the estimates of α and β are not statistically different from 0 and 1, respectively. It appears conclusively that this relationship is rejected by the data – for example see Baillie *et al.* (1983) using data for the US dollar, sterling, the Deutschmark, lira and the French franc (1973–80) and the Canadian dollar (1977–80). There is, however, a technical econometric problem with the estimation of equations of the form given by equation 11.13 since the series are not stationary. An alternative approach is to examine the forward premium (i.e. $\{F_t - S_t\}/S_t$) as a predictor of the future movement in the exchange rate. This can be tested by running regressions of the form:

$$\Delta S_{t+k} = \alpha + \beta FP_t \qquad (11.14)$$

where ΔS_{t+k} is the change in the spot exchange rate between time t and $t + k$, and FP_t refers to the forward premium at time t for delivery of currency at time $t + k$. Again, if the forward premium is an unbiased predictor of future movements in the spot rate, it is necessary that the estimates of α and β are not statistically different from 0 and 1, respectively. It appears conclusively that this relationship is rejected by the data – see for example Fama (1984), amongst many others.

Finally in this respect, it is possible to look at the forecasting errors, e_t (defined as $S_{t+k} - F_t$), to see if they were correlated with information available to agents at time t. This can be checked by running a regression of the following form:

$$e_t = \Gamma X_t \qquad (11.15)$$

where X_t is a vector of variables known at time t. If the coefficients of Γ are not all zero, then the market is not processing all available information. This requirement is known more technically as a requirement that the errors should be orthogonal to any information available to the agents.

The types of variable in X can be divided into two categories: lagged values of e, and other information additional to lagged e (i.e. weak and semi-strong tests). Tests of both types again conclusively reject the error orthogonality – see for example amongst many others Macdonald and Taylor (1989).

Two explanations are possible for this rejection of the hypothesis that the forward rate is an unbiased predictor. First, the market is inefficient and is not processing all available information correctly. Second, speculators are not risk neutral but are, in fact, risk averse, so that they require a risk premium (which may vary over time) to compensate them for the risk of a loss following an adverse movement in the exchange rate such that:

$$\Delta E_t s_{t+k} + \rho_t = R^*_t - R_t \qquad (11.16)$$

where ρ_t is a time-varying risk premium correlated with the interest differential or forward premium. So far little progress has been made in identifying such a premium. Whatever the reason, it is apparent that the dual hypothesis of risk neutrality and market efficiency is decisively rejected by the data. Survey data on expected exchange rates have been used to try to disentangle the two effects in the dual hypothesis (see e.g. Froot and Frankel 1989). The general conclusion from this literature

seems to be that both risk aversion and failure of the rational expectations hypothesis are both responsible for the rejection of the hypothesis
of speculative efficiency.

Finally in this section we look at the performance of professional
forecasting agencies. The test examines whether forecasting agencies
can consistently outperform the market, that is, a strong test in the Fama
terminology. It is, of course, difficult to obtain information on forecasts
sold to clients. However, a limited number of tests have been carried out
by researchers, including Goodman (1979), Levich (1979), Bilson
(1983) and Blake *et al.* (1986). The studies by Goodman, Levich and
Blake *et al.* suggested that the forward rate was at least as good a
predictor as that provided by the forecasting agency. Bilson found that
the gain from combining forecasts including those of a forecasting
agency and adopting a portfolio approach involving more than just one
currency offered the prospect of gaining substantial profits.

The question of whether the foreign exchange market conforms to the
efficient markets hypothesis remains open. It seems clear that the
evidence clearly points to the rejection of the dual hypothesis of risk
neutrality and efficiency.

Chapter 12

Eurosecurities markets

12.1 Introduction

In chapter 7 we established that London is one of the main international financial centres in the world. Three main areas of international financial activity can be distinguished: banking, bonds and similar types of securities, and equities. We have already discussed the nature and extent of international (mainly eurocurrency) banking in chapter 4 and the extent of international equities trading through London in chapter 8. In this chapter we examine the eurosecurities markets which have developed out of the eurocurrency markets and then discuss some of the wider developments in international financing. The eurosecurities markets we consider, in sections 12.2 to 12.4, are those of eurobonds, euronotes and euro-equities. These markets have been the subject of a great deal of financial innovation over the past 15 years and the new financial instruments which have emerged have tended to blur the distinction between traditional international banking and securities trading. We finish this chapter therefore with a discussion of dis-intermediation. This process describes how changes in the financial environment and the changing preferences of borrowers and international banks have led to a move away from international financial intermediation through banks to direct financing through greater use of the international capital markets.

12.2 Eurobonds

In this section we examine the nature of eurobonds, the reasons for the growth in the issue of such bonds and the variety of types of eurobond issued, and the methods of issuing them. International issues of asset-backed securities are also discussed in this section, as most of these issues are classed as eurobonds.

Table 12.1   *Classification of international bonds*

| | Bond issues | |
	By residents	*By non-residents*
In domestic currency	Domestic bonds	Traditional foreign bonds
In foreign currency	Eurobonds	Eurobonds

Traditional foreign bonds and eurobonds together comprise all international bonds.

12.2.1 *Nature of eurobonds*

A large borrower wishing to raise long-term funds through bond issues can turn to either the domestic bond market, as we saw in chapter 9, or to the international bond markets. We can distinguish between two types of international bond. A traditional foreign bond is one issued by a non-resident borrower on the market of a single country and denominated in that country's currency. For example, foreign bonds issued in New York in dollars, London in sterling or Tokyo in yen are known respectively as yankee, bulldog and samurai issues. The other type of international bond is the eurobond, which is a bond issued in markets other than that of the currency of issue and sold internationally. Thus, a German company which issues a US dollar bond in New York is issuing a foreign (yankee) bond, whereas if the company issues the bond in a number of national markets, other than the US, then it is classed as a eurobond. Table 12.1 illustrates the difference between domestic, foreign and eurobond issues.

Eurobonds are generally issued 'offshore', which means that the issue of such bonds is not subject to the rules and regulations which govern the issue of foreign bonds in that currency, such as obligations to issue detailed prospectuses and any interest-withholding taxes, that is, taxes deducted at source before interest is paid for non-resident holders of bonds. This is not to say that there are no restrictions on eurobond issues and trading, since the ISMA, which is a self-regulatory body, has introduced trading rules and standardised procedures in the eurobond market.

12.2.2 *Growth of the eurobond market*

The first eurobond was issued in 1963 and their use grew at a slow rate throughout the 1960s and 1970s, and then explosively over the early 1980s. Table 12.2 shows the characteristics of international bonds issued over the 1980s and early 1990s.

Table 12.2   *Growth of international bond issues, 1980–96*

	1980	1982	1984	1986	1988	1990	1992	1994	1996
Total international bonds									
($billion)	38.3	75.5	109.5	226.4	229.7	241.7	333.7	429	709
Eurobonds									
(%)	53	67	75	83	78	78	83	86	83
Foreign bonds									
(%)	47	33	26	17	22	22	17	14	17
Currencies (%)									
US dollar	42.7	63.9	63.5	54.9	36.8	34.8	37.7	38	44
Yen	4.9	5.2	5.5	10.4	9.8	13.4	12.2	18	11
Swiss franc	19.5	15.0	12.0	10.3	11.5	10.1	5.4	5	4
Deutschmark	21.9	7.1	6.2	7.5	10.3	7.9	10.1	7	14
Sterling	3.0	2.6	5.1	4.8	10.4	9.2	6.9	7	7
ECU	0.2	2.6	2.8	3.1	4.9	7.8	6.3	2	1
Other	7.8	3.6	4.9	9.0	16.3	16.1	22.4	23	19

Source: OECD, *Financial Statistics*, various issues.

There are a number of reasons for the rapid growth of eurobond activity over the early 1980s. Over this period international interest rates fell steadily, making the issue of both equities and fixed-interest bonds more attractive to borrowers. Banks have generally been reluctant to lend at fixed rates of interest over the long term. In addition, the problems of banks over the 1980s and the greater cost of borrowing through banks, described in section 12.6, led borrowers to look more to the international capital markets as a source of funds. Whilst international bond issues grew rapidly over the 1980s, it is clear from table 12.2 that eurobond issues, starting from a roughly equal share with foreign bonds at the beginning of the 1980s, have accounted for the majority of this growth. One reason for this is the lower cost of eurobond issues compared with domestic or foreign bond issues. The ability of buyers of bonds to escape withholding tax and income tax on interest receipts enables borrowers to issue at lower yields. Eurobonds are generally issued in bearer form, eliminating the need for registration of ownership so that ownership is vested in the holder. The anonymity this brings allows owners to avoid tax on interest. The repeal of withholding tax on interest paid to foreign purchasers of domestic bonds in the US in 1984 together with changes to allow US residents to issue bearer bonds to non-resident borrowers may have been expected to make eurobonds less attractive. However, there are other advantages to issuing eurobonds, which account for the continued growth. The lack of restrictions on eurobond trading makes it easier and therefore speedier to make issues and thus take advantage of a favourable 'window' in interest rate movements or other economic changes. Also, the liberalisation of domestic capital markets in the US, Germany and Japan and the general globalisation of capital markets that took place over the 1980s have encouraged borrowers and investors to look more to international capital markets.

International bond issues are denominated in currencies which are important for international trade. This explains the importance of dollar-denominated eurobonds. However, the dollar-denominated dominance of the eurobond market is not quite as great as the dollar dominance of the eurocurrency loans market. This is because borrowers have also tended to issue bonds to tap the savings of countries which have a high savings ratio, in particular the economies of Germany and Japan. Furthermore, investors look for securities denominated in strong currencies. As we shall see in section 12.5, the use of swap contracts allows the currency denomination of the funds raised to be swapped into a different currency if required.

It should be noted that the Swiss authorities have acted to prevent the emergence of a eurobond market in Swiss francs so as to control the international use of its currency. Swiss franc issues of international bonds are therefore solely issues of foreign bonds. The prevention of eurobonds denominated in Swiss francs together with the growth of eurobonds vis-à-vis foreign bonds partly account for the decline in international bonds denominated in Swiss francs.

One feature of recent eurobond issues, revealed in table 12.2, is the growth in ECU-denominated bonds up until 1992. (ECU stands for European Currency Unit, which is a composite currency unit made up of the currencies of the members of the EU.) Issues of ECU-denominated eurobonds grew steadily over the 1980s and early 1990s. Sovereign issues of ECU-denominated bonds provided high-quality benchmarks in the market and promoted the introduction of ECU derivative products, for example at LIFFE and MATIF (see chapter 13). The decline in ECU eurobond issues since 1992 reflects the turmoil in the Exchange Rate Mechanism in 1992 and 1993 and continuing uncertainty about the move to EMU (see chapter 15).

The geographical location of borrowers in the international bond markets in recent years is shown in table 12.3. This shows the dominance of Japanese borrowers, both banks and non-banks, until 1992. The growth in Japanese-based issues of bonds largely reflected the strength of the Japanese stock market over this period, with most of

Table 12.3   *Main issuers of international bonds by country of origin,*
1988–96 (%)

	1988	*1990*	*1992*	*1994*	*1996*
Japan	22	27	17	9	6
US	7	12	5	11	18
UK	12	11	10	8	8
France	7	9	10	8	5
Germany	5	0	6	11	16

Source: OECD, *Financial Statistics*, various issues.

these issues being equity-related bonds (discussed below). The decline in issues in since 1992 is related to the decline in the Japanese stock market over this period. A feature of the market not revealed by table 12.3 is the growth in issues by Latin American countries as growing investor confidence in their economies following Brady deals has permitted a return to the international bond markets (discussed in chapter 4).

12.2.3 *Types of eurobonds*

The eurobond market has been the subject of a great deal of financial innovation since the early 1980s and many different types of eurobond have been created. It is possible though to classify eurobonds as belonging to one of three basic types:

(i)   *Straight fixed-rate bonds*. These are the traditional type of bond with a fixed coupon payment.

(ii) *Floating-rate notes (FRNs)*. These are bonds issued with coupon payments made on a floating-rate basis. The coupon, which usually consists of a margin over a reference rate such as LIBOR, is paid at the end of each interest period, usually six months, and then reset in line with the reference rate for the next interest period. FRNs are generally medium-term bonds, that is, with maturities from 5 to 15 years.

(iii) *Equity-related bonds*. There are two types of equity-related bonds:

   (a) *Convertibles*. These give the holder the right to convert the bond into ordinary shares, with the terms and conditions of the conversion set at the time of issue.

   (b) *Bonds with equity warrants attached*. Warrants are options which give the holder the right to buy shares in a company at

Table 12.4   *Eurobond issues classified by type, 1980–96 (%)*

	1980	1982	1984	1986	1988	1990	1992	1994	1996
Straight	68	70	52	65	72	69	80	70	68
Floating-rate note	22	22	39	25	11	18	13	21	25
Equity related	9	9	8	8	17	14	7	9	7

Source: BIS, annual reports, various.

a given price in the future. Warrants are attached to the bonds but are securities in their own right and so can be stripped from the bond and sold separately. This distinguishes them from convertibles, where the conversion rights are an integral part of the issue.

A breakdown of issue volumes by type is shown in table 12.4.

Floating-rate notes were the fastest-growing section of the eurobond markets in 1983, 1984 and 1985 and the first half of 1986. There were various innovations on the standard FRN, and issues by UK building societies and other UK financial institutions pushed sterling into the second largest currency for FRNs. The FRN market is dominated by financial institutions, banks in particular, which both issue and invest. A particular form of FRN, the perpetual FRN, so called because it is never redeemed, was popular with banks as it qualified as primary capital. All these developments receded with the virtual collapse of the FRN market at the end of 1986. This was due to a variety of reasons, including excess competition in the issue side of the market driving down yields on some issues to unattractive levels and concern from central bankers that perpetual FRNs both issued and held by banks did not properly spread risk outside the banking system. A further contributing factor to the decline of the FRN market at that time, namely growing interest in the eurocommercial paper market, is discussed below.

The FRN market appears to have recovered to some extent since 1992 as investors looked to longer-term issues of bonds and away from short-term notes such as commercial paper. One of the reasons for this is that investors are attracted to long-term floating-rate debt when interest rates are expected to rise and there was an expectation in the market in 1992 that US interest rates in particular had reached a trough.

Another factor behind the renewed interest in FRNs by borrowers is the increased use of structured FRNs. These are designed to respond to investors' views of future interest rate trends but do not expose the issuer to associated interest rate risk. About 30 per cent of issues of FRNs were structured in some way in 1993. There are three principal types of structured FRNs.

(i) Reverse FRNs are structured to produce rising coupons as a floating-rate reference rate falls. The notes contain an implicit interest rate cap, with a strike price equal to the fixed-rate element, as well as non-negativity clauses to prevent rates falling below zero.

(ii) Collared FRNs contain caps and floors, thereby generating maximum and minimum returns. They contain two embedded options and in effect the issuer purchases a cap from the investor and at the same time sells the investor a floor.

(iii) Step-up recovery FRNs (SURFs) pay coupons linked to yields on comparable longer-maturity bonds. With a rising yield curve they therefore pay the higher yield available at the longer maturity.

So, in 1993, with investors' expectations that US interest rates were reaching a trough, there was a high demand for collared dollar FRNs. Investors with views on the shape of the US yield curve could have alternatively purchased SURFs. However, in Europe in 1993 investors expected interest rates to fall further in many countries and thus were keen to invest in reverse FRNs. These swap-related derivative strategies (caps and floors) are discussed further in chapter 13.

The equity-related issues of international bonds saw rapid growth over the latter part of the 1980s. These issues have been predominantly of bonds with attached warrants issued mainly by Japanese investors denominated in US dollars. As noted above, this was related to the strength of the Japanese stock market in the late 1980s, which made the issues attractive to investors. As the Japanese equity indices have fallen in the 1990s then issues of equity-related bonds, which are related to these indices, have fallen.

12.2.4 *International asset-backed securities*

Asset-backed securities are tradable instruments supported by a pool of loans or other financial assets (see chapter 4). These allow both financial and non-financial institutions to securitise illiquid assets on the balance sheet, so that they can be taken off the balance sheet. The majority of ABSs are issued into the domestic US market. However, there has been a growth in international ABSs (essentially eurobonds, as they are targeted at non-resident investors) in recent years, as demonstrated by table 12.5.

Table 12.5   *Asset-backed bonds: announced issues in domestic and inter-national markets, 1986–96 ($billion)*

	1986	1988	1990	1992	1994	1996[a]
US						
Domestic	145.7	152.7	238.4	516.3	377.7	336.4
International	0.7	0.2	10.1	2.0	6.4	65.7
UK[b]						
International	–	5.9	3.8	1.1	4.9	4.8
Other						
Domestic	–	0.6	2.8	7.2	5.6	17.6
International	–	0.1	0.2	1.3	4.0	9.2
Total international	0.7	6.2	14.1	4.4	15.3	79.7

[a]First three quarters of 1996 annualised.
[b]All sterling issues have been euromarket issues.
Source: BIS, *International Banking and Financial Market Developments*, November 1997.

International ABS issues are dominated by those originating in the US, and hence dollar denominated (accounting for over 80 per cent of issues in 1996), with UK issues accounting for around 6 per cent. In fact the first ABS issues in the eurobond sector were eurosterling issues by UK-based specialist mortgage lenders who financed mortgage lending from inter-bank market finance (see chapter 5). This business declined in 1992 following a decline in new mortgage commitments. In recent years there has been a growth in international ABS issues from continental Europe (including issues from Ireland, Spain, Germany and France). It is predicted (see Janneau 1996) that international ABS issues will increase as institutions and their regulators see the advantages afforded by securitisation.

12.2.5 *Methods of issue of eurobonds*

Since the 1980s the standard method of issuing eurobonds is by way of a bought deal. This involves a lead manager buying the entire issue at an agreed price prior to the announcement of the issue. The issue is then resold (i.e. syndicated) after the announcement.

Since the late 1980s, members of the syndicate enter into a contractual agreement not to resell at a lower price until the full issue has

Table 12.6 *Euronotes: amounts outstanding at year end, 1986–96 ($billion)*

	1986	1988	1990	1992	1994	1996
Euronotes	29.4	72.3	111.3	177.1	378.7	834.1
of which:						
short-term notes[a]	29.0	66.7	89.4	115.7	119.3	172.0
medium-term notes	0.4	5.6	21.9	61.4	259.4	662.1

[a] Combines eurocommercial paper and other short-term notes.
Source: BIS, annual report, various years.

been completed. In US terminology this is termed a 'fixed priced reoffer' technique.

The secondary market in eurobonds is mainly OTC, with settlement being achieved via one of the international clearing systems (i.e. Euroclear or Cedel).

12.3 **Euronotes**

In contrast to the longer-term eurobonds, the euronote markets encompass the various types of short-term securities issued to tap the eurocurrency markets. There are three basic types of euronotes, although there are many variations on these. The original euronotes were note-issuance facilities (NIFs), which first appeared in 1978. The other types of euronote instruments, namely eurocommercial paper (ECP) and medium-term notes, were based on the NIFs and made a significant appearance in the mid-1980s. NIFs and eurocommercial paper are classed as short-term notes. The amounts outstanding of the various types of euronotes over the decade 1986–96 are shown in table 12.6.

12.3.1 *Note-issuance facilities*

These are formalised, syndicated, underwritten medium-term loans which enable borrowers to issue a stream of short-term bearer notes, usually of one, three or six months' maturity, on a rollover basis. These are generally issued through a tender panel and if the borrowers are unable to sell the notes at a given spread over LIBOR to investors in the market, then the underwriting banks guarantee to purchase the notes themselves. Thus, borrowers obtain medium-term funds, generally for seven to ten years, financed by successive issues of short-term notes. NIFs therefore transform short-term funds into long-term funds, a transformation which is normally carried out through banks in their role as financial intermediaries. In this situation banks are, however, simply earning fee income for arranging and underwriting the facility and, as long as the notes are placed at the maturity dates without problems, then the business is off the balance sheet.

Note-issuance facilities were developed as an alternative to syndicated loans and partly performed that role in 1984 and 1985 as issues of these facilities increased at a rapid rate. Issues have declined relative to other types of short-term notes since the late 1980s, largely because of the action of central banks, which sought to ensure that banks increase their capital when underwriting NIFs for borrowers with low credit standing. This led to banks limiting NIFs to borrowers with high credit standing and, partly in response to this, new types of short-term credits have emerged, in particular ECP.

12.3.2 *Eurocommercial paper*

The issue of ECP is a more recent development in the euromarkets, making a significant appearance in late 1984, although the issuance of commercial paper dates from the mid-nineteenth century in the US (see chapter 10, section 10.3, on domestic money markets for a description of commercial paper). ECP programmes differ from NIFs in two important respects: first, they are not underwritten; and second, borrowers use a small group of appointed banks and dealers to distribute the notes on a 'best efforts' basis. In addition, the paper generally has more flexible maturities than NIFs, which can be tailored to investors' preferences. Dealers impart marketability to the paper by agreeing to repurchase them from holders before maturity. An important difference between US commercial paper and ECP is that the former is always credit rated. When ECP first appeared, very few of the issues were credit rated, although in recent years the majority of new issues have had a credit rating. This trend towards a fully credit-rated market appears to have been accelerated by defaults by some ECP issuers in 1988 and 1989. As shown in table 12.6, the greater emphasis on credit ratings appears to have had a slowing effect on the market for ECP in the early 1990s, as lesser-rated borrowers who were originally attracted to the market in 1986–88 found it difficult to establish facilities. Another factor behind the slowdown in the growth of issues in the ECP market is competition from the newly developing domestic commercial paper markets in Europe and the more mature US market. Also, in recent years ECP has faced competition from the more flexible euro medium-term notes (EMTNs).

12.3.3 *Euro medium-term notes*

These are borrowing facilities backed by issues of paper where the paper generally has a maturity of over one year. The maturity of the paper can in theory be any length of time up to infinity but in practice is limited to around ten years. The market has shown steady growth since its emergence on a significant scale in 1986, with an acceleration in growth since 1993. One factor behind the recent growth has been the relaxation of issuing constraints in several countries. Japanese companies have been permitted to tap the EMTN market directly since July 1993 and in a number of European countries deregulation measures have been taken to facilitate the use of the national currency in EMTN programmes. Another feature of the market in recent years has been that more than half the issues have been linked to derivative instruments (structured). There are a number of reasons to suggest that the EMTN market will expand in the future and in particular will take business away from the international bond markets. First, medium-term notes (MTNs) are more flexible instruments than bonds. The maturity of the note issues together with the characteristics of the drawings under a MTN facility can be varied to meet the needs of investor and borrower. Second, the liquidity of a bond issue is to a large extent determined by its size and investors may require some minimum issue size in order to attract them to hold the bond. In contrast, the liquidity of MTNs is provided by the guarantee of dealers to buy and sell the security. Finally, recent developments in the US domestic market, where corporate borrowing appears to have shifted from bonds to MTNs, suggest that this may carry over to the international capital markets.

12.4 **Euro-equities**

Euro-equities or international equities are equities issued for sale outside the issuer's domestic market. The term 'international equity issues' is used to refer to both primary issues of shares and secondary placements

Table 12.7 *Volume of international equity issues, 1986–96 ($billion)*

	1984	1986	1988	1990	1992	1994	1996
International equity issues	0.2	14	11	15	26	62	83

Source: BIS, *International Banking and Financial Market Developments*, November 1997.

of existing shares. The equity instrument is the same as that issued in domestic markets, so the only difference between domestic and international issues of equities is the method of distribution. One method of international equity issue is to obtain a simultaneous listing on more than one national exchange. This method has become less popular as it can be costly owing to widely different listing procedures across the various exchanges. A method that is increasingly used is the two-tranche issue, where all the issue is listed on a domestic exchange but one tranche is targeted at foreign investors. The distribution of the foreign tranche is increasingly organised through a syndicate made up of one financial institution in each country where the issue is targeted.

There are no reliable data available on international equity issues but table 12.7 shows approximate figures for the volume of international equity issues since the mid-1980s. Up until 1987 growth of international equity issues was rapid owing to rising world stock markets and an increasing tendency towards international portfolio diversification following both liberalisation of financial markets and the abolition of capital controls in many countries. This growth was reversed following the world stock markets crash of 1987. However, growth has resumed in the 1990s as world stock market indices have grown, and such growth appears likely to continue, fuelled by the continuing trend towards international portfolio diversification.

There are a number of advantages to a company from an international issue of its equity. First, it has the effect of widening the ownership of the company beyond that of the domestic market. Secondly, it may be possible to issue at lower cost in foreign markets. Finally, it provides an escape from the size constraint of the domestic market. This is particularly the case for companies in some European countries with small stock markets. At present the management of international equity issues can be more profitable for a bank than an international bond issue. Greater competition in the future, however, is likely to reduce margins and therefore issue costs.

12.5   Use of swaps in eurosecurities markets

The nature of swaps is discussed in chapter 13, on derivative instruments. Swaps are widely used in international capital market transactions and were one of the forces behind the rapid growth of the eurobond markets over the 1980s. Swaps enable a borrower to raise funds in the market in which it has a comparative advantage and then swap into a liability with preferred characteristics. For example, a borrower, X, may have a competitive advantage in the fixed-interest bond market but a preference for floating-rate funds to match its

Table 12.8   *Over-the-counter derivative markets, 1988–95: notional principal outstanding ($billion)*

	1988	1989	1990	1991	1992	1993	1994	1995[a]
Interest rate swaps	1,011	1,503	2,311	3,065	3,851	6,177	8,816	12,811
Currency swaps	320	449	578	807	860	900	915	1,197

[a] Figure for 1995 not directly comparable to previous years owing to a broadening of the reporting population.
Source: BIS, annual reports, various issues.

floating-rate assets. Thus, the borrower can raise funds at a competitive cost through the issue of a fixed-rate bond but swap for a floating-rate obligation with borrower Y, which has a competitive advantage in the floating-rate market but is looking for low-cost fixed-rate funds. As long as the interest rates swapped into by the two parties are lower than the interest rates obtainable from direct borrowing through the markets where they do not have a competitive advantage then the swap is worthwhile. This fixed/floating-rate swap is a classic type of interest rate swap and, if the floating rate is one linked to LIBOR, is known as a 'plain vanilla'.

A second type of swap transaction used in the international capital markets is the currency swap. Here the swap involves an exchange of interest payments and principal denominated in one currency for payments in another. Again, borrowers will borrow in the currency in which they have a comparative advantage and then swap into the preferred currency. There are two main types of currency swap in the capital markets: fixed/fixed currency swaps, and fixed/floating currency swaps. The latter, referred to as cross-currency interest rate swaps, involve both a currency and interest rate swap. More complex swaps have been developed in recent years and the interested reader is referred to Walmsley (1988).

Table 12.8 indicates the size of the interest rate and currency swap markets in recent years. There has been a dramatic increase in the use of swap contracts, and interest swap contracts in particular. This growth partly reflects the growth in international bond issues, where a large proportion of fixed-rate bonds involve an interest rate or currency swap. Another factor behind this growth is the continuing volatility in interest rates and currency markets. The growth in other swap-related derivatives reflects the growing use of derivatives such as collars and caps with issues of FRNs and MTNs (see discussion above). The US dollar market

accounted for approximately 70 per cent of the interest rate swap market
and 85 per cent of activity in the currency swap market involved the US
dollar on one side of the transaction.

12.6   Dis-intermediation

Major borrowers can raise funds in the international markets in three
ways: they can borrow from the banking system, issue equities, or issue
debt securities such as bonds or notes.

As we established in chapter 2, the basis of banks' existence as
financial intermediaries is that of transaction and information costs. This
applies as much to international financing as it does to domestic
financing. Over the 1980s international banks have been beset by
problems such as bank failures in the US and the sovereign debt crisis,
which have reduced the credit standing of many banks and thus the
competitiveness of their lending rates. It has therefore been suggested
(see for example Bank for International Settlements 1986) that banks
have been losing their comparative advantage in international financing.
In addition, information costs have fallen because of the emergence of a
large number of credit rating agencies over the 1980s. As a consequence, many of the larger borrowers with good credit ratings have
found they can raise funds more cheaply through the international
capital markets. That is, there has been a greater preference, during
some periods since 1980, for direct financing rather than indirect
financing through a bank intermediary. This can be seen in table 12.9,
which shows the relative volumes of the various forms of international
finance since the 1980s.

Net international bank lending, which is made up of syndicated
credits as well as short-term lending, was a declining proportion of total
net international financing over the period 1980 to 1985. This is because
of a switch from bank financing to indirect financing through the capital
markets, a process known as dis-intermediation, for the reasons outlined
above. Eurobonds were the main alternative long-term funding security
to bank intermediation in the early 1980s. In the mid-1980s short- to
medium-term direct financing through the issue of euronotes also
emerged to compete with syndicated bank lending. However, this process of dis-intermediation (i.e. a switch from bank lending to securities
issues) was halted in the latter half of the 1980s. The reason for this was
principally the renewed growth in bank lending, which can be explained
by the ambitious expansion of the Japanese banks over this period
(discussed in chapter 7) and the increase in corporate restructuring in
the US and UK financed largely by debt. In addition, issues of
international securities are subject to considerable volatility owing to

Table 12.9 *Breakdown of international financing, 1980–96 ($billion)*

	1980	1982	1984	1986	1988	1990	1992	1994	1996
Net international bank lending[a]	160	95	90	206	260	465	195	190	410
Net international bond financing[b]	28	59	84	158	139	132	119	145	275
Net euronote placement[c]			5	13	20	33	40	140	224
Total international financing	188	154	179	377	419	630	354	475	909
minus double counting[d]	8	9	24	82	69	80	75	60	196
Total net international financing	180	145	155	295	350	550	279	415	713
Bank lending as % of total financing	89	66	58	70	74	85	68	45	56

[a] Net figure excludes inter-bank lending but allows for banks' own use of external funds for domestic lending.
[b] Completed international bond issues (as distinct from announced bond issues recorded in table 12.2) minus redemptions and repurchases.
[c] Completed euronote placements (as distinct from announced issues recorded in table 12.6).
[d] Purchases of bonds by banks and bonds issued by banks to underpin international lending activities.
Source: BIS annual reports, various issues.

linkages with stock markets. The global stock market crash in 1987 halted the growth in international securities issues, with bond issues reaching precrash levels again only in 1989. In the early 1990s bank lending slowed down considerably as a consequence of a slowdown in growth in many developed countries, and related to this is banks' poor performance on the domestic front (particularly in Japan), which has constrained their international lending as a result of having to set aside high loan loss provisions. The recent expansion of bank lending is partly accounted for by a growth in syndicated lending to borrowers with low credit ratings in emerging markets. These borrowers do not generally have access to the international securities markets.

Looking to the future, the factors which led to the expansion of bank lending in the late 1980s look unlikely to be repeated, whilst the spread of dis-intermediation habits to Europe and the growth in the credit rating industry suggest that dis-intermediation may be a long-run trend.

It is a mistake, however, to equate dis-intermediation with a decline in the role of banks. Banks are actively involved in the securities markets in arranging the issue of securities and underwriting or providing guarantees of liquidity in the euronote markets. Banks are also the important players in the derivative markets, such as swaps, futures and options, which underlie many security market transactions. Banks often act as counterparts in swap transactions or perform a transformation of characteristics as they construct tailor-made option and futures retail contracts from the wholesale standardised contracts traded on the exchanges. It can be argued then that dis-intermediation has not led to a greater exclusion of banks from the international financing process but that banks have transferred intermediation business that appeared on the balance sheet to fee-earning business that is conducted off the balance sheet. Banks can be seen to have adapted, and more importantly innovated, in response to the changing preferences of international borrowers. The innovation that has taken place has tended to blur the boundaries between traditional intermediation and securities transacting.

12.7   Conclusion

In this chapter we have looked at the development of eurosecurities markets, which are the international equivalents of domestic securities markets discussed in chapters 8, 9 and 10. These have grown rapidly since the 1980s and represent one facet of the internationalisation of finance.

Chapter 13

Financial derivatives

13.1 Introduction

Financial derivatives can be defined as instruments whose price is derived from an underlying financial security. The price of the derivative is linked to the price of the underlying asset and arbitrage maintains this link. This makes it possible to construct hedges using derivative contracts so that losses (gains) on the underlying asset are matched by gains (losses) on the derivative contract. In this chapter we will examine the main derivative contracts used in financial markets: financial futures, options, swaps and forward contracts. Derivatives can be categorised according to the type of trade. First, there is the category of exchange-traded instruments and in this case the instruments are purchased or sold on an organised financial exchange or market. This category includes financial futures and traded options. The second category refers to those instruments bought directly from a bank or other financial institution and these are called OTC derivatives. OTC derivatives include swaps, forward contracts and options.

The organisation of this chapter is as follows. In the next section we consider reasons for the development and growth of trading of financial derivatives over the last 20 or so years. In section 13.3 we examine the organisation of trading on LIFFE, the second largest derivatives exchange in the world and the largest in Europe. In the remaining sections we examine the nature of financial futures (section 13.4), options (section 13.5), swaps (section 13.6) and forward rate agreements (section 13.7). In section 13.8 we summarise a selection of the studies that have examined the efficiency of derivatives markets before concluding in section 13.9.

13.2   The development and growth of financial derivatives

Exchange-traded financial derivatives were first developed in the US, by the Chicago Board of Trade (CBOT) in 1975. This was followed in September 1982 with the establishment of LIFFE, which became the first financial futures market in Europe. Traded options were a later development, appearing in the early 1980s. The first recognisable swap contracts also appeared in the early 1980s. So financial derivative contracts are a fairly recent development. The exception to this is the forward currency contract, which has a much earlier history. In addition, derivative contracts on commodities, such as gold, other metals and agricultural products have existed for centuries.

As shown in figure 13.1, financial derivative contracts have seen a very rapid rate of growth over recent years. In fact the figures for OTC contracts omit the following: forward rate agreements, currency options, forward foreign exchange contracts and equity-related and commodity-related derivatives. So the true rate of growth of derivatives trading is truly spectacular, with the OTC sector growing the fastest.

One of the reasons for this spectacular growth is the high degree of volatility experienced in interest rates, inflation and exchange rates since

Figure 13.1 *Derivatives contracts: notional amounts outstanding at end of year, 1987–96 ($billion). Source: BIS,* International Banking and Financial Market Developments, *February 1998*

Table 13.1 *Top ten derivative exchanges: futures and options contract volume (million contracts), 1997*

Exchange	Contract volume (January–December 1997)
Chicago Board of Trade (CBOT)	242.7
London International Financial Futures and Options Exchange (LIFFE)	209.4
Chicago Mercantile Exchange (CME)	200.7
Chicago Board Options Exchange (CBOE)	187.2
B, M and F (Brazil)	122.2
Deutsche Terminbörse (DTB)	112.2
American Exchange (AMEX)	88.1
New York Mercantile Exchange (NYMEX)	83.9
Marché à Terme International de France (MATIF)	66.6
London Metal Exchange (LME)	57.4

Source: Futures Industry Association.

the collapse in 1971 of the fixed exchange rate regime established by the Bretton Woods agreement (see chapter 14, figures 14.1 and 14.2 for more details). In particular, the growth in the quantity of primary securities issued has led automatically to a higher volume of secondary market transactions and therefore a greater demand for hedging instruments and hence financial derivatives. The rapid growth of information technology and consequent reduction in transaction costs has also played a role by stimulating the development of new trading strategies which enabled agents to use financial derivatives as a means of reducing risk. This aspect of the role of financial derivatives is considered in greater detail in chapter 14.

Table 13.1 shows the relative importance of the various derivative exchanges. Because US exchanges were the first to develop futures contracts, they dominated the trading of financial derivatives until recently. The Chicago markets still accounted for about 33 per cent, by volume, of total exchange-traded financial derivatives in 1997 but that share had diminished from the 95 per cent they achieved in the mid-1980s because the other markets had experienced a faster rate of growth over recent years. In particular, LIFFE achieved the ranking of second largest exchange in 1997 for the first time. LIFFE volume grew by 23 per cent over 1997, compared with growth of 9 per cent for CBOT, 13 per cent for the Chicago Mercantile Exchange (CME) and 8 per cent for the Chicago Board Options Exchange. However, the fastest rate of growth, at 45 per cent, was experienced by the DTB, the German derivatives exchange, which has overtaken the Marché à Terme International de France (MATIF) as the second largest exchange in Europe.

The structure of derivatives exchanges, throughout the world but particularly in Europe, is changing. A number of mergers between derivatives exchanges have taken place and more are planned. In addition, cross-border cooperation between exchanges is taking new forms. In the UK, the London Traded Options Market merged with LIFFE in 1992 and then in 1996 LIFFE and the London Commodities Exchange merged. LIFFE has also introduced cross-listing of some of its contracts with other exchanges. Cross-listing allows contracts associated with one exchange to be listed on another exchange, usually in a different time zone so that contract can continue to be traded when the first exchange is closed. LIFFE entered into a cross-listing agreement with the Tokyo Stock Exchange for trading the Japanese government bond and with CBOT for trading LIFFE's German bond contract (on CBOT) and CBOT's Treasury bond contract (on LIFFE). The objective of generating additional turnover was generally not achieved and LIFFE ended its agreement with CBOT in late 1997. A more important development is the agreement between the German and Swiss derivatives exchanges, DTB and the Swiss Options and Financial Futures Exchange, to establish a common trading and clearing platform for their products, in late 1998, to be called Eurex. Other exchanges have been invited to join. This link-up is motivated by competitive pressures in the run-up to EMU from January 1999, when short-term interest rates on European currencies in EMU will converge, leaving just one short-term interest contract on the euro. CBOT and the CME have also recently announced that they are merging their clearing operations and CBOT and Eurex have entered into an agreement for cross-listing of products. More mergers and alliances between derivatives exchanges are expected in the next few years.

In the next section we outline the general organisation of LIFFE, which, given its relative importance as indicated in table 13.1, will provide an indication of how futures markets typically operate.

13.3   The organisation of LIFFE

A range of financial and commodity futures and options are traded on LIFFE. In this chapter we are interested in the financial derivatives products traded. We consider the nature of financial futures and options in more detail in sections 13.4 and 13.5, but we begin here with a brief definition of these two types of contract. A financial futures contract can be defined as an agreement to sell or buy a quantity of a financial instrument on an organised market or exchange at a future date and at a price specified at the time of making the contract. In contrast, an option confers the right, but not the obligation, to the purchaser to buy (a 'call' option) or the right to sell (a 'put' option) an underlying financial instrument at a standard price and times in the future. The practical distinction between traded and OTC options is that the former can be bought from and sold to parties other than the original writer (i.e. seller) of the option. The market in the underlying or actual financial instrument is called the cash market and the options or futures market the derivative market. One characteristic of traded derivative contracts is that certain features are standardised. This of course enables them to be traded, unlike OTC derivatives, for which the terms of the contract are negotiated. On LIFFE the standard unit of trading is £500,000 for three-month sterling futures, US$1,000,000 for three-month eurodollar futures, and £50,000 for the long gilt futures. The minimum unit of trading decreases as the maturity of the underlying cash market security increases, owing to the increase in its price volatility – this is evidenced by the difference in the notional principal of the short sterling and gilt contracts. Delivery of the security is also made on specific dates according to a fixed sequence of months, with the cycle of March, June, September and December being the most common. The cycle usually extends up to two years in advance but in some cases can extend up to four years. These standard features reduce the flexibility of the contracts available compared with, say, the provision of tailor-made forward foreign exchange contracts provided by the banks, as was discussed in chapter 11. On the other hand, the provision of standardised contracts enables trading to be carried out at a low cost since the buyers and sellers know precisely what they are trading.

The second general point to note is that although the transactions are originally made between two parties on the exchange, the two resulting contracts are then transferred to the London Clearing House, which clears and guarantees all transactions carried out on LIFFE and a number of other London exchanges. Consequently the Clearing House has a zero net position since it has acquired both sides of the trade. This system has a number of advantages. First, the risk of default is eliminated for both parties to the transaction since it is borne by the Clearing House. In order to protect itself against default, the Clearing House requires both parties to deposit cash against the transaction (the 'initial margin') and this margin is revalued daily to take account of movements in the price of the underlying security (the 'variation margin'). A further protection is gained by restriction of dealing facilities to 'members' of LIFFE who, themselves, are representatives of a wide range of financial

Table 13.2 *Financial futures and options contracts available at LIFFE[a] as at April 1998*

Short-term interest rate futures	*Government bond futures*
One-month euromark	*(long-term interest rate)*
Three-month euromark*	German government bond (Bund)*
Three-month sterling*	Long gilt*
Three-month eurolira*	5-year gilt
Three-month euro-Swiss*	Italian government bond (BTP)*
Three-month ECU	Japanese government bond (JGB)
Three-month euroyen	German government Bobl bond*
Equity index futures	*Other equity products*
FTSE 100 *	Options on individual shares
FTSE 250	

* Option on that futures contract is available.
[a] Commodities futures and option products not listed.

institutions. Second, it enables transactions to be 'closed out' before the maturity date since the party wishing to terminate the agreement merely takes out an exactly opposite liability. In fact over 90 per cent of agreements are closed out before the maturity date and we discuss the reasons for this in section 13.4.

The contracts available on LIFFE in March 1998 are shown in table 13.2. It should, however, be remembered that this list can only be indicative of what contracts will be available as it is likely that new ones will be developed. For those contracts marked with an asterisk in table 13.2, LIFFE also provides options on the futures contracts. Up to 1990, LIFFE also provided facilities for trading in futures and options in currencies but these were suspended in 1990. For the pound against the US dollar, traded options are still available on the Philadelphia Stock Exchange (units of £31,250 per contract) and futures contracts on the CME (units of £62,500).

The relative importance of the various contracts traded at LIFFE over the years since its formation is shown in table 13.3. The table shows the dramatic growth in total number of transactions, from 0.24 million contracts in September–December 1982 to 209 million contracts in 1997. The statistics also demonstrate the relative importance of short-term interest rate and bond contracts. The decline of currency futures and options is also apparent. The probable reason for this is that the OTC market (i.e. the 'forward' market discussed in chapter 11) offers

Table 13.3 *LIFFE financial futures and options trading volume (million contracts), 1982–96*

	1982[a]	1984	1986	1988	1990	1992	1994	1996
Futures								
Short-term interest	0.16	1.36	2.07	5.19	12.26	26.84	51.73	63.51
Government bond	0.03	0.94	4.23	8.12	16.01	26.68	68.82	68.63
Currency	0.05	0.20	0.07	0.02	–	–	–	–
Equity index	–	0.07	0.12	0.47	1.44	2.62	4.71	6.81
Total futures	0.24	2.57	6.49	13.80	29.78	56.14	125.26	138.95
Options								
Short-term interest	–	–	0.04	0.52	1.69	4.70	7.02	8.10
Government bond	–	–	0.33	1.22	2.68	5.03	11.96	12.28
Currency	–	–	0.11	0.01	–	–	–	–
Equity index	–	–	–	–	–	2.57	4.79	6.81
Individual equities	–	–	–	–	–	3.53	4.31	4.30
Total options	–	–	0.48	1.75	4.37	15.83	28.08	31.49
Total, all contracts	0.24	2.57	6.97	15.55	34.15	71.97	153.34	170.44

[a] September to December only.
Source: LIFFE.

comparable products which are perceived by traders to be more advantageous. As far as currency futures are concerned, the forward market provides a similar and flexible opportunity to hedge against future exchange rate changes through either fixed-dated or option-dated forward contracts. This eliminates the necessity of having to sell the instrument in the market, although similar resale facilities are available if required by entering into a spot sale of the currency in the market which offsets the original forward contract. However, on 12 September 1994, CME launched two new currency forward contracts (i.e. dollar/Deutschmark and dollar/yen) which can be used in conjunction with the currency spot contracts to replicate OTC currency swaps. As was noted in chapter 11, the swap segment of the market formed the major component of the forward market. Similarly, OTC options contracts can be arranged with banks which meet the trader's precise requirements. It is understood that such contracts have shown a considerable degree of growth, with London as an important centre, though no official statistics exist.

Dealing on LIFFE must be carried out through members. On receipt of an order from a customer, the member then transmits this order to her or his booth on the trading floor. Trading is carried out by the open-outcry system for most contracts during the period 8 a.m. to 4.15 p.m. and by LIFFE's automated pit trading system between 4.30 p.m. and 6.00 p.m (allowing a short change-over period). However, there are variations on this; for example, the three-month euro-Deutschmark contract trades from 7.30 a.m. to 4.10 p.m. by open outcry and then from 4.25 p.m. to 6.59 p.m. on automated pit trading. Whilst scenes from the trading floor or pit initially convey the impression of utter chaos, it is claimed that this system ensures that all orders receive equal treatment and that it is therefore fair. As noted earlier, the order is then transferred to the Clearing House. Immediate day-to-day supervision of the market is vested in the Board of the Exchange, which has established a market supervision department to carry out self-regulation. Ultimate supervisory authority lies with the Bank of England, which exercises general surveillance over all London exchanges.

However, all this may change. LIFFE is developing an electronic trading system, LIFFECONNECT, for its individual equity option products, which will permit electronic trading of equity options during normal trading hours. In addition, LIFFE has announced that this electronic trading system will be extended to allow electronic trading of its futures products from the fourth quarter of 1999 at the latest. It is expected that open-outcry trading of futures contracts will continue alongside electronic trading, though if traders prefer electronic trading then this will probably lead to an abandonment of open outcry. Although there are cost advantages with electronic trading, as discussed in chapter 7, there are liquidity advantages with open-outcry trading and so heavily traded futures contracts are likely to remain predominantly open-outcry traded for the foreseeable future.

13.4   The nature of financial futures

In order to demonstrate the nature of financial futures it is necessary to describe their function. As is the case for all traded financial instruments (see chapter 7), three uses of financial futures are traditionally identified. These are hedging, trading (or perhaps more appropriately speculation) and arbitrage. In practice, however, it may be difficult to make this a clear-cut and unambiguous distinction since financial institutions are making greater use of derivatives markets for the purpose of asset/liability management.

13.4.1 *Hedging with financial futures*

Hedging can be considered a defensive operation by risk-averse operators to insure themselves against adverse movements in, for example, interest or exchange rates. As an outline of this function prior to consideration of particular hedging operations in detail, consider the position of an operator who buys a three-month sterling deposit financial future. If current actual interest rates fall then the value of the future will increase since it is offering higher rates than can be obtained in the marketplace. Conversely, if current actual interest rates rise then the value of the financial future will fall since actual deposits will earn higher rates of interest. Consequently, the price of the financial future will move in the opposite direction to the movement of interest rates. Thus, it is possible for an agent to offset – at least partially – the effects of movements in interest rates by profits or losses on the value of the financial future by selling the futures contract back to the market. The basic trading rule is that if the trader's cash position will be adversely affected by higher than anticipated interest rates, then a futures contract should be sold. Conversely, if it is lower rates that worry the trader, then a futures contract should be bought.

We now illustrate the procedure more precisely using as an example the three-month sterling interest rate futures contract. A company has obtained a loan of £1,000,000 at a rate of 12 per cent from the money markets which is due to be rolled over on 1 June. The company is concerned that interest rates will change, with a probability that the loan will be rolled over at a higher rate. In order to protect itself the company sells two three-month sterling interest rate financial futures (each valued £500,000) which are due for delivery after 1 June – it is of critical importance that the delivery date of the futures contract is later than the date when the risk to be hedged disappears, otherwise there will be a period of time when potential changes in prices of the cash instrument are not hedged. Assuming the current interest rate is 12 per cent, the price of each contract is (100 – the annual rate of interest), that is, 88 in this example. The price of the contract will move up or down in minimum amounts of 0.01 per cent, which are known as a 'ticks' or basis points. The value of a tick varies for each type of financial future but may, in this case, be derived by applying the 0.01 per cent rate of interest to the face value of a £500,000 contract for one-quarter of a year and is therefore £12.50. On 1 June the company will buy the two contracts back from the exchange. We can now examine the effect of this transaction if interest rates had risen to 14 per cent per annum on 1 June. The first point to note is that the company will bear extra borrowing costs of £5,000 for the next quarter due to the rise in interest rates of 2 per cent per annum. We next look at the futures market transaction and we initially assume that the futures price has also moved in line with the cash market rate. The company:

(i)   sells two contracts at 88 (rate of interest 12 per cent);
(ii)   buys back two futures at 86 (rate of interest 14 per cent) on 1 June;
(iii) gains 200 ticks per contract (i.e. 400) at £12.50 = £5,000.

In this case the higher cost of interest is exactly matched by the profit on the two futures transactions. If, on the other hand, interest rates had fallen, then the company's borrowing cost would have fallen but this would have been offset by the loss on buying back the futures contract. This clarifies what the company has gained from its financial futures operation, namely that the uncertainty surrounding the future interest rate on its borrowing cost has been removed. It is important to realise that the company has not necessarily made a gain on its futures trans-actions. In fact in the case of an interest rate fall it would have incurred a loss, but it would have reduced the uncertainty of future costs. This example also illustrates the reason why most contracts are 'closed out' (i.e. reversed) before the time for delivery of the futures contract, since the offsetting gain/loss on the futures contract is realised when the futures contract is closed out.

Basis risk
The precision of the hedge in the above example is due to the fact we have assumed that the price of the futures contract has moved exactly in line with the cash market rate. This degree of precision is unlikely to occur in practice and, to understand why, we need to consider a concept known as basis. This may be defined as:

basis = cash price − futures price.

In the example quoted above the basis is zero at the start and the finish of the hedging operation. It is quite common, however, for a non-zero basis to exist since the cash and futures prices are subject to different influences. In particular, the futures price will reflect the market's view of the level of the interest rate in the future. If we return to the above example, and consider the case where the futures price at the time the hedger sells the contracts is not 88 but rather 87.50: the existence of a futures price of 87.50 and an analogous cash price of 88.00 (100 − 12) implies that the market expects interest rates to rise in the period up to the date of the futures contract. The basis at the start of the hedge is therefore (88.0 − 87.5) or 0.5. If the basis is different at the time the hedger 'closes out', then the hedge will not be perfect. To illustrate this point, consider the position if the futures price had been 86.00 on 1 June (i.e. a zero basis given an interest rate of 14 per cent) then the gain on the hedge would have been 150 (8,750 − 8,600) ticks per contract, or

£3,750 in total. In this case a partial hedge has been achieved since the gain on the futures contract does not cover the additional interest charges on the rolled over loan. It is also quite possible that the change in basis could work in favour of the hedger. For example, if the futures price was 85.00 on 1 June (i.e. a basis of 1.0) then the gain would have been 250 ticks per contract or £6,250 in total. A further point worth noting is that, if the futures contract purchased by the hedger had been for delivery in June, then it is quite likely that the basis on 1 June would have been close to zero. This is because as the delivery date on the futures contract approaches, then the cash price and the futures price tend to equality because the influences on the two contracts are identical on the delivery date. As is shown below, any difference between the two prices would lead to arbitrage.

A non-zero basis can occur for a number of reasons. Thus, if the basis is close to zero when the contract is being taken out then it is sensible to choose futures contracts that mature soon after the disappearance of the risk to be hedged. In general, however, cash and futures prices of similar instruments do exhibit a fairly high degree of correlation, so that basis risk (the risk of movements in basis) is less than outright risk (the risk of an unhedged position) as long as the characteristics of the instrument being hedged are not very different from those of relevant futures instrument.

13.4.2 *Speculation with financial futures*

We now turn to examine the role of trading or speculation in the operation of financial futures markets. Providers of a hedge can protect themselves by negotiating an offsetting contract. In the example of the company quoted above, the purchaser of the futures may at that time be able to identify a customer who wishes to buy two similar contracts. In this instance the financial institution providing the hedge has incurred no risk since it has two offsetting contracts with windfall gains on one contract matching windfall losses on the other. In practice it is highly unlikely that the quantity of hedging demanded for a change in one direction will exactly match that required in the opposite direction, so traders fill the gap by making the market and therefore provide a useful economic function. Trading is basically a non-defensive activity undertaken by those agents willing to bear the risk of price changes. Their income comes from two sources which in practice may be difficult to distinguish. First, there is the reward for undertaking risk, and second the potential profits to be earned from taking a correct view of the future course of the prices of the underlying cash market securities. Financial futures are a particularly useful vehicle for speculation since transaction costs are low and there is no need to purchase or sell the underlying instrument and the cash outlay is restricted to the initial margin (typically varying between 0.1 per cent and 6 per cent of the face value of the contract) and the variation margin, thus offering potential for high degrees of leverage. If the price of the underlying security is expected to rise, speculators will go long, that is, buy financial futures, or if the price is expected to fall they will go short, that is, sell financial futures. Clearly, this is a risky operation and losses will be incurred if the prices move in the opposite direction to those anticipated by the trader. We use the long gilt futures contract as an illustration of the potential for trading contracts. Again we would like to emphasise that this is just one particular example of a wide range of potential trading activities available.

As was pointed out in chapter 9, prices of gilts are sensitive to interest rate changes and the degree of sensitivity increases directly with the outstanding maturity of the stock in question. Assume that a trader feels that the next round of publications of the various official statistics will be more favourable than has hitherto been the case. He also feels that this is likely to lead to a reduction in interest rates which has not fully been reflected in the current prices of gilt-edged stock. He therefore purchases one unit of gilt futures £50,000 nominal value for the next delivery date after the publication of the last in the round of the official statistics he considers relevant. Assume that the relevant contract is trading at £102–25, that is, £102 and 25/32nds. The minimum price movement is 1/32nd with a tick valued at £15.625 for this contract. If he is correct and the statistics on balance are sufficiently favourable to permit a fall in interest rates then gilt prices will rise and so consequently will the gilt futures contract, so that the trader will make the expected profit. It should be emphasised that the profit is entirely dependent on the accuracy of the trader's forecast as against that implicit in market prices.

13.4.3 *Arbitrage in financial futures markets*

The third activity in futures markets refers to arbitrage to take advantage of price anomalies between either the underlying cash market instruments and the futures or different futures contracts. Such price anomalies are likely to be quite small and short lived since other traders will quickly perceive the opportunity of making a profit with minimal risk. As one example we consider the position of the long gilt futures contract. This contract can be carried out by delivery of gilts from a list of deliverable gilts. For example, for the September 1998 long gilt futures contract, the list refers to any stock maturing between the years

2008 and 2012 inclusive but excludes convertible and index-linked stocks. Thus, if the prices of the futures and underlying stocks are misaligned it may be possible to borrow funds, purchase the misaligned deliverable stock and sell an appropriate futures contract. This is called cash and carry arbitrage. Little risk is attached to such an operation provided all the contracts are undertaken simultaneously. Anomalies between the prices of futures contracts may occur between different types of contracts such as between the various three-month interest rate futures noted in section 13.3 or between different delivery dates of the same futures contract. This latter arbitrage is known as spreading. We now demonstrate the process of cash and carry arbitrage more formally.

Assuming continuous discounting, then the following condition must hold if no arbitrage possibilities exist:

$$F = Se^{r(T-t)} \qquad (13.1)$$

where F is the forward price, S the price of the underlying security, r the risk-free rate of interest, T the time when the contract matures and t current time. If, for example, $F > Se^{r(T-t)}$ then profits can be made by borrowing S for the period $T - t$, buying the asset and selling (taking a short position) the forward contract. At time $T - t$, a profit equal to $F - Se^{r(T-t)}$ has been obtained. The converse would apply if $F < Se^{r(T-t)}$, that is, the forward contract would be purchased and the asset sold with the proceeds from the asset being invested at the risk-free interest rate until the forward contract matures. To illustrate this point consider a share where the market price is £40, the risk-free rate of interest is 4 per cent per annum and, for sake of ease of exposition, the time period involved ($T-t$) is one year (note if the futures matured in three months' time, then $T-t = 0.25$). Given this information, the equilibrium futures price is given by equation 13.1 as (£40 × $e^{0.04}$), or £41.63. If the actual market price of the forward contract is £40, then sale of the stock would produce £40, the proceeds would be invested to obtain £40 × $e^{0.04}$, or £41.63, as compared with the £40 required to purchase the forward contract in one year's time. Conversely if the forward price is £42, then £40 is borrowed for the year at the risk-free rate of 4 per cent, and the asset purchased for £40. In one year's time the asset would be sold for £42 in accordance with the forward contract as against the cost of borrowed funds of £41.63. This analysis applies strictly to forward contracts but would also apply to futures if either the risk-free interest rate is constant and the same for all maturities or is a known function of time. The intuitive reason for differences between forward and future prices is that the latter involve margin payments whereas the former do not. Also, equation 13.1 ignores costs involved in carrying the instrument. In the case of financial assets this is likely to be very near zero, so equation 13.1 can be regarded as depicting what is known as the 'cost of carry' relationship between the spot and the futures price. This cost would be reduced if the futures instrument yielded some known dividend or return and can be described by:

$$F = Se^{(r-i)(T-t)}$$ (13.2)

where i is the return on the futures instrument. In the case where the dividend is not known, i will represent the average dividend.

13.4.4 *Portfolio management using futures contracts*

In addition to the three traditional uses discussed above, futures markets can be used to vary a portfolio's overall maturity structure by altering the maturity of individual securities. For example, the average maturity of a portfolio can be 'synthetically' reduced by the sale of, say, a long gilt futures contract in five months' time and using a 'deliverable' gilt from the portfolio to complete the transaction. Thus, the maturity on the security has been changed from its previous term to five months and the new redemption value is the price implied by the futures contract. Similarly, the average length of a portfolio of short-term securities can be lengthened by purchasing a series of short-term contracts.

13.4.5 *Nature of currency futures*

Before turning to a discussion of the nature of options in section 13.5, it is worthwhile examining, albeit briefly, the nature of foreign currency futures on the International Money Market (IMM) at CME. The four major currencies traded are the Deutschmark, Swiss franc, Japanese yen and sterling. The largest of these four types of contract concerns the Deutschmark and the market report for this contract in the *Financial Times* quoted a latest price of $0.6351 (the equivalent of a closing price) for delivery in March. We use this quotation to demonstrate the principles of this market. As is the case for other futures contracts, settlement is made on a specific date and can be by way of cash settlement or delivery of the currency. IMM quotes the rate as dollars per 1 Deutschmark and the size of the contract is 125,000 Deutschmark so the buyer of the contract has agreed to pay $79,387.5 for 125,000 Deutschmark for delivery in March (125,000 × 0.6351). If the price of the Deutschmark rises to 0.6400 the value of the contract rises to $80,0000 and the buyer has made a profit of $612.5. As in the case of LIFFE and other futures contracts, the seller of the contract would have to pay and the buyer receive additional margins.

Clearly, on the expiry date the underlying (i.e. the spot) rate and the futures price would coincide. Before this date there will be a gap between the current spot rate and the futures price and this is called the 'swap'. The level of the swap reflects the interest differentials and can be calculated according to the following formula (assuming interest is paid at discrete intervals):

swap = (spot exchange rate) × (eurodollar rate – euromark rate)
   × (days to delivery/360)

(Most contracts are worked out on the basis of 360 days.)

Thus, for example, suppose at the close of trade on a particular day, the eurodollar and euromark three-month deposit rates were 6.5 per cent per annum and 5.5 per cent, respectively, and the spot exchange rate $0.6500 per Deutschmark. On a contract which has, say, 90 days to delivery, the swap is:

$$0.6500 \times (0.065 - 0.055) \times (90/360) = 0.001625$$

The trader could then add the swap to the current spot rate to arrive at a theoretical futures price of 0.6516. If the actual futures price were less than 0.6516, a trader could make a profit by selling Deutschmark spot and buying futures. Similarly, if the futures price were above 0.6516 the trader could buy Deutschmark spot and sell futures. Of course in practice the differential would have to exceed transaction costs, which in any case are likely to be low.

13.5   The nature of options

Options give the purchaser, in return for a premium, the right to buy (a 'call' option) or the right to sell (a 'put' option) a financial instrument at an agreed exchange rate (the 'striking' price) at a specified date or dates. No obligation is imposed on buyers to carry out the obligation so they will choose to do so only if it is profitable for them. Two classes or types of options can be distinguished. As was discussed in section 13.3, an option can be either an OTC option or a traded option. OTC options have either to be exercised or allowed to lapse. Traded options offer the additional choice to the holder of reselling them on the market. In fact, as we shall see later, it is more likely that a traded option will be resold rather than exercised. Trading on organised options markets can be for the purposes of both speculation and hedging and it is the presence of speculators which provides liquidity for the market. Options can be further categorised into American and European options. An American

Table 13.4   *Examples of LIFFE equity options*

	Strike/exer-cise price	Calls			Puts		
		January	*April*	*June*	*January*	*April*	*June*
BP	420	13	23	31½	10½	17½	24
(*421)	460	1½	8	16	39½	43	48
ICI	700	53	66½	75½	3½	20	25½
(*746)	750	19	35½	47	20	43½	49

* Underlying security price.
Source: *Financial Times,* market report dated 17 December 1994.

type of option can be exercised at any date up to the expiry of the option whereas the European type can be exercised only on a specified date. The options traded on LIFFE are generally of the American type. Premiums for traded options are quoted in market statistics and we show in table 13.4 the relevant details at the close of trading on 16 December for just two of the share options (BP and ICI) which are traded at LIFFE as reported in the *Financial Times*.

The detail contained in table 13.4 can be interpreted in the following way. A trader can purchase a call option (i.e. the right to buy BP shares) expiring in January 1995 at a strike/exercise price of 420p per share for a premium (i.e. price) of 13p per share. For April 1995 expiry and the same strike price the premium is 23p per share. Similarly, the purchase of a put option (the right to sell) with a strike price of 460p per share and June 1995 expiry would require a premium of 48p per share. A similar interpretation is easily derived for ICI shares. Shares have to be purchased in quantities of 1,000.

We use the quotation for April calls and puts at a strike price of 420p per share to derive the diagrams used to illustrate the profit and loss situation for the purchaser and the writer of the option.

In the first example the purchaser of a call option will exercise it to purchase BP shares only if the market price rises above 420p per share. At market prices lower than this price it is more profitable for the trader to purchase BP equity in the market so that the loss is restricted to the 23p premium paid on taking out the option. The break-even point occurs when the actual market price is 443p per share so that the premium just matches the gain on the option contract of 23p. In effect, therefore, the purchase of the call option has fixed the maximum price to be paid for BP shares at 443p per share. As the market price rises above 443p per

Figure 13.2   *Profit/loss profile of a call option*

share the purchaser obtains profits which in theory are unlimited but in practice are limited to the likely range of market fluctuations. The position for the seller (i.e. the 'writer') of the option is the mirror image of that of the purchaser. Figure 13.2 illustrates the above situation.

The position in the case of the purchase of a put option is the reverse of that in the case of a call option and is illustrated in figure 13.3. For an exercise price of 420p per share the option will be exercised only when the market price for BP equity falls below 420p per share. At prices above 420p it is more profitable to sell the shares in the market. Consequently, the break-even price for the purchaser is 402½p per share, when the profit on the sale of shares just matches the premium paid (i.e. 17½p per share). As the actual market price falls below 402½p per share the purchaser makes gains which in theory are only limited by a market price of zero but, in practice, are again limited by the likely range of fluctuations. As for the case of a call option, the position of the writer is the mirror image of that of the purchaser.

Figure 13.3   *Profit/loss profile of a put option*

Remember, the exercise of an option lies entirely in the hands of the purchaser. The writer has no control over whether the option is exercised or not. It is in the nature of a contingent liability which may or may not be incurred. As far as the purchaser is concerned, an option contract is analogous to an insurance policy with the premium for the option representing the premium paid for the policy and the risk insured is the downside risk of an adverse movement in the share price with the purchaser taking all the benefits of a favourable movement.

13.5.1 *Pricing of options*

The price of an option contract can be divided into two components:

(i)   The *intrinsic value* is the gain which would be realised if an option were exercised immediately. In the case of a call option it is the excess of the spot price over the exercise price. This represents the gain that can be made by exercising the option immediately and selling the share in the market. For a put option the intrinsic value is the excess of the exercise price over the spot rate, which represents the profit derived from buying the share in the market and exercising the option to sell the shares at the strike price. In the above example the current market price for BP shares was 421p per share at the close of trading on 16 December 1994. For a strike price of 420p per share the intrinsic value for a call option for April 1995 delivery is 1p per share. Similarly, for a put option at a strike price of 460p per share for April delivery the intrinsic value is 39p (460 – 421). The intrinsic value is always positive or zero.

(ii) The *time value* represents that part of the premium not represented by the intrinsic value. For the call example given above, an intrinsic value of 1p per share and a premium of 23p per share (April call option), the time value is 22p per share; similarly, the time value for the put quoted above is 4p per share (43 – 39). Time value cannot be negative and will approach zero at an increasing rate as the option nears expiry. This can be seen from table 13.4, where the time value of a call option at a strike price for ICI shares of 700p is 7p for January delivery (current price = 746p, hence intrinsic value = 46p, which with a premium of 53p gives a time value of 7p), 20½p for April delivery and 29½p for June delivery.

When a non-zero intrinsic value of an option exists the option is said to be 'in the money'. For a put option, if the strike price is less than the current spot rate, then the option is said to be 'out of the money'. A call option is said to be 'out of the money' if the strike price is more than the current price. If the exercise (strike) price is equal to the spot price then the option is 'at the money'. Time value is at its maximum for a given expiry date when an option is at the money and tends to zero for options deeply out of the money or deeply in the money. This can be rationalised intuitively by considering the position of an option deeply out of the money. The further the option is away from the strike price the more unlikely it becomes that it will be exercised. Hence both the value to the holder and the risk to the writer are reduced, thus lowering the premiums required for taking on the risk. For an option in the money, intrinsic value exists so that the holder incurs the risk of this value being eroded by adverse movements in the spot price. As far as the writer of the option is concerned, the adverse movement to the holder would be a gain. The larger the intrinsic value the greater is the risk of erosion of the intrinsic value. Thus, the premium will compensate the buyer of the option with a reduced time value in the premium and the writer will be willing to grant the lower premium owing to the lower risk involved. The presence of the time component in the price of an option means that it is likely that the holder will sell the option in the market rather than exercise it. To illustrate this point consider again the case of the call option expiring in April with a strike price of 420p per share. The premium is 23p per share, which exceeds the intrinsic value of 1p, so that sale of the option in the market would permit the holder to extract the time value for herself or himself.

The price of an option mainly depends on the factors listed below:

(i)   the strike or exercise price,
(ii)   the current market price of the underlying asset, in the case of BP or ICI shares 421p and 746p, respectively (see table 13.4),
(iii) time to the expiry of the option,
(iv)   the volatility of the price of the underlying asset,
(v)   the risk-free interest rate.

The precise relationship between these factors is derived by various mathematical formulae, of which perhaps the most well known is the Black–Scholes formula. Discussion of the mathematical methods necessary to derive such relationships is beyond the scope of this text but it is possible to identify intuitively how these factors influence the price of an option.

In the case of a call option, the lower the exercise or strike price the more likely it is to be exercised and therefore the higher the price. The second factor is the current spot price. In this case the higher the spot price the more likely the option is to be exercised. Two other factors are the volatility of the price of the underlying cash asset and the maturity of the option. The option is more likely to be exercised if the price of the cash instrument is volatile and/or the greater is the length of time before the option expires. Anything which increases the probability of the option being exercised raises the price of the option, that is, the premium. In the case of a put option the premium would be raised if the direction of the first two factors is reversed; that is, the option will be more valuable the lower the price of the underlying cash instrument and/ or the higher the strike or exercise price. Finally, a rise in the risk-free rate of interest is likely to be accompanied by expectations of increased growth rate of the price of the share. However, the increased interest rate will reduce the present value of any future cash flows associated with the holding of the option. Both these effects will reduce the value of a put option. In the case of a call option, following a rise in the risk-free interest rate, the first effect discussed above raises its value but the

Table 13.5   *Philadelphia Stock Exchange sterling/dollar options as at close of trading 16 December 1994 (£31,250) (cents per £1)*

Strike price	Calls			Puts		
	December	January	February	December	January	February
1.500	6.17	6.18	6.35	–	–	0.18
1.525	3.67	3.84	4.24	–	0.12	0.55
1.550	1.22	1.91	2.51	–	0.64	1.29
1.575	–	0.67	1.33	1.18	1.88	2.54
1.600	–	0.15	0.60	3.62	3.80	4.23
1.625	–	–	0.22	6.12	6.13	6.33

Source: *Financial Times*, market report, 17 December 1994.

second effect lowers it. However, the first effect dominates so that a rise in the risk-free rate of interest always increases the price of call options.

The effect of changes in the strike/exercise price and time can easily be seen from the detail contained in tables 13.4 and 13.5. The effect of changes in the exercise price can be observed by looking down the columns and in time by looking along the rows.

13.5.2 Currency options

So far our exposition has been in terms of options on individual shares. Options exist, however, for other financial assets such as stock indices, foreign currency and futures. Options on foreign currency are mainly conducted on an OTC basis but traded options are available on the Philadelphia Stock Exchange. The *Financial Times* market quotation for the end of trade on 16 December is reproduced as table 13.5.

The interpretation of the table is similar to that for share options. The exception is that the option is to purchase sterling in amounts of £31,250 with the option price quoted per £1. Thus, the total cost for an option to purchase £31,250 for February delivery at a strike price of $1.500 per £1 is $1,984.375 (31,250 × 0.0635). For the purposes of comparison, the spread for the spot exchange rate at close of trading on 16 December 1994 in the London forex was $1.5625 to $1.5635 per £1.

13.5.3 Exotic options

In addition to the standard American-type and European-type options so far discussed, a number of options with non-standard or more complicated pay-offs exist. These are termed 'exotic options'. They are generally OTC options and are designed by banks to meet the specific needs of their customers. A large number of such options exist and we mention only a few to illustrate their nature. One such option is called a 'Bermudan' option, which, like American-type options, can be exercised up to and including the maturity date but, unlike American-type options, such early exercise is restricted to specific dates. Another type is 'forward start options', for which payment is made now but the option does not start until a later date. Similarly, options can be made up of a package of options in the manner discussed in chapter 14, where pay-offs of a combination of options are illustrated. One further example is provided by 'compound options', which are in fact options on options. As noted earlier, the types of exotic options are exceedingly numerous and our examples are designed merely to point out how departures from the standard European and American types of options can be engineered. We now turn to a discussion of swaps.

13.6   Swaps

A swap is an agreement between two parties to exchange future cash flows in accordance with a previously agreed formula. Normally such arrangements involve a bank acting as an intermediary rather than being directly between two companies. In this case the bank has entered into two contracts, one with each party. This causes the bank/financial intermediary to incur the additional risk that one party may default, leaving the bank with an open contract. It is often the case that only one customer has approached a bank to arrange a specific swap. In this case the bank may assume the position of the counterparty until such time as the second part of the swap can be arranged. In this case the bank is said to 'warehouse' the swap. Again, additional risk is incurred by the bank until the offsetting transaction is arranged. Swaps are OTC derivatives and arise in a variety of forms. We commence our discussion with the simplest and most common form of a swap, between fixed and floating interest rate payments in the same currency. This is called a 'plain vanilla' interest rate swap.

13.6.1 *Example of a plain vanilla interest rate swap*

Consider the matrix of borrowing costs for two companies, A and B, shown in table 13.6. Suppose also that B wishes to borrow at fixed rates and A at floating rates. It may appear that since A can borrow more cheaply at both fixed and floating rates that no profitable swap is possible. This is not so, since the gap between the two fixed rates is

Table 13.6 *Hypothetical example of borrowing costs of two companies*

	Fixed rate	*Floating rate*
Company A	8%	0.5% above LIBOR
Company B	9%	1.0% above LIBOR

different from that for the two floating rates. Company A pays 1 per cent less than B for fixed-rate loans but only 0.5 per cent less in the case of floating-rate loans. Thus, company A has a comparative advantage in the fixed-rate loan market and company B in the floating-rate loan market. The two companies profitably exploit this situation through:

(i)   A borrowing at fixed rates and lending to B at, say, 8.2 per cent;
(ii) B borrowing at floating rates and lending to A at say LIBOR + 0.5 per cent.

For the sake of ease of exposition we shall assume that the loan period is one year. The two companies' cash position is as follows.

> *Company A*:
> borrows at 8 per cent,
> lends to B at 8.2 per cent,
> pays B LIBOR + 0.5 per cent.
> Hence net cost of a floating-rate loan to A is LIBOR + 0.3 per cent.

> *Company B*:
> borrows at LIBOR + 1 per cent,
> lends to A at LIBOR + 0.5 per cent,
> borrows from A at 8.2 per cent.
> Hence net cost of fixed-rate loan to B is 8.7 per cent.

Note that the cost of the preferred type of borrowing is lower for both companies after the swap. This is the case even though company A has cheaper access to finance than company B in both markets. It is the existence of comparative advantage that matters.

In practice, as we have already noted, the swap would be arranged via a financial intermediary and the margins of lower cost in our hypothetical example show that the financial intermediary could easily exploit the situation to obtain a profit for itself. Also, it is important to realise that the principals themselves would not be exchanged, merely the net difference between the two streams of interest payments at periodic intervals as set out in the agreement.

It is interesting to speculate why such differences would occur. One reason put forward, as illustrated in the above example, is the existence of comparative advantage. However, this view does come up against the problem of why such differences are not eliminated by arbitrage in the manner indicated above. One possible explanation centres around the term of a loan and the possibility of default. If during the period of the loan contract the default risk of a company which had borrowed at floating rates increased, the desired margin over LIBOR would also increase. Normally the lender has the option of reviewing the margin during the period of the loan. The providers of fixed-rate loans do not have this option so the comparative advantage of A in the fixed-rate loan market may reflect differing probabilities of default in the future. Thus, B has secured a fixed rate of interest lower than would otherwise be the case.

13.6.2 *Other types of swaps*

A second type of swap is a 'plain deal currency' swap. Suppose company D wished to borrow in dollars and company C in sterling but the comparative advantages favoured dollar borrowing for C and sterling for D. In this case company C would borrow in dollars and company D in sterling. They would exchange the two sums borrowed and agree to pay the interest rates associated with the swapped sums (C in dollars and D in sterling). At the end of the period of the loan, they would again exchange the original principal sums so that no risk would arise from exchange rate changes. Again, the reason for this type of swap is probably differences in comparative advantage. As was the case for plain vanilla swaps, such a contract would normally be arranged via a financial intermediary who is likely to 'warehouse' the swap if a counterparty is not immediately available.

A number of variations of the simple swaps discussed above exist and we discuss below some such possibilities. It is possible to combine a plain vanilla swap with a plain deal currency swap so that fixed-rate borrowing in one currency is swapped for floating-rate borrowing in another currency. Another alternative is an amortising swap, whereby the notional principal is reduced in a similar manner to a scheduled amortisation on a loan. Deferred or forward swaps are available and in this case the swap is negotiated now but comes into operation at a later date. Similarly, swaps can be 'extendable' (i.e. one party has the right to extend the life of the swap) or 'puttable' (i.e. one party has the right to terminate the swap). Finally, options are available on swaps and these are called 'swaptions'.

13.7 Forward rate agreements

A forward rate agreement (FRA) is very similar to the interest rate futures discussed in section 13.4. It is an agreement in which two parties agree on the level of an interest rate to be paid on a notional deposit for a specific maturity at some specified time in the future. For example, a contract could be arranged for an agreed interest rate to be applied to, say, a six-month deposit commencing in three months' time. This particular contract would be quoted as 'three against nine months'. As in the case of interest rate futures, the deposit itself cannot be exchanged, so cash settlement is practised. Settlement takes place at the commencement of the contract, after three months in our example. The actual settlement is the difference between the interest rate agreed in the contract and a reference rate, which is normally LIBOR. If LIBOR is higher on the settlement date than the agreed rate then the buyer of the FRA receives from the seller the gap between the two rates (assuming of course that LIBOR is the reference rate). Conversely if the agreed rate is lower than LIBOR, the buyer pays the seller the gap between LIBOR and the agreed rate. In effect then, a FRA is an OTC interest rate futures contract.

We now discuss briefly the nature of the FRA market. FRAs are usually traded for standard periods such as three, six, nine or twelve months. The market is primarily an inter-bank market although banks do conclude a number of agreements with their customers. FRAs are predominantly a US dollar market although contracts are specified in other currencies. Individual contracts are quite large, with agreements for $20 million being quite common by late 1985 and some contracts amounting to $50 million (Cross report – Bank for International Settlements 1986). London is one of the main centres of the market and the Cross report estimated that about 40 per cent of total FRA market activity occurred in London in 1985.

Forward rate agreements are popular as a means of managing interest rate risk. Thus, in the example quoted above, the buyer of the FRA has protected himself/herself against a rise in interest rates as represented by the reference rate. Whatever happens to market rates of interest in three months' time, the buyer is locked into the agreed rate. The position for the seller is the converse. The seller has been assured of receiving the agreed rate, again irrespective of what happens to the reference rate. Both parties have purchased interest rate certainty and have given up the chance of random gains or losses. In other words it is a risk-averse strategy. For the policy to work the reference rate must be chosen to be representative of interest rates in general, hence the choice of LIBOR. Clearly, FRAs also offer the opportunity of speculating against future interest rate movements.

13.7.1 *Example of the use of an FRA for hedging*

We now demonstrate the calculation of payments on FRAs. The standard formula is:

$$\Pi = P \times (S - R) \times (m/\text{year})/(1 + S(m/\text{year})) \qquad (13.3)$$

where Π is the payment to be made to the buyer by the seller if $S > R$, or to the seller if $S < R$, S is the reference rate at the settlement date and R the agreed rate; m is the number of days in the FRA. For the purpose of calculation, a year can consist of either 365 days (UK or Australia) or 360 days (e.g. US). Note that the payment is discounted by the market rate of interest (S) for the length of the FRA because the payment is made at the commencement of the contract.

To illustrate this formula consider the example quoted at the beginning of this section ('three against nine months') and assume that the agreed rate was 7 per cent and LIBOR 8 per cent on the settlement day and the agreement was for $1,000,000. The buyer would receive from the seller of the FRA the following amount:

$$\Pi = \frac{1,000,000 \times (0.08 - 0.07) \times (182/360)}{(1 + 0.08(182/360))}$$
$$= \$4859.03$$

The buyer of the FRA has successfully locked himself/herself into a rate of 7 per cent at the end of the FRA period. This can easily be seen from the following calculations:

> Borrowing at LIBOR:
> $1,000,000 @ 8 per cent for 182 days   = 40444.44
> less receipt on FRA invested until end of agreement:
> $4859.03 \times \{1 + 0.08(182/360)\}$ = 5,055.55
> net payment   = 35,388.89
> borrowing cost at 7 per cent:
> $1,000,000 \times 0.07(182/360)$ = 35,388.89

This numerical example demonstrates that the buyer of the FRA has, in effect, a fixed-rate loan at 7 per cent. Similarly, the seller has supplied a loan at a fixed rate of 7 per cent. In this example, the buyer has gained and the seller lost compared with transactions at LIBOR in three months' time. If interest rates had fallen, the loss would have been borne by the buyer of the FRA. The significant point is that both parties have guaranteed themselves the fixed rate of 7 per cent for their respective transactions.

13.8 Efficiency of derivatives markets

Futures and options are derivatives markets, so their prices are a function of the anticipated movements in the price of the underlying cash market asset. It is therefore possible to impute equilibrium prices from the prices of options and futures. Efficiency requires that these imputed prices should provide accurate forecasts. The literature on the efficiency of these markets is more limited than that for the cash markets and so our survey of the evidence is more restricted. We describe studies of the role of options prices in the stock market and foreign currency markets, and futures in relation to the foreign currency markets and the US Treasury bill futures market.

The method adopted by Manaster and Rendleman (1982) in respect to the stock market was to use option prices to calculate the market's implied equilibrium stock price using the Black–Scholes formula for close-of-market option prices on all listed options exchanges for the period 26 April 1973 to 30 June 1976 (approximately 37,000 observations). This price was compared with another estimate of the equilibrium price given by the actual observed stock price and the divergence between these two estimates of the unobservable equilibrium price calculated. If this divergence is related to future movements in stock price then there is a suggestion that option prices contain some information not contained in the observed price. Manaster and Rendleman found that a relationship does exist between these two variables but simulation of an 'ex ante' trading rule suggested that this information was not sufficient to generate significant economic profits.

The method used by Manaster and Rendleman was adopted by Tucker (1987) for a study of the foreign exchange market using the implied exchange rates in comparison with the forward rate to derive a profitable trading strategy. The database consisted of 608 observations of options for sterling, Deutschmark, Swiss franc, and Japanese yen over the period November 1983 to August 1984. The assumption of IRP and the observed forward rate were incorporated into the calculation of the implied equilibrium exchange rate. This resulted in a trading rule which suggested that when the implied spot rate is greater than the observed spot rate, then the currency options market assessment is that the forward rate is underpriced, so the currency should be bought forward. In a result similar to that obtained by Masters and Rendleman, Tucker also found that whilst the deviation between the observed and implied spot rates was a statistically significant determinant of future returns, this information was insufficient to generate significant economic profits.

Cavanaugh (1987) looked at the potential to use futures contract prices to generate profits. The data represented daily changes in the logarithm of futures prices for delivery of currency on specific days. Fifteen series for the Canadian dollar and sterling were examined by Cavanaugh and he found evidence of serial correlation. Tests of simulated trading strategies suggested that this dependence could have been exploited by members of the exchange to generate profits in excess of those obtained by a policy of buy and hold. Because of the higher costs of trading involved, it was also suggested that these opportunities for profit could not have been exploited by non-members.

Elton *et al.* (1984) based their study on intra-day quotations for Treasury bills (cash and futures) for the period 6 January 1976 through to 22 December 1982. Elton *et al.* note that an investor can purchase an N-day Treasury bill in either of two ways using the futures market:

(i)   purchase an N-day Treasury bill in the cash market,
(ii) purchase a $(91 + N)$-day Treasury bill in the cash market and sell a Treasury bill in the futures market for delivery in N days, then deliver the $(91 + N)$-day bill against the futures contract.

An efficient market implies that the returns on the two strategies should be the same after allowance for transaction costs. Three strategies are examined. First, there is the simple strategy of purchasing the lower-priced instrument. Second, an arbitrage strategy could be followed whereby the lower-priced instrument is purchased and this is financed by shorting the higher-priced instrument. The third strategy examined was a swap, whereby holders of the higher-priced instrument liquefied their holdings and used the proceeds to purchase the lower-priced instrument. Elton *et al.* found that profits can be made from all three strategies, which suggests that the US Treasury bill futures market is not perfectly efficient. Since the study did not depend on any assumptions concerning an equilibrium model, these are direct tests of efficiency rather than joint tests of efficiency and a particular equilibrium model as was the case for the earlier tests discussed.

Finally we mention assessment of market efficiency through an examination of the volatility of option prices. It is possible to derive an estimate of the expected volatility of option prices through use of the Black–Scholes model. All the other variables in the model are known so it is relatively easy to calculate the implied volatility and compare this figure with the actual volatility observed in the market. A number of studies have been carried out using this method and the general conclusion is that the implied measure of volatility is biased (see e.g. Beckers 1981; Gemmill 1986; Gwylim and Buckle 1994). While this does not prove the market is inefficient, it does tend towards the rejection of the combined hypotheses that the Black–Scholes model is appropriate for the valuation of option prices and that the market is efficient. Unfortunately it does not suggest which (or perhaps both) is irrelevant.

13.9 Conclusion

We have surveyed the development of the financial futures markets in London and found that these markets have grown rapidly. The conditions for this rapid growth, that is, the observed volatility of asset prices in the related cash markets, are likely to continue and use of these markets is therefore likely to grow both in volume and in number of securities traded in the future as they offer traders some opportunity to hedge against adverse price movements. The question of the efficiency of these markets is, like that of the other markets surveyed, an open question. In this connection it is relevant that many of these markets are relatively new and that the operators may still be on a learning curve. Finally, as we have noted in the main body of the text, the development of derivatives markets has increased the risk attached to the operations of banks. This raises the question of how far prudential control of banks by the authorities can control such risks. This aspect is discussed in chapter 18.

Chapter 14

Managing risk via the financial markets

14.1 Introduction

In this chapter we survey the various methods that are open to traders to manage risk. The risks we are concerned with arise in connection with unforeseen changes in exchange rates and interest rates. Quite obviously a rise in interest rates raises both costs to borrowers and also returns to lenders. Similarly, changes in exchange rates alter the domestic currency equivalent of foreign currency. This is easily demonstrated by reference to the sterling equivalent of $500,000 at exchange rates of $1.95 per £1 and $2.0 per £1. At the former rate the sterling equivalent is £256,410 but only £250,000 at the latter rate. Thus, a person making a payment denominated in dollars benefits as sterling appreciates from $1.95 to $2.0 per £1 but the recipient of a payment denominated in dollars loses out. This causes problems for the traders. In a similar way changes in interest rates cause problems for the borrower and lender when these are made at floating rates of interest.

In this chapter we discuss how firms may attempt to manage this risk. This type of risk has increased in severity since the beginning of the 1970s owing to the increasing volatility of prices on security markets, although recent years have seen a decline in such volatility. This is demonstrated in figures 14.1 and 14.2, which show changes in volatility in representative exchange and interest rates since 1968.

In the case of figure 14.1, the volatility of the dollar/pound exchange rate is represented by the moving 12-month standard deviation of percentage monthly changes. The picture shown before 1970 is one of relative stability. With the change from fixed to floating exchange rates at the beginning of the 1970s a steep increase in volatility can be observed and this increase persisted until 1992. Interest rate volatility is also measured by the moving 12-month standard deviation of monthly

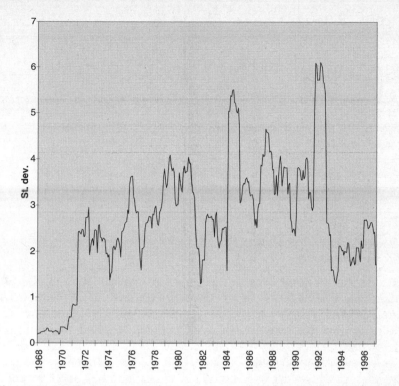

Figure 14.1   *Exchange rate volatility: moving 12-month standard deviation of monthly changes (sterling/dollar rate, 1968–97). Source: CSO,* Financial Statistics, *various issues*

changes. It seems inappropriate to use percentage changes when the level of the rate itself is subject to such a range of values and the cost/benefit to the trader depends on the absolute magnitude of the change. The changes themselves depicted in figure 14.2 are more volatile than those for exchange rates shown in figure 14.1 but generally interest rate volatility was more pronounced in the 1970s and 1980s than during the 1960s. This is particularly true of the late 1970s and early 1980s. The general picture revealed by these two figures is then one of increasing volatility of exchange and interest rates from the early 1970s to the early 1990s, which in turn enhanced the uncertainties faced by firms. The reduction in volatility since 1992, particularly in terms of interest rates, is partly explained by the reduction in inflation since that time and the relative stability this has created in the economic environment.

In section 14.2 we discuss in more detail the precise nature of exchange and interest rate risk before proceeding in section 14.3 to

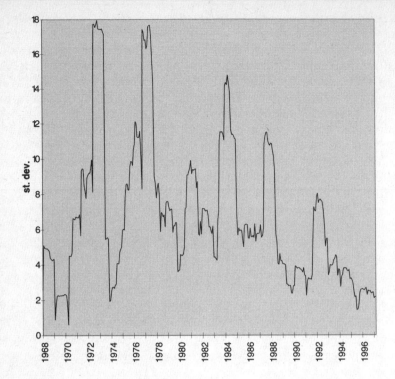

Figure 14.2   *Interest rate volatility: moving 12-month standard deviation of monthly changes (Treasury bill discount rate, 1968–97). Source: CSO,* Financial Statistics, *various issues*

discuss how firms can use internal methods of managing exchange rate risk. In section 14.4 we discuss external methods of managing exchange rate risk and in section 14.5 the management of interest rate risk. In section 14.6 we consider some of the problems that have occurred (in a spectacular manner) when hedging or trading with derivatives. Finally in section 14.7 we present our conclusions.

14.2   Nature of exchange and interest rate risk

Exchange rate risk can arise in a number of different ways. First, there is transaction risk, which arises because the exchange rate has changed between the date of the commitment and the date the payment is made or received. For the exporter uncertainty is increased by the possibility of exchange rate changes if the commodity is invoiced in foreign currency and costs are primarily defined in terms of domestic currency. A similar problem arises for importers, who find the domestic currency costs of their inputs denominated in foreign currency rising and falling in an unpredictable manner. This raises the possibility of unforeseen windfall losses or profits, making foreign trade considerably more risky than domestic trade. It also makes it difficult for firms engaged in foreign trade to quote prices for fear of exchange rate changes altering costs. It is important to define when this risk is incurred. It arises from the date the commitment is entered into. In the case of exports, this dates from the time the price quotation has been communicated to the purchaser. This may be a special quotation or it may date from the time a price list is circulated to actual or prospective customers. In a similar manner for importers, the risk dates from the time they have communicated their acceptance of the purchase of the goods from the foreign company. It is also important to realise that, when the trade is priced in one currency and payments to be made in another, it is the currency in which the payment is priced that is subject to exchange rate risk. If, for example, payment is to be made in dollars, then if both the domestic currency and that used as the unit of account move against the dollar in the same proportion, then no extra exchange rate risk is involved.

The second type of exposure to exchange rate changes is defined as translation risk. This arises when it is necessary to value overseas assets and liabilities for their incorporation into a consolidated balance sheet. If a company has a net surplus or deficit of assets defined in non-domestic currencies, then the balance sheet valuation will change as the relevant exchange rate alters. This particular exposure would not pose serious difficulties if the changes in the exchange rates were purely random around a relatively constant value. In fact since the abandonment of fixed exchange rates in 1972, long swings in exchange rates have been observed. Again, the nature of the commitment of the asset or liability is relevant. The translation exposure on a short-term liability or asset which is likely to be realised in the fairly near future (say one to five years) is similar to transaction exposure since their renewal might occur at the time of an unfavourable exchange rate. Therefore potential serious translation risk exists for the firm unless these risks are hedged. In contrast, permanent investment in subsidiaries can be treated as non-renewable and therefore impose a much lower incidence of exposure, though this could be serious if the currency in which the asset/liability is priced has shown a long-trend movement against the domestic currency.

The third type of exposure is economic exposure. In this case changes in exchange rates alter the relative prices of exports and imports. Over time this can adversely affect the position of firms where exchange rates have moved against them or alternatively help those firms whose products are made relatively cheaper by the exchange rate change. This type of exposure is of a long-term nature and is brought about by changes in the volume of sales following a change in the exchange rate. One example of this type of exposure is the pricing of oil in dollars. Thus, if the domestic currency depreciates against the dollar, the price of oil rises, adversely affecting those companies whose products have a large oil component. It should be emphasised that the exchange rate which matters for international trade is the real exchange rate, which may be defined as the nominal rate corrected for price changes. Thus, if nominal rates always moved to correct differing rates of inflation in the countries concerned then the dangers arising from economic exposure would be considerably reduced. In fact there is a considerable volume of evidence suggesting that PPP does not exist in the short run so that changes in real exchange rates do occur. There is little a company can do to protect itself against this type of risk except to diversify its products and production centres.

The final type of risk can be termed hidden exposure. A firm may not be directly affected by exchange rate changes since its products may be sold entirely to domestic customers and its raw materials bought from domestic producers. Despite this concentration on the domestic market, the firm would be exposed to indirect transaction and economic risk via one of its suppliers. Similarly, exchange rate change may beneficially affect potential competitors from abroad. An alternative form of indirect exposure can arise from the operation of a subsidiary which is itself affected by exchange rate changes in a third market even if the currencies of the principal and its subsidiary are linked together by fixed exchange rates.

So far we have concentrated on exchange rate exposure, but interest rate exposure may be analysed in the same way. Transaction exposure occurs through changing interest payments or receipts following a change in the interest rate structure. Translation exposure can occur through changes in the value of financial assets held originating from changes in interest rates. This is particularly applicable to the position of investment institutions, which hold large volumes of long-term financial securities. Economic exposure arises from changes in interest rates, which affect the general business environment as well as having an impact on firms according to the degree of leverage, that is, the proportion of capital raised by way of loans as distinct from equity finance. Thus, a rise in interest rates will reduce consumer demand and, generally, raise the cost of investment and impose costs on particular firms which have undertaken to raise finance by way of loans subject to interest rate adjustment.

In the following section we discuss how firms may reduce exchange rate exposure by methods internal to the firm and in section 14.4 the role of methods external to the firm.

14.3 Managing exchange rate risk: internal methods

A number of methods exist to manage exchange rate risk which are internal to the firm. These include: doing nothing; forecasting exchange rate movements; invoicing or accepting invoices denominated only in domestic currency; and operating a foreign currency bank account. In summary, the individual firm has a choice of doing nothing or hedging. The first option offers the lowest cost but the least protection against exchange rate exposure whereas hedging offers the highest degree of protection but also the highest cost because of the number of transactions involved.

The first method of managing exchange rate risk is therefore to do nothing and accept the spot rate at the time the payment is made or received. Appeal to the efficient markets hypothesis suggests that the current spot rate may well be the best available forecast of the future spot rate. In this case the most profitable policy for the firm would be to rely on the future spot rate for conversion of the foreign currency. Two problems arise with this approach. First, there is a distinct possibility that the foreign exchange market does not conform to the efficient markets hypothesis and that therefore the current spot rate is not the 'best' forecast of future exchange rates. Second, the firm may value certainty or near certainty of the domestic currency equivalent of the foreign currency receipt or payment, or in other words it may be risk averse in this respect. To illustrate this point, a firm is able to plan its pricing policy if it knows in advance the sterling value of future imports and exports. This may well be preferable to a trading system that lowers the average domestic currency cost of imports and raises the average domestic currency receipts for exports if this policy involves relatively large gains and losses around the average. It is quite possible that the firm, in these circumstances, may place a higher value on certainty than profitability in areas where it lacks expertise.

The policy of relying on the future spot rate to convert foreign currency into domestic currency is really nested in the second option, that of forecasting. In reality, doing nothing is equivalent to using the current spot rate as the optimal forecast of future spot exchange rates. It may, however, be the view of the firm that it can improve on the current spot rate as a predictor so that it forecasts the future pattern of spot exchange rates itself. The policy for the firm to manage exchange rate risk would then be to forecast and to choose between the use of internal and external methods of managing the risk in the light of a comparison of its internal forecasts and the constellation of market spot rates, forward rates and option prices. In a similar manner the firm could speed up payments in foreign currency (or purchase of the foreign currency) when the domestic currency was expected to depreciate and retard conversion of foreign currency receipts into domestic currency. The converse behaviour would occur when the domestic currency was expected to appreciate. This overall strategy of forecasting would be consistent with the view that the foreign exchange market does not conform to the efficient markets hypothesis. Apart from the comments made above with respect to risk aversion, the strategy of forecasting the future pattern of exchange rates also suffers from the defect that it requires resources to develop the expertise necessary to provide accurate forecasts. The firm may feel that its available resources are more profitably directed towards its primary functions.

The third internal method is to require invoices to be denominated in domestic currency. In this case there is no exchange rate exposure as far as the transaction component is concerned. However, this exposure has not been eliminated but rather transferred to the foreign purchaser or supplier of the goods. It is also more than likely that the foreign purchaser of goods would not be willing to accept invoices denominated in the domestic currency of the supplier and, given the existence of competition, this would be likely to cause loss of orders. In effect, transaction exposure has been changed into economic exposure.

The final internal method of managing exchange rate risk is to operate foreign currency bank accounts. Thus, as long as receipts and payments are in balance over a reasonable period of time, the exposure on receipts would match and offset the exposure on payments in a specific foreign currency. This type of account could also be allowed to run into deficit by way of an overdraft for a short period of time provided this overdraft was eliminated by future receipts of that currency. This type of risk management has only a limited application since it does require receipts and payments of that currency to cancel each other out over a reasonably short period of time. A persistent balance, particularly a persistently growing balance (either in deficit or in surplus), leaves the firm open to exchange rate exposure on both a transaction and a translation basis.

It was seen that internal methods offer the firm only limited scope to manage exchange rate risk, so we now turn to discussing the external methods open to the firm.

14.4 Managing exchange rate risk: external methods

In this section we discuss how a firm might manage exchange rate risk by having recourse to the financial institutions and markets. A number of such methods exist and these are the use of: the forward exchange market; temporary foreign currency deposits and loans; forfaiting; options; and back-to-back loans. Currency futures offer another method, but we do not consider these in this section because they seem to play a less important role in the management of exchange rate risk than in the case of other financial risks. However, a brief discussion of the nature of currency futures is provided in chapter 13, section 13.4.5.

14.4.1 *Forward contracts*

We discussed the forward exchange market in chapter 11, where it was seen that it is possible to purchase or sell foreign currency for delivery at a future date at a rate agreed at the time of the transaction. For example, if a trader was due to receive $500,000 in three months' time, she could sell the $500,000 forward for sterling, thus fixing the rate for conversion into sterling in three months' time. Clearly, this method of managing risk provides the trader with certainty of the domestic currency equivalent of the foreign currency receipts or payments. For example, if the relevant forward rate is $1.9398 per £1, then the sterling value of the $500,000 is £257,758.53. Again, it is worth emphasising that the firm does not make a profit by trading in the forward exchange market. At the time of the conversion out of or into foreign currency the spot rate may be higher or lower than the agreed forward rate of $1.9398 per £1. In fact our survey of the empirical evidence on the efficiency of the forward rate as a predictor of the future spot rate suggests that the forward rate will deviate from the future spot rate because of the existence of a risk premium. In other words, the trader will on balance pay a premium to the provider of the forward exchange as a compensation for the transfer of risk. Thus, the trader's gains arise purely from knowing what the rate will be, that is, she has purchased certainty, which, in the case of the above example, means she is sure that she can convert the $500,000 into £257,758.53. Even here a caveat must be raised. The certainty is obtained only provided the second party (i.e. the person buying or selling the goods) does not default. If he fails to complete his part of the transaction, the original trader is left with a forward contract not matched by a future spot receipt or payment so that she then has a foreign exchange rate exposure.

A further restriction on a straight forward contract is that it applies to a fixed date whereas in many commercial transactions the precise date of receipt of or payment in foreign currency is uncertain. One way around this is to choose an option date forward contract. This provides the right to buy or sell foreign currency, typically from a bank, up to a particular date. The disadvantage with this type of purchase is that the bank will offer the contract at the rate most favourable to itself. Thus, for an option contract for three months forward to sell sterling, the bank would select the highest rate out of the spot and individual outright forward rates up to three months. Conversely, in the case of an option date forward contract for the bank to purchase sterling, it would apply the lowest of the relevant rates. The trader can mitigate the impact of the adverse (from the trader's point of view) selection of rates by entering into overlapping option date forward contracts so that, for example, receipts of foreign currency expected in instalments over the next three months might be covered by an option forward contract for one month for a proportion of the total receipts and the balance by way of an option forward contract for two to three months. A further restriction may occur because the forward market for the desired currency is very thin or, in the extreme, non-existent. This may be overcome by exercising two forward contracts. In the case of a future receipt of a thinly traded currency, for example, it may be possible, given the importance of the dollar in international financial transactions, to sell dollars forward for domestic currency and simultaneously to buy dollars forward for the thinly traded currency. By this method the firm has achieved an indirect forward sale of the currency concerned.

14.4.2 *Temporary foreign currency deposits and loans*

A firm can use temporary foreign deposits and loans to achieve the same degree of protection against transaction exposure as is afforded by forward transactions. Reverting to the example of the future receipt of $500,000, the firm can achieve protection in the following manner:

(i)   borrow $500,000 from a bank for three months at the time of entering into the contract leading to the receipt of dollars;
(ii)   convert the dollars into sterling at the current spot exchange rate;
(iii) deposit the sterling received in a three-month interest-bearing sterling deposit.

The dollar loan is then paid off by the $500,000 receipt in three months' time. The sterling equivalent of the $500,000 depends on the two interest rates (the dollar borrowing and the sterling deposit) and the spot exchange rate. Since all these rates are known, this strategy fixes the sterling equivalent of the future receipt of dollars. In the case of a payment of $500,000 by a firm, steps (i) to (iii) above are reversed, that is:

(i)   borrow the sterling equivalent of the quantity of dollars which will increase to $500,000 when invested; alternatively the firm could use any spare cash holdings to finance step (ii);

(ii)   convert the dollars into sterling at the current spot rate;

(iii) invest the dollar receipts from (ii) above into a three-month interest-bearing dollar deposit.

On maturity of the deposit, the dollars are used to make the dollar payment.

In principle the cost of using this type of strategy should be the same as using the forward exchange market since it is in effect equivalent to covered interest arbitrage discussed in chapter 11 and IRP would imply that no profits can be made through moving funds between various centres.

14.4.3 *Forfaiting*

The third method of avoiding transaction exposure is to use a technique known as forfaiting. This involves transferring the risk to a bank by obtaining domestic currency from the bank in return for the transfer of the foreign currency debt to the bank. The most common types of debt instruments transferred are promissory notes and bills of exchange and the usual currencies are Deutschmarks and US dollars. The base interest rate for the transaction would be the relevant eurocurrency rate and, in addition, the bank would charge a commitment fee representing the delay between the agreement and the delivery of the instrument and the risk of exchange rate changes.

14.4.4 *Options*

Options also offer a method of managing exchange rate risk. As noted in chapter 13, options give the purchaser, in return for a premium, the right to buy (a 'call' option) or the right to sell (a 'put' option) at an agreed exchange rate (the 'striking' price) at a specified date or dates. No obligation is imposed on buyers to exercise the option so they will choose to do so only if it is profitable for them. Remember, the exercise of an option lies entirely in the hands of the purchaser. The writer has no control over whether the option is exercised or not. As was demonstrated in chapter 13, an option contract is analogous to an insurance policy, with the premium for the option representing the premium paid

Table 14.1   *Philadelphia Stock Exchange sterling/dollar options (£31,250)* *(cents per £1)*

Strike price	Calls				Puts			
	Oct.	Nov.	Dec.	March	Oct.	Nov.	Dec.	March
1.875	9.10	9.20	9.33	9.79	–	0.70	1.41	3.56
1.900	6.60	7.04	7.31	8.02	0.04	1.22	2.01	4.56
1.925	4.11	5.17	5.57	6.49	0.07	2.02	2.91	5.71
1.950	1.97	3.61	4.11	5.20	0.29	2.88	4.05	7.06
1.975	0.53	2.43	3.00	4.12	1.37	4.24	5.47	8.55
2.000	0.07	1.65	2.08	–	3.29	5.89	7.11	–
2.025	0.01	1.08	1.56	–	5.67	7.77	8.94	–

for the policy and the risk insured is the risk of an adverse exchange rate movement, with the purchaser taking all the benefits of a favourable movement.

Options are also particularly useful in the case of contingent exposures, for example in the case of a tender in foreign currency. If the firm does not win the contract, there is no need for the foreign currency and the option will be exercised only if it offers the chance of immediate profit because it is 'in the money'. Similarly, the firm may wish to take out options because the precise quantity of foreign exposure is not known, for example in the case of an uncertain volume of sales of goods abroad or in the case of domestic sales requiring imported raw materials. In such cases the firm can use options to provide a hedge against foreign currency exposure.

Over-the-counter options would be arranged as a private contract with a bank and offer the advantage that the conditions attached to the contract exactly match those required by the purchaser. In contrast traded options are standardised and may not therefore match the precise quantity requirements of the purchaser. For example, the sterling options quoted on the Philadelphia Stock Exchange are denominated in units of £31,250. On the other hand they offer the additional benefit of being able to be sold on the market rather than just being exercised or allowed to lapse. The suspension of currency options on LIFFE suggests that the disadvantage of standardised contracts outweighs the advantage of tradability.

Various option strategies are possible and we use the quotations for December delivery on the Philadelphia Stock Exchange listed in table 14.1 to illustrate them – note in the following examples the spot rate is assumed to be $1.9750 per £1 for illustrative purposes.

In the case of options, the trader has a choice of exercise rates. If he or she purchases, for example, a call option with a strike price of $1.875 per £1 the premium is 9.33 cents, implying a maximum price for the purchase of pounds of $1.9683 per £1 (1.875 + 0.0933). Thus, the trader is sure that the minimum quantity of sterling obtained for a future receipt of $500,000 is £254,026.32. If the spot rate at the time of receipt of the dollars is less than $1.875, then the option will not be exercised and the trader will purchase the sterling in the market at the lower price but losing the option premium. Similarly, at strike prices of $1.975 and $2.025 per £1, the maximum prices rise to $2.005 and $2.0406, respectively. In a similar manner buying put options with strike prices of $1.875, $1.975 and $2.025 per £1 fixes the minimum prices obtained by the sale of sterling at $1.8609, $1.9203 and $1.9356, respectively. It can be seen that the analogy to insurance is very close. The higher the premium paid the greater is the degree of protection against the down-side risk of adverse changes in the spot exchange rate. This leaves the trader a choice of strategies in which there is a trade-off between protection and cost. More complex strategies are discussed below.

Vertical spread

One such strategy goes by the name of a vertical spread, involving the simultaneous purchase and sale of options with different exercise prices. In the case of a vertical bull call spread (so called because of the expectation of rises in the exchange rate) the trader would buy a call option with a strike price of, say, $1.975 per £1 at a premium of 3.0 cents and write (sell) a call with a higher strike price, say $2.025 per £1 at a premium of 1.56 cents. Thus, the premium income incurs a loss of 1.44 cents (3.0 − 1.56) or equivalently $0.0144. At a spot rate below $1.975 per £1 neither option is exercised and the trader's loss is 1.44 cents. At spot rates between $1.975 and $2.025 only the purchased call option is exercised, so the trader benefits from the increasing profitability of this option. At the rate of $2.025 per £1 the trader's profit (compared with the spot rate) is at a maximum since thereafter any profit on the purchase of the call option is matched on a one-for-one basis by the loss on the option sold. At a spot rate of $2.025 per £1, the trader's profit (as compared with the spot rate) is given by the profit on the option purchased minus the loss on the premium, that is:

$$(2.025 - 1.975) - \$0.0144 = \$0.0356 \text{ or } 3.56 \text{ cents.}$$

In this case the trader has given up the potentially unlimited gain above a spot rate of $2.005 per £1 offered by a simple call option purchase with a strike price of $1.975 per £1 in return for a lower premium, that is, 1.44 cents as against 3.0 cents. In terms of hedging the trader has ensured a minimum sterling equivalent, for say $500,000, of £251,332.06 {500,000/(1.975 + 0.0144)} provided the spot exchange rate remains below $2.025 per £1. As the rate rises above $2.025 per £1 the trader is fully exposed to potential losses. Traders would use this strategy where they thought that the exchange rate is likely to rise above the current spot rate but not by any great amount.

In an analogous manner a trader who believed that the spot rate was likely to fall from the current level but not to any great extent would buy a put, again say with a strike price of $1.975 per £1 (premium 5.47 cents) and sell a put with a lower strike price, say $1.950 per £1 (premium 4.05 cents). At an exchange rate greater than $1.975 per £1 neither option would be exercised and the trader's loss is limited to the premium deficiency of 1.42 cents per £1. At rates below $1.975 per £1 but above $1.950 per £1 only the put option purchased is exercised and below $1.950 per £1 both options are exercised. Thus, the trader's maximum profit at $1.950 per £1 is $0.0108 or 1.08 cents per £1 ($1.975 − $1.950 − $0.0142). Again, the trader has given up the opportunity of obtaining an unlimited profit at rates below $1.950 per £1 in return for the lower premium of 1.08 cents per £1. In terms of hedging, the trader, who has to make a payment of $500,000, has ensured a maximum sterling cost of £254,556.56 provided the spot rate remains above $1.950 per £1 {500,000/(1.975 − 0.0108)}. As the spot rate falls below $1.950 per £1, the trader is fully exposed to potential losses. This type of strategy is called a vertical bear spread.

The vertical spread strategy is also called a 'collar' because of the restricted range of protection as compared with a traditional option.

Figure 14.3   *Profit and loss for vertical spreads*

Note that this restricted range of protection is obtained through payment of a reduced premium. This type of trade can be gainfully used by either a hedger or a speculator. In the case of a hedger, it is no longer a pure hedge since the firm has taken a view on the likely direction and magnitude of future exchange rate movements. A diagrammatic presentation of profit/loss situations is shown in figure 14.3.

Volatility trading with options
The concluding types of option trading strategies examined are concerned with volatility trading. These are straddles, strangles and butterflies. In each case the operator takes a view on the likely course of movements in exchange rate volatility and backs this view by entering into an appropriate option strategy. For this reason these strategies are more likely to be adopted by speculators and writers of options than firms using the market as a facility to hedge.

(i) *Straddle*. A straddle involves writing or purchasing a call and put option at the same strike price. In the case of a sale of a straddle (sometimes called a short straddle) the writer could, for example, write (sell) a December call and a December put each with a strike price of $1.975 per £1. The combined premium received from the sale would be 8.47 cents per £1 (5.47 + 3.0). At the strike price (i.e. $1.975 per £1) neither option would be exercised. At spot exchange rates below $1.975 per £1, only the put option would be exercised and the break-even point for the writer of the option occurs where the loss on this option is just matched by the combined premium receipts. This occurs at a spot exchange rate of $1.8903 per £1. In a similar way, as the spot exchange rate rises above $1.975 per £1, only the call option is exercised and the break-even rate is $2.0597 per £1 (i.e. $1.975 + $0.0847). Whilst the rate remains within the two bounds ($1.8903 and $2.0597) the speculator will profit but otherwise faces unlimited loss. This type of trade is likely to be used by a speculator who believes that volatility is not likely to increase to any great extent and it is often therefore called a bear straddle.

In contrast, a speculator who believes that volatility is likely to increase will buy a straddle (a 'long' or 'bull' straddle). In this case he or she would purchase a call and put option for the same delivery date and strike price. Using the above example as an illustration the speculator could purchase a December call and put each with a strike price of $1.975 per £1. In this case he or she pays out the combined premium of 8.47 cents per £1 and this is the maximum loss. The profit is potentially unlimited as the spot exchange rate rises above $2.0597 per £1 or falls below $1.8903 per £1.

In both cases of long and short straddles, the speculator is not forming a view as to the direction of the exchange rate movement but

Figure 14.4   *Profit and loss for a straddle*

rather its volatility or the likelihood of it moving beyond specified limits. The profit and loss situations for both types of straddle are shown in figure 14.4.

(ii) *Strangle.* The second type of volatility strategy is a strangle. It is similar to a straddle and has the same underlying rationale but two different strike prices are involved and this lengthens the area of maximum profitability in the case of a short strangle or maximum loss in the case of a long straddle. In the case of a short strangle, the speculator could write a December call with a strike price of $2.000 per £1 (premium 2.08 cents) and a December put with a strike price of $1.950 per £1 (premium 4.05 cents). The combined premium income is 6.13 cents per £1 (2.08 + 4.05). At spot rates below $1.950 per £1 only the put option is exercised so that the break-even point is $1.887 per £1 ($1.950 – $0.0613). Between rates of $1.950 and $2.000 per £1, neither option is exercised so the speculator earns a profit of 6.13 cents per £1. At rates above $2.000 per £1, only the call option is exercised and the break-even point is $2.0613 per £1 (2.000 + 0.0613). The case of a long strangle can be illustrated by the same example but in this case the speculator purchases the two options. Consequently her or his maximum loss is given by the combined premium income and positions of profit are given when the spot exchange rate either falls below $1.887 per £1 or rises above $2.0613 per £1. Diagrammatic representations of the profit and loss situations for strangles are shown in figure 14.5.

Figure 14.5   *Profit and loss for a strangle*

(iii) *Butterfly*. The final option strategy considered is a butterfly. A butterfly strategy is also similar to a straddle and has the same under-lying rationale of trading against movements in the volatility of exchange rates. In this strategy, however, a floor is provided for the maximum loss or a ceiling to the maximum gain. Purchase of a butterfly (a long butterfly) entails buying an out-of-the-money call, writing two at-the-money calls and buying an in-the-money call. As an illustration of this strategy the calls purchased could be as shown in table 14.2.

The combined premium income represents a net loss of 1.13 cents. At a spot rate below \$1.925 no option is exercised so the maximum loss is the negative premium income, that is, 1.13 cents per £1. Up to a spot rate of \$1.975 per £1, only the in-the-money option is exercised so the point of maximum gain is \$(1.975 − 1.925 − 0.0113) per £1, that is, \$0.0387 per £1 or 3.87 cents per £1. At rates above \$1.975 per £1 but

Table 14.2   *Illustration of a butterfly*

	Strike price (\$ per £1)	Premium (cents per £1)	Spot rate when exercised (\$ per £1)
In-the-money (purchased)	1.925	5.57	>1.925
At-the-money (sold)	1.975	3.00	>1.975
Out-of-the-money (purchased)	2.025	1.56	2.025

Figure 14.6 *Profit and loss for a butterfly*

Table 14.3   *Illustration of a condor*

	Strike price ($ per £1)	Premium (cents per £1)	Spot rate when exercised ($ per £1)
In-the-money (purchased)	1.925	5.57	> 1.925
Option (i) (sold)	1.950	4.11	> 1.950
Option (ii) (sold)	1.975	3.00	> 1.975
Out-of-the-money (purchased)	2.000	2.08	> 2.000

below $2.025 per £1 the two at-the-money options (written) are exercised so losses on these offset the profits gained on the in-the-money option purchased. The maximum loss occurs at a spot rate of $2.025 per £1 because after this point the out-of-the-money call is exercised. Consequently the gain on the two call options purchased is matched on a one-for-one basis by the loss on the two call options sold. The maximum loss is therefore the gain on the option with a strike price of $1.1925 per £1 less the loss on the two options written with a strike price of $2.000 less the net premium deficiency: $((2.025 − 1.925) − 2(2.025 − 1.975) − 0.0113) per £1, which is $0.0113 per £1 or 1.13 cents per £1.

Selling a butterfly (a short butterfly) would entail the reverse procedure, that is, writing an in-the-money call, buying two at-the-money calls and writing an out-of-the-money call. The profit and loss situation would be precisely opposite to that illustrated for the above example, that is, a maximum loss of 3.87 cents per £1 and a maximum profit of 1.13 cents per £1. The profit and losses for this situation are illustrated in figure 14.6.

As noted above, figures 14.5 and 14.6 illustrate the essential difference between a butterfly and a straddle, that is, the maximum loss or gain is restricted to a fixed amount.

A variant of a 'butterfly' is a strategy known as a 'condor'. The general principle is the same but, in the case of a purchase, the two options sold are at different prices. An example is given in table 14.3 and interested readers are advised to derive for themselves the graph of the profit/loss situation arising from this transaction. As in the case of a butterfly, for writing a condor the transactions are reversed.

Hidden premium options
One of the problems for traders using options as a strategy to manage risk is that the premium has to be paid in advance, or 'up front' in the jargon. Partly in response to the reluctance to make payments up front, a

number of variants have been developed in the OTC sector. These variants have been given a number of names according to the marketing strategy of the institution itself, but a generic title would be 'hidden premium' options. These are a sort of hybrid between normal forward contracts and options. The trader due to receive dollars would enter into a forward contract to purchase pounds but one with a break point at which the trader could break out of the forward position and transact at the spot rate. No up-front premium is involved as the cost would be incorporated into the forward rate. Clearly, in view of the added protection, the forward rate would be less advantageous than for a standard forward contract; it would be a higher rate in the case of purchases of, or a lower rate in the case of sales of, pounds. As an illustration, consider again the situation of the receipt of $500,000. The normal forward rate discussed earlier was assumed to be $1.9398 per £1. For illustration of the principle behind hidden premium options, we assume that the rate for a forward contract with a break at $1.90 per £1 is $1.9980 per £1. This gives the trader the right to break the contract if the spot rate at the maturity of the contract is less than $1.90 per £1. If on maturity the spot rate was $1.80 per £1 the following transactions are implied, leaving the trader with net receipts of £264,870.14:

sale of $500,000 at the forward rate (1.9980)	£250,250.25
purchase of $500,000 at the break rate (1.90)	-£263,157.89
sale of $500,000 at the spot rate (1.80)	£277,777.78
net receipts	£264,870.14

Note that by this strategy, the trader is protected against the loss of falls in the spot rate against the forward rate below the break rate. At the same time the trader is protected against rises in the spot rate above the agreed forward rate. The protection strategy in the case of sale of sterling would be the mirror image of that discussed above for the purchase of sterling. The trader would enter into a contract with an enhanced forward rate but one which provided a break if the spot rate rose above a specified break rate.

14.4.5 *Back-to-back loans*

The final method of using the market to hedge exchange rate risk is to arrange a back-to-back loan. Back-to-back loans can take two forms: parallel loans or swaps. Multinational corporations use these types of loans for subsidiaries wishing to raise finance in foreign currencies. Assume there are two parent companies, one in the UK and one in the US, each with a subsidiary in the country of the other parent company.

Thus, the UK parent company lends in sterling to the subsidiary of the US company located in the UK and the US parent company lends in dollars to the subsidiary of the UK company located in the US. Each subsidiary company has a loan and cash denominated in the currency where it operates and has, therefore, avoided exchange rate exposure. If each parent company had borrowed in its domestic currency it would then have to transform the loan into foreign currency for the use of its subsidiary and it would therefore be exposed to exchange rate risk. Swap loans involve the exchange of debts denominated in different currencies. Thus, a firm with easy access to the UK capital market may wish to finance an investment in the US. If it is possible for that firm to find a corresponding US firm which has easy access to the US capital market but wishes to finance a sterling investment, then it is possible for both firms to gain by swapping their respective liabilities for repayment of the debt principal and interest payments. Such parallel and swap loans may be arranged through banks.

Finally, we look at currency exchange agreements, which are in essence similar to swap loans. Returning to the example used to illustrate the parallel loan, the two parent companies would agree to lend to each other, the US company to the UK company in dollars and the UK company to the US company in sterling. These loans would then be passed on to their subsidiaries, and hence each subsidiary has a loan denominated in the desired currency. Swaps are discussed in more detail in chapter 13, section 13.6. The repayment terms, including any interest differentials, would be agreed at the time of the original loan, thus removing any exposure to subsequent exchange rate movements.

We now turn to examine strategies to manage interest rate risk.

14.5   Managing interest rate risk

We shall spend rather less time discussing interest rate risk, not because we regard this type of risk as being of less importance than exchange rate risk but rather because many of the strategies have already been discussed in the previous section. Internal methods of managing interest rate exposure take the form of doing nothing or forecasting, with all the inherent problems examined at the beginning of section 14.3. External methods of managing risk include use of the futures market, of options and of interest rate swaps. In chapter 13 section 13.4.1 we illustrated the position of a company which wished to hedge against a rise in rates of interest by selling a financial futures short-term deposit. We also noted that the hedge may be less than perfect due to a change in basis. We also emphasised that the hedger should sell futures if the company was harmed by rising interest rates but buy futures if its position was adversely affected by falls in interest rates.

14.5.1 *Interest rate futures*

As was noted in table 13.3 of chapter 13, a range of interest rate futures are provided, including domestic and foreign rates of interest, short- and long-term rates. This provides a number of possible strategies to manage interest rate exposure. However, a single interest rate contract is likely to involve more than one instance of exposure. Thus, a loan which is to be rolled over every three months for one year involves four instances of, rather than a single, risk. This can be covered by utilising a strip hedge, that is, taking out sales of four futures contracts, one for each time the loan is to be rolled over. This may prove to be difficult if the market for distant futures is illiquid. An alternative strategy is to employ a rolling hedge. Successive hedges are obtained on the earliest interest rate revisions only. An alternative strategy is to take out a 'piled up' hedge, in which futures amounting to a multiple of the loan would be taken out. Thus, if the interest rate on the loan is to be reassessed four times, futures contracts equal to four times the loan would be sold. These contracts would be closed out and renewed at each of the reassessment dates. The advantage of piled-up hedges is that they avoid distant futures but on the other hand they incur a large number of contracts and therefore commission charges.

14.5.2 *Interest rate options*

Over-the-counter options are provided by some banks and LIFFE also offers options on interest rate futures on some of the most important contracts (see table 13.3 for details). This provides hedging opportunities, in the same way as was discussed for exchange rate exposure in the previous section, for fixing maximum and minimum rates of interest. An interest rate cap gives a borrower an opportunity to purchase an agreement that will compensate the borrower if interest rates rise above a specific level. Similarly, an interest rate floor gives an investor the opportunity to purchase an agreement that will compensate the investor if interest rates fall below a certain level. In return for these facilities the borrower or investor will pay a premium to the seller and this cost can be seen as an insurance against adverse interest rate movements. As an example, consider the case of a company borrowing $10 million from a bank on a floating-rate basis linked to three-month LIBOR. The treasurer is concerned that interest rates may rise over the next three years and so purchases an interest cap at 8 per cent based on three-month LIBOR for a period of three years. If three-month LIBOR rises to 10 per cent on the first settlement date the company would be paid an amount by the seller to compensate for the 2 per cent difference between the cap rate and the LIBOR rate. The cap rate will continue to be checked against LIBOR at each settlement date (every three months) until the end of the three-year period. If interest rates were to fall to say 6 per cent, then the company would receive no benefit under the cap facility but would be able to take advantage of the lower rate on the underlying loan. Thus, the advantages of the cap facility are that the borrower can quantify maximum borrowing costs over the term of the facility and that, unlike futures or fixed-rate funding, the borrower is protected from rising interest rates but is able to benefit from any downturn in rates.

An interest rate floor is an option contract which compensates investors for falls in interest rates but allows them to take advantage of interest rate rises. A collar, as discussed in section 14.4, on exchange rate hedging, is effectively a combination of an interest rate cap and floor. One party to the agreement will sell the cap and the other party will sell the floor. A borrower therefore will buy the cap to establish a maximum borrowing cost and simultaneously sell a floor, which will set a minimum borrowing cost. The value of the floor will be used either partially or fully to offset the cost of the cap. In practice the value of the floor agreement is usually less than the value of the cap agreement and so a net payment is required. The advantage of the collar agreement over the cap is the reduction (or elimination) of charges. However, this saving is achieved by giving up some part of the gain that could be achieved if rates fall. A collar can also be used by an investor. An investor would buy a floor and sell a cap, which would give protection against rates falling below the floor level but by sacrificing some of the potential gain available when rates rise above the cap level.

The preceding discussion of caps, floors and collars related to OTC option contracts. Traded options on interest rate futures can also be used to provide the same sort of protection. With a traded option, instead of the seller of the option compensating the buyer for adverse changes in interest rates, the protection is obtained by first buying an option and then selling before maturity with the net gain providing compensation. For example, a lending floor can be obtained by buying call options that will increase in value if interest rates decline. Assume the option selected is a December 89.00 call with a premium of 0.61. This option achieves a minimum effective lending rate of 10.39 per cent:

interest rate implied by exercise price =   11.00 per cent (100 – 89)
less call premium   -0.61 per cent
= minimum effective lending rate   10.39 per cent

If the interest rate underlying the option falls before the option expires then the value (premium) of the option will rise. If, say, interest rates fall from 11 per cent to 10 per cent and the call option value increases to 1.00, then the option can be sold and a gain of $1.00 - 0.61 = 0.39$ is made. This gain compensates the investor for a fall in the underlying interest rate. The effective lending rate has thus been fixed at 10.39 per cent:

lending rate	10.00 per cent
plus gain on option	0.39 per cent
= effective lending rate	10.39 per cent.

14.5.3 *Interest rate swaps*

Finally in this section we discuss the nature of interest rate swaps. An interest rate swap entails the exchange by two parties of interest rate payments of a different character based on a notional principal amount. Three types of swap are probably the most important. These are coupon swaps, basis swaps and cross-currency interest rate swaps. In chapter 12 (section 12.5) we described the dramatic growth in the interest rate swap market in recent years, partly reflecting the growth in fixed-rate euro-bond issues. In chapter 13 we discussed the nature of the interest rate swap. The classic example of this type of swap is to exchange a floating-rate loan for a fixed-rate one. This may be carried out to eliminate the risk of changes in interest rates. Note again that the benefit of this strategy is the substitution of certainty for uncertainty. This swap may be carried out directly by the two liability holders or through a bank acting as an intermediary. In the latter case anonymity is preserved. The second type of interest rate swap is a basis swap, where a loan with interest rates based on one key rate is swapped for another loan based on an alternative key rate (e.g. a LIBOR rate for a local authority rate). In both cases it may be possible for a borrower with a low credit rating to obtain a lower charge than would otherwise be the case. Finally, we have examined the nature of the cross-currency interest rate swap in section 13.6.2.

14.6   Problems arising from hedging or trading derivatives

Although derivatives can be and are used to manage financial risk, they are not themselves inherently riskless. This is evidenced by the detail in table 14.4, which lists some well publicised examples of companies incurring losses through derivative products.

Table 14.4 *Examples of companies incurring losses through the use of derivatives products*

Company	Estimated loss reported in the media
Allied Lyons	£150 million
Atlantic Richfield	$22 million
Barings	£860 million
Codelco	$200 million
Gibson Greetings	$73 million
Maryland County Administration[a]	$1.3 million
Metallgesellschaft	$1.3 billion
Orange County[a]	$1.7 billion
Proctor and Gamble	$100 million

[a] US local authorities.

With the exception of Barings (where the loss was due to fraud and inappropriate internal control procedures), all the other companies are users of derivatives rather than suppliers. This suggests that there is a relatively high degree of ignorance on behalf of users.

The first point for any user to note is that hedging an exposure by writing (selling) options incurs a considerable risk since writing an option involves the seller incurring potential losses which are unlimited. Reference to figures 13.2 and 13.3 demonstrates this point in the case of a simple (single) transaction. In the case of both call and put options the writer faces unlimited losses if the price moves against the writer so that it is profitable to exercise the option. This contrasts with the position of the purchase of options where the maximum loss is limited to the premium paid for the option. Consequently hedging using options should be carried out by purchase of rather than by writing options.

Obviously when using the futures market, it is essential that the price of the instrument of hedging moves in parallel with the instrument hedged. A hedger is always trading a greater price risk for the (hopefully) smaller basis risk. In other words hedgers are speculating on 'basis'. However, other problems exist and we will use the Metalgesellschaft (MG) and Barings cases to illustrate these.

14.6.1 *Case study of Metalgesellschaft*

This section draws heavily on work by Franklin Edwards (see Edwards and Cantor 1995). Briefly, MG Refining and Marketing (MGRM), a subsidiary of MG, wished to establish long-term relationships with customers and so entered into contracts to supply approximately 160 million barrels of gasoline and heating oil to end users over the next ten years. Mark-ups of $3–$5 over current prices were established. This marketing strategy carries a massive risk of price rises. There are three ways of minimising this risk, but each has problems:

(i)   buy the quantity of fuel necessary to meet the contract at the outset – this has the major problem that it involves massive warehousing costs and these would make the deal unprofitable;

(ii) buy futures contracts to purchase the oil with a time profile that matches the delivery contracts – but no exchange-traded contracts exist for ten years' maturity and the cost of negotiating OTC contracts for such a maturity would be enormous;

(iii) buy exchange-traded contracts within the existing maturity trading arrangements and roll them over (renew them) periodically.

MGRM used strategy (iii). They purchased the contract with near maturities and rolled them over periodically – that is, they followed a short-term stacking policy – reducing the derivative commitment in respect of any oil delivered. Even without the benefit of hindsight this strategy involved considerable risk since any price changes would involve MGRM in margin payments/receipts in the opposite direction to spot price changes *before* the receipt of cash from the relevant oil deliveries. In fact the price of oil fell consistently during 1993 so MGRM was continually making margin payments leading to MGRM having to post nearly $900 million to maintain its hedge. Note, however, that if the price of oil had risen then MGRM would have received substantial inflows of margin payments. The danger of having to make large margin payments on a hedging contract is known as 'funding risk'. This type of risk is endemic in any hedging contract using futures.

    An additional risk occurs at the time of the renewal of the contracts in the case of hedging risks with a longer maturity than that of the relevant financial instruments which are readily available in the markets. This necessitates purchasing a sequence of short-term securities, that is, 'rolling over' the contracts. If the price of the new contract is above the price of the old contract additional losses are incurred in the hedge on the roll-over date – if nearby prices are below deferred prices the market is said to be in 'contango'; the converse is referred to as 'backwardation'. In fact, throughout 1993, the market was in contango virtually every month thus adding to the losses on the strategy. In part this was not foreseeable since over the period 1983–92 the market was, on average, in backwardation. Critics have also pointed out that the strategy was prone to credit risk through the possibility of default by the counterparties. This did not arise.

MRGM's strategy was probably defective in construction in other respects as well. They appear to have hedged the contract on a one-for-one basis; that is, each delivery of one barrel of oil was hedged by a futures contract for one barrel. This is not necessarily the correct strategy. If the price of the futures contract fluctuates more than (but in the same direction as) the price of the underlying commodity, then a one-for-one strategy is inappropriate as a defensive mechanism and a ratio of less than one for one would be appropriate. In fact the formula for the minimum variance hedge (h) is:

$$h = \rho(\sigma_S/\sigma_F)$$

where ρ is the correlation coefficient between the price of the futures and that of the underlying commodity, σ is the standard deviation and S and F represent spot and futures. Edwards and Cantor (1995) report h as less than one. If fewer future contracts had been entered into then the margin payments would have been smaller.

One of the problems with regard to the use of derivative instruments occurs if such instruments are 'marked to market'. As noted above, users of such instruments may incur a significant negative cash flow if the price of the instrument moves against them because margin payments have to be made. Such payments have to be made before maturity of the futures contract and hence before any profit/loss on the derivatives contracts have been offset by those on the underlying cash market transaction. The case of MG noted above illustrates this point only too well. The scale of the margin payments led the company to wind up the contracts and incur substantial cash losses, as indicated in table 14.4.

14.6.2 *Case study of Barings Bank*

Barings is one of the more recent and spectacular instances of financial disaster for a well established bank. This section draws on the official report into the collapse of Barings (Board of Banking Supervision 1995). In outline, Barings succeeded in losing an equivalent of £860 million through futures trading via the now notorious fraudulent rogue trader, Nick Leeson, engaged in unauthorised trading. All such losses were transferred to a hidden account denominated '88888', which was opened in July 1992 shortly after Leeson arrived in Singapore as a trader for Barings Futures (Singapore). The trading losses were incurred mainly through two types of activity. First, Leeson rapidly built up a long position of futures contracts on the Nikkei 225 stock index and a short position on Japanese government bonds. In both cases the market moved against him. Secondly, he also engaged in volatility trading on the options market by writing (selling) a 'call' and a 'put' at the same exercise price (i.e. 'straddle' as described in section 14.4.4) on the Nikkei index. As noted earlier, this strategy is used by a trader who does not believe that the market will move outside its existing trading profile. As soon as the index of the underlying moves outside the range as defined by the break-even points such as those illustrated in figure 14.4 then losses are incurred. Note the position of the writer is far more risky than that of the purchaser since the latter has no further obligations after payment of the premiums. In fact, the index moved outside the range of his straddle contracts, no doubt due in part to the Kobbe earthquake on 17 January 1995. His overall position on 24 February was short a total of 37,925 call options and 32,967 put options. All but one of the put options were in the money, leading to substantial margin payments from Barings to the exchange.

One salient feature of the debacle is the speed with which the losses built up. From 1 January to 27 February, Leeson's trading activities resulted in losses of £619 million. In fact, on Thursday 23 February, his trading activities succeeded in losing £144 million in one day and, to quote the succinct comment of the report, 'it was at this point that he left BFS [Barings Futures (Singapore) PTE Ltd.], never to return'. The interesting point is why Leeson engaged in these activities to such an extent and built up such a long position after a period of long decline in the index. Two possible reasons can be put forward: first, the desperate gambler trying to recoup his losses in the hope that the index would appreciate later; and second, an attempt to move the market in his favour.

Who was culpable? We would argue that it was not the existence of derivative securities per se but rather incompetent management. The report is littered with examples of what many would consider to be evidence of gross incompetence. A few examples are appended below:

(i)   Leeson was both the senior trader and manager responsible for the back office (administration), an arrangement singularly prone to fraud. Separation of the two functions was recommended in an internal audit report in August 1994. Action then would have prevented the collapse.

(ii) No organisation chart existed, with the consequence that various executives seemed to be confused as to who reported to whom.

(iii) 'At that point in time [early 1994] I never really thought much about why it is so profitable' (Ron Baker, head of Barings' Financial Products Group, quoted in Board of Banking Supervision 1995: p. 28, para. 2.47).

(iv) One executive felt that his inexperience contributed to the fiasco: 'There is no doubt that if I had ten years' experience in exchange traded equity derivatives, this would not happen. The fact is that I did not' (Ron Baker, p. 49, para. 3.61).

(v)   The massive quantity of funds was transferred for margin payments without any real query by raised by Barings' Treasury Group for the reasons behind the transfers.

(vi) Queries raised by outsiders regarding the trading activities in Asia were not checked out. The queries arose from a number of sources, including the BIS on 27 January 1995, Schroders on 16 February 1995 and an employee on the Japanese market in general on 17 February 1995. It is perhaps surprising that Barings' apparently sole response to the query from the BIS was, according to a tape of a telephone conversation: 'For the BIS to ring us was a bit embarrassing'.

14.7   Conclusion

We have examined a wide range of strategies for firms to manage exposure to risk. Since these risks have increased since the early 1960s it is not surprising that the number of instruments available to hedge risk has also increased. This is just one further example of financial innovation.

We would like to emphasise that hedging is not an ephemeral concept. In the survey carried out by the Bank of England on behalf of the BIS, of the 396 firms surveyed, 43 per cent said they used derivatives for both trading and hedging, 32 per cent for hedging alone and 14 per cent for trading and hedging and market making (*Bank of England Quarterly Bulletin* 1996). These figures give some indication of the importance of the hedging function. Further corroboration of the importance of derivative contracts is provided by a survey of 386 major international corporations reported in Price Waterhouse (1995). This found that:

(i)   73 per cent of the respondents used derivatives to manage their interest rate risk on their borrowings;

(ii) 96 per cent of the respondents partially or fully hedge their foreign exchange transactions exposure. The main vehicle used was the forward exchange market, with only 4 per cent using futures. Option-based products, swaps and foreign currency balances were also used by 50 per cent of the respondents.

The findings by Price Waterhouse (1995) also drew attention to concern over the control standards applied by the companies. This concern was more pronounced in the case of foreign exchange transactions – for example only 36 per cent of respondents imposed dealer-trading limits.

This reinforces comments made earlier in this section on the role of management.

It should also be noted that financial risk is just one of the risks facing a company. In some cases insuring against financial risk may increase the total risk incurred by a firm. To illustrate this point, consider the example of a firm which sells a product in an overseas market with the price denominated in the overseas currency. Before delivery of the product the firm's costs rise due to a higher relative rate of inflation. In a floating exchange rate regime, the exchange rate will depreciate so that the domestic currency receipts will rise compared with the level anticipated at the time of making the contract. This will offset the rise in costs. The extent of the offset will depend on the extent of the depreciation, which itself depends on the efficiency of the foreign exchange market. In contrast, if the firm hedges the exchange rate risk, no offset to the relative rise in domestic costs will have occurred.

Finally, the existence of losses on the scale noted in table 14.4 has also led to discussion over whether derivatives markets should be more tightly regulated. It is a salient feature of the losses noted in table 14.4 that, with the sole exception of Barings, all were in respect of non-financial companies. It would seem reasonable to assume that companies would operate in such markets only if they possessed the necessary financial expertise to comprehend the risks involved. In any case, customers who feel they have been misled or ill advised in any way have recourse to legal action. In fact, it was reported in the media that such action was undertaken by Procter and Gamble and Atlantic Richfield. It has also been reported that a bank, CS First Boston, has made repayments to three customers totalling $40 million in respect of derivatives advice it provided. Consequently, no further prudential control would seem to be necessary to protect customers. The case of regulating banks' operations in derivatives markets raises different issues, which are considered in chapter 18.

Chapter 15

The single European market in financial services

15.1 Introduction

The general principle of a single market for Europe was embodied in the Treaty of Rome in 1957. However, little was done in terms of achieving this over the 1960s and 1970s as the individual member states of the European Community (now the EU) concentrated attention on their own domestic economic problems. The impetus for achieving the objective of a single market came in 1985 with the publication of a white paper from the European Commission, *Completing the Internal Market*, promoted by the then Vice President of the Commission, Lord Cockfield. Momentum was achieved by setting a target date of 1992 for completion of the single market. To this end the white paper detailed 300 measures designed to remove physical, technical and fiscal barriers to trade within the Community. The introduction of the principle of qualified majority voting in the Council of Ministers on most issues, whereby no individual member state can veto a proposal, also helped to speed up the decision-making process. This is illustrated by the passing of the Single European Act in 1987, soon after the white paper.

The underlying objective for a single European market is to benefit consumers and producers by a variety of methods, but most importantly by reducing costs through the removal of non-tariff barriers to trade, increased competition and the ability to operate on a larger scale, thereby obtaining the benefits of economies of scale. These developments should in turn promote greater efficiency of firms operating within the EU and thus strengthen their ability to compete in world markets, with the prospect of increased growth in EU economies.

319

In this chapter we examine in section 15.2 the progress so far in achieving a single market in financial services. In section 15.3 we discuss some of the likely effects of a single market in financial services for UK-based financial intermediaries. Finally, in section 15.4 we briefly consider the complementary developments towards achieving EMU.

15.2   A single European market in financial services

Progress has been slower in tackling barriers to trade in financial services than in physical goods. This is despite the economic importance of financial services, which is estimated at 8 per cent of EU GDP (higher in the UK – see table 2.2). Also, the removal of barriers to trade in financial services will have effects wider than those directly impinging on the financial services industry, given the important role of the financial system in encouraging and facilitating investment and hence economic growth.

The main barriers to trade in financial services are:

(i)   market entrance requirements,
(ii)   differences in prudential standards,
(iii) differences in rules of market conduct.

In terms of (i), a basic right of establishment already exists in the EU for providers of financial services. That is, a firm from one EU member state can set up an operation in another EU member state and compete on an equal basis with other firms there, provided it establishes local offices in conformity with the rules and regulations of that member state. This falls short of a true single market and recent negotiations have been aimed at giving the right to firms to trade financial services throughout the EU on the basis of a single authorisation 'passport' from their home member state. To ease doubts about the completeness or rigour of home country regulatory regimes, attention is being directed at harmonising key prudential standards. This harmonisation aims to remove both host country concerns about the possible failure of foreign firms and concerns about 'unlevel playing fields', whereby a firm operating in one member state but subject to lighter and therefore lower-cost regulation under its home country regulations may obtain an unfair advantage in the market in which it operates.

The main headings under which financial services are being liberalised by EU legislation are collective investments, banking, investment services, insurance and capital movements. We now consider the principal developments to date in each of these areas.

15.2.1 *Collective investments*

The EU directive harmonising the laws relating to the authorisation of undertakings for collective investment in transferable securities, which for the UK refers to unit trusts, was implemented in 1989. Once authorised at home, such undertakings are free to market their units anywhere in the EU subject only to compliance with local marketing regulations.

15.2.2 *Banking*

The first attempt at harmonisation of banking across the EU was the First Banking Directive of 1977. This laid down minimum legal requirements

Table 15.1 *Business which is integral to banking and included within the scope of mutual recognition according to the Second Banking Coordination Directive*

1	Deposit taking and other forms of borrowing
2	Lending, including:
	consumer credit
	mortgage lending
	factoring
	trade finance
3	Financial leasing
4	Money transmission services
5	Issuing and administering means of payment (credit cards, travellers' cheques and banker's drafts)
6	Guarantees and commitments
7	Trading for own account or for account of customers in:
	money market instruments (bills, CDs, etc.)
	foreign exchange
	financial futures and options
	exchange and interest rate instruments
	securities
8	Participation in share issues and the provision of services related to such issues
9	Advice to undertakings on capital structure, industrial strategy and related issues
10	Money broking
11	Portfolio management and advice
12	Safekeeping of securities
13	Credit reference services
14	Safe custody services

Source: Annex to Second Banking Coordination Directive.

for credit institutions to be authorised in member states and created a basic right of establishment. The Second Banking Coordination Directive of 1989, which came fully into effect at the beginning of 1993, took the harmonisation process considerably further. Rather than large-scale harmonisation, the aim of the Second Directive was to establish the minimum harmonisation of prudential standards to entitle a credit institution authorised in one member state to provide core banking services throughout the EU under the passport scheme, outlined above. The core banking services referred to are listed in table 15.1.

In addition to the Second Banking Directive, which provides for authorisation, a number of related directives provide harmonisation of regulations. The 1989 Solvency Ratio Directive establishes an EU-wide rule that a bank's capital must be at least 8 per cent of its risk-adjusted assets and off-balance-sheet transactions (in line with the Basle accord of 1988 – see chapter 18, section 18.4). Capital is defined by the 1989 Own Funds Directive. The Directive on the Monitoring and Control of Large Exposures states that from January 1994 a limit of 40 per cent of capital will be imposed for exposures to a single client, which will be reduced over time to 25 per cent. In addition, the aggregate amount of large exposures (those exceeding 10 per cent of capital) may not exceed 800 per cent of such capital. Finally, a directive on deposit guarantee schemes provides for mandatory insurance for all EU deposit-taking institutions. The coverage per depositor is set at a minimum of ECU 20,000 (ECU 15,000 until 1999).

15.2.3 *Investment services*

The Investment Services Directive (ISD) of 1993 aims to give non-bank investment firms the same opportunities for conducting business in the EU as banks already enjoy under the Second Banking Directive. In addition, the Capital Adequacy Directive (CAD) of 1993 fulfils a similar function to the bank regulatory directives listed above and provides a similar framework for regulating investment firms as well as the securities business of banks.

The main driving force behind the harmonisation provisions of the ISD and CAD is the need to ensure competitive equality between universal banks (in which banking and investment business is mixed) and non-bank investment firms. Those countries with a long tradition of universal banking, such as Germany, favoured a conservative capital adequacy regime whereas countries such as the UK feared that if bank-style capital regulations were imposed on non-bank investment firms they would be placed at a competitive disadvantage compared with non-European firms. Indeed, there is a case for lighter capital controls for investment firms than for banks. The emphasis for banks is on solvency and hence capital is important (see chapter 18) whereas the emphasis for investment firms is on liquidity, reflecting the ability to scale down their activities.

The main structures available for a regulatory regime for banking and securities firms are set out by Dale (1994). At one extreme we have the Glass–Steagall model: the US arrangements where banks are not permitted to undertake investment business or own securities firms. At the other extreme we have the universal bank model, which is the traditional model for much of Continental Europe. The model chosen for the EU was the trading book approach, which permits banks to engage freely either directly or through subsidiaries (as in the UK). Each bank would need to separate its securities 'trading book' from the rest of its business (securities held for investment purposes). The trading book alone would then be subject to more permissive capital adequacy rules appropriate to securities trading. This creates a number of problems, discussed by Dale (1994). One particular problem is that the capital requirements for bank loans are much higher than those applicable to debt securities of equivalent default risk and maturity held on the trading book. The CAD regime may therefore provide an incentive for banks to shift their business from traditional bank lending towards securitised lending (see chapter 12 for further discussion of securitisation).

Implementation of the ISD was to have been by 1 July 1996 and its provisions brought into force by 31 December 1996. However, the directive was not implemented by the due date in Germany, Greece, Spain, France, Italy, Luxembourg and Portugal. Similar problems occurred with implementation of the CAD, although both are now generally in force. These problems illustrate that progress towards a single market in financial services is slow and harmonisation does not occur following publication of a directive. The European Commission has also become increasingly concerned about the ways in which directives are being implemented with inconsistencies impeding the operation of a single market.

15.2.4 *Insurance*

Freedom of establishment was provided in 1973 for non-life insurance and 1979 for life insurance. The next main breakthrough came with the Second Non-Life Insurance Directive, which was implemented in 1990. This provided freedom to provide cross-border insurance services for large commercial risks. In 1992 the Third Life Directive along with the Third Non-Life Directive were adopted and came into force in 1994. Under these directives an insurer with its head office within the EU can,

under the single passport principle, set up operations anywhere in the
EU. Derogations, giving extra time for implementation, were given to
Spain, Portugal and Greece.

15.2.5 *Capital movements*

A complementary Directive on the Liberalisation of Capital Movements,
requiring the removal of all capital controls in the EU, was adopted in
June 1988 and largely put into effect during 1990. Some countries,
notably Portugal and Greece, were given until 1995 to put this directive
into effect. The UK has of course been free of capital controls since
1979.

15.3   Likely effects of the liberalisation of EU financial services

To examine the potential effects of a single market in financial services
we draw upon the Cecchini (1988) report, published by the European
Commission. The Cecchini report's section on financial services is
based on an analysis by Price Waterhouse. The methodology of the
report was to make a comparison between the price charged for a
particular service in one member state and the average of the four lowest
member state prices. The member states considered were Belgium,
France, Germany, Spain, Italy, Luxembourg, the Netherlands and the
UK. A selection of the results of the study are presented in table 15.2.

The Cecchini report attempts to predict the effects of competition in
financial services with the arrival of a single market by assuming that
where prices are higher than the average of the four lowest then the
price will fall by half the difference. Such assumptions are questionable
for a number of reasons. First, the figures may not be based on a
comparison of like with like, so for example a consumer loan in the UK
may have a different default rate, and hence a different interest rate,
when compared with a consumer loan in Spain. Similarly, when
comparing insurance premiums, the variation in premium rates may
reflect variations in expected claims. In other words, some variation in
prices may be justifiable given the idiosyncratic nature of individual
markets. Also, whilst it is likely that some business will flow to low-cost
producers, assuming a competitive market emerges, this process may
take some time to occur because of, for example, price-insensitive
consumers, cultural factors which favour the home producer and the
costs involved in setting up a distribution network. With these
drawbacks in mind, the figures in table 15.2 provide some indication of
where UK producers face competition or where they have scope for
expansion into other EU countries. One area where UK consumers face

Table 15.2 *Percentage differences in the prices of standard financial products compared with the average of the four lowest national prices*

Service	Description of service	B	G	S	F	I	L	N	UK
Banking services									
Consumer credit	Annual cost to consumer of 500 ECU. Excess interest rate over money market rates	-41	136	39	n.a.	121	-26	31	121
Credit cards	Annual cost assuming 500 ECU debit. Excess interest rate over money market rates	79	60	26	-30	89	-12	43	16
Mortgages	Annual cost of home loan of 25,000 ECU. Excess interest rate over money market rates	31	57	118	78	-4	n.a.	-6	-20
Commercial loans	Annual cost (including commissions and charges) to a medium-size firm of a loan of 250,000 ECU	-5	6	19	-7	9	6	43	46
Insurance services									
Life insurance	Average annual cost of life insurance	78	5	37	33	83	66	-9	-30
Home insurance	Annual cost of fire and theft cover for house valued at 70,000 ECU with 20,000 ECU contents	-16	3	-4	39	81	57	17	90

B, Belgium; G, Germany; S, Spain; F, France; I, Italy; L, Luxembourg; N, Netherlands.
Source: Cecchini report (1988), table 6.1.

high cost is consumer credit, where interest rates are approximately 9 per cent above money market rates. It should be noted though that building societies entered into competition with banks in this market after the Price Waterhouse study was conducted, following liberalisation of building societies (discussed in chapter 5). In addition, with the four main countries of the EU at the high end of the credit price range it is doubtful that there will be much competition from other EU banks in the UK market. One area where the UK has a cost advantage is in mortgage lending. The Spanish mortgage market in particular offers the most scope to UK banks and building societies in their expansion into EU countries. However, the wide variation in legal and institutional arrangements for mortgage lending in EU countries may slow down any expansion.

The benefits of a single market in financial services are undermined by exchange rate fluctuations between EU member states' currencies, which create uncertainty and therefore would inhibit cross-border trade. Moves towards EMU and in particular to closer linkage of exchange rates through the Exchange Rate Mechanism can therefore be seen as complementary to the creation of a single market. It is to these developments we now turn.

15.4   European economic and monetary union

The Delors report, prepared in 1989 by the Committee for the Study of Economic and Monetary Union, provided a broad framework for the transition towards monetary union in Europe. The report recommended three stages in a 'progressive realisation of economic and monetary union'. The first stage began in July 1990 and was aimed at accomplishing liberalisation of financial markets (in particular the removal of exchange controls), enlargement of the membership of the Exchange Rate Mechanism (ERM) of the European Monetary System and a change in the mandate of the Committee of Central Bank Governors. The second stage, which began in January 1994, saw the establishment of the European Monetary Institute, which had the task of preparing the way for EMU. In stage 3 the European Monetary Institute is replaced by the European Central Bank, which, together with the central banks of the member states, would form the European System of Central Banks. The third stage proposed the irrevocable fixing of exchange rates, the eventual replacement of national currencies by a single currency and the transfer of monetary authority to the European Central Bank.

The proposed timetable (at the time of writing, March 1998) for establishing the final stages of EMU is outlined in box 15.1.

Box 15.1   *Timetable for the final stages of EMU*

1–3 May 1998:   Decision on which member states are eligible to participate in EMU and announcement of bilateral conversion
rates between participating members.

1 July 1998:   European Central Bank and the European System of
Central Banks established.

1 January 1999:   European monetary union to begin 'irrevocably'. Euro
becomes a currency in its own right.

1 January 2002:   Euro notes and coins enter into circulation.

A number of issues arise out of this timetable, which we now briefly comment upon. The European Monetary Institute has been set up in Frankfurt, which will also be the site of the European Central Bank. The timetable for preparation for EMU, set out in the Maastricht Treaty, has largely been adhered to and the starting date for EMU will be met. The Maastricht Treaty laid down five convergence criteria to determine the degree of economic convergence by member states before commencing stage 3. The criteria are:

(i)   price stability – inflation rate over one year should not exceed the average inflation rate of the three best-performing states, in terms of price stability, by more than 1.5 percentage points;

(ii)   interest rates – average nominal long-term interest rate over one year should not exceed the average interest rate of the best three states in terms of price stability by more than two percentage points;

(iii)   government budget deficit – the deficit should not exceed 3 per cent of the ratio of planned or actual government deficit to GDP at market prices;

(iv)   government debt – the ratio of government debt to GDP should not exceed 60 per cent;

(v)   participation in the ERM – a member state should have partici-pated in the ERM for at least two years before proceeding to stage 3 and should not have devalued or revalued its currency within the mechanism.

If a member state meets all these criteria then it is permitted to join in stage 3. The main problem in Europe in the 1990s has been the high

Table 15.3 *Performance of member states of the EU in relation to converg-*
ence

Date	Inflation[a] January 1998	Deficit (% of GDP) 1997	Debt (% of GDP) 1997	ERM partici- pation March 1998	Long-term interest rates January 1998
Reference value	2.7[b]	3	60		7.8[c]
Belgium	1.4	2.1	122.2	yes	5.7
Denmark	1.9	-0.7	65.1	yes	6.2
Germany	1.4	2.7	61.3	yes	5.6
Greece	5.2	4.0	108.7	yes[d]	9.8
Spain	1.8	2.6	68.8	yes	6.3
France	1.2	3.0	58.0	yes	5.5
Ireland	1.2	-0.9	66.3	yes	6.2
Italy	1.8	2.7	121.6	yes[e]	6.7
Luxembourg	1.4	-1.7	6.7	yes	5.6
Netherlands	1.8	1.4	72.1	yes	5.5
Austria	1.1	2.5	66.1	yes[f]	5.6
Portugal	1.8	2.5	62.0	yes	6.2
Finland	1.3	0.9	55.8	yes[f]	5.9
Sweden	1.9	0.8	76.6	no	6.5
UK	1.8	1.9	53.4	no	7.0

[a] Percentage change over 12 months of harmonised indices of consumer prices.
[b] Average of inflation rates of best three member states plus 1.5 per cent.
[c] Average of 12-month average of long-term interest rates for best three member states plus 2 per cent.
[d] Since March 1998.
[e] Since November 1996.
[f] Since October 1996.
Source: European Commission press release, 25 March 1998.

public debt levels following a severe economic downturn in the early 1990s. For the UK this occurred earlier than the rest of Continental Europe, with recovery coming earlier, and so the UK has been able to bring its public debt levels down without too much economic pain. For countries such as France and Germany, the later recession and recovery has meant that to meet the debt targets, public expenditure had to be cut at times when unemployment was high (in France, unemployment was 12 per cent in 1997). The major factor behind Germany's struggle to meet the Maastricht criteria was the cost of unification of East and West Germany. As a consequence of these problems the convergence criteria have been interpreted with some discretion. In particular, the criterion on the ratio of government debt to GDP (criterion (iv) above) has been judged according to whether the ratio is 'sufficiently diminishing and approaching the reference value at a satisfactory pace' (as stated in the Maastricht Treaty). This interpretation has permitted countries such as Italy, with a debt to GDP ratio of 122 per cent in 1997, to be recommended for acceptance into stage 3 because this ratio has been declining in recent years. Germany itself narrowly failed to meet the debt–GDP ratio criterion in 1997 and the ratio also showed a slight increase over 1997. However, it would have been inconceivable for EMU to have gone ahead without Germany. The performance of the member states of the EU against these convergence criteria are set out in table 15.3.

On the basis of the performances set out in table 15.3 the European Monetary Institute recommended in March 1998 that the following 11 countries had met the necessary conditions to adopt the single currency, the euro, on 1 January 1999: Belgium, Germany, Spain, France, Ireland, Italy, Luxembourg, the Netherlands, Austria, Portugal and Finland. These recommendations were ratified by the Ecofin Council (Finance Ministers) in May 1998. Two countries, Greece and Sweden, were judged as not meeting the criteria, the latter mainly because it has not been a member of the ERM for at least two years (criterion (v) above) and over this period its exchange rate was volatile in relation to the currencies of the ERM. Denmark and the UK negotiated a separate protocol in the Maastricht Treaty which gave them the right to opt out of EMU. Both countries have exercised this right. The UK meets all the criteria except for two-year membership of the ERM. However, in October 1997 the UK government published a further five tests against which participation of the UK in EMU had to be assessed. These were:

(i)   whether there is sustainable convergence between the UK and the economies of the single currency;
(ii)   whether there is sufficient flexibility to cope with economic change;
(iii)   the effect on investment in the UK;
(iv)   the impact on the UK financial services industry;
(v)   whether it is good for employment.

The first test is regarded as the most important by the UK government. It is argued that the UK economic cycle is out of line with the rest of Europe. Interest rates in October 1997 were 7 per cent in the UK (reflecting a booming economy which needed slowing down to achieve the inflation target) as against approximately 3 per cent in France and Germany (whose economies were growing more slowly, having come out of recession more recently). There has been some concern that if the UK did opt out of the single currency then this would damage its position as a financial centre and activity in the euro would be centred in Frankfurt and Paris. However, the government's assessment of test (iv) was that the UK is a global financial centre, with much of its business generated around the world – see chapter 7 for further discussion. London is still expanding as a world financial centre despite uncertainty about whether the UK will participate in the single currency. It is predicted that a large euro-euro market will emerge, centred on London, just as London is the main centre for euro-Deutchmarks, eurodollars and euroyen. In other words, the location of financial activity does not depend on the local currency. So in conclusion, the UK government decided not to opt into the single currency when it commences in January 1999. Further, the government announced that it is unlikely that the UK will enter the single currency this side of the next general election, which is likely to be in the year 2002. So the UK is essentially playing a waiting game, as it has always done with the development of new European institutions since the Second World War. If the single currency is successful then the UK is likely to join.

Finally, the proposed European Central Bank will be independent of any government interference and will have the primary objective of maintaining price stability. Its constitution is based largely on that of the Bundesbank (see chapter 17 for further discussion of the nature of central bank independence) and its primary objective will be the maintenance of price stability. It will also have the tasks of conducting foreign exchange operations, holding the official foreign exchange reserves of the (EMU) member states and promoting the smooth operation of payment systems. An additional support to anti-inflation credibility in post-EMU monetary policy is the stability and growth pact. This sets out the rules for government borrowing for EMU members after 1 January 1999. In particular, the Maastricht criteria of less than 3 per cent budget deficits becomes a ceiling that can be breached only in exceptional circumstances. Exceptional circumstances were defined to cover a natural disaster or a fall in GDP of at least 2 per cent over one year. Members which broke the 3 per cent ceiling would be required to make non-interest-bearing deposits with the European Central Bank. If a country fails to return to below the 3 per cent threshold those deposits become fines.

The ERM has played an important role in the move towards monetary union in Europe and we briefly review its history and recent developments in the next section.

15.4.1 *The Exchange Rate Mechanism*

The history of the ERM can be traced back to the breakdown of the Bretton Woods system of fixed exchange rates in 1971. Attempts were made to create a European successor to Bretton Woods with the establishment of the European currency 'Snake' in 1972. This arrangement was designed to narrow fluctuating margins between EU currencies. Sterling participated in the early months of the Snake but withdrew to follow a floating-rate regime. The Snake had mixed success, with other currencies withdrawing in its first years of operation, leaving just five currencies participating in 1978. The Snake was replaced by the more durable ERM in March 1979. A number of realignments were undertaken in the early years of the ERM but until the problems of the early 1990s, discussed below, there were no general realignments after January 1987. The ERM appeared to become more stable in the late 1980s and in 1989 the Spanish peseta joined, followed by sterling in October 1990. These two currencies were permitted fluctuations of up to 6 per cent around agreed central rates with other currencies, whilst the other currencies were allowed fluctuations of 2.25 per cent. Strains appeared in the ERM in the early 1990s, caused in particular by the reunification of Germany. The cost of raising living standards in the East towards equality with the West led to the German budget deficit increasing dramatically. The effect of this was to raise interest rates in Germany and consequently in the rest of the ERM states, as the currencies are tied through the ERM. However, this coincided with a downturn in the business cycle in Europe in the aftermath of the late 1980s boom, and the burden of high interest rates became onerous. Countries deep in recession, such as the UK and Italy, were seen by currency speculators as having unsustainable currency parities in the ERM and they believed that devaluation was inevitable. Selling pressure on the currencies of these and other ERM countries eventually proved too much for the authorities and the UK and Italy departed from the ERM in September 1992. Then, in 1993, a further wave of speculative pressure led the French authorities to give up the battle to prevent the franc falling below its floor with the Deutschmark. This led to an effective abandonment of the ERM although officially the system continued with 15 per cent rather than 2.25 per cent fluctuation bands. The UK has still not rejoined the ERM although Italy did rejoin in November 1996 and Austria and Finland joined in 1996 and Greece joined in March 1998.

15.5 **Conclusion**

In this chapter we have briefly summarised the main developments in the move towards greater integration amongst EU countries in terms of trade in financial services and EMU. The final outcome of these developments is uncertain, as at the time of writing the timing and extent of the moves towards integration are uncertain. What is clear though is that, given the momentum for change and the changes already agreed, a greater degree of European integration is inevitable.

Chapter 16

The efficiency of the UK financial system

16.1 Introduction

The criticisms of the UK financial system are generally based on the following rationale. Growth of UK gross national product since 1945 has been less than that of many other countries. Over this period gross domestic capital formation has been lower in the UK than in other countries and this has caused the lower rate of growth of gross national product. In turn this lower level of investment has been caused by deficiencies in the UK financial system. Complaints have focused on the excessive amount of resources devoted to speculation on secondary markets, inadequate provision of funds for investment, excessive cost of capital, and 'short termism', that is, excessive concentration on the short term as opposed to the long term. Such criticisms have come from a wide range of sources, not just the left in political terms. For example, a Conservative Chancellor referred to market operators as 'teenaged scribblers'. Nevertheless, these arguments appear to be rather tenuous in the absence of other confirmatory evidence.

It is factual to note that both the rate of growth and also the level of investment have been lower than those observed in many Continental countries. This, as any student of statistics knows, does not of necessity indicate a causal relationship flowing from the lower level of investment to the lower rate of growth. It could be plausible to argue that the lower rate of growth in the UK has led to ('caused'?) the lower level of investment or that they were both caused by a third variable. Similarly, it is a large step to assume that, in the absence of other confirmatory evidence, the lower level of investment has been caused by deficiencies in the financial system. Equally it is true to add that additional evidence may well support these criticisms.

It is as well at this stage to remind the reader of the functions of the financial system discussed in chapter 1. These are the provision of:

(i)   a payments mechanism;
(ii)   a mechanism for financial intermediation between surplus and deficit units;
(iii) primary and secondary markets so that portfolio holders can adjust their portfolios;
(iv)   various financial services, such as foreign exchange, pension provision and insurance.

As can be seen from the opening remarks, most of the complaints have centred on functions (ii) to (iv) rather than on the provision of the payments mechanism. Consequently we concentrate on these aspects of the financial system in the following assessment though, in view of the large volume of literature on this topic, we are able only to indicate the main themes of the various arguments. In section 16.2 we examine the efficiency of the various markets and in section 16.3 discuss the nature of short termism, which is perhaps the most consistent criticism raised. In section 16.4 we review some explanations of short termism and the slower rate of growth and present our remedies in section 16.5.

16.2   Efficiency of the financial system

In chapter 7 we reviewed the various meanings of the word efficiency as applied to financial markets. These were: allocative efficiency, operational efficiency and informational efficiency.

16.2.1 *Allocative efficiency*

Allocative efficiency is a broad concept and is likely to be achieved provided the market is giving out correct signals (i.e. that informational efficiency is achieved) and that incentives exist to follow the direction of these signals. There is just one proviso to this statement and this concerns the possibility that certain types of undertaking may not be able to obtain finance owing to gaps in the market.

The proposition that it is difficult for entrepreneurs to obtain small amounts of capital to finance the start-up of a company or to expand it in its early years is of long standing. In 1931 the Macmillan Committee on Finance and Industry brought attention to such a gap in the provision of finance (the 'Macmillan gap') and as a consequence the forerunner of the 3i Group (previously Investors In Industry – owned by the clearing banks and the Bank of England) was established in 1945. In 1971, the

Bolton Committee in its report highlighted both an 'equity gap' in terms of raising long-term finance below £250,000 (£1 million in current prices) and an information gap where small firms were unaware of sources of finance or could not present a reasoned request for finance. The Wilson Committee also reported on the financial problems of small companies in 1979 and also highlighted the information gap and commented on the difficulties for small firms in obtaining venture capital (i.e. for high-risk ventures with little track record).

Over the 1980s there were a number of developments which went some way to closing the finance and information gaps identified. What follows is a brief summary of these developments – more detailed surveys can be found in the *Bank of England Quarterly Bulletin* (November 1990) and Boocock (1990).

With regard to the information gap, the Department of Trade and Industry set up a number of small-firm information centres, providing free information and advice. In addition, a number of regional development agencies and other specialised agencies were established, which also provide advice. There was also a growth in venture capital providers which provide equity and other forms of long-term capital to small/medium-sized firms at both the early stages of development (e.g. seed capital) and later stages (e.g. expansion, management buyouts/ins). Institutions offering this type of financing can be divided into two broad groups. First, captive funds are subsidiaries of the major UK pension funds, insurance companies and banks. These captive funds obtain their finance from the parent company. Second, independent funds raise capital for investment from a wide variety of sources, including private investors and some financial institutions. In 1988 the independents accounted for approximately 66 per cent of the amount invested by venture capital funds, with captive funds accounting for most of the rest. The distinction between captive and independent is not so clear cut though, with most independent funds having some links with financial institutions and captive funds having some degree of independence.

The finance provided by the venture capital industry substantially increased over the 1980s so that in 1988 over £1 billion was invested. During the 1990s the sum invested further increased and in 1997 UK venture capital investment reached a figure of approximately £3 billion. However, there has been a change in the nature of the finance provided over this period, illustrated in table 16.1. There has been an increasing emphasis on financing buyouts, buyins and acquisitions at the expense of start-up and other early-stage financing. UK corporate restructuring over the latter half of the 1980s led to the sale of non-core businesses by many diversified companies as they reverted back to core activities. These sales were often to incumbent management (management buyout)

Table 16.1   *UK venture capital financing by financing stage, 1984–97 (% of total invested)*

	1984	1985	1986	1987	1988	1997
Start-up	17	13	16	8	5	2
Other early-stage	10	6	7	4	2	3
Expansion	39	36	27	22	27	22
Buyout/in and acquisition[a]	28	38	44	63	62	65
Secondary purchase[b]	5	6	5	3	4	6
Other	1	1	1	–	–	–
Total (£million)	228	279	396	795	1,006	3,066

[a] Purchase of an existing company as a going concern.
[b] Acquisition of existing shares in a company from another venture capital firm or other shareholders.
Source: British Venture Capital Association.

and financed by venture capital funds. This type of financing was attractive to venture capital funds as it was less risky than the traditional investment and usually offered a quicker exit route (i.e. realisation of the fund's investment) through a trade sale or flotation.

Two government initiatives in the early 1980s also addressed the funding gap for small companies. The first was the Loan Guarantee Scheme, which was introduced in 1981 following a recommendation of the Wilson Committee. The aim of this initiative is to encourage banks and some other credit institutions to supply medium-term loan finance (for two to seven years), up to a maximum of £100,000, where the risks involved would normally mean the loan request is rejected. The government guarantees 70 per cent of any loan approved and the borrower pays a premium on top of the normal interest rate. The scheme was extended indefinitely following a review by the government in 1989. This suggests that the government perceives there is a funding gap requiring a scheme of this sort. The scheme has been criticised though, as it provides loan finance whereas equity risk capital is considered more appropriate for small growing companies. The second government initiative was the Business Expansion Scheme, introduced in the 1983 Finance Act. This was designed to attract investors to provide equity finance to non-quoted companies, by giving tax relief to investors at the marginal rate paid for amounts up to £40,000 per annum. This tax relief was to compensate investors for the extra risks involved. Most finance of this sort was obtained by companies making a direct issue of shares to the public. The advantage to the company was that investors could not sell shares purchased under the scheme before five years had elapsed without losing the tax relief. The Business Expansion Scheme ended in December 1993 and was regarded as having achieved only limited success.

Despite the developments in funding for small business over the 1980s and in particular the growth in venture capital providers, it is still widely believed that there exists an equity gap for amounts below £100,000. There is also some evidence to suggest that a second gap exists for funding for amounts between £100,000 to £250,000. Further new developments have occurred with a number of funds being established to lend to small and medium-sized companies. One such fund is the Merseyside Special Investment Fund, which was established with £16 million of EU money and a further £9 million derived from private sources. The aim of the fund is to assist firms which are too small to utilise traditional venture capital equity finance. Similar schemes based on private and public funding are springing up elsewhere across the UK to try to meet the gaps mentioned above.

16.2.2 *Operational efficiency*

It is difficult to obtain hard evidence concerning operational efficiency but what we can obtain is indirect evidence from the structure of the financial system and also the cost of capital. In a competitive system we would expect to see inefficiencies competed away and, in the long run, profits to be 'normal', reflecting the degree of risk involved in the industry. As we have seen in earlier chapters, the UK financial system has certainly been subject to a large degree of liberalisation in areas of pricing and range of business conducted.

To take just a few examples, in recent years we have seen the relaxation of controls over the banking industry, and the death of some cartels, such as 'Big Bang' on the LSE removing fixed commissions and opening it up to a greater degree of competition. The building societies' interest rate cartel has also ended and, as a consequence, the mortgage market is now a 'competitive price-driven' market. The incidence of competition has increased not only in the domestic context but also on an international scale. The abolition of exchange controls allows residents to invest overseas without restraint. As we have seen in chapter 4, a large number of foreign banks now operate in London. Consequently it would be reasonable to expect that the increased competitive environment would have led to a greater degree of efficiency. We certainly have seen a fairly high degree of financial innovation, that is, the development of new markets and financial instruments. In chapter 13 we discussed the development in London of a major new financial market, LIFFE. The increased volume of trading on this market noted in chapter 13 indicates a successful development. New instruments have been developed and extended, such as in the commercial paper market together with all those available to manage risk as indicated in chapter 14.

Nevertheless, critics have pointed to the volume of trading carried out on the major markets and in particular the LSE and the foreign exchange market. With reference to the LSE, we noted in chapter 8, figure 8.1, the low proportion of funds raised by firms through new issues of equity and debentures and the consequent importance of internally generated funds as a source of business finance.

One other aspect of the operational efficiency of markets concerns the cost of capital. A number of commentators have argued that the cost of capital is higher in countries such as the UK and US compared with other countries such as Germany and in particular Japan. Perhaps one of the most widely quoted studies was that carried out by McCauley and Zimmer (1989), who claimed that the real cost of funds after tax was some 3 per cent higher in the UK than in Germany and Japan. The main reasons given for this difference were higher savings ratios and lower risk premiums. These reasons are not unambiguous with respect to their theoretical underpinning. If real returns on savings are lower in some countries, then, given the current level of globalisation of finance, it would be expected that international arbitrage would lead to funds moving out of countries with a lower rate of return in favour of centres with higher real rates of return. This would tend to lead to real rates of return being equalised across international centres. The second reason put forward suggests that high levels of inflation lead to volatility of nominal returns and a higher risk premium. Marsh (1990) suggests that examination of the gap between the risk-free return and the return on equities shows that risk premiums were higher in Japan than in the UK. This is supported also by the fact that the standard deviation of stock market returns were higher in Japan than in other countries. Marsh also argued that McCauley and Zimmer used an inappropriate measure of the cost of equity capital in their study, that is, the inverse of the price/ earnings ratio. This is inappropriate because it makes no allowance for future growth potential; the correct measure is the risk-free real rate of interest plus a premium for investing in equities. However, a contrary argument must also be raised at this juncture. High nominal rates of interest can cause cash flow problems, particularly for firms with high gearing. It could be claimed that nominal interest rate stability permits firms to utilise a more highly geared capital structure with its cost advantage without the danger of a financial crisis due to restrictive monetary policy. Clearly, this has not been the case for UK firms during periods of high nominal interest rates (e.g. to take just one example, Brent Walker in 1990). All in all it seems that the cost of capital may well be higher in the UK than in other countries but that the extent of the margin has been exaggerated. Furthermore, any higher cost due to higher nominal rates of interest must be the responsibility of the government for permitting higher and more volatile rates of inflation rather than that of the financial system.

One final criticism of the operational efficiency concerns the response of the financial system to firms in difficulty. It is often claimed that the financial institutions are too keen to foreclose on debt rather than allow sufficient time for a firm to recover its former position of financial strength. This is of course the classic dilemma for banks. Do they force the firm into bankruptcy and accept the loss without a chance to recoup their losses, or do they lend additional funds, thus incurring additional risk, in the hope of obtaining repayment of all lending eventually? The criticism suggests that the banks and other lenders too often follow the first course of action. There appears to be some force in this argument and the Bank of England has negotiated with the commercial banks to produce an agreed procedure to deal with companies with a liquidity crisis. This is termed the 'London approach' and full details are provided in the *Bank of England Quarterly Bulletin* of May 1996. Basically the approach is to provide funds for the company to keep it afloat until such time as a considered judgement can be made about its long-term future. The funds are to be provided by the lending banks in proportion to their existing exposure. A lead bank is to be identified to keep the other creditors informed. This is necessary because of the large number of banks often lending to a single firm. For example, in the case of the troubled Goodman International empire in Ireland, it was reported that 33 different banks were involved in lending the equivalent of £500 million. The lead bank is likely to be the bank with the largest exposure. Finally, in this interval all other lending to the company should be suspended.

16.2.3 *Informational efficiency*

It has been argued that excessive resources have been devoted to speculation as distinct from the raising of capital. A similar objection could be raised against the operation of the foreign exchange market, where the daily volume of trading dwarfs any requirement to finance UK overseas trade. The counterargument is that the speculators are necessary to ensure that prices of the various securities reflect all available information. The aim of speculators is to make a profit. They do this by identifying securities which are incorrectly priced in the market, purchasing those which are identified as underpriced and selling those identified as overpriced. In this manner the speculator contributes to market efficiency in the informational sense. Correct decision making will reward the speculator and, in the same way, the inefficient speculator, who makes wrong decisions, will be penalised. A 'Darwinian' process will ensure the survival of efficient speculators at the expense of the inefficient ones. Speculation will, therefore, be stabilising. However, it is of course perfectly possible to argue that the process is not as efficient as that described above. Whilst persistently inefficient speculators must leave the market through shortages of finance, it is quite possible (though improbable over a long period) that successive waves of inefficient speculators will appear on the market, leading to the existence of destabilising speculation.

A second criticism arising from the relative volume of speculative activity on financial markets points to the likelihood of increased volatility of market prices. It is quite probable that this increased volatility may have detracted from the efficiency of the market mechanism by obscuring the price signals given out by the market. Some casual empirical support for an adverse effect of market volatility on business operation is given by the rapid growth of hedging instruments such as financial futures since 1980. However, the real test of these criticisms must be whether the market conforms to the efficient markets hypothesis or not. Clearly, no market can be absolutely efficient in the sense that market prices always fully reflect all available information. The acid test is more sensibly one of examining whether market prices usually reflect all available information, so that the market approximates to the efficient markets hypothesis. In this connection we examined the efficiency of the stock market (chapter 8), the bond market (chapter 9), the foreign exchange market (chapter 11) and the financial futures market (chapter 12). Our conclusions were not decisive in either direction but it is certainly true to say that no conclusive evidence was presented against market efficiency in the informational sense.

A second aspect of informational efficiency concerns the advice given by City analysts about the advisability of purchasing equity in a company. In this connection the *Observer* (28 October 1990) provided an interesting commentary on analysts' reports on Polly Peck, which foundered in the autumn of 1990. Throughout 1990 a considerable number of analysts were recommending the purchase of Polly Peck shares on the ground that the shares were undervalued. At least ten analysts were quoted as recommending the purchase and some with a repetition of a buy and hold strategy even as late as September. It is patently obvious that the advice was ill-founded and this may raise doubts over this aspect of the City's work. This, incidentally, adds additional support to the efficient markets hypothesis since, at least in this case, market experts failed to beat the market.

We now turn to discuss short termism, which is perhaps the main thrust of common criticism of the UK financial system.

16.3   Short termism

In general terms, short termism can be defined as a climate in which companies concentrate on short-term profits rather than long-term investment. Associated with the concept of short termism is the view that the UK financial system suffers from myopia. One aspect of this view on short termism is the belief that the takeover mechanism contributes to companies concentrating on short-term issues because of the necessity of having to look continually over their shoulders, as it were, to identify possible predators. This is particularly true in times of falling share prices. This is largely a consequence of the type of financial system that exists in the UK. As we saw in chapter 2, the financial systems in the UK and US can be broadly categorised as market based. Thus, financial markets play an important role in terms of both raising long-term capital and changing corporate control. In contrast, in bank-based financial systems, such as those of Germany and Japan, the banks play a greater role in providing external finance. The finance provided by banks consists of loans and equity so that the banks often take a more active role in the running of the companies they finance. In particular they will often initiate changes in management and sometimes ownership. However, such changes are carried out without hostile confrontation.

Certainly it is true that expenditure on takeovers has increased over the last ten years but the question remains as to whether this will have encouraged the growth of short termism. The role of the financial system in mergers and acquisitions is highlighted by the advisory fees earned from both the predators and the victims. The fact that such fees add to a bank's profitability without incurring any of the balance sheet restraints imposed through prudential control provides an additional stimulus for banks to engage in this type of business. A counterargument would suggest that takeovers are part of the discipline of the market and are necessary to provide a spur for the stimulation of efficiency and the removal of inefficient managements. However, the discipline is rather a blunt instrument which may threaten efficient as well as inefficient companies.

Protagonists of the view that the financial system is responsible for short termism suggest that the equity of a company is subject to a dual valuation situation. First, there is what may be called the normal valuation, when the price of equity reflects the marginal trading in company shares between portfolio investors. There is, however, a second valuation, which occurs when a potential bidder is attempting to acquire control of a business and so is bidding for the whole of the company's equity. In this case the share price will rise above the normal price and the difference between the two prices is the bid premium. This provides an incentive for shareholders, particularly the institutions, to accept the bid because it is unlikely that the share price will continue to remain at that level in the absence of the predator. The source of the bid premium can be construed to be the increased efficiency with which the firm taken over is managed or alternatively increased economies of scale attributable to the integration of the firm into the predator's operations. An alternative view of the source of the bid premium is, however, that it represents the anticipated profit through asset stripping, including sale of assets and perhaps the acquisition of pension fund surpluses. In this case the bid premium represents a transfer from the other stakeholders in the firm, such as employees, to the predator company without conferring any benefit to the economy as a whole.

In the UK the investment institutions dominate holdings of equities in companies so it is their decisions which matter as far as the success of takeovers is concerned. In this connection it is also important to note that the institutions have incentives to accept takeover offers for reasons other than that described above. Fund managers prepare statistics every quarter and have therefore an additional incentive to accept bids for companies whose shares are held in their portfolios to boost the quarterly performance of the fund that they manage. This also raises the question of their commitment to the companies whose securities are held in their portfolios. In general they seem quite reluctant to become involved in the management of these firms, possibly owing to a lack of expertise. A second possible reason for this is that the possession of detailed knowledge of any firms would make it more difficult for them to deal in their securities for fear of falling foul of legislation on insider trading. A further reason for a 'hands-off' approach to the management of the companies is the number of different funds which are likely to hold the equity of any one individual company. This general situation is contrasted with the position of countries where the banks provide a major source of funds for industrial and commercial companies. It appears that these banks are more firmly committed to their clients and are represented in top management and have, therefore, a voice in the firm's policy-making process.

However, there is evidence to suggest that fund managers in the UK are taking an increasingly active role. Gartmore, the fund management arm of National Westminster Bank, and the fifth largest fund manager in the UK, in 1997 created the new post of head of corporate governance. Standard Life has circulated lists of their corporate governance proposals to the chairs and chief executives of the main quoted companies. Prudential, the UK's largest life assurance company, has set up a mechanism to enable companies to discuss strategic issues in confidence with the chair of its fund management arm. All these developments suggest that institutional fund managers are beginning to stimulate strategic change in companies.

The general tenor of the argument above depends on the hypothesis that share prices do not reflect the long-run profit potential of the company concerned, or in other words that the efficient markets hypothesis is breached since some facets of information are not fully reflected in the price of equity. Marsh (1990) disputes this with the aid of an illustration derived from the valuation of ICI shares according to a standard valuation model. The then current share price and price of capital for ICI implied:

> that the market is expecting ICI's dividends to grow at the rate of 13% per annum. In turn this implies that of ICI's current market capitalization, only 8% is attributable to the current year's dividend, only 29% can be explained by the present value of dividends expected over the next five years and only 50% by the value of the dividends expected over the next 10 years. (Marsh 1990)

Marsh admits that analysts' judgements on the cost of capital are tentative but nevertheless the figures are not suggestive of short termism in share valuation. This point seems to us to be critical since if the price of equity is representing, albeit as an approximation, the long-term profit potential of firms then the search for short-term profits by fund managers will not provoke short-term profit decisions by firms. A fund manager will seek to identify shares which are incorrectly valued and then buy any undervalued shares or sell any shares which are considered to be overvalued. Consequently, even though the manager's actions are motivated by short-term gains, he or she is in fact moving share prices towards their correct price. Clearly, if the market is not efficient in an informational sense then the foregoing argument is not correct and the manager's actions will be stimulating short-term behaviour.

A further consideration concerns the influence of investment on the price of a company's shares. There is a not inconsiderable volume of evidence derived from the US to suggest that the announcement of long-term investment often enhances the value of a company's shares – see for example McConnell and Muscerella (1985). This implies that investment is not of necessity an activity to be avoided for fear of inducing takeover bids through lower share prices. In this connection it may also be argued that the perception that investment and dividend payments are necessarily alternative sources of demand for a company's resources is incorrect. Successful investment projects will enhance a company's profit-making potential and therefore dividends in the long run.

16.4   An alternative explanation of short termism

An alternative explanation of short termism is provided by Marsh (1990). This is based on the view that it is the management itself which is subject to myopia, or 'managerial short termism'. A number of arguments are presented to support this hypothesis. The first point concerns the system of remunerating top managers. It appears that only a small proportion of managers' remuneration is directly linked to the performance of the corporation. Furthermore, the majority of executive schemes that are in existence are based on short-term indicators, such as accounting profit. The underlying argument is that such schemes may provide an incentive for executives to pursue short-term objectives at the expense of a long-term strategy. One example would be an investment proposal which provided benefits in the long run but which is perceived to have an adverse effect on profits in the next few years.

Second, there is the role of investment appraisal. It is often argued that current profitability influences the divisional allocation of capital budgets. The problem arises because profitability is assessed via accounting profits and this may provide incorrect signals for investment appraisal, which should be based on discounting methods. It also appears that, in practice, the payback method of investment appraisal is still used by UK managers to assess investment projects – see Marsh (1990) for survey evidence. The problem with this method of investment appraisal is that it concentrates on the short term only and ignores any long-term profits which occur after the break-even time has been reached. If true, this would also provide an important explanation of short termism.

The third broad strand of the argument for managers suffering from myopia can be considered under the heading of a perceived lack of investment opportunities. One reason for this could be poor labour relations, with a heavy incidence of restrictive practices leading to a dilution of the benefits from innovation and investment. A second reason could be the uncertain economic climate due to the higher inflation rates experienced in the UK which have led to the imposition of restrictive monetary policies from time to time. The resulting uncertain economic climate would not be expected to provide a spur to the development of long-term strategies by firms. A further argument offered is the lower investment in education and training in the UK as compared with other developed nations.

In the following section, we discuss possible remedies for short termism.

16.5   Remedies for short termism

Assuming that short termism is a problem for the UK economy, the proposal of adequate remedies requires identification of its causes. One reform, which would draw fairly wide support, is a change in the method of remuneration of managers by providing incentive schemes which link their salaries to the medium-term (say in the region of five years) market value of their companies. Sykes (1990) suggests that the rate would typically be in the range of 5–10 per cent and also that penalties should accrue for non-performance. This would require both an extension of incentive schemes and also the replacement of the role of short-term accounting profits within existing schemes. Presumably extension of such schemes would require fiscal incentives to be provided by government. Benefits would accrue in the form of an incentive directed towards the adoption of long-term strategies by firms. Furthermore, the risk element coupled with the incentives should assist the correct allocation of managerial resources within the UK economy.

A similar proposal advocates the extension of the appointment of non-executive directors and the separation of the duties of managing director and chairperson of a company. Advocates of this strategy claim that this would provide a more independent element in the board of directors and remove an element of passivity and self-selection. It would also facilitate a more objective assessment of past policies and remedies where appropriate. A basic requirement for this strategy to be successful is that the non-executive directors must be genuinely independent and not just 'old cronies' of the existing directors.

The above two proposals could presumably be facilitated by persuading shareholders to take a more active and discerning role in the management of firms. This in reality entails the investment institutions taking a more active role in the management because, in general, individuals' shareholdings are dwarfed by those held by the institutions, with the result that proposals by individuals have little chance of acceptance. The problem with institutions taking a more active role in the management of individual firms in their portfolio is, as we have seen earlier, twofold. First, they probably lack the expertise and would therefore be involved in additional expenditure recruiting the requisite qualified staff. Second, the possession of inside knowledge would inhibit share dealings and could therefore detract from market efficiency. For similar reasons it is advocated that banks should become more like banks in Germany and Japan by being closely identified with their borrowers. This would include lending by way of equity and becoming involved in management decisions.

Further remedies suggested depend on the view that short termism is attributable to the deficiencies of the financial system – for such a view see for example Cosh *et al.* (1990). They argue that remedies such as those indicated above will require a fairly long time to implement. It is therefore suggested that some 'grit' should be introduced into the takeover mechanism. First, terms of reference to the Monopolies and Mergers Commission should be broadened so as to enable a better distinction between takeovers which result in economies of scale and greater efficiency of operation and those which are designed to gain profits by asset stripping. Currently criteria are restricted to the effect on competition, which provides a reasonably clear framework for decisions. Extension of the criteria to incorporate public interest would permit the authorities to filter out, albeit judgementally, takeovers which were not designed to increase efficiency of operation. Further restraints could be introduced by requiring all contested bids to be submitted to the Monopolies and Mergers Commission.

Another suggestion on a similar line takes the form of restricting the voting rights from newly acquired shares for a specific period of time after the acquisition, such as 12 months. Similarly, it is also suggested that the threshold at which a predator is obliged to make an offer to all shareholders is reduced from the current 29.9 per cent to a lower figure, such as 14.9 per cent (Plender 1990). Both these measures would increase the cost and difficulty of making predatory bids, especially where they are contested.

A further proposal along these lines advocates the imposition of tax penalties on share transactions to encourage the institutions to take a longer view in their portfolio decisions. This seems to us to be a step in the wrong direction for three reasons. First, the existence of a secondary market provides liquidity, so that existing individuals as well as institutions can change the composition of their portfolios. Restriction on this important function may well reduce the willingness of individuals to hold equity in their overall portfolio of wealth. Second, as we have noted earlier, dealings by institutions is a mechanism which pushes equity prices towards their true value. Third, imposition of taxes on share dealings on the LSE would force business away to other international stock exchanges. It is quite likely that attempts to tax dealings on other exchanges would create massive scope for evasion. It would therefore in all probability be ineffective and costly to operate.

16.6   Conclusion

Certain facets of the debate appear to be clear. Short termism is generally perceived to be a problem for the UK economy. Investment has been lower in the UK economy and this is presumably owing, at least in part, to short termism. Certain of the proposed remedies command fairly widespread support. These include the proposals for the introduction of long-term incentives for managers and increased representation of genuinely independent non-executive directors. Beyond this, little agreement on either the causes or the remedies exists. Those who believe that the volume of takeovers is excessive advocate legal or quasilegal restraints on the takeover process. Believers in the efficient markets hypothesis argue that such restraints would do more harm than good. In this connection, it is interesting to note that a report by the McKinsey Global Institute (1996), entitled *Capital Productivity*, suggests that short-termism actually brings productivity gains for the US. Capital productivity was significantly higher in the US than either Germany or Japan. In the period 1990–93 Germany's and Japan's capital per head were 13 and 22 per cent higher than in the US. Yet capital productivity in the two countries were 35 and 37 per cent lower than in the US. This higher capital productivity creates higher financial returns and it is argued that concentration on financial returns stimulates managerial efficiency.

The arguments are likely to continue. For example, Will Hutton (*Guardian*, 3 January 1995) argues strongly that the 'City' has failed UK industry over a long period of time. The main criticism, due to Professor C. Mayer, is based on the alleged failure of the City to provide either 'a stable long-term ownership base' or cheap long-term debt. Similarly, arguments continue to be made that the cost of capital is higher in the UK than elsewhere because of the alleged requirement of the City for high rates of return. The problem with these arguments is that they do not provide irrefutable evidence of the failure of the financial system. As noted earlier, arbitrage, given the current freedom of international movement of capital, should stimulate movement towards equality of risk-adjusted rates of return across national boundaries. The higher rates required by the UK financial institutions could therefore reflect higher risk in the UK due to more volatile conditions partly (or perhaps wholly) due to inappropriate government macroeconomic policy. The lack of availability to private firms of cheap long-term debt may be attributable to the size of the PSBR over the postwar period. It can be argued that excessive borrowing by the government 'crowded out' private sector borrowing. Finally, we have discussed the problem of short termism at some length in the previous section.

On the other hand, we would not argue that the financial system is perfect. Financial scandals such as occurred in the Lloyd's insurance market and the Maxwell raid on pension funds are pertinent in this respect. Similarly, problems have occurred in the life assurance industry, with salespersons selling inappropriate pensions. Regulation has appeared to be questionable from time to time, both in the examples quoted above and with respect to the supervision of banking – the example of the Bank of Credit and Commerce International is relevant here (see chapter 18).

As in most cases discussed in this text, there is no clear-cut objective answer. It is a question of judgement and as we have stated above the arguments are likely to continue for some time.

Chapter 17

Central banking

17.1 Introduction

In this chapter we examine the role of central banks in the financial system. We first discuss, in section 17.2, the current position of the Bank of England following the important changes made in the autumn of 1997. Then in section 17.3 we move on to consider the role of central banks and whether, in fact, this role is necessary for the smooth running of financial systems. Finally in section 17.4 we look at the arguments for granting central banks independence in their operation of monetary policy and consider the institutional arrangements surrounding the independence of the Bank of England. Our conclusions are presented in 17.5.

17.2 The Bank of England

In the autumn of 1997 important changes were made to the role of the Bank of England (hereafter just termed the Bank). Briefly, these were:

(i) the Bank was granted independence in the sense it was given freedom to set interest rates;
(ii) prudential control of banks was transferred from the Bank to the new Financial Services Authority (FSA), which became responsible for prudential control of the whole of the financial services industry;
(iii) management of the government's debt was transferred to the Treasury.

These developments are examined in more detail below. Under the new arrangements, the Bank will be managed on a day-to-day basis by the governor and two deputy governors. One deputy governor will support the governor on monetary stability and the other on financial stability. The Bank will be accountable to a court consisting of the governor and deputy governors plus up to 16 non-executive members appointed from a wide range of interests. It is hoped that this will increase the transparency of the operations of the Bank.

The Bank was formally recognised as a central bank by the 1946 Bank of England Act, which effectively nationalised it. Prior to this Act, from its establishment in 1694, the Bank had carried out the functions of a central bank but operated as a private concern. Under the Act the subordinate status of the Bank to the Treasury was statutorily established and this was changed only in 1997. We now describe the structure of the Bank and then outline its main functions.

The Bank is separated into two departments for accounting purposes: the Issue Department, which is treated as being part of the government, and the Banking Department, which is a public corporation. The Issue Department has as liabilities notes in circulation or held by the Banking Department. Whilst it was possible to call upon the Bank to redeem these notes for gold up until 1931, since that date the note issue has been a fiduciary one backed by securities. These securities, held as assets by the Issue Department, include government securities as well as privately issued securities such as commercial bills.

The Banking Department obtains its deposits from two main sources. First, acting as banker to central government, it has the item referred to as 'public deposits', which represents the consolidated accounts of the various revenue collecting and spending departments of the government. Second, it has 'bankers' deposits', which include the mandatory deposits of UK banks and building societies, set at 0.15 per cent of eligible deposits. The remainder of the Banking Department's liabilities are made up of accounts held by other bodies such as overseas governments and central banks, capital and reserves. The assets of the Banking Department include: first, government securities, which comprise government bonds, Treasury bills and ways-and-means advances to the government; second, advances and other accounts, which include short-term loans to discount houses and holdings of commercial bills; and third, notes and coins, which represent the reserve held by the Bank to meet any deposit withdrawals. Details are shown in table 17.1.

By holding balances at the Bank, banks are able to settle any inter-bank indebtedness in a convenient way. This works through the operation of a clearing house, so that at the end of a working day the net debts between any two banks are settled by means of an appropriate transfer of funds between the two banks' accounts at the Bank. In fact, there has been a move to 'real time' settlement, that is, almost immediate

Table 17.1 *Bank of England: balance sheet as at 31 December 1996 (£million)*

Liabilities		Assets	
Issue Department			
Notes in circulation	22,609	Government securities	14,579
Notes in Banking Department	11	Other securities	8,041
Banking Department			
Public deposits	202	Government securities	1,253
Special deposits	0ᵃ	Advances and other accounts	2,313
Bankers' deposits	2,442	Premises, equipment and	
Reserves and other accounts	3,249	other securities	2,331
Capital	15	Notes and coin	10

ᵃ This item refers to additional interest-bearing deposits, which the Bank reserves the right to call from banks. Such deposits constitute an additional instrument in the Bank's armoury for monetary control purposes but have not been used since the early 1980s, hence the 0 entry.

settlement of payments for all wholesale transactions so that these items are settled as they arise rather than waiting for the end of the day. The idea of real-time gross settlement is to avoid settlement risk through the knock-on effects of the failure of a counterparty. One example of this risk is provided by the Herstatt bank failure in 1974 when, because of time zone differences, customers with some foreign exchange contracts were left unpaid although they had completed their own side of the transaction.

A further role played by the Bank under this heading is that of note issuing. If the general public increase their demand for notes then this will show up as a decrease in notes held by the banks. The banks can then replenish their stocks by exchanging for notes their balances held at the Bank. The Banking Department in turn can replenish its stock of notes, if required, by authorising a change in the fiduciary issue from the Issue Department. The resulting transfer of notes from the Issue Department to the Banking Department will generate a corresponding balancing transfer of securities in the opposite direction.

Although not responsible for supervision as far as protection of depositors is concerned the Bank is still responsible for the stability of the financial system, which involves the collection of regional and sectoral information. It is not clear how this split of responsibility for supervision between depositor protection and stability will work in practice. For example, where does the dividing line between rescue of a bank and its prudential supervision lie? Presumably the Bank will retain its role in the future development of markets so as to maintain the position of London as an international financial centre. Support to the banking sector is also provided on a day-to-day basis through the Bank's operations in the money markets, which were examined in chapter 10. When the banking system as a whole runs short of cash, then it is ultimately the Bank which restores the cash position of the banks. The Bank also operates as lender of last resort to any bank or group of banks experiencing liquidity problems. The Bank's aim here is to maintain the stability of the banking system. As the banking system is based on confidence then the failure of one or more banks can rapidly lead to a collapse in confidence in the banking system generally. A classic example of the Bank acting in this role was the operation of the 'lifeboat' to help a number of secondary banks in 1974/75. We examine the 'lifeboat' operation in more detail in chapter 18.

Perhaps the main change in the role of the Bank in the financial system is the assumption of the operational decision making with regard to the determination of interest rates to achieve price stability as defined by the government's inflation target. Decisions on the level of interest rates will be taken by a new monetary policy committee eventually comprising nine members. Five of the members will be Bank staff (including the governor and two deputy governors) and the other four recognised experts, who will be permitted to engage in other activities which do not 'give rise to a conflict of interest' (Chancellor's letter to the governor). Decisions on the level of the 'repo' rate (see chapter 10 for a discussion of money market intervention by the Bank) will be on the basis of a majority vote with the governor having the casting vote in the event of a tie. A representative of the Treasury will be entitled to attend the meetings of the monetary policy committee but in a non-voting capacity. It can be seen therefore that the Bank has been given limited independence in that it is responsible for setting the repo rate but only so far as to achieve the inflation target set by the government. The case for independence and the degree of 'democratic' control is examined in section 17.4.

17.3   The role of central banks

Central banks generally provide both microeconomic and macro-economic services. The macroeconomic services arise from their participation in monetary policy and their microeconomic services from their support and control of the institutions and markets comprising the financial system. In this section we are interested in the question of why it should be necessary for a financial system to have, in effect, a 'super' bank responsible for the operation of the financial system. Other industries may form trade associations but these are rarely endowed with legal powers to control the industry in question. Some examples do occur in the professions, where societies such as the Chartered Accountants for England and Wales, the Law Society and the British Medical Association are at least in part responsible for the regulation of the conduct of their members. There is of course the counterargument put forward by the 'free banking' school, who argue that regulation would be best left to the market. This argument is examined in chapter 18; in this chapter we content ourselves with an examination of why central banks may be necessary.

Fama (1980) notes that banks provide two services: operation of the payments mechanism, and portfolio services such as the acceptance of deposits and lending. Many have argued that this dual function necessitates the presence of a central bank to avoid the risk of systemic failure (i.e. failure within one institution leading to failure in others) within the financial system due to bank inter-indebtedness arising from their participation in the payments mechanism. A number of suggestions have been made to avoid such a risk. These include 'narrow' banking, daily revaluation of bank assets and mutual fund banking. The first suggestion has been endorsed by the two Nobel Prize winning economists, namely Milton Friedman and James Tobin. Briefly, the idea is that banks engaged in the payments mechanism should be required to hold highly liquid government securities to back checkable deposits and that these securities should be specifically allocated to these deposits. This would remove any risk of failure. One problem with such a plan is that the profitability of such bank operations would be severely restricted, leading to rises in charges for payments. On the other hand, if payments services attract the full cost, this could provide incentives for economic use of the services, leading to a better allocation of resources. Nevertheless, as Goodhart (1989, p. 182) has pointed out, narrow banking is the 'reverse of the evolution of banking', which has traditionally been based on fractional reserves.

The second suggestion, put forward by some US economists (e.g. see Benston *et al.* 1986), is that banks should be required to revalue all assets at market prices at the end of the day. If the revalued assets fell such that their net capital was approaching zero (i.e. before bankruptcy occurred) the bank would be closed as a separate entity and either merged with another bank or taken over by the regulatory authorities. The advantage claimed for this system is that a financial cost would not be involved since the bank would be approaching bankruptcy but not yet be bankrupt. The disadvantages spring from three sources. First, the revaluation sets up costs for all banks. Second, there is the creation of an incentive to fraudulent revaluation as the bank approaches bankruptcy, which would necessitate increased monitoring costs borne by the authorities. Third, revaluation would be difficult in the case of some assets such as loans for which there are limited markets. To some extent the force of this objection is being reduced due to the creation of ABS markets (see chapter 4 for discussion of ABSs).

The third suggestion put forward by Goodhart (1989, ch. 8) is that the liabilities (i.e. deposits) of the banks used for transaction purposes are revalued. Currently, checkable deposits are guaranteed in nominal terms with complete convertibility as and when required. The idea of the mutual fund intermediary is that such deposits would be revalued according to the assets of the fund, again on a daily basis, although the cheques would be defined in terms of a constant 'numeraire'. In order to provide for unforeseen fluctuations in the value of the fund (and there-fore the value of individual deposits) between the time of writing and the presentation of the cheque, the fund could impose minimum balance requirements on deposit holders and also set up emergency overdraft facilities. This latter provision would eliminate the problems for customers should the value of the fund decline for a significant period of time even though the fall in value was likely to be reversed at a later date. Apart from the question of revaluing assets, the problem for this latter suggestion is customer acceptance. It may appear to be unlikely that the general public would wish to hold transaction balances in a form in which the value is uncertain.

The suggestions examined above provide for a change in the role of the central bank as far as monitoring or supporting the financial system is concerned rather than elimination of the central bank itself. Further arguments can be made for unsupervised banking, that is, 'free bank-ing', and their adoption would render central banks redundant. The question of free banking is examined in chapter 18.

17.4   Independence of central banks

As we have noted above, prior to 1997 the politically controlled Treasury had the ultimate say on the monetary policy objectives pursued by the Bank. In such a situation there was a temptation for a government to finance its current borrowing requirement and to reduce its real burden of accumulated debt through increasing the money supply and thereby inflation. There are also some suggestions that over the period 1950–79 the government relaxed monetary policy at politically con-venient times, for example in the period leading up to a general election, rather than pursue the monetary policy most appropriate for reducing or

controlling inflationary pressures. This has prompted serious consideration of the question of central bank independence. Examples of
independent central banks are the German Bundesbank, established in
1957, and the US Federal Reserve System ('the Fed'), established in
1913. The legislation governing both these central banks includes the
pursuit of price stability. However, this is just one of many economic
and monetary objectives in the governing legislation and neither central
bank is legally required to make price stability its prime concern. The
legislation does assign a great deal of power over economic and monetary policy to these unelected bodies, which may inevitably bring them
into conflict with the elected government of the country. Indeed, the
lack of accountability of an independent central bank is often cited as a
counterargument to independence. However, this argument fails to take
into account the fact that the independence of a central bank is not
permanently guaranteed, as the government could introduce new
legislation to remove its independence. Central banks such as the
Bundesbank and the Fed maintain their autonomy by being accepted as
legitimate. The Bundesbank obtains its legitimacy through the widespread popular support it enjoys in Germany, which has come from its
achievement of low and stable inflation, and this has assisted the
economic success of the country. The legitimacy of the Fed has been
achieved largely as a result of successive Fed chairmen exploiting the
conflict between President and Congress built into the US constitution.

'Credibility' of the central bank becomes the main theoretical argument supporting the granting of independence to central banks. The
argument proceeds along the lines that democratically elected governments have an incentive to boost the economy prior to an election so as
to achieve re-election (as noted above in the case of UK governments
during the postwar period). The proposition was put forward by Barro
and Gordon (e.g. Barro and Gordon 1983a, 1983b) that there is a strong
incentive for governments to 'cheat' in their conduct of monetary policy.
Having both adopted declared policies of a specified inflation target and
convinced the general public of its serious intent (i.e. attained credibility), the government has an incentive to cheat and renege on its
commitment to the specified rate of inflation in order to achieve a lower
rate of unemployment. In the long run such policy changes are ineffective if the long-run Phillips curve is vertical at the natural rate of
unemployment. Furthermore, after episodes of reneging on commitments, the government loses credibility and its policy announcements
will not be believed. One solution is to delegate price stability to a
central bank unfettered by the political consideration of re-election and
which, it can be argued, would then pursue the desired price policy with
greater determination than elected governments.

In recent years many countries have adopted or made progress towards adopting legislative proposals removing their central banks from government control. Between 1989 and 1991 the central banks of New Zealand, Chile and Canada were made independent. From 1992, following the Maastricht Treaty, the central banks of the EU member states have introduced legislation or are committed to introducing legislation to make their central banks more independent. In 1993 the governments of Brazil and Mexico announced proposals to make their central banks more independent. In view of these developments it is therefore helpful to examine the empirical evidence on the relationship between central bank independence and economic performance.

One of the first empirical studies of this kind was that of Bade and Parkin (1988), who examined the relationship between the degree of central bank independence and inflation for 12 countries of the Organization for Economic Cooperation and Development (OECD) in the post-Bretton Woods era. Central bank independence was split into two types: financial independence, as measured by the government's ability to set salary levels for members of the governing board of the central bank, to control the central bank's budget and to allocate its profits; and policy independence, as indicated by the government's role in appointing members of the governing board of the bank, government representation on the board and whether the government was the final policy authority. Bade and Parkin found that financial independence was not a significant determinant of inflation outcome, but policy independence had a role to play. Alesina (1989) extended the Bade and Parkin study by adding four more countries to the analysis and also found an inverse relationship between the degree of central bank independence and inflation outcome. Grilli *et al.* (1991) found a negative relationship between inflation and central bank independence over the full sample period (1985–88) and over the post-Bretton Woods subsample. A more extensive study has been undertaken by Cukierman (1992) for the period 1950–89. He extended the work of the previous studies by using not only legal or 'de jure' measures of independence but also practical measures which attempted to capture the actual or de facto independence of the central bank. The measures of de facto independence included the frequency of turnover of central bank governors and the response to a questionnaire from qualified individuals from central banks. In addition, Cukierman extended the study to 70 countries by including less developed countries in addition to the developed countries examined in the previous work. Cukierman also found the degree of central bank independence affected the rate of inflation in the expected negative direction, with the relationship being stronger for developed countries.

Most of the empirical evidence therefore suggests that creating an independent central bank will improve a county's inflation performance. There are, however, a number of weaknesses with studies of this kind, as highlighted by Pollard (1993). Most of the studies create indexes of independence by identifying a relevant set of factors and then looking for compliance with the factors in the central bank charters, with each factor being given an equal weight in constructing the index. Thus, in the study by Grilli *et al.*, the factor that the governor's term of office must exceed that of the political term of office is given the same weighting as the factor that no government approval is required for the central bank in setting monetary policy. Clearly, the latter factor has more bearing on the central bank's actions. The only study that attempts a weighting of the criteria is that of Cukierman, but here, per force, the weights are subjective. Another problem with the analysis is that most of the studies use a legal or de jure measure of independence, which may not reflect the actual or de facto experience of central banks. Cukierman, in fact, examined the relationship between a legal index of independence and a measure of de facto independence based on his questionnaire results. A correlation of 0.33 between the two measures suggested that the legal measure may give misleading results. A further concern with these studies is that most of them consider only central bank independence as a determinant of inflation. When other determinants of inflation are included in the analysis, it is possible that central bank independence may have no role to play. As a final point, a negative correlation between central bank independence and inflation does not imply causality. Countries averse to inflation, such as Germany, may formalise this aversion through the creation of an independent central bank. Thus, it is inflation aversion in a country which may be the causal factor in explaining low inflation so that the policy of making a central bank independent, where there is insufficient aversion to inflation, may not yield the desired outcome in the long run.

The UK government has granted the Bank operational independence. This means it is free to select the level of interest rates it considers appropriate to the state of economy so as to achieve the target rate of inflation set by the government. Democratic control is retained through the government setting the target rate of inflation. This contrasts with the situation in other countries where the central bank also determines the rate of inflation consistent with the general aim of price stability. In one way the delegated powers to the Bank and its monetary committee could be regarded as a technical rather than a policy matter. However, as a new arrangement, the Bank may wish to obtain credibility and so may use its discretion to act as a hawk on inflation, thus aiming for overkill. Only time will tell whether this poses a real danger to the economy.

Additional controls have been built into the system to meet the criticism of a 'democracy' deficit. First, the Bank will report to the House of Commons Treasury Committee. It has also been suggested that the Commons Committee should hold 'confirmatory' hearings following the appointment of new governors or members of the Monetary Policy Committee. This would place restraint on the government filling key appointments with its own supporters, thus vitiating the grant of independence. It remains an open question as to whether the government will agree to this suggestion. The second control arises from the broadening of the composition of the court to represent broad sectors of the economy. Third, each time inflation is 1 per cent below or above the target, the governor and the Monetary Policy Committee will be required to write an open letter to the Chancellor explaining why the target has been missed. The letter will also have to contain a statement of the remedial measures to be undertaken by the Bank and a prediction as to when inflation will return to the target level. Note that a level of inflation below the target is also considered a failure of policy. This latter measure is directed to ensuring that the Bank pursues the government target rather than one of its own.

17.5   Conclusion

There has been a radical change in the position of the Bank of England. It has been granted operational independence in the conduct of monetary policy but, unlike many of its counterparts, is subject to the constraint of the government determining the policy target. In the operation of monetary policy, the Bank is assisted by the monetary policy committee. On the other hand, powers of prudential control and management of the national debt have been transferred to the FSA and to the UK Treasury (the new Debt Management Office), respectively. The Bank retains responsibility for the financial system and it will be interesting to see how the division of responsibility between the Bank and the FSA works out in practice. As these changes have been recent, it is too early to judge their efficacy. The interested reader is advised to keep up to date on this topic through reference to the financial pages of the quality newspapers and other media.

Chapter 18

Regulation of the financial system

18.1 Introduction

The type of regulation we discuss in this chapter is termed prudential regulation since it is designed to ensure prudent behaviour by financial institutions. In contrast to the rest of the financial sector, prudential regulation of banks has been the subject of analysis over quite a long period of time. Consequently the major part of the discussion in this chapter is directed to prudential control of banks. We briefly review the system of prudential control of the investment industry in section 18.5 and present our conclusions in section 18.6. We begin with a brief survey of recent bank failures and an examination of the type of risks faced by the banking industry.

18.2 History of bank failures

Regulation of banks must be examined against the background of bank failures. Any major problem results in changes in the regulatory environment as the regulators try to block any loophole in the rules. Concentrating on events this century, the greatest incidence of bank failure occurred in the US between the years 1929, when there were 25,000 banking firms, and 1934, when the number had been reduced to 14,000. These failures led to the introduction of fairly restrictive bank legislation such as single-state operations, which have remained characteristic of the US banking scene until today, although these restrictions are currently under review. Broadly speaking, there were no further major problems until 1973, which saw the start of the fringe bank crisis in the UK. Over the early 1970s, following rapid credit expansion, which was a consequence of the introduction of the policy of competition and credit control, many secondary or 'fringe' banks increased their deposits rapidly and lent a large proportion of these funds to property-related companies. Following a slump in property values in 1973 the secondary banks began to experience difficulties. As a consequence the inter-bank market, upon which the secondary banks were heavily dependent for deposits, dried up for all but banks of good standing and in addition deposits were withdrawn from the secondary banks. At the end of 1973 the Bank of England, seeing the problem as one of illiquidity, stepped in and organised a rescue of the secondary banks which has come to be known as 'the lifeboat'. Under this operation the Bank of England sought the help of the clearing banks in recycling the deposits they had gained following the withdrawal of deposits from the secondary banks. However, the problems in the property market, which had caused the loss of confidence in the secondary banks, deteriorated further over 1974 and several of the banks receiving support under the 'lifeboat' moved into a position of insolvency. Whilst a few banks were allowed to fail the majority were kept going. The Bank of England's intervention was justified in the following way (*Bank of England Quarterly Bulletin*, June 1978):

> The Bank thus found themselves confronted with the imminent collapse of several deposit-taking institutions and with the clear danger of a rapidly escalating crisis of confidence. This threatened other deposit-taking institutions and if left unchecked, would have quickly passed into parts of the banking system proper. While the UK clearing banks still appeared secure from the domestic effects of any run ... their international exposure was such that the risk to external confidence was a matter of concern for themselves as well as for the Bank. The problem was to avoid a widening circle of collapse through the contagion of fear.

At the height of the rescue operations, total lending amounted to over £1,000 million. This crisis led to a rethink of banking supervision and subsequently to the introduction of the Banking Act of 1979, which provided the first legal codification of the Bank of England's regulatory powers. This Act required the licensing of banks and deposit-taking institutions and also transferred the duty of supervision entirely to the Bank of England.

Further major failures occurred in 1974, namely Bankhaus Herstatt (Germany) and the Franklin National Bank (US). The latter was the twelfth largest bank in the US. Also in the US, 1984 saw the failure of Continental Illinois Bank, which was the eighth largest bank in the US. In this year the Johnson Matthey Bank failed in the UK – this failure is discussed in detail below. Other bank failures occurred over a range of countries, including Denmark, Canada and Ireland.

The Johnson Matthey Bank (JMB) faced financial difficulties, which resulted in the Bank of England purchasing JMB for £1 on 1 October 1984 from its parent company Johnson Matthey p.l.c. and subsequently reselling it. This was the first rescue of an ailing bank by the Bank of England since the lifeboat operation of 1974. The Bank of England sought to justify the rescue of JMB with arguments similar to those used to justify the lifeboat operation, in particular the fear of contagion if JMB were to collapse. There were also reasons put forward which were specific to the JMB case. JMB was one of a group of five gold bullion dealers which jointly fixed the price of gold on a twice-daily basis in London. It was feared that the other gold bullion price fixers may have encountered liquidity problems if JMB were allowed to collapse, which would have put in jeopardy London's position in the international bullion market. The rescue of JMB, like the lifeboat operation of 1974, involved the participation of other banks and the clearing banks in particular. These banks were persuaded by the Bank of England to provide indemnities against potential loan losses by JMB in order to keep JMB's credit lines open. This time, however, the clearing banks publicly objected to being forced into a rescue. As Goodhart (1988) argues: 'In today's more competitive conditions, the banks at the centre of the system frequently see the failing bank as being a relatively imprudent competitor. Why then, they feel, should they penalise their own shareholders for the sake of such a competitor?' Goodhart goes on to argue that the clearing banks' reaction in the JMB affair 'is a clear warning now that the Bank of England, and other central banks, may find it increasingly hard, if not impossible, to persuade other commercial banks to assist them in future rescue packages'. Goodhart suggests this should lead to a consideration of alternative strategies to deal with a future illiquidity/insolvency problem, and we consider one such alternative (namely deposit insurance) in section 18.4.7.

There are other issues highlighted by the JMB affair (see Hall (1987) for further discussion) which merit comment. It can be argued that the act of rescuing JMB introduces moral hazard into the banking system; that is, other banks may act less prudently in the belief that the Bank of England will not allow them to fail. The Bank of England, however, has stated that the rescue of JMB was a special case and does not imply that all banks in difficulties will be rescued, but as Hall (1987) argues, 'no amount of exhortation is likely to persuade market operators to ignore the Bank's actual deeds in the market place'. The JMB affair also opens to question the adequacy of the supervisory arrangements and authorisation procedures at that time. The supervisors of JMB did not chase up late quarterly returns and allowed JMB to postpone meetings with Bank of England staff. Also, the escalating problems of JMB were not seen by the supervisors, despite the breaches of the Bank's guideline on loan exposure. The Bank expects to be notified of any single non-bank exposure of over 10 per cent of the bank's capital. In its 1985 annual report the Bank of England stated that two large exposures at the end of June 1983 were reported by JMB to be 15 per cent and 12 per cent of capital (in fact these were understated and the true figures were 26 per cent and 17 per cent, respectively) and at the end of June 1984 were reported to be 38 per cent and 34 per cent (true figures being 76 per cent and 39 per cent, respectively). Leaving aside the understatement, the Bank's guidelines on loan exposure were known to be breached, with the problem getting worse, well before JMB had to be rescued. The Bank, however, has stated that breaches of this guideline are common-place and that complete observance of this rule would be too restrictive. The catalogue of incompetence by JMB management, related in the Bank of England's annual report for 1985, also calls into question the adequacy of the vetting arrangements undertaken by the Bank. One final issue raised by the JMB affair is the role of auditors in the supervision process. The auditors of JMB, Arthur Young, were criticised and successfully sued by the Bank of England. However, at the time the auditors of a bank were not allowed to express fears to supervisors without the client's permission. Therefore the only action the auditors could take was resign or qualify the accounts, both of which risked a run on the bank, thereby complicating any future rescue.

The next significant bank failure in the UK was the collapse of the Bank of Credit and Commerce International (BCCI), which was forced to close its operations in July 1991. BCCI was first registered in Luxembourg in 1972 and opened its first UK branch a year later. By 1977 it had 45 branches in the UK and planned to increase the number to 150 but the Bank of England refused this expansion because of concerns regarding its Middle Eastern connections. In 1980 the Bank of England refused BCCI full banking status but allowed it to act as a second-tier licensed deposit taker. Over the 1980s a number of incidents occurred which cast doubt on the competency of management at BCCI and revealed criminal activity in its operation. For example, in 1985 BCCI reported large losses on its futures and options trading. After this BCCI moved its treasury operations out of London to the Gulf region. In 1990 BCCI was found guilty in a Florida court of conspiring to launder money for a Colombian drug cartel. Later on that year the bank's auditors revealed the use of false accounting practices and fictitious loans. In 1990 BCCI moved its operations to Abu Dhabi, making it less accessible to its regulators. Also in that year the auditors of BCCI produced a report to the Bank of England estimating that £1.5 billion was required to cover potential losses. Early in 1991, after a tip-off to the auditors revealing fraudulent activity on a massive scale, the Bank of England initiated a further study from the auditors. This found that accounts had been falsified for a number of years, that transactions had been disguised and that BCCI was insolvent. The Bank of England shut down BCCI in July 1991. It later emerged that BCCI had worldwide debts of $10 billion (in the UK £400 million). UK depositors were entitled to receive only 75 per cent of their deposits, up to a maximum of £20,000, under the deposit insurance scheme (see below).

The main criticism of the Bank of England in this case was why it failed to close down BCCI during the 1980s when there was evidence of fraudulent activity. Indeed, the Bank of England attempted to restructure BCCI in 1990 to save it from closure. In order to investigate this and other aspects of the supervision of BCCI, the government and the Bank of England set up the Bingham inquiry, which reported in October 1992. The inquiry cleared the Bank of England of any negligence in its supervisory activities. However, the inquiry did comment on the slack supervisory regime, which took too long to investigate reports of fraud and close BCCI down. The report can be summarised in the following points.

(i)   The auditors of BCCI may not have pursued evidence aggressively enough, nor did they pass on their concerns to the Bank of England as fully as they may have done.

(ii) The Bank of England failed to understand BCCI's legal status, wrongly leading it to rely on the Luxembourg authorities' judgement.

(iii) Although fraud was brought to light by other parties, the Bank of England did not investigate; the Bank did not see itself in an investigatory role.

(iv) When BCCI faced closure, the Bank of England tried to restructure it and did not take enough notice of reports of lack of fitness and properness.

Among the recommendations of the Bingham inquiry was the establishment of the Special Investigations Unit in the Bank of England (now set up) to examine any warning signs received by the Bank. One of the main lessons to come out of the BCCI affair though was that banking group structures which deny supervisors a clear view of how business is conducted should be outlawed. This has since been addressed by the Basle Committee and is discussed in section 18.4.4.

The most recent major bank failure was that of Barings in February 1995. Barings was placed in administration following a failed attempt by the Bank of England to secure a buyer. Since then the Barings group operations have been taken over by the Dutch financial services group ING. A case study outlining the details of the collapse of Barings Bank is provided in section 14.6.2. Here we examine the regulatory implications. The failure of Barings was brought on by losses incurred on unauthorised transactions in derivatives undertaken by a single trader operating in a Singapore subsidiary of the group. The size of the losses (which turned out to be £860 million) exceeded the bank's capital. The cause of failure in this case appears to be inadequate internal controls within the Barings group. However, the Bank of England, in its role as lead regulator, was also criticised for its failure to heed earlier warnings of problems in the Barings Singapore subsidiary and its failure to ensure that the group had adequate internal controls. As with BCCI, when the Barings group was faced with closure the Bank of England's preferred solution was a rescue by a bank or syndicate of banks. Justification for such a rescue was weak, as the systemic risks associated with failure were relatively low. Although Barings was allowed to fail in the end, thus sending signals to the marketplace that banks in difficulty will not automatically be bailed out, the signal was not as clear as it could otherwise have been.

18.3   Reasons for the prudential control of banks

As indicated above, the occurrence of bank failure provides the trigger for further regulation but, before looking at the detail of the system of control, we examine why financial institutions are subject to a degree of prudential regulation and supervision. This contrasts with the position of industry and commerce in general where imprudent behaviour (other than illegal activities such as fraud) likely to lead to bankruptcy is the concern of the owners and shareholders rather than any supervisory authority. In discussion of the reasons for prudential control of the financial system, we follow the direction of most of the early literature on this topic, which was focused on prudential control of the banks rather than the financial system as a whole.

18.3.1 *The risks faced by banks*

First of all we need to examine the nature of the risks faced by banks. These can be categorised as:

(i)   systemic failure arising from deposit withdrawals;
(ii)   price risk;
(iii) default risk;

(iv) fraud and mismanagement risk;
(v) regulatory risk.

Systemic risk arises from the fact that banks' assets and liabilities have a particular feature which may render them liable to financial difficulties even when they are basically sound. Their liabilities are very liquid, often withdrawable on demand, whereas a large proportion of their assets are in the form of loans and advances which are illiquid owing to both the difficulty of securing repayment at short notice and the absence of a wide secondary market in bank debt. Consequently exercise of the right to withdraw by a large number of depositors (i.e. a run on the bank) may cause failure of a bank which is perfectly viable in the sense that the discounted value of its assets exceeds that of its liabilities. This problem is enhanced by the procedure followed by banks in the event of a run occurring. Until insolvency is declared the bank is obliged to pay out the full amount of any deposit withdrawn. Once insolvency is declared the depositors must await realisation of the bank's assets in the company of other creditors and have their claims assessed by the courts. Thus, in the event of a rumour of difficulties being faced by a bank, there is likely to be a run on that institution since it is in the interest of each depositor to be at the head of the queue. In fact the risk is wider than that so far discussed since, for similar reasons, the 'run mentality' can spread to other banks even though these banks may not be in difficulties. This is because depositors have only imperfect information about a bank's safety. If they see one bank in difficulty they do not have the information to assess whether the problems are specific to that bank or affect all banks. In such circumstances it is rational for depositors to withdraw funds from sound banks in order fully to guarantee safety for their deposits. Thus, the run can spread through the banking system. This danger is reinforced because the individual banks are linked together through both the payments system (see section 3.5.3 for a discussion of payments risk) and the inter-bank markets. Hence failure of one bank will adversely affect the financial position of other banks. An un-regulated banking system is therefore susceptible to swings in public confidence and this provides one of the main reasons why the banking system is regulated. This danger is termed 'systemic risk' or contagion.

Price risk refers to the possibility of asset prices changing in a manner which will have adverse effects on the bank's financial position. A good illustration of price risk is given by the current position of the savings and loans associations in the US. If assets are held with a longer maturity duration than liabilities, then unanticipated rises in interest rates will cause losses unless the lending is at floating rates of interest. It is estimated (see for example Benston and Kaufman 1988) that at least

500 savings and loans associations were merged or failed in the 1980s because of this type of risk. Open currency positions also incur a price risk since unanticipated changes in the relevant exchange rate will result in windfall gains or losses to the bank concerned. Involvement of a bank in futures or options also leaves it exposed to the risk of price changes. The final type of price risk occurs when an institution is forced to sell an asset to obtain funds quickly. The necessity of a speedy sale may prevent the bank from seeking out the most advantageous deal, thus incurring some form of loss. This is in effect a liquidity risk. Price risk in general has increased because of the rising volatility of asset prices, illustrated in figures 14.1 and 14.2.

The risk of default is endemic in bank lending and arises for example from changes in economic climate, which will induce the failure of some firms. The impact of monetary restraint, with its accompanying high interest rates, on firms with a large percentage of capital in the form of debt provides a good illustration of increased risk of default due to a changing economic climate. Another potential source of debt failure arises from country risk, which refers to the failure of foreign governments and other borrowers to repay loans. The problem of sovereign lending was examined in chapter 4. As was discussed in chapters 3 and 4, a bank can reduce the incidence of default risk by spreading its lending activities (i.e. portfolio diversification) over a wide number of customers, so that failure of any one customer imposes only a light burden on the bank, and over different categories of borrowers (geographical or type of industry/person), so as to reduce the risk of failure. Banks can also further reduce the incidence of this type of risk by applying an adequate system of scrutiny to loan applications. Nevertheless, default risk is always present for banks.

Fraud and mismanagement offer further risks to banks. In the UK the closure of BCCI in 1991 – discussed above – was a direct consequence of fraud on a massive scale on the part of the management. In the US it seems that fraud was the reason for the failure of some savings and loan associations. Yang (1987) reported that fraud and other misconduct were the principal reasons for the failure of some 30 associations in California between 1983 and 1986. Mismanagement is a fairly general cause of difficulties for all concerns, financial or otherwise, and was probably one of the main reasons for the 1984 failure of JMB in the UK.

The final type of risk faced by a bank is the potential impact of the regulatory environment, which may impair the safe and efficient operation of a bank. One example of this type of risk in the UK was that in the past banks were subject to imposed lending restraints as part of the government's monetary policy. Similar restraints were not imposed on lending by the building societies.

For the sake of ease of exposition, we have examined these risks as though they were independent of each other. In fact they are interdependent in a number of ways. Thus, for example, inefficient management is likely to lead to inadequate scrutiny of loan applications and hence greater default risk. Price risk can be reduced by appropriate interest-rate pricing and taking a balanced currency position. Liquidity risks can be avoided by holding a sufficient level of highly liquid assets. Fraud can be prevented by good internal supervision as well as the supervision provided by auditors.

18.3.2 *Reasons for regulating banks*

We now turn to the justification for external regulation of banks in the light of the risks examined above. The first reason offered concerns systemic risk. It is argued that the financial system is subject to waves of confidence and so external regulation is necessary to prevent financial panics.

A second reason offered for the control of banks is that the social costs of a major bank failure are far more wide reaching than the failure of a single firm. Failure of any firm affects shareholders. The difference is that the customers (i.e. the depositors) of a bank are likely to be much larger in number and wider in geographical distribution than with a comparable commercial undertaking. In addition, there is the adverse impact on the function of channelling savings to prospective investors which is likely to lower the aggregate level of investment within an economy.

A third reason offered for prudential control is the possible lack of sophistication of the general public. It is argued that they lack the expertise to differentiate between safe and risky investments. One consequence of this is that the public would be likely to accept a higher return offered for investment in one direction without analysing any extra risk which may be involved. This problem is reinforced by the difficulty of obtaining adequate statistics to assess the risk or safety of an individual institution. Balance sheets tend to conceal the type of lending and the risks involved. In addition, as we saw in chapter 2, banks' existence is partly based on asymmetric information since banks have access to information not available to depositors. Adequate risk assessment requires information supplementary to that contained in the financial reports. The justification of regulation under this heading may be conveniently summed up as depositor protection.

As we have seen in chapters 3 and 4, banks often find themselves under a considerable degree of pressure for a variety of reasons, such as the sovereign debt overhang, bad debts arising from company failure

due to high interest rates and falling property values and keen competition. These facets provide a fourth reason for supervising banks,
which is the prevention of banks undertaking excessively risky
operations in an effort to restore their financial position. There is also
the feeling that excessive competition may lead to underpricing of
services which, in turn, has an adverse effect on long-run profitability
and, therefore, the viability of banks. This fear is compounded by the
fact that the 'correct' price for a new service may be difficult to
determine without experience extending over an adequate period of
time.

The final reason offered for prudential control of banks is the prevention of the entrance of undesirable firms or individuals into an
industry in which the preservation of confidence is so vital. A supporting argument is that the industry offers considerable scope for fraud
and that, therefore, this restraint is essential.

It should be noted that the arguments so far presented favour regulation of banks. Nevertheless, certain caveats can be entered against the
exercise of excessive prudential control over banks. The first
consideration is the incontrovertible fact that regulation imposes costs in
the form of real resources on both the regulators and the regulated. The
central bank has to employ the expertise necessary to carry out the
prudential control and the banks have to employ resources to complete
the returns required by the controller. These costs can be relatively high
and it is therefore a question of cost–benefit analysis to determine
whether the benefits gained by prudential regulation outweigh the costs
incurred. The budget for the operation of the FSA (the new bank
regulator in the UK, from the summer of 1998 – see section 18.5) for
the financial year 1998/99 has been set at £153.9 million. This cost
represents the cost to the taxpayer in real resources and does not include
costs imposed on the banks to complete the necessary returns and so on.
It is significant and is suggestive of the argument that the burden of
proof for/against prudential control rests on the advocates of such
control rather than those who favour a free-market approach. Second,
there is the danger of the regulation becoming so excessive as to reduce
competition, raising costs and lowering the pace of financial innovation.
A similar argument is often presented in terms of the institutions
'capturing' the regulator by the introduction of practices favourable to
themselves, as for example the introduction of a cartel restraining
competition and raising profits. A further argument against regulation is
that the form of the regulations will distort the market mechanism by
diverting resources to fields of activity favoured by the regulators.

Finally by way of arguments opposed to regulation is the danger that
onerous regulations imposed in one centre will merely lead to the

movement of the activity to centres where regulation is more relaxed. This is of course one of the main reasons for the development of offshore banking and is perhaps the main incentive for a common regulation system across banks operating in different countries, often termed a 'level playing field'. This aspect of prudential control is discussed in section 18.4.8. In recent years a small but growing group of economists have argued that banking markets are no different to any other markets and so the principle of laissez-faire should also apply. These 'free bankers' believe that banks should be allowed to operate in a truly competitive market environment with no restrictions on the types of assets they hold or the liabilities they issue and in addition no protective restrictions such as restrictions on entry to banking, deposit insurance (see later) or lender of last resort. In such a competitive banking system depositors would be aware that they would lose their funds if the bank failed. Depositors would want reassurance that their funds were safe. Bank managers would want to keep depositors' confidence because if depositors had any doubts about the safety of the bank they would start to withdraw deposits. Bank managers would therefore want to reassure depositors that they were not taking excessive risks and would expose their policies to outside scrutiny. Bank managers would also want to maintain adequate capital, again to reassure depositors. Competition would ensure that bankers struck the right balance between return to investors and depositor protection. According to Dowd (1993), history shows us that banks in relatively unregulated systems maintained strong capital. Dowd also argues that bank runs were usually constructive events that weeded out the weaker banks.

One interesting suggestion put forward by Benston (see e.g. Benston and Kaufman 1988) is for a bank's assets and liabilities to be revalued at market prices and that, when economic capital becomes negative (or perhaps positive but only by a small margin), the bank should be reorganised or taken over. One of the main advantages claimed for this system is that the cost of any bank rescue would be quite small. Second, it is argued that depositors would have increased confidence in the banking system, so that runs on banks would become less frequent. Third, the requirement for much of the system of prudential control would be removed. Implementation of such a system would require periodic revaluation of assets and this would cause major difficulty given the high proportion of UK bank assets in the form of loans, which, as we have already seen, are difficult to recall or sell on a secondary market. Nevertheless, this option may become more viable in the future if and when the secondary market in loans further develops.

In summing up the arguments for and against prudential regulation of banks, perhaps the most telling argument is the lack of expertise and knowledge possessed by the individual depositor to assess the quality of the bank. It can, therefore, be argued that retail banking should be subject to fairly rigorous control (some options are examined in section 18.4) whereas wholesale banking should be subject to a much lighter measure of prudential control. The reason for the suggested difference between the degree of regulation imposed on the two types of banking lies in the perceived expertise of their customers. Wholesale customers are (or should be) financially aware whereas it is arguable that at least some of the customers of retail banks will be financially illiterate.

The argument in favour of prudential regulation of the financial industry has been framed in terms of banks but most of the arguments can easily be extended to incorporate prudential regulation of financial institutions in general. The remainder of this chapter will concentrate on the regulation of banks (section 18.4) followed by the investment institutions (section 18.5).

18.4   The UK system of prudential control of banks

The UK system of authorisation and prudential supervision of banks was operated by the Bank of England until the summer of 1998. At this time control was passed to the FSA, which has been established to regulate the whole of the financial services sector. The system of control in the UK is based on regulating the entry of banks into the banking industry and then once a bank is established it is supervised by the regulator to ensure that it acts in a prudent manner.

18.4.1 Authorisation of banks

The Banking Act of 1987 requires banks to be authorised by the Bank of England (now the FSA) before operating as a bank. The authorisation procedure requires the regulator to be satisfied that the systems of capital, liquidity and internal control are adequate and the quality of management is consistent with banking status. The connection between this requirement and the danger of undesirable firms/individuals entering the banking industry is obvious. Those that meet the standards are referred to as 'authorised institutions' although it is only those institutions with more than £5 million in capital (or which are incorporated outside the UK) that are accorded the title of 'bank'. In addition, the European Commission's Second Banking Coordination Directive (see chapter 15) permits banks that are incorporated in other EU states (now extended to cover the countries of the European Economic Area) to set up branches throughout the EU on the basis of authorisation by their home supervisor. The main responsibility for prudential supervision of branches of banks within the European Economic Area in the UK lies with the home supervisor.

18.4.2 *Prudential supervision*

The FSA is responsible for ensuring that authorised banks continue to operate in a prudent manner. The aim of ongoing supervision is to minimise the risk of bank failure and not to guarantee that banks will not fail. Where banks do fail (as in the case of BCCI) then separate arrangements exist to ensure that depositors receive (limited) compensation (see below, section 18.4.7).

In order to ensure that banks are managed prudently the supervisor will monitor banks on an individual basis and issue instructions where needed to ensure this. The ultimate sanction open to the supervisor is to restrict or revoke a bank's authorisation. Although there are quantitative assessments of a bank's risks and control procedures which play a role in the supervision process – for example the adequacy of a bank's capital (section 18.4.4) – the judgement of those undertaking the supervision of the bank also plays a key role.

A new systematic framework for risk-based supervision is currently being implemented in the UK. At the time of writing (March 1998) this was still at the consultative stage and there may be revisions. However, this risk-based approach to supervision has been adopted in a number of countries, including the US, and the broad outline that follows is likely to form the basis of the final framework. One of the aims of this approach is to ensure a greater consistency of supervision across banks. The new framework is called Risk Assessment, Tools and Evaluation (RATE) and it will apply to all UK incorporated banks. Under RATE a supervisory period is introduced which is the length of time between undertaking formal risk assessments of a particular bank. This will normally be one year but can be varied between six months and two years according to the risk profile of the bank. A shorter period would apply to banks with a relatively high-risk profile. In each supervisory period, the supervisor will perform a risk assessment, take appropriate supervisory action, apply the tools of supervision and undertake a formal evaluation.

The formal risk assessment is based on nine evaluation factors. These factors can be separated into those that help identify the business risks of a bank and those that focus on the adequacy and effectiveness of the bank's internal controls and management. To assess the business risks of a bank, five quantitative factors and one qualitative factor are considered. The quantitative factors are accorded the acronym CAMEL and refer to capital, assets, market risks, earnings and liabilities. Some of the issues considered under each of these headings are listed below (for further details see annex II of Bank of England (1997)):

(i)   capital – composition and quality, adequacy (see section 18.4.4), access to capital;
(ii) assets – composition, concentration, provisioning and arrears, maturity and marketability;
(iii) market risk – composition of the trading book, track record and risk appetite (see section 18.4.3);
(iv) earnings – overall performance of the bank, sources and costs;
(v)   liabilities – composition, concentration and liquidity (see section 18.4.3).

The CAMEL assessment will focus in particular on the key business risks of credit, market and liquidity. We cover each of these three areas in more detail below. A further analysis of the bank's overall business and external environment, under the heading of the 'Business factor', will provide a context for the CAMELB analysis, which will assess the business risk profile of the bank. The second element of the assessment will focus on a qualitative analysis of the internal controls, organisation and management of the bank. This COM assessment will focus on issues such as the procedures for identifying, evaluating and monitoring risks in the organisation, whether reporting lines are clearly defined and the fitness and properness of directors and managers.

A brief outline of the process of a RATE assessment would be, first, to undertake a preliminary risk assessment of a bank. This would involve collecting background information including management accounts, strategy documents, organisational profiles and so on. Second, an on-site visit by supervisors would take place. This would provide the supervisors with an opportunity to improve their understanding of the business risks of the bank and to clarify points arising out of the preliminary risk assessment. The most important aspect of an on-site visit will be to assess internal controls within the bank as part of the COM evaluation. After a visit the supervisory team will undertake a formal evaluation of the CAMELB and COM factors. This will enable the supervisor to determine the overall risk profile of the bank and prepare an appropriate supervisory programme. This programme will identify those areas where the supervisors have specific concerns and require remedial action. To ensure consistency of treatment across banks an advisory panel, consisting of staff not directly involved in the supervision of the bank under review, will assess the supervisory programme. Finally, the supervisors will provide the bank with formal feedback of its findings.

We now turn to examine some of the key elements of this risk assessment in more detail. These are:

(i)   the assessment of liquidity risk;
(ii) the assessment of credit risk and the adequacy of capital in relation to this risk;
(iii) the assessment of market risks;
(iv) liaison between auditors or reporting accountants and supervisors.

18.4.3 *Liquidity risk*

As we have discussed above, one feature of the asset and liability structure of banks which suggests prudential control is the liquid nature of their liabilities and illiquid nature of their assets. A bank can fail through inability to meet deposit withdrawals through lack of liquidity even though it is viable in the long run. Liquidity can be provided in a number of ways, including:

(i)   holding sufficient cash or assets which are easily liquefied;
(ii) holding an appropriately matching portfolio of cash flows from maturing assets;
(iii) maintaining an adequately diversified deposit base in terms of maturities and mix of depositors.

The supervisors have the duty to ensure that banks maintain an appropriate mix of all three. With specific reference to the liquidity position, no minimum overall liquidity ratio is applied to all banks because it is felt that the allocation of specific assets to a liquidity category is bound to be arbitrary. Banks engage in maturity transformation, so that the term structure of their assets is longer than that of their liabilities. Hence assessment of the liquidity risk of a bank can be achieved by preparing a maturity ladder, showing the accumulated mismatch of short-term assets and liabilities over a variety of time periods up to one year. In this ladder marketable assets are shown as maturing immediately but are subject to a discount for valuation in the liquidity ladder so as to reflect potential variations in market price; for example, CDs with less than six months remaining to maturity are subject to 5 per cent discount and those up to five years 10 per cent discount. The time periods of this maturity ladder are: sight to eight days; eight days to one month; one to three months; three to six months; and six to twelve months. It would be expected that the maximum point of excess of liabilities over assets will occur in the first six months. Each bank will be given its own mismatch ratios for control purposes for the various periods of the analysis by the supervisor. The bank is expected to monitor its mismatch positions and report breaches of the control ratios to the supervisor. A recent revision to this approach has been to switch to an analysis of mismatch positions on the basis of cash flows rather than maturities. This cash flow approach captures interest payments and receipts, other income and expenses and off-balance-sheet cash flows and therefore provides a more detailed picture of the liquidity risk of the bank.

18.4.4 *Capital adequacy*

As we have noted in the last section, liquidity is essentially a short-term concept referring to the ability of an institution to meet day-to-day cash outflows, whereas solvency is a longer-term concept referring to the prospective ability of a bank to meet all its liabilities as they fall due. The distinction between liquidity and solvency is not as clear cut as these definitions imply. There is a view that if a financial institution is confidently believed to be solvent then it should be able to borrow through the markets to meet any short-term liquidity difficulties. It follows therefore that the existence of liquidity problems that cannot be resolved through the markets implies that other market participants believe the risk of insolvency for that institution to be high. The reverse is generally not the case as it is possible to face insolvency problems without any illiquidity problems first showing up, as was the case with JMB. The view that 'banks with liquidity problems that cannot be solved through the markets implies the bank is likely to be insolvent' was seen by Quinn, then the Executive Director of the Bank of England with responsibility for banking supervision, to be one which is 'absolutist and neglects the vital role that time plays in assessing the quality of a bank's assets, quite apart from being a high risk strategy' (*Bank of England Quarterly Bulletin*, May 1988). Quinn argued that there are great difficulties in establishing the value of a bank's assets and that it is possible for assets to gain or lose value very quickly, thus creating liquidity problems. A bank's management may be able to turn round the problem over time or the problem may disappear through an improvement in external circumstances. However, if a bank is denied short-term funding, its capacity to recover claims is put in doubt and other debtors may then stop paying, believing that the institution is likely to become insolvent, thus compounding the problem. Thus, the Bank of England has placed increasing emphasis on banks managing their liquidity as part of the overall policy of minimising the risk of insolvency. However, the most important aspect of the Bank's policy (now the FSA's) in this regard relates to its monitoring of each bank's capital adequacy.

The capital of a bank is seen as financing the infrastructure of the business and providing a cushion to absorb any losses on its assets. As we saw in chapter 2, a bank can minimise credit risk with regard to its loans by:

(i) limiting the risk of default on individual loans through appropriate selection of borrowers;
(ii) reducing the overall risk of its loan portfolio by diversifying;
(iii) pooling its risk so as to make the overall risk of default more predictable.

This last point enables the bank to cover its expected losses by incorporating a premium in its loan rate of interest. Unexpected loan losses are then covered by the bank's profits in the first instance and ultimately by its capital. Thus, the level of a bank's capital is important in assessing its solvency in adverse circumstances. The underlying principle is that it is the shareholders rather than the depositors who should bear the risks of the business undertaking.

The question of capital adequacy was first addressed by a working party set up by the Bank of England in 1974, which reported in 1975 (see *Bank of England Quarterly Bulletin*, September 1975). This working party recommended the use of two ratios: the free resources (gearing) ratio and the risk–assets ratio. These ratios were further revised in 1979 and the system of assessing capital adequacy that operated throughout most of the 1980s is set out in the *Bank of England Quarterly Bulletin* of September 1980. The gearing ratio is a very simple measure, essentially relating the value of a bank's free resources, that is broadly the bank's capital minus the value of its infrastructure, to the value of its deposits. Thus, it takes no account of the riskiness of the bank's assets and as a consequence is rarely referred to nowadays for supervisory purposes. The risk–assets ratio has become the key ratio in monitoring capital adequacy and this relates the value of a bank's capital to the value of its assets weighted according to their inherent riskiness. However, it does so only to the extent that these activities appear on the balance sheet. As we have discussed in chapter 4, since the early 1980s banks have increasingly undertaken activities which do not result in a balance sheet entry under normal accounting procedures ('off-balance-sheet' business). Thus, in order to measure the adequacy of a bank's capital to all, or at least most, of the default risks it is exposed to, the risk–assets ratio has recently been modified to incorporate 'off-balance-sheet' business.

Basle capital accord

The new system of risk weightings and capital definitions was proposed in an agreement reached by the Basle Committee on Banking Supervision (1988). This accord, which provides for a common system of prudential control for banks operating in the major industrial countries, came into effect at the beginning of 1993. Under this approach banks' assets are divided into various categories and each category is given a weighting according to its perceived relative riskiness. Each asset is multiplied by this risk factor and the total of the risk-adjusted assets then related to the bank's capital. For example, cash has a risk weight of 0, loans to discount houses 10 per cent and commercial loans 100 per cent. A two-step process is involved for off-balance-sheet items. First, they are transformed into an on-balance-sheet item using standard conversion ratios. Second, the risk weightings are then applied to the converted values. The capital base itself consists of two components: core capital, or tier 1, and supplementary capital, or tier 2. The first component broadly comprises shareholders' equity and published accumulated profits, and the second consists of medium- and long-term subordinated debt instruments (i.e. debt ranking after all other debt for winding up purposes), general provisions and unpublished profits. Three restrictions are imposed. First, the total of tier 2 components should not exceed a maximum of 100 per cent of the total of tier 1 items. Second, subordinated debt should not exceed a maximum of 50 per cent of the total of tier 1 items. Third, general provisions should not exceed 1.25 per cent of weighted risk assets. A minimum level for the risk–assets ratio of 8 per cent is prescribed but it is not expected that all banks will

Table 18.1   *Example calculation of a bank's capital base, categorised into two tiers, for an assessment of the risk–assets ratio*

Tier 1 items	Value (£million)	Tier 2 items	Value (£million)
Equity	40	Current year's unpublished profit	4
Accumulated profits	8	General provisions	7
		Subordinated term debt	27
Total tier 1	48	Total tier 2	35[a]

Capital base = tier 1 capital + tier 2 capital = £48 million + £35 million = £83 million.

[a] In calculating tier 2 capital, only £24 million of subordinated debt is permitted as subordinated debt cannot exceed 50 per cent of tier 1 capital.

Table 18.2 *Example calculation of a bank's risk-weighted assets, for an assessment of the risk–assets ratio*

Assets	Value (£million)	Weight (%)	Weighted value (£million)
Cash	30	0	0
Treasury bills	7	10	0.7
Secured loans to discount market	80	10	8
Other eligible bills	40	20	8
UK government stocks	60	20	12
Commercial loans	350	100	350
Personal loans	200	100	200
Mortgage loans	100	50	50
Total on-balance-sheet assets	867		628.7
Off-balance-sheet risks:			
guarantees of commercial loans	50	100	50
standby letters of credit	80	50	40
Total risk-weighted assets			718.7

work to this figure and capital adequacy will be considered for each bank against the background of its operations; for example, a higher ratio will be set for a bank with inexperienced management or a high concentration of risks.

To illustrate the calculation of the risk–asset ratio, consider tables 18.1 and 18.2. From the former, the capital base (tier 1 capital + tier 2 capital) is £83 million, and from the latter, the total risk-weighted assets are £718.7 million. The risk–assets ratio is therefore (83/718.7) 11.6 per cent. This illustration is not meant to represent a typical bank but is used to show how the ratio is constructed. However, the weights shown in table 18.2 are the actual weights used by regulators.

The theoretical basis of the risk–asset ratio is perhaps suspect since it is based on the assumption that the risks are independent, otherwise it would not be possible to add the risk-adjusted assets together. Portfolio theory suggests that risks may be interdependent in some instances; for example, a general recession will induce failures of a number of companies. On the other hand, portfolio theory suggests that diversification should make the risk of the whole portfolio less than the aggregation of the risks of the individual securities. It is difficult, however, to design a scheme which would take this factor into consideration. A second problem arises if the risk factors do not accurately measure the relative degree of risk in each asset. This problem is made worse because the effect of the risk weightings is likely to induce lending favourable to the arbitrarily imposed risk factors and may therefore distort the market mechanism. Another serious concern with the new system relates to the 100 per cent risk weighting applicable to commercial loans to the private sector. The implication is that the capital requirement for a loan to an AAA-rated multinational company (see section on credit ratings in chapter 9) is precisely the same for a loan of the same size to a small company with a lower credit rating. As banks' main assets are loans it is not clear why the designers of the system did not allow for differential risk weightings in this area. One consequence may be that aggressively managed banks may be tempted to shift their lending towards high-risk (high-return) borrowers, thus increasing their exposure to the risk of default, while cautiously managed banks are not rewarded for their prudence.

Heavy exposure to individual companies imposes a risk over and above that captured by comparing asset risks and capital, as evidenced in the failure of JMB. A bank is therefore required to notify exposure to any individual customer in excess of 10 per cent of its capital (calculated in the same manner as for the risk–asset ratio). Any exposure in excess of 25 per cent of the capital base is permitted only in exceptional circumstances.

18.4.5 *Market risks*

The increased amount of trading activities by large banks has focused attention on a bank's exposure to market risk, defined as the risk of loss from adverse movements in financial market rates and prices. The risk–asset ratio introduced by the Basle capital accord of 1988, discussed above, addressed a bank's exposure to credit risk. An amendment to the Basle accord set new minimum capital requirements for a bank's market risk exposure. The Capital Adequacy Directive for EU incorporated banks undertaking trading activities (see chapter 15) is also being amended to bring it into line with the Basle amendment (Basle Committee on Banking Supervision 1996). These requirements are to be introduced into UK bank supervision during 1998. Under these requirements a bank must separate its long-term investments in securities from its trading book. Trading refers to positions taken with a view to resale or short-term profit, rather than to holding the securities until maturity. Thus trading book exposures are treated as short term and valued on a mark-to-market basis (i.e. at the current price at which they could be sold in the market). The long-term investments (mainly its loan book) would be subject to the original credit risk capital requirements under the 1988 accord. The bank's trading book positions in debt, equity and derivative securities are then subject to the market risk capital requirements. In addition, commodity and foreign exchange positions held by the bank (both inside and outside the trading book) are subject to the market risk capital requirements.

An innovative feature of the market risk requirements is that they provide for the use of banks' own internal value at risk models for measuring market risks. Briefly, a value at risk model calculates an estimate of the maximum amount a bank can lose on a particular portfolio over a given holding period with an associated degree of statistical confidence. These estimates are normally derived from the recent behaviour of underlying risk factors, such as interest rates and exchange rates. The estimate is then multiplied by a scaling factor to produce a capital charge that the bank is required to hold. The advantage of using a bank's own internal models for calculating the minimum capital requirement is that the resulting requirement should more accurately match a bank's true risk exposure. Of course, the supervisor will require a bank to perform testing exercises and provide other information to check the validity of these models. Those firms that do not have a comprehensive internal model will apply a standardised measurement framework. The market risk capital requirements introduce a new element of bank capital, tier 3 capital, which comprises short-term subordinated debt. This should have an original maturity of at least two years and will be limited to 250 per cent of a bank's tier 1 capital that is allocated to support market risks. Tier 3 capital is only eligible to cover market risks.

In addition, the Basle Committee on Banking Supervision (1997) has published a set of principles for the assessment and management of banks' interest rate risks. Interest rate risk refers to the difference between the interest rate structure of loans and deposits. These principles apply to interest rate risk arising from both trading and non-trading activities. There are no explicit capital requirements in these principles but emphasis is placed on banks having appropriate measurement, monitoring and other control systems to deal with these risks and, of course, prudent behaviour would require a bank to hold capital to cover such risks. Appropriate action on dealing with excessive risk taking in this area is left to the discretion of the supervisory authority.

18.4.6 *Liaison with auditors/reporting accountants*

Auditors/reporting accountants provide a potentially fruitful source of information concerning the financial position of banks. However, a conflict of duty may arise since the auditors have a prime responsibility to the shareholders of the banks whereas the role of the supervisors is the protection of the depositors. Following the Banking Act 1987, a relationship between the auditors and the Bank (now the FSA) was provided for. The relationship is based on trilateral meetings between the auditors, the institution and the supervisors at the Bank (FSA). Matters discussed include the statutory accounts and the auditors' reports. The reporting accountants are also required to report on the institution's accounting and other internal control systems and the returns provided for prudential control purposes. Meetings are normally called by the Bank (FSA) or by the auditors via the institution concerned. In exceptional cases, however, the auditors or reporting accountants can report direct to the Bank (FSA). Such exceptional circumstances would have to be of a serious nature, such as situations where the integrity of the directors or senior management is being questioned.

The connection between the role of auditors and the failure of management in connection with JMB, accompanied by inadequate internal systems of control and provision of inaccurate returns, is self-evident.

18.4.7 *Deposit insurance*

The final component of the UK system of prudential control is the existence of insurance of deposits. In the event of failure, depositors would have 90 per cent of their deposits refunded, up to a maximum pay-out of £18,000. The scheme is financed by a flat-rate contribution by banks in proportion to their deposits. The advantages claimed for deposit insurance are threefold. First, such schemes are designed to provide for speedy compensation for depositors, who then have no need to wait for the completion of the winding up of the institution. Second, systemic risk should be reduced since the incentive to be first in the queue to withdraw deposits is reduced. This point is critically dependent on the public being aware that deposits are insured in this manner. This is far from evident. As an interesting exercise the reader should try asking friends or a class of students if they know that their deposits are insured! Third, perhaps the hidden rationale for the scheme is that it provides the finance for compensation of depositors without recourse to the government.

Deposit insurance is not without its critics since it is open to a number of objections. It can be argued that the existence of deposit insurance increases the problem of moral hazard. As far as the banks are concerned the wrath of the depositors may be averted because of the knowledge that they will obtain compensation for any deposit loss. This could act as an incentive to the bank managers to take excessive risks since any profits gained will be theirs but any loss will be borne by the insurer. For similar reasons the depositors may be less careful in their monitoring of banks and may select institutions which offer the highest rate of interest on deposits regardless of the risks involved because they know any loss will be reimbursed by the insurer. Presumably the restriction of reimbursement to 90 per cent and a maximum pay-out of £18,000 are both attempts to overcome the moral hazard problem and a recognition that large deposits are likely to be made by persons or institutions with an awareness of the financial risks involved. Apart from the question of moral hazard, there is doubt over the precise form of insurance charge levied in the UK and most other countries. The charge is levied on the quantity of deposits at a flat rate. Many argue that the charge should be linked to the risk involved, in the manner of car insurance. The problem with this suggestion is who is going to make the risk assessment? It is likely that a central bank would baulk at that type of decision for fear of complaints of discrimination. It also remains a moot point whether ratings provided by private agencies would be satisfactory for the purpose of fixing deposit insurance rates. Nevertheless, the Federal Deposit Insurance Corporation in the US has introduced a system of risk-based insurance premiums whereby premiums for banks rated as well capitalised and well managed, by the supervisory authority, are set at 4 cents per $100 of deposits. In contrast, banks regarded as risky have to pay the much higher premium of 31 cents. This provides a rough and ready approximation to a risk-related premium.

The last point to be made about deposit insurance is that it is not likely to be an adequate substitute for prudential control unless regulators are prepared to permit banks to become bankrupt so that insurance would be seen as protection rather than compensation. In particular, there is a belief that the regulator would not permit a large bank to fail because of the effect on confidence in the banking sector. The evidence is mixed as far as the Bank of England is concerned, as the JMB was rescued whilst BCCI and Barings were allowed to fail.

In the 1980s the US system of banks and particularly thrift institutions saw a dramatic increase in the number of institutions failing, putting the Federal Deposit Insurance Scheme under a tremendous strain. The Federal Savings and Loan Insurance Fund was overwhelmed and federal taxpayers had to bail the Fund out to the tune of several hundred billion dollars. This prompted a lively debate in the US about reform of the deposit insurance system and the interested reader is referred to a series of essays which examine reform from a variety of angles (Russell 1993).

18.4.8 *International cooperation in banking supervision*

Banking is an international function, with many banks operating outside
the country where their head office is located. Types of foreign banking
establishments comprise branches, subsidiaries and joint ventures or
consortia. Thus, some difficulties could occur for effective prudential
control because of ambiguities as to the precise division of the responsibility for supervision. In 1975 the Basle concordat set out guidelines
defining the responsibilities of the parent and the host country for
supervision. This was reformulated again in 1983. The main principle of
these guidelines was that no foreign banking establishment should
escape adequate supervision. It was agreed that supervision of consortia
should be exercised by the authorities in the country of incorporation.
With respect to the remaining two categories, host authorities are
primarily responsible for supervision of their liquidity and foreign
currency positions. Capital adequacy is the responsibility of the parent
country. As described above (section 18.4.4), in July 1988 the Basle
Committee launched a major new regulatory initiative with an agreement by the Group of 10 industrial countries to establish minimum
capital adequacy standards for international banks. A reassessment of
the Basle approach to banking regulation was prompted by the supervisory weaknesses revealed by the collapse of BCCI in the summer of
1991. In particular, the BCCI collapse demonstrated the ease with which
a fraudulent bank could exploit weakly regulated offshore centres. This
led in July 1992 to the Basle Committee issuing a new set of minimum
standards for the supervision of international banks. The main requirement is that all international banks should be supervised by a
home-country authority 'that capably performs consolidated supervision' (Basle Committee on Banking Supervision 1992). That is, the
authority concerned should:

(i)   monitor banks' global operations on the basis of verifiable con-
       solidated data;
(ii)   be able to prohibit the creation of corporate structures that impede
       consolidated supervision;
(iii) be able to prevent banks from establishing a presence in a suspect
       jurisdiction.

In 1996, the Basle Committee issued new proposals to extend the 1988
accord to cover market risks (the 1988 accord was principally concerned
with credit risk).

Finally in this section, regulatory agencies around the world have
become increasingly concerned about the rapid growth in derivatives

trading by banks (see chapters 13 and 14 for discussion) and the potential risks arising out of this. The main concerns are that the complexity of these instruments may impede effective risk control by bank management and supervisors and the market linkages created by derivatives increases the potential for financial contagion. This latter concern is another form of the systemic risk problem discussed in section 18.3. A number of regulatory authorities, including the US Federal Reserve, the Bank of England and the BIS, have undertaken reviews of the derivatives situation and each has expressed concern. These concerns were heightened by the collapse of Barings in February 1995 following losses sustained in derivatives trading (discussed in section 18.2). The capital adequacy regime arising out of the Basle capital accord covers the credit risk side of derivatives and the new market risk proposals cover derivatives market risks. Differences may exist between exchange-traded derivatives, which are transparent, and OTC derivatives, which are more opaque. Hence further developments in this area are likely to focus on encouraging institutions to disclose more information about their risk positions and risk control systems. This control refers to banks, not customers. The latter may be assumed to have expertise in assessing risks although recent examples of losses made by companies through misuse of derivatives (e.g. MG, and Procter and Gamble) may suggest otherwise.

We now turn to an examination of the supervision of investment institutions.

18.5   Control of investment business

Before 1986, the control of investment business was carried out under the provisions of Prevention of Fraud (Investments) Act 1958. However, at the beginning of the 1980s doubts were expressed concerning the effectiveness of this Act and these led to the appointment of Professor Gower to review the protection of investors. The Financial Services Act 1986 was based on the Gower report. In this section we briefly review the general nature of the machinery of control.

In general the 1986 Act provided for the legislation of investment business. An investment was widely defined to include securities issued by companies, public corporations, central and local government. Units in collective investment schemes were also included, as were futures, options and long-term insurance. Investment business was also widely defined and included dealing, arranging deals, managing collective investment schemes and investment advice. Basically the legislation requires that any person or company carrying out such investment business must obtain authorisation. Certain institutions and persons can gain exemption from the need to be authorised, as 'exempted persons'. Exempted persons include Lloyd's underwriters, the Bank of England and recognised investment exchanges (see below). Provision was included for removal of authorisation in the case of wrongdoing. A compensation fund was set up and provisions made for dealing with complaints by the general public.

The overall regulatory function was delegated to the Securities and Investment Board (SIB). Second-tier regulatory bodies were also set up for the various subdivisions of the investment business and these were called self-regulatory organisations (SROs). The SROs require approval from the SIB before they can operate. The SROs currently in existence are:

(i)   the PIA;
(ii)   the Securities and Futures Authority;
(iii)   the Investment Management Regulatory Organisation.

The PIA was set up in 1994 and regulates investment business conducted with private investors chiefly relating to 'packaged products' such as life assurance policies and unit trusts. The PIA was established to take over the regulatory tasks previously undertaken by the Life Assurance and Unit Trust Regulatory Organisation and the Financial Intermediaries, Managers and Brokers Regulatory Association, and both these bodies have now been terminated. The Securities and Futures Authority regulates firms that are primarily concerned with dealing in securities, including derivatives, as a member of an investment exchange, and firms advising on corporate finance. Finally, the Investment Management Regulatory Organisation regulates firms that manage investments. Supervision of the conduct of business is entrusted to these SROs and they have had to produce rule books for operations within their trade which are at least equivalent to the rule book of the SIB.

The SIB was renamed the FSA in October 1997. However, this was more than just a change of name as the FSA is to now the single regulator for the whole of the UK financial services industry. The FSA will take over all aspects of financial regulation from the following regulators:

(i)   the Building Societies Commission;
(ii)   the Friendly Societies Commission;
(iii)   the Insurance Directorate of the Department of Trade and Industry;
(iv)   the Investment Management Regulatory Organisation;
(v)   the PIA;
(vi)   the Registrar of Friendly Societies;

(vii) the Securities and Futures Authority;
(viii) the SIB.
(ix) the Supervision and Surveillance Department of the Bank of England.

The FSA will acquire its full range of regulatory responsibilities in two stages:

(i)   Following enactment of the Bank of England Bill, the FSA will assume responsibility for supervising banks, wholesale money market institutions and the foreign exchange clearing house. The Bill is expected to receive Royal Assent in the summer of 1998.
(ii) Enactment of a proposed financial regulatory reform bill will provide the FSA with the remaining regulatory functions outlined above. At the time of writing, this bill is expected to be implemented in late 1999.

Investment exchanges may also apply for recognition by the FSA. A recognised investment exchange is classed as an exempted person as regards investment business done in its capacity and therefore does not require authorisation. Recognised investment exchanges currently recognised include the LSE, LIFFE and the main commodities exchanges in London. A second category of investment exchange created under the SIB's rules is the designated investment exchange. This is an investment exchange engaged in the dealing of international securities but not subject to UK regulation. An example of a designated investment exchange is the ISMA, which organises a market in international bonds from London. Transactions effected on a designated investment exchange by an authorised person need not be reported to the FSA. Finally, overseas exchanges can also be recognised under the Financial Services Act. Once recognised, an overseas exchange is classed as an exempted person in respect of investment business done in the UK. Examples of overseas exchanges obtaining such recognition are NASDAQ and the Sydney Futures Exchange.

The other main part of the investment regulatory environment is the Criminal Justice Act 1993, which deals with insider dealing offences. The Drug Trafficking Act, 1994, deals with money laundering offences.

The overall objective of the legislation is to achieve protection for investors with involvement of government being the minimum necessary to achieve an operation of a financial system which provides fair rewards without fraud. The strategy adopted was one of self-regulation within a statutory framework. Some felt that a more legalistic approach would have been desirable, on the lines of the US Securities and

Exchange Commission. The opposing argument is based on the idea that practitioners are better placed to spot abuses and breaches of rules than an external body carrying out legal obligations. It is probable that the system adopted will be more flexible and faster in the provision of remedies than a court.

18.6   Conclusion

We have surveyed the UK system of prudential control of financial institutions. The main thrust of our argument has been concerned with the banks. Because of the central position of financial institutions as intermediaries between lenders and borrowers, it is generally (but not always) agreed that some form of external control should be exercised over their behaviour to ensure that they act in a prudential manner. However, all financial behaviour involves risk and prudential control should not be too excessive otherwise competition may be restrained in a manner which leads to excessive operating costs and a lack of financial innovation.

Chapter 19

Conclusions

In this chapter we provide a brief summary of the nature of the UK financial system as presented in this book. In chapter 2, we defined the financial system as a set of markets and institutions which provide the means of raising finance, and which supply various financial services. The institutions we have considered in this book can be usefully sub-divided as follows:

(i)   the banking sector – retail and wholesale banks (chapters 3 and 4, respectively);

(ii)   other deposit-taking institutions – building societies and finance houses (chapter 5);

(iii) long-term investment institutions – pension funds, life assurance companies, investment and unit trusts (chapter 6).

In a similar manner, discussion of markets proceeded as follows:

(i)   introduction to markets (chapter 7);

(ii)   equity markets (chapter 8);

(iii) the bond market, including the term structure of interest rates (chapter 9);

(iv) the sterling money markets (chapter 10);

(v)   the foreign exchange markets (chapter 11);

(vi) the eurosecurities markets (chapter 12);

(vii) the newer derivatives markets, that is, financial futures, options and swaps markets (chapter 13).

This was followed by a discussion of the role of these markets in the management of risk (chapter 14), The nature of central banks was discussed in chapter 17.

The operation of the financial system raises a number of issues. The first concerns how far prudential control should be exercised over the institutions/markets. This was considered in chapter 18. The impact of a single European market and EMU between member states of the EU was discussed in chapter 15. Efficiency of the system was examined in two ways. First, consideration of the application of the efficient markets hypothesis took place against the background of each of the markets. An agnostic conclusion was reached for all markets, implying that the hypothesis was still an open question. Second, the broader aspect of the efficiency of the UK financial system was discussed in chapter 16, and here again our conclusions were not firm but tended to point towards efficiency.

By any standard, the UK financial system described above is a sophisticated system. It is also an open financial system, without restriction of flows of funds into or out of the country for either residents or non-residents. It is also a financial system which has seen a considerable degree of change in recent years in the development of both new markets (e.g. financial futures) and new instruments (e.g. commercial paper), and liberalisation in the sense of the removal of controls restricting competition between institutions. At the same time, the incidence of prudential control has increased.

The pace of change has continued to be fast. Since the second edition of this book, major changes have taken place in the nature and role of the Bank of England. Similarly, the operation of the gilt-edged, equity and money markets has changed dramatically. Similar changes will continue to take place in the future and the interested reader is recommended to keep abreast of future changes by reading the financial reports of the quality press and other media.

Glossary of technical terms and abbreviations

ABS	Asset-backed security – a tradable instrument backed by a pool of loans.
ADR	American depository receipt – confers ownership rights to UK shares and traded in its own right. Avoids the need to register change in share ownership and transactions do not involve stamp duty.
Adverse selection	A problem created by asymmetric information. Refers to the problem that the people who are most undesirable from the other party's point of view are the ones who are most likely to want to engage in the financial transaction.
AIM	Alternative Investment Market – opened in June 1995.
Arbitrage	Buying and selling securities in order to profit from price differences without incurring risk.
Ask price	The price at which a market maker is prepared to sell a security.
Asymmetric information	Refers to the situation where one party to a transaction has more information relating to that transaction than the other party.
ATM	Automated teller machine.
BACS	Bankers' Automated Clearing Services.
Banker's acceptance	A bill of exchange endorsed by a bank, i.e. the bank is guaranteeing the bill. It commands a low rate of discount – see *bill of exchange*.

Basis	The spread or difference between two rates, such as the difference between the futures price and that of the underlying cash instrument.
Basis point	One one-hundredth of 1 per cent.
BCCI	Bank of Credit and Commerce International.
Bearer bond	A bond which is owned by whoever holds it. No registration of ownership is involved – see *bond*.
Bill of exchange	An order in writing telling a person to pay a certain sum of money to another at a specific time in the future. Bills are mainly used in foreign trade. The person who promises to pay is said to accept the bill. A prime bank bill is a bill accepted by a high-class bank. A fine trade bill is a bill accepted by a trader with a first-class reputation. A bill bears no interest rate and is said to be discounted when it is sold for a price less than its maturity value.
BIS	Bank for International Settlements – a settlement bank for the major central banks.
Bond	Title issued by the public sector or a company acknowledging the existence of debt. Normally a bond commands a fixed rate of interest based on its nominal value.
Broker	A person who arranges deals between buyers and sellers on behalf of a third party. A broker is not trading on her/his own account but earns a commission on the deal called a brokerage fee.
BSA	Building Societies Association.
CAD	Capital Adequacy Directive.
CAMEL	Capital, assets, market risks, earnings and liabilities.
Cap	A derivative instrument designed to fix a maximum level to which a price or interest rate can rise.
CBOT	Chicago Board of Trade.
CD	Certificate of deposit – a negotiable instrument issued by a bank or building society acknowledging an interest-bearing time deposit.
CHAPS	Clearing House Automated Payments System – automated end-of-day net settlement system for sterling wholesale payments.

CME	Chicago Mercantile Exchange.
Collar	A derivative instrument designed to fix both a maximum and minimum level to which a price or interest rate can rise or fall.
Collateral	Security given for the repayment of a loan.
COM	Controls, organisation and management.
Commercial paper	An unsecured promissory note issued by commercial firms promising to pay a fixed sum of money normally with a maturity of less than 270 days. This security is usually sold at a discount, i.e. for less than its nominal or face value.
Consortium banks	A subsidiary set up by a number of banks for the purpose of making a large loan(s).
Contingent liability	Debt which comes into existence on the occurrence of some contingency.
Coupon	Fixed rate of interest payable on bonds.
Covered interest arbitrage	Investing in a security denominated in a foreign currency and covering against the exchange rate risk by taking out an offsetting forward transaction.
Crest	London Stock Exchange settlement system.
CSO	Central Statistical Office.
Debt rescheduling	Formal rearrangement of both debt service payments and repayment of the principal with new maturities.
Default	Failure of a borrower to make a payment of either interest or principal on the due date.
Discount	The payment of an immediate sum in settlement of a sum due at a later date.
Discount houses	A group of institutions whose main function is to discount bills of exchange and other short-term financial instruments.
Dividend	Income return on ordinary shares.
DTB	Deutsche Terminbörse.
ECB	European Central Bank.
ECP	Eurocommercial paper.
ECU	The European Currency Unit. It is made up of a weighted total of the currencies of the member states of the European Union.

Efficient markets hypothesis	This puts forward the view that market prices reflect all available information.
EMTN	Euro-medium-term note.
EMU	Economic and monetary union.
Equity	The part of total capital of a company belonging to the shareholders. In terms of a company's balance sheet it is the residual after deducting liabilities except those due to shareholders from total assets.
ERM	Exchange Rate Mechanism – the system of semi-fixed exchange rates of participating countries of the European Union.
EU	European Union.
Euro	New single currency for members of the European Union participating in stage 3 of economic and monetary union. Comes into existence in January 1999.
Eurobank	Financial institution that accepts deposits and makes loans in currencies other than that of the country in which it is located (i.e. the 'host country').
Eurobond	A bond issued in a currency other than that of the country where it is issued, for example a bond denominated in dollars issued in London.
Eurodollar	Dollar deposits held at banks located outside the US. More broadly the term can be used for a deposit denominated in any currency other than that of the host country.
Euronote	Short-term note or debt issued in the syndicated loan market. Short term usually refers to one-, three- or six-month maturities.
European Monetary Institute	Now replaced by the European Central Bank.
European System of Central Banks	The central banks of Europe all acting independently of domestic governments under an agreement on monetary union, under the control of the European Central Bank.
Exercise price	The specified price at which *options* can be taken up or exercised.
Factoring	The act of a financial institution taking over the debts owed to a firm. The price paid for the debts

would be less than the nominal amount outstanding, i.e. the debts are discounted and the rate of discount will reflect the relevant interest charge and an allowance for the riskiness of the debt.

FIL	Financial investment opportunities line.
Financial futures	A standardised contract providing for the purchase or sale of a fixed quantity of a financial commodity such as foreign exchange, bank deposit, etc. The underlying financial instrument is known as the cash instrument.
Floating rate	An interest rate which is reset at regular intervals – the adjustment usually being made with reference to a key rate such as *LIBOR*.
Floor	A derivative instrument designed to fix a minimum level below which a price or interest rate cannot fall.
Foreign bond	A *bond* issued by a borrower in the capital market of another country.
Forex	Foreign exchange.
Forfaiting	Buying a client's debts without the right to reclaim in the event of a *default*.
Forward contract	A contract specifying a price for the delivery of a commodity or financial instrument at an agreed date in the future. This contract differs from a futures contract since the contract is not standardised and can be adjusted according to the needs of the purchaser.
Forward premium	The gap between the forward exchange rate and the ruling *spot rate*. If the forward rate is less than the current spot rate then the currency is at a discount. The premium/discount can be expressed as an annual percentage or in the form of cents, etc., per £1.
FRA	Forward rate agreement.
FRN	A floating-rate *note*, i.e. a note issued with provision for revision of the rate of interest at periodic intervals (normally three or six months) in line with a key market rate such as *LIBOR*.
FSA	The new Financial Services Authority, which is responsible for prudential control of the whole financial services industry, including the banks.

FT-SE 100	Financial Times Stock Exchange Index of the 100 leading shares, in terms of market value, traded on the LSE.
GDP	Gross domestic product.
GEMM	Gilt-edged *market maker* – an institution which 'makes' the market in gilt-edged securities.
Gilt-edged security	A *bond* issued by the UK government.
Hedge	The reduction of risk on exposure to changes in market prices/rates through taking an offsetting position.
Hedge fund	An investment fund drawn up in such a manner as to avoid the main investment protection legislation. It is usually highly *leveraged*.
ICC	Industrial and commercial company.
IDB	Inter-dealer broker.
IMF	International Monetary Fund – a multilateral agency that assists countries with payments difficulties by arranging rescheduling of debts or new credits.
IMM	International Money Market.
Index fund	An investment fund which is constructed to track an appropriate stock market index, e.g. the FT-SE All-Share Index.
Investment bank	A bank that is involved in the commencement, underwriting and distribution of new issues of securities.
IRP	Interest rate parity – the requirement that the difference in interest rates between two countries should be matched by the forward exchange rate premium/discount.
ISD	Investment Services Directive.
ISMA	International Securities Markets Association.
JMB	Johnson Matthey Bank.
Junk bonds	High-risk, high-return *bonds*. Substantial volumes were issued to finance buyouts (leveraged buyouts) in the US during a wave of corporate restructuring in the late 1980s. A junk bond has a credit rating of less than BBB.
LDC	Less developed country.

Lender of last resort	An institution, normally the central bank, which underpins the financial system by lending to banks, or more occasionally domestic firms, which are facing a liquidity crisis but are basically sound in the long run.
Leverage	A high proportion of debt in the capital structure.
LIBOR	The London inter-bank offer rate, i.e. the rate at which banks are willing to lend funds in the London inter-bank market.
LIFFE	London International Financial Futures and Options Exchange.
London inter-bank bid rate (LIBID)	The rate of interest paid on deposits in the London inter-bank market.
LSE	London Stock Exchange.
Management buyout	The purchase of an existing company by its incumbent management, usually financed by a venture capital fund.
Market maker	An institution which undertakes to sell and buy a commodity(ies) or financial instrument(s) on a continuous basis. This ensures that others can always buy or sell, thus providing liquidity.
Matching	The practice of securing a distribution of assets which is equal to that of the liabilities in respect of characteristics such as maturity or currency denomination.
MATIF	Marché à Terme International de France.
Maturity	The time to the expiry of a loan/debt. Original maturity is the time to expiry when the loan was issued.
Merchant bank	Banks which make profits from carrying out services for corporate customers in addition to lending. The types of services are portfolio advice, new issues advice and underwriting, accepting bills of exchange, advising on takeovers and mergers, foreign currency services, etc.
MFR	Minimum funding requirement.
MG	Metalgesellschaft.
MGRM	Metalgesellschaft Refining and Marketing.
MIRAS	Mortgage interest relief at source.
MMD	Money market deposit.

MTN	Medium-term note – paper issued with an original maturity of more than one year but less than five years.
NASDAQ	National Association of Securities Dealers Automated Quotations System – the computerised price information system used by dealers in the over-the-counter market (*OTC*) in the US.
NAV	Net asset value per share – the value of assets less liabilities divided by the number of issued shares.
NIC	Newly industrialising country.
NIF	A note-issuance facility whereby a bank (or more commonly a syndicate of banks) arranges and guarantees the availability of funds from the issue of a succession of short-term notes (commonly three or six months). In the case of these notes not being taken up by the market, the banks will provide the funds.
NMS	Normal market size – the SEAQ classification system for LSE-traded shares which replaced the old alpha, beta, gamma system. NMS is a value expressed as a number of shares used to calculate the minimum quote size for each share.
Note	A short-term financial instrument similar to a *bond*. Unlike a bond, a note is essentially a short-term instrument.
OECD	The Organization for Economic Cooperation and Development. Membership includes Australia, Austria, Belgium, Canada, Denmark, Finland, France, Germany, Greece, Iceland, Ireland, Italy, Japan, Luxembourg, Netherlands, New Zealand, Norway, Portugal, Spain, Sweden, Switzerland, Turkey, the UK and the US.
OEIC	Open-ended investment company – a type of collective investment fund which came into existence in January 1997. They have a company structure like investment trusts but are similar to unit trusts (i.e. are open-ended) in that the number of shares or units can vary from day to day.
Off-balance-sheet business	A type of business which does not create liabilities or assets for banks (or other businesses). Fees are usually generated along with contingent liabilities. Examples are *NIF*, forward exchange contracts, option writing, etc.

Offer price	The price at which a *market maker* is prepared to sell securities.
Offshore bank	A subsidiary bank, such as a *eurobank*, which operates in a currency other than that of the host country. An alternative definition emphasises business carried out with non-residents in addition to the currency definition.
OFT	Office of Fair Trading.
OPEC	Organization of Petroleum Exporting Countries.
Options	The right *but not* the obligation to buy (a 'call' option) or sell (a 'put' option) a commodity or financial instrument in return for the payment of a premium. The seller of an option is called the 'writer'. An over-the-counter (*OTC*) option is an option which is tailormade for the purchaser and which cannot be sold. A traded option is an option in the form of a standardised agreement which the purchaser can sell on an organised market. A European-type option can be exercised only on a specific date and an American-type option can be exercised on any date prior to the expiry date.
OTC	Over-the-counter market. An informal dealer-based market.
Perpetual FRN	A *note* issued without provision for redemption.
PIA	Personal Investment Authority.
PIL	Physical investment opportunities line.
p.l.c.	Public limited company.
PPP	Purchasing power parity.
Primary market	A market for new issues of securities.
PSBR	Public sector borrowing requirement – the amount of money required by the public sector not otherwise raised by taxation.
Public sector debt repayment	Repayment of debt by the public sector when it has a surplus.
RATE	Risk Assessment, Tools and Evaluation
Real-time gross settlement (RTGS)	All inter-bank transactions are settled in the accounts of the central bank as they occur.

Repurchase agreement (repo)	An agreement to sell securities and repurchase them at a later date, both prices being agreed at the time of the initial sale. This is in effect an agreement to lend money with *collateral* and the two prices would reflect this.
Rollover credit	A loan that is renewed (rolled over) at fixed intervals, with the interest rate being altered in line with a key rate such as *LIBOR*.
S&P	Standard and Poor's.
Savings and loans association	In the US, an institution which accepts deposits deposits and makes loans, the bulk of which are in the form of mortgages. The equivalent of building societies in the UK.
SEAQ	Stock Exchange Automated Quotations System.
SEATS	Stock Exchange Alternative Trading Service.
Secondary market	A market for the sale and purchase of existing securities, as opposed to a market for the sale (or issue) of new securities, which is termed the *primary market*.
Securities and Exchange Commission	US investment regulatory body.
Securitisation	The process by which existing non-negotiable debt (such as bank loans) is changed into a security which is marketable. The term can also be used in a broader sense to indicate the change of procedure through which debt which was formerly obtained by bank lending (i.e. non-negotiable) is issued in marketable forms such as *NIF* etc.
SERPS	State Earnings-Related Pension Scheme.
SETS	Stock Exchange Automatic Trading System.
SIB	Securities and Investment Board.
SIP	Statement of investment principle.
Spot rate	The rate (most commonly exchange) which refers to transactions completed now rather than at some future time. In the case of foreign exchange rate transactions, settlement must be completed within two days.
Spread	The gap between the institution's buying and selling rates for financial securities and foreign exchange. It can also refer to the margin above the base rate, such as *LIBOR*, at which a specific loan is priced.

SPV	Special-purpose vehicle.
SRO	Self-regulatory organisation.
Stripping	The process of separating a conventional coupon-bearing bond into its constituent interest and principal payments.
Subordinated debt	Debt which ranks after all other debt for repayment in the event of liquidation.
SURF	Step-up recovery *FRN*.
Swap	An exchange of currencies or of debt with different characteristics such as interest rate type.
Syndicated loan	A loan which is made by a group of banks. Normally one bank or banks act as the lead bank(s) and then arrange to sell all or some of the debt to other banks, which are termed participating banks.
Underwriting	A process whereby financial institutions guarantee that a debt or *equity* issue will be taken up at a specified price. In the event of the market not purchasing all the issue, the institutions will purchase the balance.
Withholding tax	A tax which is deducted at source prior to payment of interest on dividends.

References

Alesina, A. (1989) 'Politics and business cycles in industrial democracies', *Economic Policy*, 8, 55–98.

Alexander, S. S. (1954) 'Price movements in speculative markets: trends or random walks', *Industrial Management Review*, 5, 25–46.

Allen, T. J. (1990) 'Developments in the international syndicated loan market in the 1980's', *Bank of England Quarterly Bulletin*, February, 71–83.

Arrow, K. J. and Hahn, F. H. (1971) *General Equilibrium Analysis*, Holden Day Inc.

Bade, R. and Parkin, M. (1988) *Central Bank Laws and Monetary Policy*, University of Western Ontario, mimeograph.

Baillie, R. T., Lippens, R. E. and McMahon, P. C. (1983) 'Testing rational expectations and efficiency in the foreign exchange market', *Econometrica*, 51, 553–64.

Bank for International Settlements (1986) *Recent Innovations in International Banking* (the Cross report), BIS.

Bank for International Settlements (1996) *Central Bank Survey of Foreign Exchange and Derivative Market Activity*, BIS, May 1996.

Bank for International Settlements (1997) *International Banking and Financial Market Review*, BIS, November 1997.

Bank of England (1997) *A Risk Based Approach to Supervision (The RATE Framework)*, Bank of England.

Barro, R. J. and Gordon, D. B. (1983a) 'Rules, discretion and reputation in a model of monetary policy', *Journal of Monetary Economics*, 12, 101–21.

Barro, R. J. and Gordon, D. B. (1983b) 'A positive theory of monetary policy in a natural rate model', *Journal of Political Economy*, 91, 589–610.

Basle Committee on Banking Supervision (1988) *International Convergence of Capital Measurement and Capital Standards*, Basle Committee.

Basle Committee on Banking Supervision (1992) *Minimum Standards for the Supervision of International Banking Groups and Their Cross-border Establishments*, Basle Committee.

Basle Committee on Banking Supervision (1996) *Amendment to the Capital Accord to Incorporate Market Risks*, Basle Committee.

Basle Committee on Banking Supervision (1997) *Principles for the Management of Interest Rate Risk*, Basle Committee.

Baumol, W. (1982) *Contestable Markets and the Theory of Industrial Structure*, Harcourt Brace.

Beckers, S. (1981) 'Standard deviations implied in option prices as predictors of future stock price variability', *Journal of Banking and Finance*, 5, 363–81.

Benston, G. J., Eisenbeis, R. A., Horvitz, P. M., Kane, E. J. and Kaufman, G. G. (1986) *Perspectives on Safe and Sound Banking: Past, Present and Future*, MIT Press.

Benston, G. J. and Kaufman, G. G. (1988) *Risk and Solvency Regulation of Depository Institutions: Past Policies and Current Options*, Monograph 1 in Finance and Economics, Saloman Brothers Centre for the Study of Financial Institutions.

Bilson, J. F. O. (1983) 'The evaluation and use of foreign exchange rate forecasting services', in R. J. Herring (ed.), *Managing Foreign Exchange Risk*, Cambridge University Press.

Bjerring, J. H., Lakonishok, J. and Vermaelen, T. (1983) 'Stock prices and financial analysts' recommendations', *Journal of Finance*, 38, 187–204.

Blake, D., Beenstock, M. and Brasse, V. (1986) 'The performance of UK exchange rate forecasters', *Economic Journal*, 96, 986–99.

Blume, M. E. and Friend, I. (1974) 'Risk, investment strategies and the long-run rates of return', *Review of Economics and Statistics*, 56, 259–69.

Board of Banking Supervision (1995) *Report of the Inquiry into the Circumstances of the Collapse of Barings*, HMSO.

Boocock, J. G. (1990) 'An examination of non-bank funding for small and medium sized enterprises in the UK', *Service Industries Journal*, 124–45.

Brady Commission (1988) *Report of the Presidential Task Force on Market Mechanisms*, US Government Printing Office.

Bryant, C. (1987) 'National and sector balance sheets 1957–1985', *Economic Trends*, no. 403, May, 92–119.

Cantor, R. and Packer, F. (1994) 'The credit rating industry', *Federal Reserve Bank of New York Review*, 19, no. 2, 1–26.

Cavanaugh, K. L. (1987) 'Price dynamics in the foreign currency futures market', *Journal of International Money and Finance*, 6, 295–314.

Cecchini, P. (1988) *The European Challenge 1992: The Benefits of a Single Market*, Gower Publishing Group.

Clark, J. (1993) 'Debt reduction and market reentry under the Brady Plan', *Federal Reserve Bank of New York Quarterly Review*, 18, no. 4, 38–62.

Copeland, L. (1994) *Exchange Rates and International Finance*, 2nd edition, Addison-Wesley.

Cosh, A., Carty, J., Hughes, A., Plender, J. and Singh, A. (1990) *Take-Overs and Short-Termism in the UK*, Institute of Public Policy Research, Industrial Policy Paper no. 3.

Cukierman, A. (1992) *Central Bank Strategy, Credibility and Independence*, MIT Press.

Dale, R. (1994) 'Regulating investment business in the single market', *Bank of England Quarterly Bulletin*, November, 333–40.

Davis, E. P. (1990) *International Financial Centres – An Industrial Analysis*, Bank of England Discussion Paper no. 51.

Davis, E. P. (1996) 'The role of institutional investors in the evolution of financial structure and behaviour', in *The Future of the Financial System*, Reserve Bank of Australia.

Davis, E. P. and Latter, A. R. (1989) 'London as an international financial centre', *Bank of England Quarterly Bulletin*, November, 516–28.

Delors, J. (1989) *Report on Economic and Monetary Union in the European Community*, Committee for the Study of Economic and Monetary Union.

Demery, D. and Duck, N. W. (1978) 'The behaviour of nominal interest rates in the United Kingdom 1961–1973', *Economica*, 45, 23–37.

Diamond, D. (1984) 'Financial intermediation and delegated monitoring', *Review of Economic Studies*, 51, 393–414.

Diamond, D. (1989) 'Reputation acquisition in debt markets', *Journal of Political Economy*, 97, 728–62.

Diamond, D. (1991) 'Monitoring and reputation: the choice between bank loans and directly placed debt', *Journal of Political Economy*, 99, 689–721.

Diamond, D. (1996) 'Financial intermediation as delegated monitoring: a simple example', *Federal Reserve Bank of Richmond Economic Quarterly*, summer, 51–66.

Dimson, E. and Marsh, P. (1984) 'Unpublished forecasts of UK stock returns', *Journal of Finance*, 39, 1257–92.

Dooley, M. P., Fernandez-Arias, E. and Kletzer, K. M. (1994) 'Recent private capital inflows to developing countries: is the debt crisis history?', *NBER Working Paper No. 4792*.

Dooley, M. P. and Shafer, J. R. (1976) *Analysis of Short-Run Exchange Rate Behavior: March 1973 to September 1975*, International Finance Discussion Papers no. 76, Federal Reserve System.

Dowd, K. (1993) 'Deposit insurance: a skeptical view', *Federal Reserve Bank of St Louis Review*, January/February, 14–17.

Edwards, F. R. and Cantor, M. S. (1995) 'The collapse of Metallgesellschaft: unhedgeable risks, poor hedging strategy or just bad luck?', *Journal of Futures Markets*, 15.

Elton E. J., Gruber, M. J. and Rentzler, J. (1984) 'Intra-day tests of the efficiency of the treasury bills futures market', *Review of Economics and Statistics*, 129–37.

Fama, E. F. (1965) 'The behaviour of stock prices', *Journal of Business*, 38, 33–105.

Fama, E. F. (1970) 'Efficient capital markets: a review of theory and empirical evidence', *Journal of Finance*, 84, 499–522.

Fama, E. F. (1975) 'Short term interest rates as predictors of inflation', *American Economic Review*, 65, 269–82.

Fama, E. F. (1977) 'Interest rates and inflation: the lessons in the entrails', *American Economic Review*, 67, 487–96.

Fama, E. F. (1980) 'Banking in the theory of finance', *Journal of Monetary Economics*, 6, 7–28.

Fama, E. F. (1984) 'Forward and spot exchange rates', *Journal of Monetary Economics*, 14, no. 3, 319–39.

Fama, E. (1991) 'Efficient capital markets II', *Journal of Finance*, 46, 1575–617.

Fama, E. F. and Blume, M. E. (1966) 'Filter rules and stock market trading', *Journal of Business*, 39, 226–41.

Fama, E., Fisher, L., Jensen, N. and Roll, R. (1969) 'The adjustment of stock prices to new information', *International Economic Review*, 10, 1–21.

Flood, M. D. (1991) 'An introduction to complete markets', *Federal Reserve Bank of St Louis*, 73, no. 2, 32–57.

Frenkel, J. A. and Levich, R. M. (1975) 'Covered interest arbitrage: unexploited profits?' *Journal of Political Economy*, 83, 325–38.

Frenkel, J. A. and Levich, R. M. (1977) 'Transactions costs and interest arbitrage: tranquil versus turbulent periods', *Journal of Political Economy*, 85, 1209–24.

Froot, K. and Frankel, J. A. (1989) 'Forward discount bias: is it an exchange rate premium?', *Quarterly Journal of Economics*, 104, 139–61.

Gemmill, G. (1986) 'The forecasting performance of stock options on the London Traded Options market', *Journal of Business, Finance and Accounting*, 13, 535–46.

Gibbons, M. and Hess, P. (1980) 'Day of the week effects and asset returns', *Journal of Business*, 54, 579–96.

Goodhart, C. A. E. (1988) 'Bank insolvency and deposit insurance: a proposal', in P. Arestis (ed.), *Contemporary Issues in Money and Banking*, Macmillan.

Goodhart, C. A. E. (1989) *Money, Information and Uncertainty*, 2nd edition, Macmillan.

Goodhart, C. A. E. and Gowland, D. (1977) 'The relationship between yields on short and long-dated gilt-edged stock', *Bulletin of Economic Research*, 29.

Goodman, S. J. (1979) 'Foreign exchange forecasting techniques: implications for business and policy', *Journal of Finance*, 34, 415–27.

Grilli, V., Masciandaro, D. and Tabellini, G. (1991) 'Political and monetary institutions and public financial policies in the industrial countries', *Economic Policy*, 13, 341–92.

Gurley, J. and Shaw, E. (1960) *Money in a Theory of Finance*, Brookings Institute.

Gwylim, O. and Buckle, M. (1994) *Volatility Forecasting in the Framework of the Option Expiry Cycle*, European Business Management School Discussion Paper, University of Wales.

Hall, M. (1987) 'UK banking supervision and the Johnson Matthey affair', in C. Goodhart, D. Currie and D. Llewellyn (eds), *The Operation and Regulation of Financial Markets*, Macmillan.

Hirschleifer, J. (1958) 'On the theory of optimal investment analysis', *Journal of Political Economy*, August, 329–52.

Janneau, S. (1996) 'The market for international asset backed securities', in

International Banking and Financial Market Developments, Bank for International Settlements.

Kasman, B. (1992) 'A comparison of monetary policy operating procedures in six industrial countries', *Federal Reserve Bank of New York*, 17, no. 3, 5–24.

Keim, D. B. (1986) 'The CAPM and equity return regularities', *Financial Analyst Journal*, 42, 19–34.

Kleidon, A. W. (1986) 'Variance bounds tests and stock price valuation models', *Journal of Political Economy*, 74, 639–55.

Lancaster, K. (1966) 'A new approach to consumer theory', *Journal of Political Economy*, 74, 132–57.

Lever, H. and Huhne, C. (1985) *Debt and Danger: The World Financial Crisis*, Penguin Books.

Levich, R. M. (1979) 'On the efficiency of markets for foreign exchange', in R. Dornbusch and J. A. Frenkel (eds), *International Economic Policy*, Johns Hopkins University Press.

Lewis, M. K. (1987) 'Off-balance sheet activities and financial innovation in banking', *Banca Nationale del Lavoro*, 387–410.

Lewis, M. K. (1991) 'Theory and practice of the banking firm', in C. J. Green and D. T. Llewellyn (eds), *Surveys in Monetary Economics, vol. 2, Financial Markets and Institutions*, Blackwell.

Lewis, M. K. and Davis, K. T. (1987) *Domestic and International Banking*, Philip Allan.

Llewellyn, D. T. (1985) *The Evolution of the British Financial System*, Gilbart Lectures on Banking, Institute of Bankers.

Llewellyn, D. T. (1991) 'Structural change in the British financial system', in C. J. Green and D. T. Llewellyn (eds), *Surveys in Monetary Economics, vol. 2, Financial Markets and Institutions*, Blackwell.

Llewellyn, D. T. (1996) 'Banking in the 21st century: the transformation of an industry', Loughborough University Banking Centre Research Paper No. 105/96.

Logue, D. E. and Sweeney, R. J. (1977) 'White noise in imperfect markets: the case of the franc/dollar exchange rate', *Journal of Finance*, 32, 761–8.

Macdonald, R. and Taylor, M. P. (1989) 'Economic analysis of foreign exchange markets: an expository survey', in R. Macdonald and M. P. Taylor (eds), *Innovations in Open Economy Macroeconomics*, Basil Blackwell.

Malkiel, B. G. (1966) *The Term Structure of Interest Rates*, Princeton University Press.

Manaster, S. and Rendleman, R. J. (1982) 'Options prices as predictors of equilibrium stock prices', *Journal of Finance*, 37, 1043–57.

Mankiw, G. and Summers, L. H. (1984) 'Do long-term interest rates overreact to short-term interest rates?' *Brookings Papers on Economic Activity*, 1.

Marsh, P. (1990) *Short Termism on Trial*, IFMA.

Massimb, M. and Phelps, B. (1993) 'Electronic trading, market structure and liquidity', *Financial Analysts Journal*, 50, no. 1, 39–50.

Mayer, C. and Alexander, I. (1990) *Bank and Securities Markets: Corporate*

Financing in Germany and the UK, Centre for Economic Policy Research Discussion Paper no. 433.

McCauley, R. N. and Zimmer, S. A. (1989) 'Explaining international differences in the cost of capital', *Quarterly Review Federal Reserve Bank of New York*, summer, 7–21.

McConnell, J. J. and Muscerella, C. S. (1985) 'Corporate capital expenditure decisions and the market value of the firm', *Journal of Financial Economics*, 14, 399–422.

McCulloch, J. H. (1981) 'Misintermediation and macroeconomic fluctuations', *Journal of Monetary Economics*, 8, 103–15.

McKinsey Global Institute (1996) *Capital Productivity*, McKinsey Global Institute.

Meiselman, D. (1962) *The Term Structure of Interest Rates*, Prentice-Hall.

Miles, D. (1989) *Financial Liberalisation, the Housing Market and the Current Account*, Birkbeck College mimeo.

Modigliani, F. and Shiller, R. J. (1973) 'Inflation, rational expectations and the term structure of interest rates', *Economica*, 40, 12–43.

Modigliani, F. and Sutch, R. C. (1966) 'Innovations in interest rate policy', *American Economic Review*, 56, 178–97.

Newberry, D. J. (1989) 'Futures markets, hedging and speculation', in J. Eatwell, M. Milgate and P. Newman (eds), *The New Palgrave Dictionary of Finance*, Macmillan.

Pilbeam, K. (1992) *International Finance*, Macmillan.

Plender, J. (1990) 'Throw sand in the take over machine', *Financial Times*, 24 July.

Pollard, P. S. (1993) 'Central bank independence and economic performance', *Federal Reserve Bank of St Louis*, July/August, 21–36.

Price Waterhouse (1995) *Corporate Treasury Control and Performance Standards*, Price Waterhouse.

Russell, S. (1993) 'The government's role in deposit insurance', *Federal Reserve Bank of St Louis Review*, January/February, 3–9.

Rybczynski, T. (1988) 'Financial systems and industrial restructuring', *National Westminster Bank Quarterly Review*, 3–13.

Sachs, J. (1986) 'Managing the LDC debt crisis', *Brookings Papers on Economic Activity*, 397–440.

Sachs, J. and Huizinga, H. (1987) 'US commercial banks and the developing-country debt crisis', *Brookings Papers on Economic Activity*, 555–606.

Santoni, G. J. (1987) 'The great bull markets 1924–1929 and 1982–1987: speculative bubbles or economic fundamentals', *Federal Reserve Bank of St Louis Review,* November, 16–30.

Sargent, T. (1972) 'Rational expectations and the term structure of interest rates', *Journal of Money Credit and Banking*, 4.

Sarkar, A. and Tozzi, M. (1998) 'Electronic trading on futures exchanges', in *Current Issues in Economics and Finance*, Federal Reserve Bank of New York.

Securities and Investments Board (1994) *Regulation of the United Kingdom Equity Markets*, Discussion Paper of SIB.

Shiller, R. J. (1979) 'The volatility of long-term interest rates and expectations models of the term structure', *Journal of Political Economy*, 87, 1190–2119.

Shiller, R. J. (1981) 'Do stock prices move too much to be justified by subsequent changes in dividends?', *American Economic Review*, 71, 421–36.

Stickel, S. E. (1985) 'The effect of Value Line investment survey rank changes on common stock prices', *Journal of Financial Economics*, 14, 121–43.

Sykes, A. (1990) 'Bigger carrots and sticks', *Financial Times*, 31 October.

Taylor, M. P. (1987) 'Covered interest parity: a high-frequency, high-quality data study', *Economica*, 54, 429–38.

Taylor, M. P. (1995) 'The economics of exchange rates', *Journal of Economic Literature*, 33, 13–47.

Taylor, S. (1986) *Modelling Financial Time Series*, John Wiley.

Tobin, J. (1984) 'On the efficiency of the financial system', *Lloyds Bank Review*, 153, 1–15.

Tucker, A. L. (1987) 'Foreign exchange option prices as predictors of equilibrium forward exchange rates', *Journal of International Money and Finance*, 6, 283–94.

Twinn, C. (1994) 'Asset backed securitisation in the UK', *Bank of England Quarterly Bulletin*, May, 134–43.

Walmsley, J. (1988) *The New Financial Instruments: An Investors' Guide*, Wiley.

Yang, J. E. (1987) 'Fraud is the main cause of failure at S&Ls in California, Congress says', *Wall Street Journal*, 15 June, 6.

Index